SELF-RULE

A CULTURAL HISTORY

THE UNIVERSITY OF CHICAGO PRESS

SELF-RULE

OF AMERICAN DEMOCRACY

ROBERT H. WIEBE

CHICAGO AND LONDON

Robert H. Wiebe is professor of history at Northwestern University and the author of numerous books including *The Opening of American Society, The Segmented Society,* and the classic *The Search for Order.*

The University of Chicago Press, Chicago 60637
The University of Chicago Press, Ltd., London
© 1995 by The University of Chicago
All rights reserved. Published 1995
Printed in the United States of America

04 03 02 01 00 99 98 97 96 95   1 2 3 4 5

ISBN: 0-226-89562-9 (cloth)

Library of Congress Cataloging-in-Publication Data
Wiebe, Robert H.
    Self-rule : A cultural history of American democracy / Robert H. Wiebe.
        p.   cm.
    Includes bibliographical references and index.
    1. United States—Politics and government.   2. Political culture—
United States—History.   I. Title.
E183.W54   1995
320.973—dc20   94-33957
                                                                      CIP

FOR SAM WARNER

CONTENTS

||||||

ACKNOWLEDGMENTS

——— The first sketch of this book formed three Carl Lotus Becker Lectures in 1987 at Cornell University, where Michael Kammen served as the most gracious host imaginable. I very much appreciate Stuart Blumin's encouragement at that stage. By pointing out the limitations of those lectures, Jane J. Mansbridge, Robert J. Norrell, Mary Beth Norton, James Oakes, and Robert Westbrook spurred me on to better things. Sara Evans, John Higham, and Susan Hirsch provided a similar service in response to a paper summarizing another set of my views on American democracy. Shlomo Avineri, who as commentator at a conference of 1987 in Jerusalem accused me of "following the Communist line," deserves special mention for creative criticism.

Josef Barton, John L. Thomas, and Sam Bass Warner, Jr., suffered through a very rough draft of the manuscript—the ultimate test of collegial commitment—and bade me continue. James T. Kloppenberg and James J. Sheehan gave thoughtful readings to a later version, and Ellen Carol DuBois provided a thorough evaluation of part 2. Robyn Muncy's excellent comments on the penultimate version guided me through the final revisions. I am deeply grateful to all of them. I also appreciate the readings by Robert Bellah and Michael Schudson.

James Campbell, Arthur F. McEvoy, and Harold Perkin pointed me to useful sources. Harry Watson shared with me some of his extensive knowledge about early 19th century politics and Henry Binford some of his about late 19th century cities. Roland Guyotte helped me organize my thoughts on contemporary democracy, and Joyce Seltzer helped me organize my manuscript into chapters. Members of my family took an interest in the project. Douglas Wiebe and Richard P. Wiebe suggested books to read. Eric Wiebe and Patrick Wiebe challenged my views on the merits of electronic voting. Tobey Wiebe expressed confidence that eventually I would have ideas, as did James E. Sheridan and Clarence L. Ver Steeg; and Richard L. McCormick, Peter Parish, and Ryo Yokoyama expressed excitement about some of them. At the University of Chicago Press, Kathryn Gohl, Douglas Mitchell, and Rina Ranalli were invariably responsive and helpful. All of these contributions boosted my morale.

A Lloyd Lewis Fellowship from the Newberry Library gave me time in a congenial environment to write a preliminary draft. Richard H. Brown, then academic vice president at the library, was particularly encouraging. The generosity of the Spencer Foundation and of an anonymous donor speeded the completion of the manuscript. Throughout its years of preparation, Rudolph H. Weingartner and Lawrence B. Dumas, successive deans of the College of Arts and Sciences at Northwestern University, never failed to support this project. I also owe special thanks to Steven L. Bates, John R. McLane, and Adair L. Waldenberg, who went out of their way to make sure I got the full benefit from my leaves. I can rail at the stars if I like, but I cannot cry poor.

And then there are the intangibles that made this book, and a good many other things, possible. To Joe Barton and Barbara Speicher for taking in a waif; to Peggy Anderson and Jim Sheehan, Barbara and Herb Bass, Barbara and Lloyd Gadau, Barbara and Jerry Linderman, and Dorothy and John Thompson for providing occasions of understanding and affection; to Barbara Heldt and Gerry Smith for loyally shoring me up; to Anita Fellman for checking to see that I was making it; to Pat Graham for offering her unique combination of practical assistance and personal warmth; to Pamela Loewenstein for expressing a steady confidence; and to Sam Warner for sharing one damn thing after another, I feel enormous debts.

||||||||

INTRODUCTION

_____ **A**mericans act as if democracy were too important to define. Keep it elastic enough, they seem to be saying, to accommodate what we find best in our nation's life. Hence, in everyday usage, democracy may refer to our treatment of one another in public or in private; to conservative, liberal, or radical economic programs; to the individual's rights against majorities or the majority's rights against all comers; to color-conscious or color-blind public policies; to the downfall of dictatorial power abroad or the rise of executive authority at home; to a leveling of distinctions or a glorification of differences; and a good deal more. As the indispensable term for whatever we like, it has come to cover so much in general not to mean much of anything in particular.

In fact, democracy is too important not to define. As America's most distinguishing characteristic and its most significant contribution to world history, democracy demands the kind of clear-eyed, close examination we reserve for those issues that enable us to understand our own lives. I join a gathering of people who in recent years have been separating democracy out for rigorous examination in its own right. My contribution to these conversations is special attention to the sweep of democracy's history in America. How did American democracy arrive? How has it related to other patterns of behavior around it? How has it changed over the centuries? How is it situated in contemporary America?

But first, a few more words about its meaning. Although the recent rise of interest in democracy has invested the subject with a new seriousness, it has not given it a new clarity. A confusion of definitions— some explicit, more implicit—competes for our attention. By drawing on what a core of sixty-odd studies have said about democracy over

1

the last quarter century, let us try to make sense of this mix.*

Despite the initial impression—an important one—that many of these sixty-odd voices are simply talking past one another, some areas of agreement do emerge from our sample. To begin with, almost all of them share one piece of common ground: democracy is a process of self-government that includes elections. Very few leave the matter there, however. In fact, most commentators hurry along to compile a list of conditions that will legitimize the elections and anything else they associate with self-government. Here the complexity commences.

Some of their conditions state what must go into the political process, others what must come out of it. On the input side, prerequisites divide in two parts: one specifying the structure for self-government, that is, constitutions, laws, rules, and procedures; the other the character of the participating citizens, that is, the beliefs, commitments, and knowledge of people like you and me. At the far end of the process, essential outputs fall into three broad categories: freedom, usually referring to individual liberties; justice, usually focusing on matters of social equity; and effectiveness, almost always prizing the ability to resolve major problems promptly and authoritatively. Conditions have a way of accumulating very rapidly, as anyone might guess from the sheer scope and the natural appeal of these considerations: political structure and civic character going in; freedom, justice, and effectiveness coming out. After all, who wants a warped framework or an incompetent public, an inequitable system or a faltering government? Yet the higher various commentators on democracy mound their conditions, the deeper our sole common ground—the process of self-government—gets buried, and as a consequence the more the subject of democracy comes to resemble a great pile of everybody's pet concerns.

Adding to the confusion, contemporary commentators themselves tend to separate into groups—philosophers, publicists, and social scientists—and to talk only with their own kind. Philosophers, who usually treat democracy as a moral problem, keep the individual to the forefront, come late in their arguments to democracy itself, and stress its outcomes: they tell us how things ought to be. Publicists, perhaps because many of them are journalists, begin with a crisis in public affairs, connect it to democracy, and lay out a menu of necessary reforms: they tell us how things must be. Social scientists start with politics and government, look for democracy in them, and concentrate on

*Citations to works from this core are by author and publication date. For full citations, see "Special Debts and Further Readings," section on Introduction and Conclusion, pp. 279–281.

procedural improvements: they tell us how to make things work. When the car rattles, the social scientist lifts the hood, the philosopher asks where we think we are going, and the publicist looks for a cop. Philosophers and publicists, who are attracted to issues of freedom and justice, shy away from close examinations of structure; social scientists, on the contrary, give priority to structure and effectiveness. Publicists have the weakest sense of history: their crises are almost always unprecedented. Philosophers have the strongest: their ideas almost always have a lineage. Social scientists show the greatest appreciation for the status quo, philosophers the least. Even after discounting for the inevitable exceptions, including the difficulty of categorizing some participants, three such disparate groups, each with its own vigorous discussion of democracy under way, help to explain why so many different prescriptions swirl around the subject.

In almost all cases, dissatisfaction begins at the far end of the line, with democracy's outcomes. Perhaps the individual's freedom is being frustrated, as the philosopher Robert Nozick and legal theorist Roberto Mangabeira Unger might agree; or social justice is being denied, as the consumer's champion Ralph Nader and the political commentator Kevin Phillips would argue; or the governmental system is producing paltry results, as the journalist E. J. Dionne, Jr., and the political scientist James Morone would claim. When critics shift attention from the output to the input end, they almost always want to insert something that will correct these flawed outcomes. Social scientists commonly favor a revitalization of political parties, additional rules on how election campaigns are financed (also popular among publicists), and ways of disciplining unruly legislatures, such as allowing line-item vetoes or (here both publicists and philosophers join in) mandating equitable economic policies. Some publicists and philosophers advocate lengthening the list of constitutionally protected rights. All of these are alternative ways of changing what goes into the process in order to increase the justice or the efficiency of what comes out of it.

Most proposals seek to compensate for deficiencies in the general public: stronger political parties because ordinary citizens need focus and leadership; limits on campaign spending because voters are defenseless against soundbite propaganda; mandated rights because the weak need protection against the strong, minorities against majorities. What is electoral politics, charge the political scientists James MacGregor Burns and L. Martin Overby, but "domination by the media and money; the long ballot that bewilders voters; the avoidance of real issues; and the endless demagoguery, sensationalism, and trivialization." The scholar Moses Finley takes for granted our agreement on citizens' wholesale "ignorance," their "glaring lack of consistency . . .

lack of knowledge, lack of political education, and apathy." With an even sharper edge, the academician Frank Sorauf describes American politics as "driven by mass fears, mass opinion, and mass voting, a politics easily inflamed" and incorrigibly personalized. The public staggers on the defensive. Rather than government demonstrating that it deserves the voters' support, voters need to demonstrate that they deserve the government's attention. It is the obligation of the citizenry, the historian Christopher Lasch has stated, to shake free of modern society's infantilizing pressures and "show that democracy embodies a demanding, morally elevated standard of conduct." Robert Bellah and his colleagues suggest making the very definition of democracy "a political system in which people actively attend to what is significant." [1]

Not surprisingly, the hierarchically arranged world of James Madison and Thomas Jefferson, in which the few expounded the issues and the many listened, enjoys a special popularity among those most skeptical of the public's qualifications. The philosopher William Riker calls any other form of democracy "absurd" and "indefensible." [2] The widely admired ideal of public life derived from the philosopher Jürgen Habermas presupposes just such an educated, dispassionate, and receptive citizenry open to persuasion by rational argument—Habermas's attempt, as Adam Seligman astutely remarks, to revive for our time the values of the 18th century Enlightenment. Commentators as different as the columnist Flora Lewis and the philosopher John Rawls echo this demand for a rational citizenry.

Not many participants in these discussions advocate curing the ills of popular rule with more of it. That solution makes no sense where public participation itself is part of the problem: "more democracy" only "exacerbates the confusion of the American public sector." If but only "if people are informed and caring," in the political scientist Thomas Cronin's paternal phrasing, "they can be trusted with self-government." [3] But how could it be otherwise? Dissatisfaction with outcomes feeds dissatisfaction with inputs. Almost by definition, the wrong consequences coming out of the process are linked to the wrong public values going into it, and a democracy worthy of the name waits upon a higher quality of raw material. Moreover, those who start by demanding better results eventually come full circle looking for them: new structures and new civic values matter only if they produce the prescribed outcomes in freedom or justice or effectiveness. If the public does not focus on what the Bellah group considers a significant issue, democracy by their standard fails.

Contemporary critics signal their distress with the existing system of inputs and outputs by certain code words, the most common of which is *truly,* as in the philosopher Philip Green's desire to achieve a democracy "of truly equal citizens," or the political scientist James Fishkin's search for "a truly adequate version of democracy."[4] Variations include affirmations of a *genuine* or *real* democracy, in obvious contrast to the current phony, false versions; or, approaching from the subject's underside, the use of such dismissive terms as the philosopher John Dunn's "capitalist democracy" and the social scientist Göran Therborn's "bourgeois democracy," presumably in contrast to the inviting array of proletarian, anarchist, theocratic, and traditionalist alternatives. Others keep us focused on outcomes by threatening us with the worst of them if we don't watch out. In case democracy takes a wrong turn, the publicist Irving Kristol conjures for our consideration a Hobbesian horror of a society: "vicious, mean, squalid, and debased."[5] The philosopher Alan Gilbert repeatedly trots out the Nazis to scare us. If we cannot abide these repulsive outcomes, the argument goes, we have no choice but to ensure the right ones.

Almost inevitably, this preoccupation with consequences, causes, and more consequences shrinks the common ground in between, the political process. Advocates of freedom and justice favoring more absolute rights, for example, set out quite openly to curb popular government. Rights are mandates beyond popular choice, the legal theorist Ronald Dworkin makes clear, "the majority's [absolute] promise to the minorities." After the philosopher Amy Gutmann inserts in her model of the just constitution "universal welfare rights and a relatively equal distribution of income," among many other entitlements, governments are largely administrative, and elections ritual. The political process slips into the modest role of a dependent variable. Ruy Teixeira, an expert on low levels of voting, recommends increasing turnouts not to expand popular participation but largely to give leaders "sufficient legitimacy to pursue desired policies"—and then only if "the costs of reform are not too great."[6]

Occasionally the common ground disappears altogether. Although few commentators on democracy say it outright, the heavy emphasis on results always places a popular political process at risk. If it fails to prove its worth, why preserve it? A few definitions do abandon it, as those of two sages in the social sciences illustrate: for Seymour Martin Lipset, democracy is simply "the good society itself in operation"; for Ralf Dahrendorf, it is no more than "political change without revolution." Democracy in this dispensation floats. With no firmer moorings than these, the call for a "democratic transformation of all our institutions," for example, reads like a throwaway line.[7]

Once airborne, democracy may just stay aloft. Commentators who believe that the system itself corrupts the outcome demand a new system—anarchism for the philosopher Robert Paul Wolff, revolutionary socialism for the publicist Michael Parenti. Parenti joins Frances Fox Piven and Richard Cloward in deciding that, in fact, the United States has at no time been democratic. By their own high standards, the political philosophers Benjamin Barber and Robert Dahl agree: genuine democracy, in Barber's words, "has never existed" in America. "For feminists," the philosopher Carole Pateman writes in an extension of that argument, "democracy has never existed [anywhere]; women have never been and still are not admitted as full and equal members and citizens in any country known as a 'democracy.' "[8]

Perhaps, as William Greider suggests, high standards transform democracy from a social system into "an unfulfilled vision of what the country might someday become."[9] Less ambiguously, the philosopher John Dryzek has decided that an open, egalitarian democracy can only be an ideal, always beyond realization. Certainly Dahl's full-scale treatment of democracy establishes criteria for popular participation that no society will meet: an inclusive electorate of all mentally competent adult residents, each with an equal opportunity to prepare the agenda of public issues, equal rights in determining the mechanisms for decision-making, equal access to relevant information about those issues, and equal weight in shaping their solution. The very height of these ideals accentuates the depths to which the United States has sunk, measured in the end by the vast distance separating it from true, real, genuine democracy.

As a logical proposition the definition of democracy need not have any connection with actual happenings. But what passes in logic fails in history. Something profoundly important occurred in early 19th century America that acquired the name democracy. Once out, its influence spread worldwide. Since then hundreds of millions of people have operated on the assumption that democracy exists, and definitions of democracy must be sensitive to that fact. In the flood of commentaries since the 1960s, remarkably few reckon with this history of social experiences.

In two ways, an awareness of history loosens the criteria for what must go into democracy and what must come out of it. First, it questions certain prerequisites that by today's standards seem indispensable to a sound democracy. For example, those who argue that poverty as we define it disables citizens and that education as we define it empowers them pay no attention to a contrary 19th century record. During most of the century, with a substantially lower standard of living and no safety net, the American electorate invested significantly higher levels of energy in the entire political process, including voting.

Depressions—free-fall experiences for countless citizens—seem to have deterred no one. Education through families, churches, and common schools, through popular webs of oral and written communication, and through participation itself created a far more assertive, self-confident electorate in the 19th century than an increase across the board in formal schooling has produced in the 20th. Those who counter that circumstances have changed dramatically in the 20th century, citing in particular the mind-boggling complexity of modern government and the mind-deadening effects of mass media, apparently are not aware of almost identical charges of an ill-equipped, manipulated public which were already coin-of-the-realm early in the 20th century—before the era of big government and before the age of radio, let alone television. Phrases like "the complexity of modern life" and "the power of mass media" are cultural artifacts, not scientific truths.

Charges that gerrymandering undermines democracy, scurrilous campaigning demeans it, and open balloting corrupts it are just as dubious. One person–one vote as the higher law of representation is a very recent obsession. Harsh language has often communicated how much politics matters, and open balloting has just as commonly strengthened the organizational ties expressing those passions. The short funereal lines outside a modern voting booth would have alarmed a 19th century democrat at least as much as the thought of the 19th century's boisterous, partisan crowds seems to distress commentators today.

As a second tempering influence, history challenges the notion that democracies need to come complete, that any aspect falling below universalistic standards sinks the whole enterprise. What ever arrives in finished form? Only the mentality insisting that today and today alone reveals the truth—a mentality that guarantees the obsolescence of today's truth tomorrow—denies other generations and other cultures a good deal of leeway in finding their own routes to democracy. In the long run not only are we all dead; we are all wrong. Other societies with other values have created other democracies. Indicatively, those commentators with the most demanding requirements show the least comfort with 19th century America's democracy, which they see at best as a faulty preliminary to our time: a partial polyarchy to Dahl, for example, or premodern "courts and parties" to Piven and Cloward, borrowing the political scientist Stephen Skowronek's belittling phrase. Even as a "bourgeois democracy," Göran Therborn has decided, the United States did not qualify until about 1970.

Tolerating deficiencies has its limits, of course. It may be, for example, that white men's prolonged monopoly of the franchise in 19th century America exceeds even a flexible meaning for democracy. Nevertheless, no one could have expected a comprehensive adult suffrage to arrive in a blinding flash early in the 19th century. Some exclusions—hence some areas for growth, some conflicts over boundaries—were well nigh inevitable. Moreover, exclusions that existed at the outset, even on grounds that now seem outrageous, carry a meaning different from later exclusions that stripped citizens of rights they once had. In terms of democracy's historical development, disenfranchisement is much deadlier than an initial failure to enfranchise. Call the one an agenda for challenge, the other an agenda for demolition.

A feeling for historical variety, in other words, encourages us to burden the definition of democracy with just as few contemporary conditions as possible. That plants our feet once again on the original piece of common ground, popular self-government. Here is democracy's heartland. Instead of shunting aside the political process because it threatens our values, we rein in our values to make room for the political process.

A cluster of contemporary commentators, including Peter Bachrach, Walter Dean Burnham, John Dryzek, William Greider, Sidney Verba and Norman Nie, and Michael Walzer, have been preserving this ground for us. And despite the fact that Benjamin Barber and Robert Dahl set exalted specifications for their ideal worlds, they have been giants in the cause of popular participation. "If democracy is interpreted as rule by the people," Verba and Nie state with disarming simplicity, "then . . . the more participation there is in decisions, the more democracy there is." Democracy, in Walzer's formulation, is "a process that has no endpoint, an argument that has no definite conclusion . . . No citizen can ever claim to have persuaded his fellows once and for all." [10]

This approach, widened sufficiently to give us a historical view, provides quite a spare definition of democracy. Its first principle is popular self-government. Hence it is necessarily political, and as it encompasses many people, it involves tallying judgments and choices in order to register popular decisions. Although opinion polls, group demands, and even individual market choices may have some role to play in the process, elections remain the crucial procedure, and guarantees of that procedure the cardinal rule in democratic politics: voting majorities can never be allowed to eliminate voting minorities from the electoral process.

By itself, voting is not enough. All kinds of governments hold elections. To make political participation effective, citizens need the information and the possibilities for association that give them access to the political system, and they need government officials who respond to popular decisions. In addition to these core requirements of access and responsiveness, democracy also needs adequate scope. Though it can tolerate some undemocratic institutions inside its own boundaries, it cannot function inside a larger hostile system. A town meeting in an 18th century monarchy does not qualify: the sovereign power must be the democratic one.

Finally, democracy is something else. As it takes root, it acquires a cluster of characteristics peculiar to that time and place, and eventually those characteristics become an inextricable part of its democracy. Social welfare programs, for example, filled this space in most of the European democracies emerging around the turn of the 20th century. After the Second World War, Japan's democracy assimilated institutions of deference. As indelibly as these clusters mark each country's democracy, however, they remain its secondary characteristics. Popular self-government without welfare policies still qualifies as a democracy; welfare policies without popular self-government, as numerous authoritarian states have illustrated, do not. In sum, democracy is invariably popular self-government and variably something else—something culturally specific that has adhered to it. In the United States, that something else has been individual self-determination.

History and theory operate reciprocally: accommodating the definition to history, circumscribing the history with definition. If history reminds us that democracy has been many things at many times in many places, a definition reminds us that it is not everything all the time anywhere. Democracy is not a facet of political economy, nor does it favor capitalism, socialism, or any of their variants. Its separability, its adaptability to many settings, helps to account for its global force. Democracy is not a set of social outcomes. It promises no one good health, adequate leisure, a rising standard of living, or an equalization of rewards. Democracy is not synonymous with a particular array of supports—two-party politics, constitutions, a vigorous press, abundant voluntary associations, and the like. No institutional context can stand proxy for popular self-government. Nor does democracy contain cures for cruelty and oppression: it has no corner on compassionate impulses or social sensitivities. Although it has some theoretical affinity for doctrines of liberty, equality, and fairness—hence the frequency with which these terms show up in discussions of democracy—it does not provide reliable, concrete support for any of these grand concepts. Democracy, in other words, reveals our humanity, not our salvation. We may not like it.

Democracy is one among competing ways to conduct public affairs. History gives it no advantages. To ask why democracy does not exist at a particular time or in a particular country is on the face of it a distorting question. Its absence does not compel explanation. Nor does any nation have a special claim on its future. Appreciating its historically contingent nature allows us to recognize how breathtaking its arrival was, how extraordinary its spread has been, and how uncertain its prospects are.

I have written a cultural history of democracy in its country of origin. Here *culture* refers to the webbing of values and relations that enables a society to function. In one sense, therefore, my study is situated at the intersection between beliefs and actions: what Americans said and what they did; what they said about what they did, and what they did about what they said. Nevertheless, it consciously steers clear of a systematic history of ideas on one side and a detailed history of political behavior on the other, either of which would have produced a very different account. Hence, in answer to whether there are aspects of American democracy, including the culture of American democracy, that this study does not cover: I certainly hope so. It scarcely requires mention that I make no effort whatsoever to provide rounded discussions of the many, familiar topics my study touches: the development of a constitutional republic, the several party systems, periodic reform movements, business law and economics, an evolving consumer culture, and the like. Although I proceed more or less chronologically, I pick and choose in the spirit of the interpretive essay, not the comprehensive synthesis.

Certain themes do recur in my account. One is the way in which new relations between work and authority have framed the major changes in American democracy. A second is how those major changes have included strikingly different interactions between democracy's two major components, collective and individual self-rule: now companions, now competitors. A third is the tension between the inherently radical nature of democracy, which entails an equality among all participants, regardless of their standing in other settings, and ongoing attempts to use the institutions of democracy to limit or nullify its effects.

These and other matters weave their way through ten chapters, divided into three parts, and a conclusion. Part 1 concentrates on those years roughly from the 1820s to the 1890s when the United States had the world's only democracy. Chapter 1 explains why, from the vantage point of the 18th century, the original democracy of the early 19th century represented a sharp break from the past. Shifting to a transatlantic perspective, chapter 2 examines how tellingly visitors from abroad identified the radical character of this democracy, both in comparison with contemporary European societies and as a driving force in American life. Chapter 3 discusses the operation of various 19th century democratic publics, including a nationwide public, the People. As a context for the People, chapter 4 places its white fraternal world of equals in a larger environment where other Americans, who differed by measures of class, race, and gender, developed their own relations to democracy.

Part 2 turns to the transition years between the 1890s and the 1920s, when America's original democracy broke down and the shape of its replacement emerged. Chapter 5 analyzes basic changes in class relations at the bottom of American society. Covering the same years, chapter 6 demonstrates how basic changes in class relations at the top of American society created a three-class system that fundamentally altered the dynamics of public policy. In a final run through the transition, this time emphasizing the years of the First World War and its aftermath, chapter 7 explains how a progressive weakening of majoritarian democracy culminated in the demolition of the People.

Part 3 picks up the history of American democracy in the 1920s and carries it to the present. In chapter 8, individualism, integrated with collective self-governance in the 19th century, separates itself as 20th century democracy's most vital force. Chapter 9 explains how during the second quarter of the 20th century other ways of defining good government and sound public policy shunted majoritarian practices to one side. Taking the newly polarized politics of the 1960s and 1970s as its point of departure, chapter 10 describes how the possibilities in public policy have changed and how the preying of class on class sharply limits democracy. Finally, the Conclusion assesses the prospects for American democracy by combining its history, as I have explained it, with the judgments of the same sixty-odd contemporary commentators I have incorporated into this Introduction. Understanding the rest of my study does not require reading the Conclusion, but understanding the Conclusion requires reading the rest of my study.

In anticipation of two questions about my own prejudices. Yes, I am a partisan of democracy. Though I have no record to prove it, I believe as an act of faith that human beings can work out a richer, fuller life through popular self-government. No, I do not feel any nostalgia for 19th century democracy. It came as part of a package that I have no desire whatsoever to reclaim. In any case, that was then. What matters now is democracy's role in the 21st century.

PART ONE

THE AMERICAN EXCEPTION
1820s-1890s

‖‖‖‖‖ **D**emocracy developed as part of a vast, differentiating process that originated with the deterioration of early modern European
society, spread rapidly in the 18th century, and transformed the western world by the 19th. Out of this process a distinctive bourgeoisie
emerged. It overhauled capitalism to accommodate the first wave of
the industrial revolution. It carved out a public life where a new kind
of citizen defined his relations with the state, and it separated women
into a private realm that was construed as the opposite of the public
one. On a global scale it fixed racial divisions that justified an emerging
white imperialism. Phrased in another way, this differentiating process
gave both individuals and groups in Western society new attributes
and heightened self-consciousness. As a consequence, centuries later
we accept as simultaneously true a way in which as individuals we
live utterly alone and a way in which our lives have no meaning apart
from their social environments. The history of American democracy
is one expression of these twin truths and of the changing relation
between them.

As individuals were disentangled from family and status networks,
they acquired what were in effect property rights over themselves.
Owning themselves, individuals owned what their labor created.
Hence their skills—what enabled them to produce—were integral
parts to what they owned—their property—and, of course, to who
they were. This personalized understanding of property made industriousness and the fruits of industriousness central to the meaning of
modern individuals and of the societies where they predominated.
John Locke was particularly persuasive in promoting these values.
Drawing on Locke's heritage almost a century later, American revolu-

tionaries laid claim to a republican virtue by contrasting their society's dedication to honest labor with a corrupt Britain's plague of aristocratic drones.

Individuation through industry was largely a characteristic of bourgeois men. Other members of society, obliged to transfer rights to their labor to superiors, relinquished their independence and, as they did, an essential component of their individuality. By the same token, citizenship, a function inextricable from personal independence, did not percolate below the level of the bourgeoisie. Individuation through citizenship involved activities that both validated the government and separated citizens from it, a combination that in deference to the writings of Jürgen Habermas has become associated with *the public sphere*. With the powers of the autocratic state around them, bourgeois individuals chipped out spaces of their own—places to meet and talk, to raise and debate public issues—and from there addressed the authorities with autonomous voices. Because these public networks relied on printed matter, the new citizenship championed a new freedom of the press.

The more citizenship became self-consciously public, the more *public* stood in opposition to *private*, the one a realm of affairs where men gathered and decided, the other a hierarchical realm that denied women a visible presence in civil society. When family status gave order to civic affairs, women, acting from time to time for their families, exercised some of those prerogatives. Individuation, raising men in bas relief and enshrouding women, closed off that option. Women who once used their family standing to participate in civic life discovered that it was now the restrictions of the family above all else which denied them a standing in civic life.

Late in this individualizing process, democracy arrived in one corner of the Western world. Although its rise roughly paralleled the spread of the industrial revolution, the connection was not close. Otherwise democracy would have originated in Britain, where the industrial revolution first flourished, rather than in backwater, commercial-agrarian America. Nor did it grow from 18th century Enlightenment values, Europe's fullest expression of rational individualism, which clashed more profoundly with democratic practices than with the turmoil of the French Revolution and Napoleonic imperialism. Nor, finally, did democracy evolve out of the American Revolution, from which it received a powerful symbolic vocabulary but little else. The Revolutionary generation should be allowed to rest on its laurels. These men broke from established authority and designed a new state, but their accomplishments had no calculable links to democracy.

Early in the 19th century, in a sprawling country of exploding enter-prise, democracy arrived when the primary privileges of these recently differentiated individuals—self-ownership and citizenship—were opened indiscriminately to everybody in one critical category, the soci-ety of white men: not just to respectable bourgeois white men but to all comers. Europeans recognized right away how clearly this stunning proposition distinguished American life from theirs, even as the United States remained in many other ways merely an offshoot of Eu-rope. But as Bruce Ackerman has observed, to qualify as a revolution does not require *"total* change": "it is enough [to] make big changes in the political system."[1] That kind of revolution—democracy—set America apart from the rest of the world.

Circulating the same privileges among all white men gave American society both an unusual fluidity and a special cohesion. Where each one of them was equally a citizen, rights became portable, and the interchangeable carriers of those rights combined and recombined with one another as circumstances required. A different democracy, with a tradition dating back to Periclean Athens, depended on an ex-isting community, small and stable, functioning as the body politic. American democracy, on the contrary, flowed with its mobile citizenry.

At the same time, *self-government* acquired its collective meaning in America. The European Enlightenment construed it as an individual matter, as personal self-regulation, and hence as personal responsibil-ity. By that light, the visiting British geologist Charles Lyell dismissed America's claim to any kind of group self-government as a transparent moral evasion. Democracy followed a different logic. Since all white men governed themselves equally as individuals, all white men com-bined as equals to govern themselves collectively. Individually, each white man made his contribution to the whole, an additive idea about citizenship that could be traced back to Aristotle. Collectively, all white men formed the governing people, a holistic idea about civic life that only congealed early in the 19th century with the new democracy.

Democracy's self-governing citizens filled public space in America. If, as Habermas has described the process in 18th century Europe, bourgeois citizens there had to shape a public sphere in the crevices of an institutionalized society, democratic Americans simply poured into a vacuum. The state did little and intruded less. By Max Weber's famil-iar definition of the state as the agency that monopolizes violent means of coercion, America was virtual anarchy. In myriad combinations, white men designed their own loosely knit, expandable institutions to carry on public life—indeed, their many public lives in many settings. Politics expressed not only what these publics wanted but how they felt about what they wanted. At odds with the Enlightenment tradition of rational dialogue and reasoned decisions, democracy's politics was passionate and celebratory.

As its public life flourished, democracy changed the relations between public and private. On the one hand, it hardened lines of differentiation: a democracy of white men defined itself against white women and people of color. In the process, previous disabilities were reinforced. White women, already caught up in customary family patriarchies, were domesticated at marriage with a new thoroughness that European visitors found excessive. Not only were blacks still enslaved; slavery in America was more relentlessly circumscribed than in any of its other settings. In both cases, that is to say, white men brought a new consciousness to denying certain people a public existence. On the other hand, the looseness, the porousness of democracy's multiple publics kept open the possibility of outsiders experimenting with publics of their own—perhaps to challenge white men, perhaps to join them, perhaps even to ignore them. In the course of these shifting, ambiguous interactions, Americans lived out the truth in one of Alexis de Tocqueville's most astute propositions: "Democratic institutions awaken and foster a passion for equality which they can never entirely satisfy."[2]

CHAPTER 1

DEMOCRACY

As democracy came crashing across early 19th century America, what stood in its way were the hierarchies that had organized 18th century life everywhere in the Western world, including America. In economic opportunities and political prerogatives, in dress and language, in the control of information and the right to speak, in all aspects of public life, obvious and subtle, hierarchy's privileges came graded along a social scale, and society's functioning depended upon a general acceptance of those differences. From time to time the hierarchy's rules were broken—perhaps dramatically, as the occasional toppling of kings illustrated—but the broad structure survived. Those hierarchies were adept at repairing piecemeal violations; only wholesale breakdown could open enough space for a new social order. Beginning around 1800, accelerating between 1815 and 1825, then consolidating one success after another during the 1830s, just such a general collapse occurred in the United States.

Because white men's hierarchies in 18th century America were flimsier than their European counterparts, eliminating them might have seemed like an easy task. Colonial America's scattered population, skeletal government, competitive Protestantism, and scant military presence were poor material for building hierarchies in the first place. Indicatively, when British officers tried to impose their version of hard, clear military discipline on the Massachusetts and Virginia militia during the 1750s, the colonists' assumptions of a looser, more reciprocal arrangement between superior and inferior frustrated them. Moreover, wave after wave of change rattled the rafters of America's hierarchies during the 18th century. In the 1730s and 1740s those recurring assaults on established Protestantism called the Great Awakening coursed up and down the colonies. In the 1770s the American Revolution shattered an imperial hierarchy, and in the 1790s the French Revolution threatened a traditional order in almost all its forms. In conjunction with the revolutions, white men in America mounted campaigns against primogeniture, pomp in government, and English common law, all props to hierarchy, and an impressive number of citizens, some well down the social scale, asserted new freedoms by banding together in revolutionary committees and democratic-republican clubs, mobbing hated authorities, and cursing privileges generally. It became commonplace for Europeans to note the bluntness, the lack of a deferential language, among America's common folk, especially in the coastal towns.

But those American hierarchies were as resilient as they were soft. Churches that spun off from the Great Awakening by and large replicated a customary 18th century order of leaders and followers. Revolutionary committees and democratic-republican clubs had short lives, and their most prominent members, rather than fight for a new social system, usually climbed the existing one. Mobs remained strikingly responsive to an overall structure of authorities as they targeted specific enemies within it. For those who cursed their officials once too often, there were still sedition laws. Who deferred to whom in 1800 determined matters ranging from the organization of political parties to the predictions of which citizens would make it to heaven and which would not.

What radicalism the American, then the French Revolution let loose did no structural damage to America's loose, adaptable hierarchy. If Pennsylvania established a subversive unicameral government in 1776, its constitution in 1790 reverted to the standard separation of powers. At the end of the century, clusters of local notables still dominated government, a wealthy few still monopolized its economic favors, small strata still controlled the learned professions, and gentlemen officers still recruited their own commands, much as elites in these hierarchies had a quarter century before. In 1802 when Tom Paine returned after a long absence to the United States, he slipped into isolation, a revolutionary out of time.

The sustained attacks on authority that did topple American hierarchies originated at the turn of the century. Challenges to a Protestant establishment, for example, began with a round of revivals that spread from Kentucky along the Appalachian chain during the first years of the 19th century. Although the revivals themselves relied on a familiar hell-fire-and-damnation appeal, they spun off a few itinerant evangelists who extended the revivals' momentary affront to denominational authority into an assault on its foundation: a learned clergy's unique ability to explain their god's inscrutable ways, and in the process to justify the selection of a few—commonly a well-to-do few—for salvation and the consignment of the rest to various realms of doubt and damnation. Carrying their much simplified and more optimistic message through the backcountry, these radical itinerants met enthusiastic responses wherever they went.

After the War of 1812, Methodists, whose theology already allowed the possibility of anyone's salvation, and Baptists, many of whom now abandoned their craggy doctrines of predestination, evangelized the east as well as the west with their versions of the good news. Neither denomination featured an educated clergy. As Baptists and Methodists shot ahead in the race for new members, some Presbyterians and Congregationalists fell in behind them. One of them, Charles Grandison Finney, stirred another wave of revivals in the 1820s as he moved from western New York into the seaboard cities. Together these evangelists leveled the path to heaven. "Conversion," one minister declared in behalf of the entire movement, ". . . is a plain, common-sense, practical business, intelligible to all."[1] An ingenious Baptist, holding up his hand and instructing his audience to follow after him, turned the steps to salvation into an elementary five-finger exercise. No mystery there: no convoluted theology that only an elite could comprehend, no complicated hierarchies to distribute the denomination's wisdom and benefits down the line. Salvation lay open to those who would seize it. In the Cane Ridge revivals at the turn of the century, sinners were told not to inhibit the mysterious workings of the Lord; in the Finney revivals of the 1820s, sinners were told to take charge of their own souls. Everything depended upon what individuals did for themselves.

So, according to another popular movement, did a person's health. Coming out of the 18th century, orthodox medicine relied heavily on abstract calculations of the body's internal balance and precise regimens to maintain it that made patients dependent on a doctor's continuing directions. State laws secured his exclusive rights, and substantial fees restricted his practice. After years of guerrilla warfare against official medicine, opponents who saw themselves as the people's champions found an authority of their own in Samuel Thomson, whose neatly titled and immediately successful *New Guide to Health* (1822) laid out botanical remedies that ordinary Americans could readily grasp and apply. Bands of Thomsonians, flaying the medical aristocrats, allying themselves with an evangelical ministry, and condemning monopolists everywhere, distributed their self-help message nationwide under the motto "Every man his own physician."

Homeopaths, Grahamites, practitioners of hydropathy, and sundry eclectics, self-defined and self-taught, came in their wake. Special

training carried no particular authority. As one historian of the profession has characterized these years, "a medical practitioner in America
could lack an M.D. degree, be unlicensed, belong to no professional
society" and still be generally accepted as a doctor: "All the elements
of professional identity pivoted upon action."[2] Unquestionably the
regular doctors' poisonous doses of mercury and antimony, their painful blistering, and their debilitating use of leeches and lances—treat-
ments that emphasized the discipline of a suffering subordinate to a
medical superior—contributed their share of converts to the opposition. Beginning in 1833, public pressures in state after state either
weakened or eliminated the legal protections for orthodox medicine.
Traditional practitioners were outraged, as the Cincinnati physician
Daniel Drake expressed in utter scorn for Andrew Jackson's endorsement of the Thomsonians: "he fought a great *battle*, and is therefore
a great *doctor!*"[3] But the tide swept past Drake. In place of a single
professional hierarchy, citizens now had a menu of choices, many of
which did transform them into their own doctors. Nothing testified
more dramatically to how many Americans took a new responsibility
for their health than the astonishing drop in America's per capita alcohol consumption, by 1850 to about one-quarter what it had been thirty
years earlier.

In fact, popular books and permissive legislation opened the exercise of almost any professional function to almost any enterprising individual. What saved the soul and healed the body could also build
houses and construct bridges: generally applicable formulas were
available for all of them. Simplified texts, casebook summaries, and
lenient examiners created a sea of lawyers surrounding the few remaining islands of professional hierarchy. "The common law," that
grand buttress for an array of 18th century hierarchies, "has no more
characteristic feature," one of its popularizers claimed, "than its *strong
common sense.*"[4] In local courts—"reactive, particularistic, and extremely informal"—ordinary citizens took on the role of public prose-
cutors, lawyers and laypeople cooperated to create the new American
system of plea bargaining, and judges accommodated to the values of
those who elected them.[5] Native wit had replaced traditional authority.

Authority in politics followed the same trajectory from hierarchy
in the 18th century to popular diffusion in the 19th. The American
Revolution actually enhanced the authority of the patriot elite who had
directed it and who as a consequence could draw on large reservoirs
of gratitude in public life. Revolutionary republicanism, in Alan
Kraut's nice summary, was government "by a small, select minority
atop a social hierarchy."[6] For at least another generation, one revolutionary leader or another was honored as the "first character" in his

state politics. Everyone recognized George Washington as first character of the nation; indeed, the assurance that he would be president legitimized an otherwise dangerous expansion of executive powers in the Constitution.

Not surprisingly, America's original nationwide political parties, the Federalists and Republicans of the 1790s, were constructed from these luminaries downward, starting with such authentic heroes as Washington, Thomas Jefferson, and John Adams at the peak, then scaling down through their national lieutenants to sympathetic state leaders to clusters of local notables who rallied the people around them. Interpretations of events and agendas for action came down the same channels; a national election was the grand mustering of party hierarchies. Although no one denied the theoretical sovereignty of the people, day by day even local notables expected to enlighten them and decide in their behalf. When from time to time assemblies or groups of citizens gave legislators precise instructions on this or that issue, their efforts at control were less popular assertions than local defenses against pressures and bribes from farther up the hierarchy.

The single most important source of authority for these sharply peaked political parties was national security, always a friend to hierarchy. As long as the European wars over the French Revolution and the Napoleonic Empire spilled across the Atlantic to threaten the new nation, Federalists and Republicans dominated American politics. Then with the lifting of international crisis after 1815, this kind of party disappeared. Within a few years the thought of Federalists or Republicans mustering the hierarchy to battle for independence seemed absurd. President James Monroe, the costumed embodiment of bygone days in his ruffles and britches, won widespread affection as a national museum piece, but no support whatsoever as the nation's leader. Other centers of hierarchical power were falling around him. Legislative caucuses, the standard means for selecting party nominees, including its candidate for president, withered under attacks that they hid themselves from the public. Open conventions emerged the new favorite. In democracies, Yaron Ezrahi has written, "seeing and witnessing"—and the irrefutable evidence they are expected to provide—"are inseparable from the attempts to define politics as a realm of plain observable facts which are accessible to all."[7] By the late 1820s, as Alexis de Tocqueville noted, it was already American practice in politics to "strip off . . . whatever conceals it from sight, in order to view it more closely and in the broad light of day."[8] Precisely this insistence on transparency gave the sudden eruption of anti-Masonic politics in those years such popular force: Masonic secrecy meant aristocratic subversion.

Even while Federalists and Republicans were battling over the terms of independence, another politics—state-based, development-oriented—rapidly gained strength after 1800. It focused on the corporate charters, or little monopolies, that state governments still bestowed one by one, ostensibly to serve the general welfare. Perhaps fifty of these, gilding the privileges of elites in a few cities, existed at the turn of the century. The itch to share those privileges—to open a bank, to establish an insurance company, to build a toll road—spread to lesser gentlemen in the major centers, to leaders in smaller coastal towns, and finally to enterprising folk throughout the backcountry. In the name of economic development, these ambitions mobilized whole localities, increased turnouts at state elections, and intensified pressure on the legislatures. By 1816, the number of state-chartered corporations had leaped to about 1,500. The original party system was collapsing by then, and state parties were filling all political spaces. Attempts to revive the authority of a central government by controlling the distribution of public land, empowering a central bank, raising the tariff, and funding a network of interior transportation—sometimes labeled the American System—called the roll of policies that the enemies of hierarchy would topple in the 1830s and 1840s. Development planning in the state capitals had no better luck. Projects mushroomed everywhere; power dispersed.

Centrifugal politics produced leaders with an ordinary look about them, men who were comfortable mixing with their constituents, not standing above them. Authority came in humble garb, and the men who wore it were obliged to prove that they deserved it. Leaders such as Henry Clay and Daniel Webster, whose careers spanned the old and new politics, were in special danger of appearing aloof and arrogant because when they entered politics, they had been expected to appear wealthier than they really were. Now, to undo the damage, they recreated their life stories so that they would appear poorer than they actually were. The patrician Clay acquired an impoverished boyhood and a self-trained mind, the aristocratic Webster a link with pioneer life in a log cabin. Calling Mr. Jefferson "Tom" or Mr. Madison "Jemmy" declared them too common to lead an 18th century hierarchy; calling Clay "Harry of the West" and Andrew Jackson "Old Hickory" sanctioned them for 19th century leadership. When Jefferson became president, he told associates to leave the affairs of government in James Madison's, Albert Gallatin's, and his own skilled hands: they defined their party. In the early 19th century, Martin Van Buren and William Henry Harrison seemed eager to disappear inside their own administrations: their parties defined them. Orders no longer came from the top; scant power remained in the center.

Less noisily but just as profoundly, a companion process remade the norms of work in the white men's world, replacing the timeless assumption that most of them would labor in dependence on a few landowners, masters, and employers with the astonishing proposition that white men would control their own working lives. The new norm of self-directed work struck at the very heart of the social order, for societies organize around the rules of who works for whom, and the beneficiaries protect those rules in the name of all that is good in this world and holy in the next.

In early modern Europe, as white colonials were pushing their way into North America, most work revolved around land, which a small fraction of the population owned and an overwhelming majority cultivated under complexly differentiated schemes of tenancy, serfdom, and day labor. These belonged, in Adam Smith's wording, to "the labouring poor, that is the great body of the people," whom Smith along with virtually all his peers consigned to lives of unremitting toil at the edges of survival. Despite the upheavals of the French Revolutionary period, peasants' prospects of bettering their lot actually shrank in the hundred years between the mid-18th and the mid-19th century, as Europe's population soared from around 140 million to around 250 million. Without surplus lands to absorb it, this explosion simultaneously drove millions off the land and heaped heavier burdens on those who stayed. In stretches of central and eastern Europe, more and more peasants slipped back into serfdom. In the Irish countryside, gradations from precarious to abject dependence created increasingly desperate conditions until famines swept away the most vulnerable. Even in England's relatively free agricultural system, rural dependence retained much of its power, as Thomas Hardy's novels of the hardscrabble West Country illuminated. Corvées, those moments of unpaid labor for a local grandee that defined a whole fabric of relationships, were still being performed in mid-19th century France.

Across the centuries, Europe's towns and cities offered literally a life-saving alternative to increasing numbers of these countrypeople. As much as propertied Englishmen feared the flux of "masterless men" on the loose, they were already integral to British life by the 17th century. Nevertheless, with the possible exception of a successful life in crime, nothing in their marginal, often hand-to-mouth existence lifted them out of dependence. Nor did any of them participate in the bourgeois spirit of what C. B. Macpherson has called "possessive individualism." Whether wage labor in the 18th and 19th centuries raised or lowered these people's standard of living—a matter of continuing dispute—the so-called free labor market certainly did not mean freedom from a superior's control. On the contrary, attempts to tighten work discipline increased with the flow of migration. Always the spur in the workers' flanks was hunger, with the threat of starvation just behind. Welfare policy in 19th century Britain was carefully built to preserve those incentives.

White men functioned under quite different circumstances in colonial North America, with its great expanse of arable land and its chronic shortage of labor. If reality never matched the myth of a farm for every white settler, ownership by any European standard was extraordinarily widespread. Most of Europe's graded privileges and obligations relating to land usage also disappeared. *Freehold*, which in the complicated British system referred to the right of certain tenants to hold lands for some period of years free of servile or arbitrary exactions, was flattened by the white colonists into another term for ownership: there free meant free. Where the towns had no walls and the countryside no manor houses, white moved more or less at will in search of opportunities, a striking difference in its own right from the restrictions that imposed a maze of barriers across Europe.

Nevertheless, patterns of dependent work were embedded deep in this white world. Perhaps half of the white immigrants to these colonies arrived legally bound—redemptioners, criminals or jailed paupers under contract, young apprentices, and other indentured laborers. Although terms and tenures varied, almost all these people, by custom and by law, stood at their master's disposal to drive and discipline as he chose. Whatever advantages a freeholder might enjoy in colonial life, they did nothing to alleviate the lot of the unfree. By and large, the conditions of indentured servitude in the colonies were even "harsher than practices that prevailed in English service."[9]

Other 18th century uses of *servant* revealed an even wider range of subordinate, coercive wage relationships, including commodified variations on the old tradition of a lord's rights to his peasants' labor. The important legal terms *master* and *servant* meant what they said. Cycling through colonial societies, these many forms of servitude made dependent white labor a regular part of life. In fact, dependence seemed to increase after midcentury. The number of indentures from England picked up. Strings of migrants moved through one western Massachusetts town after another without finding land. Perceptions of a land shortage spread along the eastern seaboard, and more large landowners experimented with ways of binding their tenants by contract to a long-term dependence.

The American Revolution gave these work relations a softer Enlightenment glow without altering their structure. Although some states modified the terms and scope of indenture contracts, they also reaffirmed their legality. Public land was sold in such large chunks that only wealthy investors could afford to buy it from the government. It was no simple matter for ordinary people to move beyond the land speculators' private baronies. Around 1800, one-third of the white men living as far west as the Shenandoah Valley remained landless. When tenants in the Maine section of Massachusetts, invoking the Revolution to support their cause, tried to escape the old-fashioned leases that blocked them from owning the land they farmed, years of conflict won them only minor concessions in a battle they eventually lost. In these areas, traditional privileges held firm at the turn of the century.

A basic restructuring in the conditions of work followed the same chronology as the dismantling of hierarchical authority. With the 19th century came the first signs of a major change; by the 1820s, old schemes were disintegrating everywhere; in the 1830s the new dispensation consolidated a sweeping victory. The supports for a system of indentured servitude clearly weakened after 1800 in the face of spreading challenges to it, both formal and informal. Nevertheless, stubborn masters managed to preserve some version of it until a legal ruling in 1821 abruptly pulled out its central prop: the court refused to enforce such a contract against the will of an adult. If the servant could simply walk away, who was master? As courts elsewhere made the same judgment, the system crumbled. By the end of the 1820s, even immigrants, no favorites at law, could escape indentures.

Apprenticing, a form of contract that at the turn of the century still gave the master almost total control over his charge's conditions of work, followed a similar chronology in decline. After 1810, legal actions and personal assertions of independence snarled the traditional apprenticing relationship of master/father with servant/dependent in an increasingly complicated web of controversy. By the 1820s, a master's leeway was sharply restricted. Within a decade, paternalist apprenticing more or less disappeared, except as a way for the state to farm out some children of the poor. Apprentices, like former contract servants of all sorts, now negotiated for a wage just as other workers in the labor market did.

Great expanses of space broke open the monopolies of land. After the War of 1812, white farmers rushed westward, pushing Native Americans ahead of them and leaving most government controls behind. When a scattering of officials tried to enforce the rights of absentee landowners, squatter rebellions lit up the west. Rapid turnover was the first rule of the smart land investor. In time, government policy responded to the relentless landseekers, first by dropping the price per acre, then—even more important—by decreasing the minimum plot for sale from 640 acres in 1796 to 40 by 1832. During the next nine

years, the government established a policy of preemption authorizing
the outer wave of settlers to pick their own farms: they could purchase
up to 160 acres of the land they had occupied before the government
surveyors caught up with them. The results were a freeholder's paradise. Even in the southern states where the adverse effects of slavery
reputedly weighed down poor whites, at midcentury "between 80 and
90 percent of the small farmers owned their land."[10]

By the 1830s, America offered the astonishing spectacle of a society
that had relinquished almost all claims to organizing white men's
work, indeed that lacked almost all of the powers to try. Stretching
westward and multiplying little dots of enterprise far beyond the capacity of a spindly government to oversee them, white men took control over their work with them, investing everyday decisions about it
in the hands of those actually doing the work. In fact, the law did
not allow white men to relinquish that control, to contract away their
freedom, even if they wanted to. Work—of the head or the hands, as
the expression went—became a national hymn. Poor and rich alike
had the right to determine their own working lives. If hunger never
went away, it was no longer a proxy for social policy. Rich and poor
alike had the same obligation to work. Playing a 19th century American Polonius, the Boston magnate John Murray Forbes instructed his
son, "All the real work of life goes hard until you have accustomed
yourself to do it . . . and then work often becomes a pleasure."[11]

Hence the standard refrain of the 19th century that all genuine citizens were producers, that productive work was the emblem of their
independence, and that denying them the opportunity for an independent working life was tantamount to stripping them of an American
identity. As a corollary, because personal credit, extending across the
continent in endlessly filagreed networks, sustained these norms of
self-directed work, white men insisted upon access to it, not as a conve-
nience or a reward but as a birthright. Government policies and financial institutions standing in the way became the great villains of the
19th century, for this producers' ideology, in the language of one popularly attuned western legislature, mandated modest amounts of credit
on demand "to every merchant, every mechanic, and every farmer who
may desire it."[12]

At times the forces behind a self-defining authority and self-directed
work swept through the white men's world so close together that they
seemed to merge. In 1821—judicial rejection of indentured servitude;
in 1822—Thomson's *New Guide to Health*; in 1823—Finney's first great
revival; in 1824—death knell for the congressional caucus: who would
even try to disentangle their influence? The politics of anti-Masonry,
of workingmen's programs, and of liberalized land laws tumbled one

atop another late in the 1820s and early in the 1830s; Jackson's attack
on the Second Bank of the United States served the causes of popular
authority and independent work evenhandedly.

Nevertheless, the victory for self-directed work was decidedly the
more fragile, the more fortuitous of the two. As a universal norm, its
dramatic triumph could only have come during a short space of time
after 1815. So much had to combine all at once in the white men's
world: an abundance of cheap land, a general collapse of unfree labor
arrangements, a fluidity in the status of wage earners, a relentless decentralization of everyday decision-making, a remarkable expansion of
small-scale credits for farmers. In the course of the 19th century, one
element after another in this critical cluster dropped away. The ratio
between prime farm land and farmers turned against aspiring newcomers. Dispensers of credit came to use it less to keep scarce farmers
in charge of the land than to control the land itself, and sometimes to
keep debtors laboring on it. Machines altered work relations in both
agriculture and industry, and wage earning, no longer the experience
of a minority—perhaps only a temporary condition at that—drew
more and more people into patterns of lifelong dependent work. By
seizing the moment at the beginning of the 19th century, white men
were able not just to expand control over their working lives but to fix
that control as a basic American right. Riding the momentum of this
success, the right of self-directed work remained a national norm long
after it could have reestablished itself under its own power.

Building something new early in the 19th century depended first on
breaking down something old: the prerequisite to construction was
destruction. The senior Henry James grasped this intimate interdepen-
dence when he identified democracy with "a dissolution and disorganization of old forms. It is simply a resolution of government into the
hands of the people, a taking down . . . and a recommitment."[13] Although the movements that leveled authority and spread control over
work relied less on the sledgehammer than the centrifuge—a spinning
beyond official range, a scattering of enterprise and conflict—they
spared nothing that stood in their way.

Democratic lore turned this critical process of destruction into a series of stock stories about the hero who persisted unflinchingly until
the enemy fell. By his own account, Samuel Thomson, the tribune of
self-medication, wrestled against all odds with one representative of
the medical hierarchy after another in his efforts to relieve the suffering
of the sick, until his book finally secured victory for the people. The
tale of tales in this vein pitted Andrew Jackson as the lonely warrior
against scheme after scheme of elite privilege: first the congressional

caucus; then a "corrupt bargain" between John Quincy Adams and Henry Clay that stole the presidency from Jackson, the people's choice; and finally the monster Bank of the United States, with its tentacles squeezing the common man's credit throughout the country. In a world of giant killers, an organization such as the Masons that wedded hierarchy, loyalty, and secrecy found it had no defenses, and enemies battered it virtually out of existence. Other hierarchies toppled as if they had been fated to go. Late in the 1830s, the Benevolent Empire, an attempt to spread evangelical Protestant morality nationwide from a New York City headquarters, collapsed into its parts.

At the risk of treating a fluid process too schematically, we might think of the initial consequence of this breakdown as many contemporaries did: radically individualizing white men's lives. In the 18th century, looking down the hierarchy, a vision of atomized individuals was invariably conservative, a way of splintering the sovereign people and disabling them for group action. Centralizers such as James Wilson and Alexander Hamilton, for example, pictured the new Constitution creating a direct connection between individual citizens and the national government that would short-circuit collective assertions at the state level. As hierarchies fell in 19th century America, however, individualization communicated just the opposite—strength, not weakness. It empowered white men, one by one, to make choices and act on them. In Britain, where the assumption that a superior few must show the way to an inferior many held firm, as serious a 19th century reformer as John Stuart Mill, contemplating ordinary workers in the role of citizens, saw only the daunting task ahead of him: "The prospect of the future depends on the degree in which they can be made rational beings."[14] In the new American scheme of things, on the contrary, that responsibility was spread evenly among white men, each of whom had his exclusive right to decide what he thought and what he did.

Among the most striking implications of this atomized sovereignty was the way in which, with one grand sweep, it eliminated the whole range of concerns about democracy's extendability that had bedeviled the Revolutionary generation. Now as white men set out into the world, they carried democracy wherever they went and as far as they went, without diminishing any of its essential attributes—any of its force or legitimacy or authority. Each of them quite literally embodied democracy. Pictured from another angle, these individuals comprised tiny sovereign units, infinitely interchangeable—hence instantly functional—however and wherever they came together. Scope no longer had any bearing on the definition of democracy; the democrats themselves determined its scope as they determined where to go.

When these sovereign atoms came together, they gave entirely different meanings to what at first glance looked like familiar behavior under a familiar label. There were political parties, for example, both before and after the democratization of public authority and working life. On the one side, the Federalists and Republicans, originating in the 1790s, were directed, legitimized, and defined by a thin stratum of gentlemen. On the other, the parties congealing in the late 1820s and 1830s affirmed and reaffirmed the common sovereignty of all white men. Electing nonentities and rotating officeholders served as practical devices for challenging the old assumptions about obedience, for demystifying government, and for circulating political power back through the electorate. In the early 19th century, the very existence of workingmen's parties—unthinkable in Revolutionary times—marked a vast distance between the original party system and the new democratic politics. Patronage, once a vertical bond between a client and his benefactor, now cemented above all else a lateral attachment to the beneficiary's democratic group within one of the new political parties. Parades in the 18th century gave public expression to social distinctions and occupational layering, their partisan replacements in the 19th century to a homogenized popular authority.

In the process, voting also underwent a basic change in meaning. Take, for example, the practice of open balloting. In the late 18th century, despite the Revolution's loosening of vested interests, leaders still assumed political office as their right and instructed the people as their duty. Although voters might repudiate officials, elections pitted gentleman against gentleman, with voters sometimes quite literally lining up behind their candidates. In this scheme of things, open balloting ratified local hierarchies. James Fenimore Cooper, a stanch defender of those traditional ways, caught their meaning in an episode in *Homeward Bound*, where the entire crew of a ship has been dispossessed by an enemy force. The captain and first mate—natural leaders both—put it to the seamen: are they up to the dangerous business of retaking their ship? The sailors cheer their assent. Only Cooper's cowardly democrat, Steadfast Dodge, holds back. "'The ballot might have given it the other way,' muttered Mr. Dodge; 'there can be no freedom of election without the ballot.'" [15]

Dodge, of course, was absolutely correct, and early in the 19th century ballots helped to separate the act of voting from the endorsement of a superior. Yet no sooner was an electorate of sovereign equals in place than variations on open balloting reappeared in new guises: color-coded paper ballots to distinguish one party from another, public boasts of party allegiance at the polls, voting in partisan bands, and the like. European visitors threw up their hands. Why would Americans nullify their own secret ballot reforms? Once again, the same thing had become entirely different. In the 18th century, voting itself signified hierarchical location: nonvoters, voters, minor officials, major officeholders, leaders, with higher qualifications commonly written into law at each point along this rising scale. Who could visualize the men at the top—a George Washington or a John Hancock—actually voting? Balloting openly in this scheme affirmed a man's place. Only in the 19th century did the franchise come to express equality. Now open balloting celebrated the new age of leveled sovereignty: independent voters standing publicly and proudly by their choices, their comrades, their party.

The most fundamental of these changes disguised as continuities involved the connection between the franchise and citizenship. In the 18th as in the 19th century, the ballot not only denoted citizenship but also vouched for the citizen's independence. The customary evidence of independence was at least a modicum of property. William Blackstone's negative phrasing captured the traditional Anglo-American rationale behind the property qualification: "to exclude such persons as are in so mean a situation that they are esteemed to have no will of their own." In most circumstances, it was assumed, property conferred other desirable attributes as well: a faith in the law, a commitment to social order, a capacity for dispassionate reason. On these grounds, British publicists disqualified the large majority of its population— "the common people"—whose "labour," Adam Smith concluded, "is both so constant and so severe, that it leaves them little leisure and less inclination to apply to, or even to think of any thing else." [16] Property alone provided an escape hatch from that miserable, mindless existence.

As an immigrant country, colonial North America adopted significantly more lenient standards of citizenship for its white men: greater flexibility in the types of qualifying property and less of it. As a result, on the eve of the Revolution, America's electorate was already impressively large, perhaps two out of three white men by contrast with about one out of four in Britain. Nevertheless, leaders in America as in Britain, seeking evidence of a citizen's independent will, assumed that property, however modest in amount, drew the appropriate line. After the Revolution, state legislatures enfranchised army veterans not just by making them voters but by granting them land which then qualified them as voters.

It was the new norm of self-directed work that turned the old assumptions about property and independence inside out. Where every white man was responsible for his own working life, even the least prepossessing among them had the autonomy, the self-sufficiency to make decisions by the light of what Frederick Grimke, using redundance for emphasis, called the American's "free liberty of choice."[17] Adulthood conferred independence. No white man had to achieve it or prove it; it was his democratic birthright. After breaking the traditional link between property and citizenship, 19th century democracy then fashioned a new one that flipped Blackstone's dictum on its head. If in the 18th century becoming a landowner established a putative claim to independence, in the 19th century each citizen's independence established a putative claim to becoming a landowner.

As property ceased to create citizens, it also lost its power to shape their character. If democracy required such qualities as solidity, reason, and commitment in its citizens, they needed other means to acquire them. The adult years would be too late: full citizenship came automatically with a white man's majority. Into this breach rushed the educational reformers—Horace Mann, Henry Bernard, and their associates—who promised to shape these democrats' public character during the malleable, habit-forming years of common schooling. What property no longer accomplished, schoolmarms and schoolmasters would. Democratic citizens, Mann declared, had "the *absolute right* to an education" and their society an equally compelling stake in their receiving one.[18]

Nothing better demonstrated how important breakdown was to the arrival of democracy than its absence. If democracy had evolved gradually out of 18th century traditions, New England would surely have been in the lead, with Massachusetts and perhaps Boston ahead of the rest, for their institutions gave them a clear head start: the widest colonial franchise in Massachusetts, a history of congregational autonomy in the churches, persistent battles for liberty against the British, and above all town meetings, not only the pride of the New Englanders themselves but also the envy of history's favorite protodemocrat, Thomas Jefferson. Yet matters developed otherwise. In what was virtually a unanimous judgment, visitor after visitor from abroad early in the 19th century singled out some part of New England—often Massachusetts, sometimes just Boston—as the least democratic part of America. On the contrary, they reported, it contained the best ordered, the least leveled, the most deferential portion of American society; its citizens held their peace, abided by the law, and listened to their betters. "In New England," Alexis de Tocqueville wrote, "where . . . the common people are accustomed to respect intellectual and moral superiority and to submit to it without complaint . . . the democracy makes a more judicious choice than it does elsewhere."[19]

Like other apparent precursors to democracy in 18th century

America, New England's institutions reflected its distinctive hierarchies. As the colonial Massachusetts militia illustrated, inferiors were bound to superiors through an implicit trade of obedience for welfare. Though soldiers refused to jump when British officers barked, they did follow orders from colonial gentlemen who paid some attention to their needs and wishes. Even the agrarian rebels in Maine who at the end of the 18th century demanded homesteads as their right sought to reestablish a "protection covenant" whereby responsive elites looked after the general interests of loyal citizens. Similar forms of reciprocity were also honored in churches and preserved through town meetings, whose consensus ethos stood polar opposite to 19th century democratic individualism.

New England's hierarchical institutions proved remarkably elastic during the upheavals between the 18th and 19th centuries. Revolution did not weaken them. In the 1790s no region expressed greater hostility than New England to the idea of "self-created" organizations—that is, group action outside the accepted order of authority—an idea that would soon be glorified in America's democratic restructuring. In each of the major battles to level authority, New England's institutions were the most resistant. There orthodox medicine and an educated bar retained their strongest supports at law. Alone in the United States, Massachusetts and Connecticut entered the 19th century with vestiges of an established church, and New England gave the new egalitarian revivalism its coldest response. Appropriately, it was New England theology that the great revivalist Finney had to crack in order to lay open the choice of salvation to his audiences. In a gesture symbolic of the region's response to these powerful democratic currents, Boston's equally famous minister Lyman Beecher—a man who proved too liberal in turn for his own church peers—declared that he personally would bar the dangerous Finney at the gates to New England.

In the United States at large, the first party system of Federalists and Republicans splintered beyond recall after 1815, and new parties—Democrats and Whigs—had to be built anew from all sorts of local and state initiatives. In New England, however, Federalists from the 1810s reconvened as National Republicans in the 1820s who reconvened as Whigs in the 1830s, a continuity in majority parties that preserved important elements of 18th century conservatism and even fooled some historians of the late 20th century into believing that Whigs generally, rather than this special Massachusetts-based variety, held tenaciously to hierarchical values in a democratic society. Just as many New England employers clung to paternalism and deference in their shops, so many of its politicians refused to abandon the old equations between property and citizenship. It was northeastern Whigs, the better to cover the nakedness of a shamelessly broad franchise, who misled Europeans into believing that almost all white men in the United States deserved to be citizens because almost all of them held property. Only in New England, with Massachusetts showing the way, did voters face compulsory registration laws early in the 19th century. At a time when by popular demand states everywhere were moving the sites for their capitals to make government seem less intimidating and more accessible, only the Massachusetts capital stood fast in a large coastal city, Boston. At midcentury, Massachusetts still had not authorized the secret ballot. Where there was no collapse of the old ways, in other words, no destruction to clear space for something new, democracy arrived slowly, limping from the weight of a good deal of hierarchical baggage.

Democracy's meaning in public discussion revealed even more starkly the differences between the 18th and 19th centuries. To the Revolutionary generation, democracy was a minor matter. What importance it did have derived largely from its relationship with other types of government. The standard trio of these forms was monarchy, aristocracy, and democracy—rule of the one, the few, the many—grounded in Aristotle, elaborated by various classical writers, and used in the 18th century as building blocks in public commentary on both sides of the Atlantic. Revolutionary Americans claimed to combine the three in a republic that retained the special benefits of each—monarchy's energy, aristocracy's corruption, democracy's representativeness—while avoiding each one's special pitfall: monarchy's tyranny, aristocracy's corruption, democracy's disorder. From deep old habits, their republic never lost its resemblance to the parent British government: Crown, House of Lords, and House of Commons stripped of their holy, hereditary authority and dressed in the homespun of secular ceremonies and generic titles became the American executive, upper house, and lower house.

Beneath this scheme Revolutionary leaders set the sovereign people, more or less where 18th century British commentators located the people but in this case investing them with the ultimate authority that Crown and Parliament used to have. Securing the Revolution's republican identity and inviting the widest public allegiance, the sovereignty of the people, once in place, never budged. Henceforth, everybody dealing with government in America began there. Atop those sovereign people, however, revolutionaries erected various structures that still relied for their legitimacy on a correct balance of governing branches. If the democratic component, even under the name of the people's branch, exceeded proper limits, it threatened the whole system. On its own, "democratical" meant "without any restraint or . . . counter poise." Except in the first flush of revolution, when enthusiasm for legislative power ran at its highest, to call the entire government a democracy condemned it. Richard Henry Lee and the young John Quincy Adams intended just that in labeling government under the Articles of Confederation a "Simple Democracy" because it lacked a separate executive and upper house to complement its congress of state delegates. "But between a balanced republic and a democracy," John Marshall bluntly declared, "the difference is like that between order and chaos." [20]

The Constitution emerging from Philadelphia in 1787 recast these familiar issues in novel ways. Instead of relying on each state to embody America's republican principles and gathering these republics into a league of states, the new plan cast a republican superstructure across the entire nation and in the process radically enlarged the territory that republics were supposed to cover. Even though the point of reference had expanded over the centuries from the ancient city of Athens to Britain's tight little island, the question still remained whether a people's branch of government—traditionally the lower house of the legislature—could even exist in a system as vast as the Constitution's.

Critics said no. Where America's state governments required more than 2,000 representatives to create genuinely democratic branches, one antifederalist argued, the proposed House of Representatives would have fewer than 100. How in a world of carts and country roads, another wanted to know, could representatives with residences "two hundred to five hundred miles from their constituents . . . retain any great affection for the welfare of the people?" The wrong sort would be drawn into the House. "When the number [of representatives] is so small the office will be highly elevated and distinguished," attracting the "natural aristocracy" and leaving "but very little democracy in it." Instead of balancing the aristocratic Senate, the House would merge with it. "Under the pretence of different branches of the legislature, the members will in fact be chosen from the same general description of citizens." Without popular counterweight, the Constitution would lead to "the absolute dominion of one, or a few." [21]

Stymied at the national level, opponents of the proposed Constitution found a genuine democratic component only in state government. They looked beyond the states' function as the voice of the sovereign people in ratifying a frame of government—first the Articles of Confederation, now the Constitution. Although a momentous role, that was a sharply limited one. They also looked past the mixes of monarchic and aristocratic elements inside each of these governments. Seen from a national perspective, the parts of state government, executive and legislative alike, merged into a single unit. What mattered now was that by contrast with the national government's distance from citizens, state governments seemed right next to them: "they will have a near connection, and their members an immediate intercourse with the people." "I conceive the position to be undeniable," an antifederalist summarized the new case, "that the federal government will be principally in the hands of the natural aristocracy, and the state governments principally in the hands of the democracy, the representatives of the body of the people."[22]

Shifting the grounds of discussion from branches of government to levels of government had profound consequences, some short term, some long range. For those most insistent upon a bill of rights, the first ten amendments represented not a guarantee of individual rights but a solidification of the states' democratic powers, "the text," Jefferson called the amendments, "whereby [state governments] will try all the acts of the federal government."[23] Appropriately, Jefferson applied just this understanding of the Bill of Rights when he concluded in 1798 that the Federalist administration had run roughshod over the Constitution and, with Madison, drew up resolutions for the Kentucky and Virginia legislatures repudiating the recently enacted Alien and Sedition Acts. The national government had failed liberty's test, the Kentucky and Virginia Resolutions declared, and only state governments—the people's governments—could preserve their rights.

In the long run, southerners would use this state-based resistance to justify the very different political programs behind nullification and secession, and democrats everywhere would turn it into yet another argument for local self-government. But these were 19th century concerns. Around 1800 the maneuverings between state and national governments still followed the familiar 18th century agenda of balancing the republican structure.

The popular implications of a second democratic issue, representation, were also tightly circumscribed by 18th century conceptions. When antifederalists looked to state government as a refuge for the people, they picked up a line of reasoning that Americans in the 1770s had followed into their Revolution. Distant, indirect representation, the argument went, violated republican principles. To qualify, in George Mason's words, representatives "ought to mix with the people, think as they think, feel as they feel . . . and [be] thoroughly acquainted with their interest and condition."[24] Hence a lofty House of Representatives lacked the essential characteristics of a popular branch. Only the state governments nestled close enough to the people to represent them.

In a hierarchy, however, that affinity between the people and the representatives a layer or two above them empowered the representatives far more than it did the people. A representative communed with his constituents to understand their circumstances, not to receive their instructions. In government, he then acted according to his own wisdom, not theirs. He, not they, decided what was in their best interests. Consequently it was not necessary that all of them have the right to vote, only that all of them be in the representative's thoughts. Phrased another way, representative bodies swallowed up the people. In effect, they became the people, as the influential British publicist John Trenchard had defined them several decades earlier: "*the people* (that is, such as shall be successfully chosen to represent the people." [25] Advocates of a democratic interest within America's new federalism had precisely that simple equation in mind as they praised the state governments: "in some degree a periodic assemblage of the people," "the people themselves in a state of refinement." [26] Here too 18th century democracy devolved into structural questions. Those questions never raised the issue of a people's government, only of the people's place in government. Champions of the state governments did not ask how the people might exercise greater power but which officials would exercise it best in the name of the people.

Only a final, rather vague area of democratic associations—popular assertiveness—had the potential for bursting these formal 18th century bounds. Here at least the people themselves were acting. Nevertheless, even under the most generous 18th century constructions this kind of democracy teetered on the rim of rabble-rousing, and in the 1790s, gales from the French Revolution blew it over the edge. In a sweep of events that almost defied belief, the giant of the Western world jettisoned hereditary privileges, executed its king, went to war with Europe, and turned a bloody terror on itself. As this stunning sequence unfolded, the number of Americans who could still see signs of liberty in the flames of Europe dwindled, and when the effects of its wars extended across the Atlantic, fears of both imperial powers, Britain and France, deepened further. By 1794 the terms for revolutionary extremism—Jacobin and Terror—were clamped like curses on any freewheeling expressions of popular sentiment. Within a year the most boisterous American supporters of the French Revolution, the democratic-republican clubs, disappeared. Nobody defended the Terror; nobody chose the side of chaos.

Tar from the Jacobin brush also stuck to the popular branches of government. By eliminating a recognizable executive, those French radicals had, after all, stretched legislative authority to the farthest republican limits, perhaps beyond them. Democracy always connoted tumult. When Adam Smith wanted to condemn the American colonies as troublemakers, for example, he associated them with "those rancorous and virulent factions which are inseparable from small democracies."[27] According to the Aristotelian tradition, pure democracy predictably led to anarchy, which then opened the door to despotism, and even before Napoleon's coronation, many a witness thought the French Revolution was working out that classical formula before their eyes.

To these standard structural concerns, the unfolding revolution added an immediate fear of unleashed violence. Leading Federalists made it plain that by their reading of the French experience all efforts to enhance state or legislative power were simultaneously invitations to bloodshed. In a tacit acknowledgment of the force of these arguments, Jefferson and Madison took scrupulous care to surround the Kentucky and Virginia Resolution—assertion simultaneously of state and of legislative authority—with a peaceful aura. No intimidation: the national government, they claimed, was the lone aggressor. No unseemly disturbances: they positively discouraged public protests. To no avail. In the French context, Virginia's challenge to national authority inevitably raised the specter of a military rebellion. Hamilton immediately planned for battle.

Although Jefferson survived the crisis of the late 1790s to become president in 1801, democracy as a topic for public discussion did not make it with him. Jefferson alone might have infused those 18th century concepts with new life for the next century. He had strong connections to all aspects of this democratic tradition: close ties with the antifederalists, public advocacy for the Bill of Rights, open delight in the initial destructive force of the French Revolution, great hopes for the countervailing power of state governments. Nevertheless, instead of turning that tradition toward the future, Jefferson left it behind. For one thing, democracy had become too dangerous. Whatever his professions of peace and innocence in 1798, he still plotted the Kentucky and Virginia Resolutions like a spy thriller, replete with clandestine meetings, midnight rides, and binding oaths to keep his part an absolute secret during his lifetime. Indicatively, Jefferson's final reference to democracy during the crisis carried intimations of bloodshed. Early in 1801, when he thought the Federalists might use force to deny him the presidency, he wrote that in "the present democratical spirit of America," friendly state militia would if necessary march him in arms to his inauguration.[28] Once president, as Hamilton predicted, Jefferson took comfortably to executive power. What need for legislative checks or state challenges now?

Democracy was simply in disrepute. Without supports anywhere, its 18th century themes slipped from sight. Certainly nothing in Napoleonic Europe revived democracy's reputation. It required as free a spirit as the Baptist radical Elias Smith, harbinger of a coming age, to call out in the backcountry that, yes, his America was "a DEMOCRACY."[29] Almost everywhere else, the concept, always suspect, lay under a cover of silence.

When democracy reemerged a generation later, the ugly duckling had become a swan. Although a close observer could find family resemblances, what mattered was the miraculous transformation. In the 18th century democracy was a force to contain through formal relationships—between legislative and executive branches, state and national governments, the people and their representatives. The 19th century let it loose. Now democracy meant people in action. In 1834, looking back to the structural preoccupations of the 18th century, the Democratic editor William Leggett had no way of dealing with the curious phrase "an 'unbalanced democracy.'" Leggett simply dismissed the issue: "We have none of those fears."[30]

When Madison analyzed "public opinion" in 1791, he gave it qualities more or less the equivalent of community values. In the 19th century it acquired power. As the commentator Frederick Grimke stated, "Public opinion" was the government's "moving force." If "The people demand" a measure, Stephen A. Douglas declared, "they will never be satisfied till their wishes shall have been respected and their will obeyed." When an aroused public spotted corrupt officials, William Cullen Bryant thought, it punished them instantly. Even if the people played the tyrant, they could not be denied. Would he oppose the Mexican War, the Whig Justin Butterfield was asked in 1846? "No, by G_d, I oppose no wars. I opposed one war, and it ruined me." Now if the people want them, he declared, "I am for *War, Pestilence and Famine*." The Revolutionary generation set their hierarchy atop the people; 19th century publicists, toppling the hierarchy, ended with just the people. "The popular voice is all powerful with us," the young George Bancroft stated a bit grandly in 1826; "this is our oracle; this, we acknowledge, is the voice of God."[31]

The new 19th century people not only included all white men; it assigned significance to each of them. Leggett considered "Every man's example . . . a leading influence" in public opinion. Give one person a public role, Bancroft argued, and you get only what he has to offer. "Give power to a fraction of the people, and you have a partial exposition of justice. Give power to the whole people, and you gain the nearest expression of . . . universal reason." Though it was conceivable for the majority to err, it was not likely. "The presumption is certainly in [the majority's] favour," the normally cautious George Sidney Camp wrote, "from [its] vast combination of wisdom and of will."[32] Even a man's foolish ideas had their function. The conservative yet sanguine Grimke pictured mixtures of wrong and right clashing in democratic debate, chipping off one piece of falsehood after another, and exposing ever more of the truth.

Of course certain continuities mattered profoundly in this transition from republic to democracy. Allowing Americans to switch citizenship as they crossed state boundaries in the 18th century opened the way for America's fluid nationwide democracy in the 19th. By the late 18th century, elections had become so routine and the transfer of power so regularized that Jefferson, with a characteristically freehanded use of grand terms, called "the law of the *majority* . . . the natural law of every society of men."[33] Revolution only reinforced a commitment to carefully articulated political procedures, a preoccupation with the particular way things were done that bound majorities and minorities alike into a common culture for expressing and resolving public conflicts. Moreover, themes of a resistance to centralized power, a suspicion of government-authorized privilege, and an insistence on representatives who rose out of the people they represented—themes that were articulated by antifederalists in the 1780s and Republicans in the 1790s— lived on as qualities in 19th century American democracy.

Nevertheless, discontinuity dominated the story of democracy's arrival. When leaders of the Revolutionary generation set out the principles of government, they talked as if they were discovering truths that lay deeply embedded in human history. Democrats in the 19th century boasted of creating theirs. Gentlemen of the 18th century sought to contain the society they led, their 19th century counterparts to release its energies. The Revolutionary gentry arranged power; 19th century democrats diffused it. In those 18th century schemes, democracy only had meaning in relation to other attributes of republican government: its democratic, elitist, and executive elements leaned on one another for mutual support. Nineteenth century democracy was freestanding. It provided its own justification and generated its own purposes.

Democracy's radical new principle was self-rule: people ruled themselves collectively, people ruled themselves individually. In a very general way, the twin roots of democracy separated along those two channels. Self-defined authority gave white men the mandate to rule collectively; self-directed work gave them the freedom to strike out individually. From one trunk came community self-governance, from the other economic self-determination. Exceptions abounded: a multitude of communities committed themselves to developing their economies, a multitude of individuals to improving their characters. Never-

40

theless, in the brazenly, vibrantly petty bourgeois world of early 19th century America, white men tended to measure their individual freedom by economic means, just as they measured their collective authority by political means.

But if the roots separated, the branches became hopelessly entangled: what integrated the collective and individual aspects of democracy had far more significance than what separated them. Free individuals formed democratic communities; democratic communities sustained free individuals. The participation of citizens together gave legitimacy to their common political decisions, which then carried authority back into their individual lives. At revivals, Americans were saved as individuals in a setting of collective pressures and community supports. Bands of artisans asserted their rights as individuals. Characteristically, democratic politicians spoke as if the same rules, the same interests, governed both. "The great principle of liberty is to leave every man and every woman perfectly free in their action to the full extent that is consistent with the safety and the peace of society," Douglas declared, "and that principle should be applied to States, Territories, and political communities as well as to individuals." [34] Hence neither Jean Jacques Rousseau's general will, swallowing the individual, nor Henry David Thoreau's anarchic individual, shucking off the community, helped in understanding the new democracy. On the contrary, it left white men always on their own, never without a group.

‖‖‖‖
CHAPTER 2

THE BARBARIANS

‖‖‖‖ Masterless men in a structureless society: could it work? Was *self-rule* a new truth or a contradiction in terms? A stream of European visitors came to see for themselves, then returned home to share their findings with a curious public. Few of these witnesses had difficulty identifying the forces behind American democracy or appreciating how radical they were, for they stood in bold contrast with trends across the Atlantic. As white men in America were taking control of their working lives, new poor laws were driving the indigent into Britain's job market. The United States reversed Europe's primary demographic equation: not fixed land and expanding population, but abundant land without the hands to work it. While authority was diffusing in Jackson's America, repressive governments were beating back popular assertions in Peel's England and Metternich's Europe. Even Britain's so-called Reform Law of 1832 reapportioned political power without appreciably broadening its base. The failures of continental revolution and British Chartism in 1848–49 only highlighted these transatlantic differences.

To America's new scheme of things, these well-to-do visitors brought the temperament and values of post-Enlightenment Europe. They thought of themselves as rational and humanitarian, friends of order and friends of man. They looked forward to improvements in the condition of the human race and advocated changes to ameliorate it. Even in the most unequal human relations, they believed, standards of elementary decency should eliminate barbarous punishments and dehumanizing servitude. For many years the standard American tour included obligatory stops at one or more institutions with special new programs for criminals, the insane, the deaf, or some other disadvantaged group. Overwhelmingly Europeans came away praising these innovations and predicting their general adoption.

In most cases, their sentiments were cool, insulated by the rational principles behind them and the social distances within them. European visitors set American democracy against a mental backdrop of hierarchy, a world scaled by birth and breeding, self-evident social qualities and inequalities, and this way of thinking guided the particular evaluations that followed. As a corollary, almost all of them still held to the belief that the mass of ordinary citizens required leaders and that leaders shaped society; the standard Enlightenment assumptions, in other words, behind the existence of a "natural aristocracy" and "the multitude [who] adopt no established principle of conduct."[1] In the United States, that traditional dependence on the civic virtue of a superior few, along with other hierarchical notions, had been ground through the mill of early 19th century change into a very different proposition, one that distributed civic rights and responsibilities among all white men. But no grinder had shredded the Europeans' faith. They continued to equate society's merits with the merits of its leaders.

Almost all of these European accounts purported to be empirical responses to American society, carefully compiled field reports from amateur scientists, as it were, about a strange new world. Each did have its distinguishing quirks, personal marks in emphasis and opinion that made it a particular visitor's work. Nevertheless, what was striking about them was not their independence but their reliance on a single set of mutually reinforcing stereotypes. Although the commentators who poured through the United States between 1815 and 1860 differed on almost all other grounds—by purpose of visit, length of stay, and type of experience, as diarists, theorists, and gossips, by nationality, politics, and sex, as keen-eyed, dim-eyed, and outright fabricating observers—they dipped into the same pot of stories, summaries, and descriptions to paint basically the same images and draw very similar conclusions about American society. Moreover, it was a coherent picture, a cartoon America to be sure but like other well-conceived caricatures an arrangement of sharp, telling observations on characteristics that Americans and Europeans alike had no difficulty relating to life in the United States.

This consistency, this drumbeat repetition, had a certain self-validating quality about it, as if these visitors were indeed scientists and had in fact entered impartially into the American laboratory, only to rediscover the same truths as their predecessors and hence to annotate them once more for the international community. Many of them made a special point of presenting their conclusions as the latest in a long line of identical, informed European judgments. Standardization, in other words, strengthened the claims to authenticity. What emerged was the first authoritative definition of America's radicalism, a meaning for something new where none had existed. As culture truth, it had undeniable influence wherever it spread. These Europeans put American democracy in its place.

The revolution in self-directed work Europeans spotted at once, and unanimously they declared it over and won. One after another, they described a miracle of self-starting, self-propelling industry among white men at all economic levels. "No drones are admitted into the great Transatlantic hive," Lady Stuart Wortley announced. "There is no time to spare; [boys] must be ready, as soon as possible, to take their places and run in the great race." For the beehive, Tocqueville substituted the anthill, a particularly felicitous metaphor to communicate relentless, purposeful work with no one in charge. "There is, probably, no people on earth with whom business constitutes pleasure, and industry amusement" as it does with the Americans, Francis Grund concluded. "Labor is as essential to their well-being as food and raiment to an European." Yes, the Frenchman Michel Chevalier agreed, the United States is a "delightful" place—"in the eyes of him who prefers work to every thing else, and with whom work can take the place of every thing else." "The American lives twice as long as others," decided Frederick Marryat, "for he does twice the work during the time he lives."[2]

The effects spread throughout society. "The toils of life—the destiny of the poorer classes in Europe—form the free choice of the rich man of America . . . ," Thomas Grattan reported. "It is considered disgraceful in a man not to endeavor to add to his fortune, be its amount what it may." By the same token, Harriet Martineau concluded, "the mechanic and farming classes . . . blessed as they are beyond any class that society has ever contained," still never rested. In one Scotsman's initial view of America at Eastport, Maine, the dockworkers "did not walk quietly and soberly up the gangway with the heavy packages or wheelbarrows; they leaped, jumped, ran . . . all rushing up with their burdens and flying down for a fresh load." "Any man's son may become the equal of any other man's son, and the consciousness of this is certainly a spur to exertion," conceded Frances Trollope. Contrasting American with British wage earners, William

Chambers agreed: "The sentiment of hope is stimulated in an extraordinary degree."[3]

In material terms, the outcome validated democracy's claims to progress. During a two-year stay, Trollope wrote, "I neither saw a beggar, nor a man of sufficient fortune to permit his ceasing his efforts to increase it." Using the familiar Enlightenment measure, Alexander Mackay concluded that "there is in America no class which can strictly be denominated poor; that is to say, there is no class whose condition is incompatible with their independence."

Democracy's critics then placed these results in the worst possible light. A workaholic culture produced narrow, mean personalities: "all their energies of body and mind . . . to acquire wealth"; "their unsatiate thirst of gain." In particular, their descriptions of Yankee character slipped easily from accounts of sharp bargaining into downright dishonesty. As the ditty about all work and no play predicted, these commentators reported, "Jonathan is a very dull boy"—not merely a nation of grinds but "a very unimaginative people." In fact, Britishers had long complained that America was too much of a good thing: too much land, too much liberty, even—from Adam Smith of all people— "unnecessary and excessive enterprize." Nevertheless, beneath the caviling, the great concession of the early 19th century stood: an extraordinary experiment in self-directed work was succeeding. Whatever else happened in democratic America, its critics acknowledged, the genie of economic self-determination, once released, would never be bottled again. The energies it had set in motion now ran on their own.[4]

European visitors pronounced the second force behind democracy—the leveling of authority—equally comprehensive and complete. In this case, however, declaring the fact merely opened wide the gates of inquiry, for they found no simple way to explain the consequences. Here, as the Europeans understood it, the stakes were society itself: who set the rules in public? who had access to public spaces? who had priority there? who could take an initiative? who had the right to choreograph other people's movements? who made decisions about who spoke, about who spoke to whom, about what could be said? Manners, in the inclusive European sense of the term, were power. They controlled the functioning of public life. Visitor after visitor, piling anecdote upon anecdote, contributed to a mountain of evidence that what American democrats considered civic freedom was actually chronic disorder, and they took it as their task to reestablish society's legitimate boundaries.

Their initial reaction to American public life—an experience unlike any other, they claimed—was a feeling of powerlessness. It was not simply that they were crowded or jostled, though they mentioned both. They felt lost in a flux of people—what Henry Murray indignantly called "this incongruous herding." "When supper was announced," an astonished Mackay reported, "the race for seats was appalling. Being near the door I was pushed in without any effort of my own." The traveler, Grund advised, "must resign the gratification of his own individual tastes to the wishes of the majority . . . he must eat, drink, sleep, and wake, when they do." In the public lobby of New York's finest hotel, the new arrival encountered "groups talking, others roasting over the stove, many cracking peanuts, many more smoking, and making the pavement, by their united labours, an uncouth mosaic of expectoration and nutshells, varied occasionally with cigar ashes and discarded stumps." "In the American hotel . . . ," Reid concluded, "you are nobody." Little wonder that these Europeans wrote with unusual emotion about the unexpected boon of a private space in traveling or dining.[5]

It mattered, of course, that many of the Americans with whom they were thrust cheek by jowl they considered their inferiors, as Trollope nicely captured in her challenge to England's armchair egalitarians: shake one "hard, greasy paw" after another, breathe the perpetual stink of other people's "onions and whiskey," then praise the wonders of democracy. Yet Trollope had no aversion to touching a social inferior, as she demonstrated in nursing her sick maid. By the same token, the Scot James Stuart missed the friendly breath on his neck of "a British landlord who exerts himself to induce his guests to partake liberally." The real issue was: who set the terms? who decided whether other people came forward or hung back? Captain Basil Hall complained of "coldness and gruffness" in the western states, not because backcountry Americans were inhospitable or "ill-natured—quite the reverse"— but because they did not step up to carry his baggage: they lacked "the spontaneous desire to be civil and useful." Others cited the rudeness of train conductors who did not step lively when they were beckoned. In a variation on this theme of determining other people's comings and goings, Emanual Howitt, insisting that his dog, not the American pedestrians, have the use of the public space by his boarding house, so angered his landlady that "with a torrent of feminine eloquence" she threw him out.[6]

As these stories suggest, forms of address were important means for social ordering, ways of structuring exchanges so that all parties knew their places. Time and again travelers commented on the profligate American use of genteel titles. Where a scavenger was a *"gentleman"* and a whore was a *"lady,"* Mary Lundie Duncan grumbled, an entire society "has suffered inversion [of] the old ordering of language." Everyday was Carnival in democratic America. On first acquaintance, Charles Augustus Murray noted, "farm-assistants and labourers, called me 'Charlie'" while the tavern keeper expected to be called "General" and the local handyman "Colonel." Murray, in turn, referred quite amiably to that democratic hero, the independent farmer, as "the American peasant." Addressed in this manner, visitors discovered, America's white "lower classes . . . have a tendency to be saucy and insolent," especially "those who owe some duty or service to another." To the utter outrage of one Englishman, a hotel porter received his instructions, then walked off, never to return. The Englishman had addressed him as "d—nd rascal," the porter explained later, and since he was not a "d—nd rascal," he had simply gone his own way. The refusal of Americans to wear livery meant that very often visitors could not even find a person to call—one of the sources of their frustration with railroad conductors. In fact, Europeans commonly cited dressing above one's station as an American sin.[7]

For those many travelers who expected to write about their experiences, the rules governing public exchanges of all sorts were crucial. As they asked, listened, and watched, they could gather something worth the telling only through a great deal of American cooperation. Yet they were the ones who felt put upon. "Everybody talks to you," Charles Dickens growled. Scarcely a visitor failed to add anecdotes about the unwanted conversation. "Wherever you go, you are surround by men (who never saw you before in their lives) who immediately have a thousand questions," complained Howitt, a prospective settler who was very much adrift in America and dependent on answers to his own thousand questions. Though Americans might be "as ready to answer as to ask," they were still "impertinent catechists." Several travelers, including Dickens and Mackay, recounted with immense pleasure how they had frustrated or misled these inquiring Americans. Democrats, in other words, did not wait for someone's permission; they talked. "Diffidence," complained Reid, "is scarcely to be met with the United States, which"—he added acidly—"greatly promotes fluency of speech."[8]

"Eaves-dropping a propensity in this country," Richard Cobden noted in his diary, along with various conversations he had overheard. So was staring, Europeans decided. The ceaselessly observing Polish visitor Theresa Pulzsky could not hide her disgust with "those public meals, where hundreds of curious eyes devour every one of our glances and our movements, and our appetites into the bargain." "You are in a house of glass," reported one visitor. Some, it was clear, had the right to look, others only the right to be looked at. "The European," Baron Klinkowström declared for all of them, ". . . misses the courtesies of the old world, which Americans generally regard as signs of bondage." When Dickens pined for "the decent old restraints of home," he had in mind precisely such matters as who asked the questions and who did the looking.[9]

Hence the common agreement on a pervasive American "hostility toward all authority," as the German Moritz Busch put it. American education, reported Henry Murray, ignores "the necessity of disciplining the mind to that obedience to authority, which lays the foundation of self-control." To nobody's surprise, another concluded, the ordinary American "is naturally the worst soldier in the world, as regards obedience and discipline. He has been brought up to believe himself equal to the officers who command him." American life was a free-for-all, in Basil Hall's summary, with "no system of manners, appropriate to each class respectively," to regulate its public affairs. A rare exception proved the rule. When travelers came to the Lowell mills, a common stop on the New England itinerary, they treated them like an oasis of order in the democratic desert. Here people knew their places and the wage-earning women only spoke when they were spoken to—at least in the shadow of the factories. What a contrast to America at large.[10]

Europeans made it very plain that in sum these qualities created a serious state of affairs. Society in any reasonable sense of the term had disappeared. Their solution was to isolate democratic America—in fact, to quarantine it. Through another string of stereotypes, visitors fashioned an American democracy so obviously, often so outrageously idiosyncratic that no one could possibly think of it as applicable to Europe. Even Tocqueville, whose cryptic comments about democracy's eventual triumph in Europe implied that he might be the exception, attributed the presence of democracy in the United States to circumstances so uniquely American that no other country could conceivably match them.

European commentators then accentuated the transatlantic difference by decivilizing American democracy. Once again, visitors with many different purposes and points of view who shared little else worked the same stereotypes, the same devastating metaphors into a single, composite account. Through their images of evanescence, callousness, animality, and violence, they refused America a place in Western culture. Unlike 17th and 18th century arguments in a similar vein, these 19th century commentaries made almost no use of the old saws about Indian savagery and wilderness desolation. The new imagery pictured barbarism not as a circumstance but as a creation, as the wholesale loss of a heritage through the decision of tens of thousands of white Americans. As they boasted, their public life was of their own making. With their eyes wide open, European travelers maintained, democrats chose to decivilize their country.

In America, these visitors reported, everything changed, nothing cohered. Families scattered. Tocqueville marveled at the ease with which one generation separated from the next, and Hall pictured the consequences as a sea of atoms where "the children glide away from their parents . . . brothers and sisters stream off to the right and left, mutually forgetting one another, and being forgotten by their families." Americans, it was claimed, changed their names almost at whim. Individual self-determination uprooted men everywhere and kept them on the move in search of wealth. They never seemed to live where they were born. In a particularly striking image of rootlessness, Grattan concluded that in American cities most people lived in boarding houses. Small wonder that these transients showed "the total absence . . . of those ties of home to which we so fondly cling." In what Dickens called "that vast counting-house which lies beyond the Atlantic," matters of sentiment, loyalty, and affection dissolved into a flux of money made, money lost. "Everything is converted into cash." "In Europe," Tocqueville stated for anyone who was missing the point, "we are wont to look upon a restless disposition, an unbounded desire of riches, and an excessive love of independence as propensities very dangerous to society."[11]

Even what looked to be solid lacked substance. America's cities, the European litmus of civilization, were said to be peculiarly at risk of burning, with New York City, the nation's major center, quite literally in flames—at least one large fire every night, several visitors agreed. Their fire companies had better be excellent, Stuart Wortley warned, because "in no place under the sun, or moon, I honestly think, have they such extensive, incessant, and unlimited practice."[12] By noting the extraordinary speed with which Americans rebuilt after these fires, the city conjured a vision of ceaseless burning-building, burning-building, as if a frenetic metabolism of growth was consuming the very organism it should have sustained.

Like the perpetually moving Americans themselves and their perpetually dissolving families, the cities were perpetually disintegrating beneath the rush of daily life. They were as superficial as the human relations within them. If the surface of wheeling and dealing ceased, those cities would simply go up in smoke. Americans leave no trace of their past, Tocqueville reported, because "no one cares for what occurred before his time."[13] So it always was with savages. During these same years, Euro-American writers created exactly the same picture of American Indians as the vanishing race whose cultures had evaporated. As this imagery captured it, change was not Heraclitus's stream, it was the relentless ocean tide erasing the sandy beach.

From nothing came nothing. Using another stereotype of barbaric sensibilities, Grattan commented on "the extremely superficial nature of all the moral qualities among the people. No one feels very deeply on any subject." Hence the absence in America of fine arts, endeavors, Lieutenant Francis Hall explained, that "perhaps in mercy, [have] been assigned to those nations which have learned to feel." Matters emotionally stirring to a European never reached the American: "we found that what we though so much of," wrote Margaret Hall, "had not excited the least sensation!"[14]

Most astonishing was the American insensitivity to death. "The stabbing of a man in the streets, or the falling of a man into the river, even when attended with instant death, does not excite so much sensation . . . [as] the death of a dog, would do in the streets of any town in England," James Buckingham decided. Faced with "a terrific and awful" catastrophe, Henry Murray reported, "alas! . . . who cared?" As long as things kept moving, nothing else counted. "If [during construction work] some men were killed," Count Francesco Arese noted, "— 'No matter!', a very common phrase in America." Even after an attempted assassination of the president, another visitor was struck by "how little noise or feeling the occurrence seems to have excited." As Stuart Wortley put it, Americans "must win, do or die, and the dead on the field are trodden under foot by their eager comrades and competitors, hurrying onward." Here were consciences appropriate to the beehive.[15]

The analogy was not far-fetched. With only slight shifts of emphasis, Europeans proceeded to turn these morally dull Americans into animals. The insensate gobbling of whatever food was laid before them, at a speed that travelers standardized at 10 to 15 minutes a meal, elicited equally standardized associations with beasts. "The men ate like wolves," went a typical description of a public meal, from a selection "only fit for pigs or prisoners." In America there is no "*eating*" as an Englishman understands it, Thomas Hamilton reported; there people "*devour* . . . to which it would be difficult to find any parallel beyond the limits of the Zoological Gardens." Charles Murray linked Americans' piggishness with their insensitivity toward death: "Several persons have died in New York lately, by being choked with edibles . . . [as] a result of the *bolting system*."[16]

With animals came filth. Appropriately, travelers sprinkled their accounts of American society with images of dirtiness—the garbage in New York's street, the mud tracked into the finest establishments, and most frequently of all, the tobacco juice gushing from men's mouths. Few visitors failed to mention "this detestable pollution" and its "abominable deposits," with obvious implications of a barnyard scene. "The habitual chewer of tobacco is an animal . . . as commonly met with in American 'parlours,' as are alligators in the swamps [and] skunks in the wood." In fact, Grund reported, " 'half-horse, and half alligator' . . . in the language of the western Americans, is full as honorable a term" as knight-errant in the European chivalric code.[17]

Dickens' carefully crafted portrait of a dog-eared pig as democrat epitomized this animal imagery. He places him on a walk up Broadway, the route visitors were told to take in approaching New York City, America's grand port of entry and its most spectacular success. "Let us go forth again into the cheerful streets," he beckons. Look, some enticing "ladies in bright colours, walking to and fro, in pairs and singly," are just ahead.

> Take care of the pigs. Two portly sows are trotting up behind this carriage, and a select party of half-a-dozen gentlemen hogs have just now turned the corner.
>
> Here is a solitary swine lounging homeward by himself. He has only one ear; having parted with the other to vagrant-dogs in the course of his city rambles. But he gets on very well without it . . . He is a free-and-easy, careless, indifferent kind of pig, having a very large acquaintance among other pigs of the same character, whom he rather knows by sight than conversation, as he seldom troubles himself to stop and exchange civilities, but goes grunting down the kennel, turning up the news and small-talk of the city in the shape of cabbage-stalks and offal . . . He is in every respect a republican pig, going wherever he pleases, and mingling with the best society, on an equal, if not superior footing, for every one makes way when he appears, and the haughtiest give him the wall, if he prefer it. He is a great philosopher, and seldom moved, unless by the dogs before mentioned. Sometimes, indeed, you may see his small eye twinkling on a slaughtered friend, whose carcase garnishes a butcher's door-post, but he grunts out "Such is life: all flesh is pork!" buries his nose in the mire again, and waddles down the gutter: comforting himself with the reflection that there is one snout the less to anticipate stray cabbage-stalks, at any rate . . . perfect self-possession and self-reliance, and immovable composure, being [his] foremost attributes."[18]

What neater summary of barbaric America, where, as Mary Duncan said, whores were indeed ladies and scavengers gentlemen; where the business and the news of the day alike came out of society's garbage; where Americans checked furtively for fear of violence, responded coldly to the deaths around them, and exhibited no fellow feelings deeper than the idle chatter among acquaintances; where equality meant soiling, crowding, shoving into other people's space; and all in the name of democratic self-determination.

In these European accounts, animal imagery might communicate any number of messages: the impersonal homogeneity of American life, its mindless work, its dull society. By far the most important, however, was America's edge of violence, its creation of society at the borders of jungle terror. Trollope's dinner table captured this sense of an animal energy almost out of control. Republican wolves had shoved aside the pigs: "the voracious rapidity with which the viands were seized and devoured, the strange uncouth phrases and pronunciation; the loathsome spitting, from which it was absolutely impossible to protect our dresses; the frightful manner of feeding with their knives, till the whole blade seemed to enter into the mouth; and the still more frightful manner of cleaning the teeth afterwards with a pocket knife," built up a tension ready to explode her dining room scene. It was not a casual matter to Europeans that men came to the table armed with knives strong and sharp enough to manage rugged roasts, wild game, and assorted breads, cheeses, and nuts. In the description of a meal that echoed Trollope, Henry Murray at one point declared "clasp-knives are opened," then immediately added: "Don't be alarmed; there is no bloodshed intended, although half a dozen people strolling about with these weapons may appear ominous." [19]

Ominous indeed. The incivility of the American public table gave every unpleasant turn there a sense of genuine danger, as Howitt conveyed through a mealtime anecdote that opened with an American across the table telling him to stop demanding service from the innkeeper. Howitt told the American to mind his own business. "This was a gross insult to the free American," continued Howitt, "and he uttered a torrent of abuse and of oaths before a large company," while eating "with a voracity as savage and disgusting as his address." Was the democrat about to leap the table, knife in hand? Howitt certainly wanted his readers to ponder that possibility.[20]

In fact, American violence was a travelers' obsession. Though commonly associated with the lawless west—"where the rifle settles the dispute," Hamilton declared—this west, sometimes no more than a few miles up the Hudson, was less a location than a metaphor for the essential America, a way of assuring readers that the author had penetrated to the heart of democratic society. As they traveled, visitors collected their tales of violence like souvenirs and applied them broadcast to America. The journey itself generated many of those stories. Stage drivers, "frequently intoxicated" in Stuart Wortley's account, "are rough and reckless, cruel to their horses . . . and cruel to the passengers." In fact, the driver who abused his passengers, even on occasion beating one of them, became a stock character in their travel books.[21]

In more general terms, Americans' proclivity for vigilante justice put them in the same camp with the "hordes of pirates, banditti, or savages." Tarring and feathering made them greater "barbarians" than the Chinese. The universal presence of weapons brought bloodshed into everyday life: "against whom is the dirk-knife now sharpened? against brothers, cousins, and neighbours!" Charles Murray declared. Pistols everywhere, a grim Quaker reported, "and no one I believe would use them more unhesitatingly than an American." Indeed, what would a season in the best society be without "a street-fight with bowie-knives" between lawyers or the public cowhiding of a philandering professor by a cuckolded doctor? Visitors tried to keep a safe distance. When young rowdies publicly abused a group of old women at midday— "and not a voice was raised against it"—Henry Murray also stood aside: "If I had presumed to interfere . . . chances are, I should have been tied to one of the posts of the market-place and made to stand target for an hour." Public violence, Reid concluded, is "the greatest evil of North America—worse than slavery."[22]

Very few went that far. To most visitors slavery was the ultimate violence, proof positive of democracy's savagery. Even in the 18th century, Europeans had identified slavery with the fringes of their world where civilization lapsed and rapaciousness triumphed. In the 19th, these commentators overwhelmingly agreed, slavery fell from the dark past like a blight on civilized values. Although they usually shied from abolitionism, visitors of every persuasion early in the 19th century struck at the institution in stabbing terms. It was America's "curse," "cancer," "abomination," "deformity." Friendly critics, such as Harriet Martineau, singled it out as the contradiction that had to be resolved. To the hostile ones, slavery simply gave the lie to America as the "Land of Liberty."[23]

Here as elsewhere travelers sharpened their message about slavery by adopting standardized descriptions of it, and the image that dominated this composite account was the initial, shocking encounter with a slave market. Europeans turned it into a stock story with four major components. First came the stunned traveler's revelation that a human being would actually be sold. The spotlight then fell on the individual "being sold, just like a horse at Tattersall's," with embellishing references to yokes and chains and whips to emphasize an intolerable degradation.[24] From this animalization of the black it was a short step to the barbarization of the whites who were buying and selling. Accounts contrasted the pitiable situation of the black, crying for her children or suffering the indignities of an auction block, and the imperviousness of the whites, who matter-of-factly went about their business without a hint of remorse. Finally the traveler broke away from the marketplace, unable to endure the scene and unwilling to keep silent.

No doubt there were many, complicated messages in this formalized story. Threatened at home with a runaway commercial capitalism, Europeans were playing the edges of their own fears about people up for sale. Details of white hands poking and pushing on black flesh tapped another set of emotions about physical contact and personal violation—specifically, in the American context, their revulsion at crowding, pawing democrats. But this moral tale also expressed powerful feelings about the horrors of slavery itself. In an otherwise smug three volumes, Basil Hall's description of how, after witnessing the sale of a sixteen-year-old black, he bolted into the streets and ran wildly "to satisfy myself of the identity of my own freedom" rang out as a heartfelt cry.[25]

Even the common Anglo-American association of Africans with savagery did not soften this condemnation. Where slavery and freedom were at issue, skin color seemed pure genetic chance. "For the first time in my life," wrote one shaken visitor, "did I bless God for the whiteness of my skin."[26] In the context of the travelers' decivilizing campaign, slavery sealed the case for quarantining American democracy. Surely a society where human beings were bought and sold daily had to be barred from Western culture.

In addition to a radical leveling and individualizing, in other words, Europeans also found a radical difference in America's violent, savage proclivities. In part, their shock reflected the fact that Americans were domesticating the kind of bloody horrors that Europeans exported through imperialism. Such viciousness, the Europeans seemed to be saying, had no place at home. But that distinction did not register with early 19th century Americans. White men there would need other defenses to keep the charge of savagery from striking deep.

Cheap lives and violent ways came with the origins of white culture in America, moving through the starving times and the slaughtering of natives in the 17th century into the paramilitary settlement of farm lands in the 18th. Who had not wondered about rootless white men kicking over the traces in the bush? On the edge of Western society, North America was a place of exploitation, inviting those who could keep the pace to seize and prosper. Nobody "owned" that wilderness:

it lay there for the taking. Into the 19th century whites were still opening farm lands in the blood of natives and profiting from the broken
bodies of black slaves.

Democracy did nothing to soften these qualities. Majority rule provided no protection for the weak and the marginal; at times it actively
promoted violence against outsiders. As democracy gathered strength
during the late 1820s and early 1830s, so did racial and religious rioting. Democratic individualism included rights to carry weapons and
to use them more or less at will in resolving problems. White men
threatened one another with pistols and knives, mutilated one another
with their hands, punished one another with boiling pitch, executed
one another with a rope and a post, and otherwise embraced brutal
public practices in great variety. Only in mythic terms was the Civil
War a divine reckoning. The world's bloodiest war to date, it featured
an experiment with the novel strategy of enemy annihilation which the
victorious union army then applied in its implacable destruction of
the Plains Indians. These were not warfare's abberations; they were
expressions—extensions—of American values. Nor was the rampaging Ku Klux Klan a peculiarly southern reaction to the unique circumstances of Reconstruction. At about the same time, whites in California
turned the same tactics against neighboring Chinese. These examples
simply dramatized the larger tradition. Once comparative statistics
were available, they showed far higher American than European rates
of murder and other violent crimes.

A heedlessness about human lives went hand in glove with a passion for economic development. Where steamboats might cut shipping
costs by as much as 90 percent, Americans built and ran them with
scarcely a thought to safety. American contractors were notorious for
laying railroad track with an assumption of accidents and an expectation of laying them over again. Appropriately, as the United States
forged ahead in industrial production, it lagged behind western Europe in safety provisions not only for railroads but for mines, mills,
and factories generally. Among these industrializing nations, only 19th
century America—the incorrigible quantifier of almost everything else
economic—failed to keep a public record of its industrial accidents.

European images of barbarism served remarkably well in explaining
this range of American behavior. Although other Europeans—the
streams of immigrants to the United States, for example—gave other
meanings to the American experiment, the charges of savagery were
too telling to ignore. White Americans dealt with them in two ways:
they sought to refute them and to recast them.

American commentators went out of their way to emphasize the
solid bourgeois qualities of their society. No people on earth, the young

Edward Everett asserted, were less prone to *"a reign of terror."* They prized Tocqueville's description of them as a religious, property-loving, law-abiding people so much that they did not quibble over his price for the compliment: Americans also had dull souls. Whenever Europeans praised one aspect of their society, Americans made it proxy for the entire country's superiority. Numerous visitors made flattering reference, for instance, to the reformed penitentiaries in the northeastern states. "The amelioration of the criminal code," Frederick Grimke decided in light of these accounts, measures "the general progress of society." Other qualities that Europeans considered chaotic Americans transformed into sources of stability. America's intermingling of classes, according to Grimke, spread civilized values throughout society and increased mutual tolerance. In the same spirit, the Reverend Thomas Starr King called America's mix of many nationalities the very foundation for its "orderly and stable democracy." [27]

Many American publicists downplayed the use of the term *democracy*. George Bancroft's bold statement of 1826—"The government is a democracy, a determined, uncompromising democracy"—was not the norm. As late as 1841, the publishing firm of Harper and Brothers claimed that no American book on democracy existed. Instead American commentators tended to favor a more sedate *republican*, apparently without realizing that to Europeans that term, conjuring Jacobin Terror, carried connotations at least as dangerous as *democrat*.

Other Americans tried to meet these charges on the Europeans' terms. Who dared to claim that the heartland of the New World produced barbarians, challenged one orator. "Look at the men . . . in our western settlements, at the Jacksons, the Harrisons, the Clays, the Casses, the Grundys . . . and a host of others; and tell me, is not wilderness life adapted to form, and strengthen, and expand the character?" The democratic mind would outmatch the aristocratic, they promised. Tales early in the 19th century had the young Philadelphia gentleman, Nicholas Biddle, in England "astonishing" British scholars with his knowledge of Greek. At the unveiling of the equestrian statue of Andrew Jackson opposite the White House, the speaker of the day glorified the American sculptor Clark Mills' creation as "the work of inborn genius": "What a wonderful triumph has our untaught countryman achieved over [the most] renowned trophies of European art!" [28]

These assertions, however, were much too easy to ridicule. What qualifications did Jackson and Harrison have for the presidency, Europeans wanted to know, other than their ability to kill Indians? Biddle stories that Americans wanted to see as "astonishing" as Jesus confounding the rabbis, Europeans saw as "astonishing" as a baboon humming Beethoven. Was a lack of training not generally a disadvantage in one's profession, Frances Trollope contemptuously asked? Occasionally Americans saw through their own deception. Though the painter Thomas Cole was not in a class with the European masters, the merchant Philip Hone acknowledged in his diary, "I think every American is bound to prove his love of country by admiring Cole."[29]

At their best, these efforts left Americans picking at the edges of someone else's handiwork. Debating one part at a time of the European interpretation risked validating the larger barbaric whole. Moreover, many white Americans *had* cut ties with their past. The freedom of self-regulated work *did* scatter them broadcast. The rules of public life *were* in flux. Americans did not need to import a concern that their society might be dissolving into a mad scramble. As a second, more promising strategy, they shifted the terms of discussion. They started over again with the unexceptionable fact that white Americans were very, very active, clearing land, digging canals, and moving goods at an extraordinary pace that continued to pick up during the years of democratization. How should these nationwide exertions be understood?

European visitors framed American activities in the here and now. Focusing on what was in front of them, they turned America's enterprise into ceaseless rounds of sweaty labor, in Trollope's matter-of-fact phrasing, "a busy, bustling, industrious population, hacking and hewing their way" into a continent. Duke Bernhard, generally more sympathetic, still saw around him "nothing but a bustling present struggling for future improvement." "To clear the forest, hunt the wild beasts, scatter the savage tribes, and rout the hordes of a less hardy race than their own; then to till the soil, dig in the mines, and work out the rude ways of physical existence—these form the elements of American civilization," Thomas Grattan wrote in the 1850s. At about the same time, William Chambers offered a similar summary: "The proper aspect, therefore, in which to view America is that of a field for the reception of emigrants." The United States was that vast empty lot across the Atlantic.[30]

In a country that was no more than met the eye, visitors found nothing attractive in the disruptions of development. New York in the process of expansion, Stuart Wortley reported, "gives one the idea of a half-finished city ... littered with all imaginable rubbish ... Piles of timber, mounds of bricks, mountains of packing-cases, pyramids of stones." Foreigners found the nation's capital, with its scattering of buildings along unpaved streets, a disgrace. An often-repeated traveler's joke recounted how the newcomer taking a coach to the capital grows impatient and asks the driver to be sure to inform him when they are approaching Washington, only to be told they have already arrived. Rather than the city of magnificent distances, as its promoters called it, it became, in Dickens' famous twist, "The City of Magnificent Intentions": a vista of unoccupied avenues, a piece of Andrew Jackson Dowling's abandoned mall, a stub of the unfinished monument to Washington. Nor was the wilderness anything more than a wilderness. The Mississippi River, for example, was a muddy mess, sometimes an ominous one: "a slimy monster," with "tangled roots showing like matted hair . . . like giant leeches . . . like wounded snakes." From the same bin of forbidding romantic imagery, Thomas Cather described the river's shores as "gloomy desolateness . . . wild, savage forest, so dense . . . that sunbeams never penetrate."[31]

In this frame of mind, Boston pleased so many Europeans because it did not seem to be evolving into anything else. Its solidity stood as a rebuke to the clutter almost everywhere else. Boston alone was settled and predictable. "Instead of dirt, noise, and all sorts of irregularities, we have cleanliness, comparative tranquility, and, as it seems, a system of municipal government." Consigned to "banishment" in the United States, Grattan realized that Boston would be the best possible destination. Its society was "more like that of England than elsewhere in America," as Cobden remarked. James Silk Buckingham added the ultimate compliment: not even English towns offered greater "order, decorum, and safety."[32]

But what if those who were looking at the here and now actually saw the future? What if their mind's eye was fixed upon the final product of a development that might not yet be under way? In this dispensation, America was not what it was but what it was becoming, what it would become years hence. Basil Hall, stanch advocate of the barbaric now, collided with just such a contrary American view of reality. His subject was talk of a railroad on the mountainous route between Boston and Albany. Pure fantasy, he wrote. "The same reasoning might be applied to a hundred other projects in the United States, many of them no less impractical but which, although existing only on paper, are, nevertheless, assumed as completed, and cast into the balance of American greatness, till the imaginary scale, loaded with anticipated magnificence, makes the Old World kick the beam."[33] For all the failure, there were enough stunning successes to keep these dreams flowering: soon trains did run between Boston and Albany. If Buffalo in 1832 was no more than a settlement "erected upon the substance of things hoped for rather than things seen," by midcentury other publicists in other tiny towns could invoke the thriving city of Buffalo to sustain their own visions of a grand tomorrow.[34]

Those who saw the future in the present were able to recast European illustrations of barbarism into American evidences of progress.

Rather than setting the muddy Mississippi in a wilderness, Americans described a new civilization springing up along the banks of this magnificent artery for commerce. When Trollope accused a penny-watching family of perversely choosing squalid quarters over the decent home they could afford, her eyes and theirs were focused on very different realities. Trollope's contradiction was their enterprise. Where visitors deplored rootlessness, white Americans boasted of what a pioneer spirit would create. Where Europeans pictured an inchaote society, Americans countered with the image of a free one generating its own institutions. Muting discussion of what was there, concentrating attention on what would come, Americans used the very sources of European skepticism about the democratic present as their points of departure into a limitless future. In a way, the worse things were now, the grander America's prospects became.

Improvement, a qualitative term in England, was purely quantitative in the United States, Captain Hall reported. In what must have been the most successful piece of public relations in early 19th century America, the boosters of Cincinnati employed that American idiom in promoting their city as one of the wonders of the modern world. During the 1820s and 1830s, it ranked next to Niagara Falls on the traveler's customary western itinerary, and visitor after visitor, repeating the litany as if copying from the same handout, reported how Cincinnati had sprung from nothing around 1800 to become the Queen City of the prospering west, with however many tens of thousands in population at that moment. This was a likely occasion to put in a nice word for America: "the European, who involuntarily associates all kinds of ideas about savage life with the words *American interior* would scarcely trust his eyes if he could suddenly be transported from his home to this city," gushed one visitor. The usually harsh Charles Murray thought no other city in the world "in twenty-seven years from its foundation, could show such a mass of manufacture, enterprise, population, wealth, and social comfort."[35]

Nevertheless, publicists of American barbarism, seeing only a tidy town on a pleasant hill, also made quite plain the cultural limitations of life on the Ohio River. It required a different lens to see what Americans saw, and the reforming Englishwoman Harriet Martineau—who not unrelatedly found Boston "as aristocratic, vain and vulgar a city . . . as any in the world"—was one of the rare visitors who shared it. "Cincinnati is a glorious place," she sang. Visualizing it on a century-long continuum that spanned the past and the future, she not only marked how far it had come in the previous fifty years but then projected how far it would go in the next fifty, as an expanding center of democratic ambitions "where every man may gratify his virtuous will."[36] In this scheme of things, fluidity, rather than so much drizzle on a depressing day, became a channeled flow of exciting changes. Development itself was civilization, and what might seem barbarism in the present was really the first step toward the improvements of tomorrow. Was it just chance that Cincinnati, America's most popular model of progress, went by the name of Porkopolis, processing the pigs of Dickens' imagination into the profits of democratic enterprise?

From nothing came something spectacular indeed. At the same time, however, that same mentality turned pressing, immediate issues back into nothing. Justifying what happened now by what would surely come excused existing injustices in the name of future happenings. Later some light-fingered publicists would pick poor William James' pocket and claim that such trading of the present for the future expressed America's "pragmatic" values. In fact, it was something quite different, a development morality that America shared with other European offshoots, such as 19th century Australia and South Africa.

Moreover, what was sure to come had another side to it—to European critics a delightful promise of comeuppance but for American democrats a much darker prospect. It was a European commonplace that only America's abundance of arable land gave such buoyance to its economy and such driving ambition to so many of its citizens. As that land disappeared, the temporary suspension of economic laws in the United States would lift and the inevitable squeeze would commence: rents raised, wages depressed, cities congested, and social classes locked in battle. Countless Americans picked up the same line of reasoning. Sell public land cheap, warned Missouri's Thomas Hart Benton in this Malthusian/Ricardian spirit, or "fill the new States with tenants and the old ones with paupers." Just as the radical Karl Marx and the conservative Thomas Babington Macaulay developed these arguments abroad, so the radical Orestes Brownson and the conservative Frederick Grimke concurred in the United States. Our "democratic institutions" are "owing to causes purely accidental," Brownson wrote in 1840, and before the end of the century "the low price of land" will no longer exist to sustain them.[37]

Those transatlantic exchanges continued through the 19th century. In the 1880s, the British commentator James Bryce anticipated the day of reckoning within a generation. "As [America] fills up her western regions with inhabitants, she sees the time approaching when all the best land will have been occupied . . . the price of food will rise . . . the struggle for existence will become more severe . . . In fact the chronic evils and problems of old societies and crowded countries, such as we see today in Europe, will have reappeared in this new soil." "When the

supply [of public lands] is exhausted," echoed the American evangelist
Josiah Strong, "we shall enter upon a new era, and shall more rapidly
approximate European conditions of life." Hence when depression
struck full force in the 1890s, the old European critique, now thoroughly assimilated, gave Americans a ready explanation for their trou-
bles. Declaring "A Land Famine," the labor publicist John Swinton
could only pine for what might have happened to the nation's poor "if
land were within their reach, as it was within that of their progenitors
... [wages] would be largely increased; the prevalent misery would be
reduced in volume; and the conditions of life of the whole community
would be improved." [38]

The climax to this long discussion came with Frederick Jackson
Turner's famous essay in 1893 on the significance of the American frontier. If as a historian Turner was disputing scholarly doctrines that
placed the origins of American institutions in medieval Europe, as a
publicist he was wrestling with a whole host of 19th century arguments about barbarism, democracy, and development. Did the American experience generate barbarism? Gloriously so, Turner declared. By
stripping pioneers of the useless, cultivated ways they brought with
them, the frontier freed Americans to create their own society. Democracy did not produce barbarism; barbarism produced democracy. And
with democracy came a new, higher civilization—not the brittle European version that went into the frontier but the rugged, adaptable,
home-grown variety that came out of it and that, by American standards, crowned the achievements of the Western world. Of course brutal things happened on the frontier. But their meaning lay not in the
events themselves; it only emerged in the course of the development
to which they belonged. Out of the momentary viciousness democratic
virtue evolved. In fact, the frontier itself only made sense as development, as the ceaselessly repeating process through which democracy
renewed itself.

In the context of public debate, Turner's account, synthesizing pieces
from almost a century's worth of foreign attacks and domestic responses alike, was a brilliant rebuttal not only to America's European
critics but also to their mimics in the northeastern cities of the United
States, such as E. L. Godkin of *The Nation*, who after midcentury
pointed accusations at western America almost identical to the ones
Europeans once leveled on the entire country. But just as forcefully,
Turner's essay also validated the crucial prediction in those debates:
when the land ran out, the uniqueness of American democracy would
disappear with it. For those who believed him, Turner surrendered the
claim as he won the argument.

CHAPTER 3

THE PEOPLE

||||||| **A**t first glance, it seems astonishing how little 19th century Europeans had to say about American politics. Few came interested in it; few acquired an interest after they arrived. Federalism, the Constitution, the Declaration of Independence, yes, but not politics. Because it revealed no useful purpose of its own, it came tacked to other subjects, almost as an afterthought. By understanding society, they assumed, they automatically understood politics. Hence when they did get to politics, they had almost nothing to add.

It was obtuseness with an important insight. Dismissing politics as more of the same captured its critical representative quality. Instead of following the precepts of elite culture, as these visitors believed all genuine leaders must do, American politicians behaved much like the white men who voted for them. Moreover, the seeming incongruity between the process and its results—so much fuss, so little to show for it—which led Europeans to throw up their hands in disgust, expressed essential democratic goals: give the government little to do and keep it close at hand. Along with sameness and inconsequence, these visitors identified a third basic characteristic: from a European perspective the irritation of a perpetual politicking that gave them no peace; from an American perspective the pervasiveness of a politics that bound people everywhere in the United States through common action. Not only did *everybody* participate but everybody *participated*. In sum, what Europeans took to be the problems of democratic politics—its coarseness, its superficiality, its omnipresence—white men in America turned into the democratic solution to their problems. An open, popular politics diffused government power and united a sprawling nation.

How did Europeans arrive at their inadvertent wisdom? Here as elsewhere the usual sequence was to describe the loss of distinctions that
ordered their own societies, then treat the results as a distasteful mess.
It shocked an Englishman, Francis Hall reported, "to find the highest
magistrates and officers of the nation travelling by the same convey-
ances, sitting down at the same table, and joining in conversation with
the meanest of the people." Europeans turned it into yet another example of social inversion: "the operative or labouring class is pos-
sessed of privileges and power so great as to render it, in fact, master
both of the government and of the constitution." The worst stood first.
Who led America's "sovereign mob" but the "wild, savage" Irishman,
the very person, a visiting Protestant dignitary warned his hosts, who
invariably scorns "the example of quiet and good men, and . . . continues the same fierce, intractable, restless being." The sons of Erin were
"so ultra in their politics, and so saucy in their manners," Amelia Murray complained, that special laws excluding them from public life
would be welcome.[1]

Radically cheapening public life in this way let loose a Gresham's
law in leadership that drove out men of talent and left the field to
the purveyors of "buncombe." "The great evil of universal suffrage,"
Charles Lyell decided, "is the irresistible temptation it affords to a
needy set of adventurers to make politics a trade, and to devote all
their time to agitation, electioneering, and flattering the passions of
the multitude." An indiscriminate democracy even demanded "the
election of judges . . . for limited times only, thus placing the judgment-
seat in subservience to king mob." The men who were elevated by this
process, as Francis Tuckett described the magistrates in North Carolina, were "brawny, cadaverous-looking . . . uncultivated and with an
apparent unfeeling brutality, heightened by the length of their locks
and a wild and dirty appearance." Only "sixth-rate" officials would
serve as "the slave of their constituents." America's squalid politics
adopted appropriately "vulgar" and "ignoble" nicknames: Locofoco,
Barnburner.[2]

Vulgarity slid inevitably into barbarism. It was disgusting enough
that ordinary white men sprayed tobacco juice wherever they went; it
was intolerable to encounter chaws in the mouths of democratic legislators and mark the telltale stains on the "carpets of the Capitol" itself.
The "vile habit" of tobacco-chewing, Adam Hodgson thought,
stripped the United States Senate of any claim to dignity; at the hands
of Thomas Horton James, alias the satirist Rubio, the Honorable
Speaker of the House of Representatives became nothing more than
"a young man who was squirting his tobacco saliva in every direction."
From these political associations Frances Trollope derived her name

for the model American, "George Washington Spitchew." Similar repulsive behavior could barbarize the president himself. In transit
among the people, Rubio reported, "I have seen him, combing his hair
with a filthy comb tied up with a piece of string, in a steam-boat, and
washing himself with a jack-towel in common with fifty other dirty
passengers."[3]

In light of these standards, little wonder that ordinary citizens felt
free to invade the White House with their own outrageous variations.
Beginning with accounts of a mob celebrating Andrew Jackson's first
inaugural, stories of riotous official events, replete with images of
muddy animals and rampaging savages, circulated widely among European visitors. Thomas Hamilton's description of a White House levee
in 1831 illustrated the genre. "Such a crew! The very labourers on the
Canal were there. The refreshments were lemonade and *whiskey punch*,
which last the servants were actually obliged to *defend with bludgeons*
from the attacks of a great part of the company." Banging republican
pigs on the snout. Hamilton took special pleasure in explaining the
Americanism "Go the whole hog": "*Go-the-whole-hoggers* . . . are politicians determined to follow Democratic principles to their utmost
extent."[4]

As always, savagery meant violence. In the United States Senate
nothing inhibited such a paragon of democratic statesmanship as Missouri's Thomas Hart Benton from responding to Daniel Webster "in
the most intemperate language," Tuckett recounted. "War to the knife
and the knife to the hilt and similar denunciations were repeatedly
uttered." Bloodshed seemed almost as routine. Several visitors expressed horror at the duels between legislators. When another member
wounded the speaker himself on the floor of the House, his punishment, Charles Murray gasped, was the be *"reprimanded!"* Europeans
so commonly linked fighting with the ordinary workings of the United
States Congress that Grattan found its absence worthy of note: "some
instances of indecorum, fearful spittings, but no scene of actual violence." When politicians were not at it like blue blazes themselves, they
were fanning the embers. The United States could "lick" or "whip"
any nation in the world, visitors reported them boasting.[5]

Even flattery had only a passing effect on these European judgments. One man after another, queuing up at the White House door
for a standardized half hour's conversation with the president of the
United States, wrote about the experience in almost identical, self-
congratulatory prose. Once past the initial shock—"I could not believe
that a person could dare associate so unconstrainedly with the state's
first officer," the Swedish Baron Klinkowström marveled—they treated
the occasion as a personal honor, and in the process they described the

character of the particular president they met quite generously. Jackson, who knew they expected "to see me with a Tomahawk in one hand, and a scalping knife in the other," fared especially well: "nothing which the most rigid critic could attribute to coarseness or vulgarity," the haughty Hamilton assured his readers.[6]

Nevertheless, no president qualified as a genuine leader. It was not that the European travelers were a hopelessly tory lot who deplored the American Revolution and all its consequences. A strikingly large number, perhaps with one Napoleon or another on their mind, ranked George Washington among the world's great men. But whatever greatness America had produced lay in the past. Declension bulked large in their accounts. Usually the touchstone was the new nation's founding generation. Contrasting the golden age of Alexander Hamilton and Thomas Jefferson with the brassy age of Jackson, Alexis de Tocqueville wrote: "America has had great parties, but has them no more . . . [the] statesmen of the present day are very inferior to those who stood at the head of affairs fifty years ago." By the 1850s, death exalted the status of John C. Calhoun, Henry Clay, and Daniel Webster, in turn. Henry Murray, calling out their names as earlier visitors had invoked the founding fathers, lamented: "But alas! the mighty spirits . . . where were they?"[7]

Until the Civil War, Europeans could not see that America's leading officeholders did anything. Rather than controlling the chaos, they joined it. "Is there any kind of order or government in the land," a guide for prospective Norwegian emigrants felt obliged to ask and answer, "or can every one do as he pleases?" Politics not government was the purpose of politics, these visitors concluded. With neither a beginning nor an end, it had no logic to it other than its own perpetuation. America's democratic press only reinforced this view. If the national level of literacy impressed them—"Americans are a newspaper reading people," the Irishman Thomas Cather acknowledged—what they read in these engines of democracy appalled the Europeans. Apparently the popular press had no functions other than malice and meanness. "[N]ewspapers teem with such gross abuse and ruffian scurrility" that "truth, honour, and fairness, are continually sacrificed." They stoked the already dangerous impulses of savagery. "Then their abuse of the authorities and people in office is beyond all idea violent," reported Lady Stuart Wortley, ". . . you would sometimes think they were speaking of the most atrocious criminals." Even Harriet Martineau, who swallowed huge gulps of intoxicating abstractions about American society, spit out in disgust: "of all newspaper presses, I never heard any one deny that the American is the worst." In a particularly unsavory summary of the press's morality, Henry Murray offered what he called a proverb: "eaten its own dirt, and died a putrid death."[8]

A libelous press fit naturally into what Europeans heard as the sound and fury of America's interminable parades, speeches, and debates. Trollope called it "electioneering madness": "It engrosses every conversation, it irritates every temper." Dickens treated the entire process like a plague of flies, a ceaseless, nasty buzz "which is an unspeakable comfort to all strong politicians and true lovers of their country: that is to say, to ninety-nine men and boys out of every ninety-nine and a quarter." "The people are all naturally politicians," an irritated Cather reported. Fresh from the failed Hungarian Revolution of 1848–49, Theresa Pulzsky still found such energetic politics merely "tiresome."[9]

There in negatives was the creative heart of the 19th century America's democratic politics: its diffusion of responsibility, its resistance to institutionalized power, its blanketing of the nation. Europeans who came looking for something that was not there missed what was, even as they described it. Insisting on a distinctive class of leaders, a government that ruled its citizens, and a politics that reflected the needs of those leaders and their government, visitors deplored the absence of all three conditions and complained about the emptiness of the results.

Occasionally a sudden bright beam illuminated democracy's actual operation. A leveled popular politics, Francis Hall thought, generated qualities of alertness and activity, "good sense and information," which produced a "unique" body of citizens in America: "the art of government, that tremendous state engine [elsewhere], is no mystery here." To account for the seemingly senseless "public meetings, conventions, caucuses, platforms, demonstrations [which] are for ever going on," the Scotsman Reid explained: "In short, every man is a sovereign, perpetually occupied in governing the other sovereigns." What if anything did unite these scattered, squabbling white men? In a moment of rare insight, Francis Grund caught a glimpse of how the twin forces behind democracy, a collective authority in governance and a personal control over work, were serving that function: the "sentiments" binding Americans together, he wrote, "are principally *political,* or have reference to their *habits of industry.*"[10]

But these insights, too, flared and died. Although many Europeans stumbled on the right topics, none of them found a political context to explain politics. No sooner had Reid pictured a community of governing sovereigns, for example, than he reverted to a routine list of democracy's social sins: "Public life is fostered, home discouraged, and a morbid craving for excitement created." What confounded them was their inability to find something out there in democracy that would enable them to define politics. They failed to grasp how politics was intrinsic to the defining process: no politics, no democracy. Understanding the crucial contribution of politics—understanding, that is, what it meant to disperse responsibility, keep government small, and still unite the nation—requires a fresh look at American political life.

Nineteenth century democratic politics revolved around elections—generally speaking, the more the better. They bound electors and elected into a reciprocal validating process that did indeed have no beginning and no ending. With authority the common property of all white men, the franchise expressed their inalienable equality. Rather than the 18th century act of giving one's vote to someone else, of ratifying superior-inferior relations through support, balloting became a form of self-expression, an assertion of one's place alongside innumerable others in the collective act of self-government. By its nature, therefore, the work of the franchise was never done. De novo, each election reenacted the leveling of authority and renewed each voter's share of sovereign power.

Nobody else could give voters their rights, as, for instance, through the charters and bills dear to the 18th century. The Republican party claims you are free because the law says you are free, the Democrat Stephen A. Douglas taunted an Ohio audience. "I thought that you were all free because you chose to be free." [11] In that same spirit of choice, Douglas promoted the principle of popular sovereignty, or local self-determination, for the western territories of the United States, a position friends and enemies alike recognized as immensely appealing. When later critics complained that they could not tell at what precise stage in the sequence from settlements to territories to states the definitive vote would be taken, they missed the essential 19th century point: popular sovereignty required perpetual reaffirmation, a people choosing over and over again. When the choosing ended, so did self-government. Without constant attention to electoral politics, Americans told the Englishman Basil Hall, "their liberties would be lost for ever." [12]

On the one hand, this never-ending flow of elections placed severe restraints on officeholders. Frequent elections covering as many posts as possible kept winners from settling too comfortably into office and kept losers close on their tail. Custom obliged officials to act out their dependence on the electorate. After each session, legislators were expected to come home and talk about it: what had they done? why? what would they do next? "Christ, how I hate democracy," hissed a weary North Carolina congressman in the midst of this ceaseless chase for approval. [13]

On the other hand, officials had powerful incentives of their own for staying close to the voters. As the flow of elections empowered voters, it empowered them too: it validated their right to use their offices. Hence office seekers served themselves when they joined in the cry for ever longer ballots that included ever more posts, from minor local functionaries to state judges. Sidestepping a vote was suspicious at best. Even those who fell just outside the orbit of direct popular judgment, such as presidents and senators, often maintained a stake in other aspects of democratic renewal. Anecdotes about Abraham Lincoln's eagerness to bathe in public opinion and William McKinley's ear so close to the ground it was full of grasshoppers linked two exemplary 19th century presidents with a desire—a need—for sustaining the essentials of democratic reciprocity wherever they stood in government.

Leveling authority and dispersing power politicized the routines of white men's everyday lives. Wherever they turned, they were expected to act out their independence and express their values. Appropriately, elections validating democratic choice and democratic rule spread everywhere: club officers, schoolteachers, team captains, and spokesmen for all kinds of ordinary affairs. The many Europeans who sneered at the love of military titles in an egalitarian land missed the fact that most of these derived from militia elections. Where officers came and went by majority vote, a soldier mouthing such titles honored himself and his fellow electors as much as he did the "captain." Even practices that at first glance might seem to violate the majority principle—the adoption of seniority rules in some legislatures, for example—actually did not. Seniority followed the logic of the queue, not the hierarchy, and democratic reaffirmations—consecutive electoral victories—ordered the queue.

Democratic politics of this diffuse sort was the white man's public map—sorting friends from enemies, defining how contests would be settled, and making connections between immediate and distant issues. It required extraordinary energy to sustain. Early in the 19th century, newspapers spread far more extensively throughout the United States than anywhere else in the world. Frankly partisan, these mobilized the faithful, fought out local battles, dissected political debates, and linked with their counterparts elsewhere. To utilize this network, Americans made themselves literate. With little help from public schools, democratic communication sent literacy rates soaring between 1800 and 1840: from around 75 percent of adult whites to around 95 percent in the north, from around 50 percent to around 80 percent in the south. Talk was at least as important as print. During these same years, the norms for public rhetoric changed from the language of a gentle-

68   CHAPTER THREE

man's monopoly around 1800 to a generally accessible "civil rhetoric"—
a lightly polished everyday language—that for the balance of the 19th
century served nationally as a medium for democratic discussion.[14]

Like the politics they communicated, the incessant attacks, the incessant exhortations, the incessant repetition of the same simple messages
that this finely spun, highly efficient web of connections carried week
in, week out, had no center or starting point. It was often impossible
to say where in such an elaborate, dispersed scheme a particular idea,
slogan, or even legislative proposal originated, and generally it did not
matter. White men formed a loop of innumerable participants. Because
each of them shares "in the government of society," Tocqueville wrote
with a flourish, he devotes "one half of his existence" to this "ceaseless
agitation" of public affairs. As the editor William Leggett declared, "it
is the duty of every intelligent man to be a politician."[15]

Democratic politics was a vibrant public process: marching, chant-
ing, disputing, debating, voting. People entered this process by demanding a place. The anger at secrecy, the demand for openness, was
a functional response to situations that made democracy impossible.
Without access, citizens had no role; private dealings paralyzed them.
Noisy, seemingly chaotic political conventions with a substantial number of self-selected participants were exemplary democratic institutions. In the end, the rules for conducting public meetings usually prevailed: decisions were made, and only some voted on them. But in the
meantime others had joined in the proceedings, voted informally with
cheers and hoots, and left with their own stake in the outcome.

At a deeper level, self-selection powered the entire democratic process. No principle lay closer to the core of its operations than the one
governing participation: the way to get into American democracy was
to get into it. Ask nobody's permission, defer to nobody's prior claim.
Just do it. The fact that citizens were "perpetually acting" in public life
did not, as several Europeans suggested, signal a nationwide nervous
disorder.[16] Americans were keeping their democracy alive. At rest everything disappeared.

Diffusing political responsibility diffused the power to govern. Active
citizens conducting frequent elections not only pulled representatives
back into their communities; they denied those representatives the
wherewithal to act even if they had been inclined to strike out on their
own. No characteristic of 19th century government contributed more
to the strength of democratic self-determination than America's exceptionally low taxes. In later times, comfortable, self-serving conservatives appropriated that cause, but in the 19th century low taxes un-
derpinned an agrarian-based democracy.

Taxes evolved in Europe through a double transfer: first, the transfer of the lord's claim on his peasants from a payment in labor to a payment in money; second, the transfer of those tax rights from the lord to the lord's government. Hence aristocrats did not expect to pay taxes. Laborers did that. Although there might also be government levies on bourgeois wealth, basically taxes went with tilling the soil. That burden could crush the life out of the countryside, as Thomas Jefferson witnessed in France. Moreover, in those rural areas where taxes had to be paid in cash and specie was dear—the usual case—the necessity of finding money for taxes skewed otherwise sensible decisions about rotating crops, maintaining livestock, and avoiding the bottomless pit of usurious debt. By no means had these practices disappeared from early 19th century Europe, and a consciousness of their degrading consequences set the political agenda in agricultural America. As the Englishman William Cobbett reported early in the century, when Americans did pay taxes, they expected concrete returns. Had they been levied for a road? Then where was the road? Everything else was suspect, not because America's independent farmers were closed-minded provincials but because they were wide-awake democrats. Self-directed work had no more obvious, implacable enemy than high taxes.

Low taxes ensured small governments, tiny ones by European standards. Except for the Civil War years, according to figures compiled by Michael Mann, the ratio of government expenditures to Gross National Product in the major European nations routinely ran five or six times higher than in the United States. Of course American governments did involve themselves in public activities, some of them quite ambitious. Nevertheless, the ideological as well as the budgetary restraints were severe. The assumption that America's public resources should eventually pass into private hands, already widespread before democracy arrived, acquired bipartisan, holy fervor by the mid-19th century. Although both major parties sought government aid for their favorite private enterprises, both expected those enterprises, after an initial boost, to generate progress on their own.

Even in the area of public order, government had relatively few responsibilities: citizens expected to manage much of that informally. As a law-and-order Chicagoan explained after the Great Fire of 1871, the critical matter was not an action's legality but whether it had "the force of public opinion back of it."[17] Not until quite late in the century did governments attempt to control radicalism. "In most European states," according to one comparative perspective, "the police . . . investigate *how one thinks*, and . . . *what one says;* but in America they only ask *what one does.*"[18] Even in the policing of actions, white men looked to their own communities. The emotions producing civil war make no sense without appreciating the depth of white men's anger when they felt other white men were using a distant government to tell them what to do. In the furious constitutional debates preceding and succeeding the war, who would decide carried almost as much weight as what the decisions might be.

In the sprawling United States, therefore, small governments meant radical decentralization. America's 18th century political heritage encouraged these pulls away from the center: states resisting national power, assemblies serving constituent interests, locally rooted legislatures guarding the right to initiate—or, more likely, not to initiate—new tax laws. Unlike the Jacobin legacy for France, republican ideology in America merely deepened this distrust of a national mobilization. Hence the toppling of authority structures early in the 19th century reinforced already powerful impulses toward local autonomy. In this instance, at least, the new democracy represented continuity with the 18th century.

The greatest 19th century challenge to this proposition came in fighting a civil war. Although most of Washington's consolidating efforts sputtered to a halt within a decade after the war, the net effect was to reverse the early 19th century's decentralizing trends. Guaranteeing the union and abolishing slavery highlighted the change. New national standards in civic and economic affairs also enhanced central authority after the war. Nevertheless, as the *Slaughterhouse* cases (1873) attested, this national overlay remained exceedingly thin: states and localities still gave meaning to citizenship and still regulated their own economies. Even where national rules mattered a great deal, as in the case of the Civil War laws establishing a single United States currency, there was a major difference between uniformity and mobilization. A national currency facilitated transactions without trying to direct them.

The state of political parties illustrated both the change and the continuity in these matters of centralization between the early and the late 19th century. The major parties of early 19th century politics, the Democrats and the Whigs, did not fully congeal as national agencies until 1840. By 1846 they were beginning to unravel, and even for their six best years they were beset by a bewildering array of feuds, schisms, and defections. Their normal tendency, in other words, was to devolve into local components. Their successors, the Republicans and the Democrats, enjoyed about fifteen years of national stability, roughly from 1875 to 1890. They too suffered from a great variety of tensions and splits, most notably but by no means exclusively arising out of the

THE PEOPLE 71

Civil War and Reconstruction, but throughout the late 19th century both parties maintained considerably more state and even regional firmness than their predecessors had. Centrifugal and centripetal forces more closely approximated one another.

In all of its 19th century variations, America's low-tax, small-government democracy remained labor-intensive. The 18th century practice of rich patrons controlling a retinue of political retainers had more or less passed, and the 20th century pattern of wealthy capitalists controlling a network of centralized institutions had not yet arrived. With political power diffused in the 19th century, it was very hard to identify the right people to corrupt—let alone corrupt enough of them—to make a significant difference. Politics, like economics, was overwhelmingly petty bourgeois. New York Governor Washington Hunt's proposal in 1852—that the person caught bribing a voter should lose his own franchise—captured the essentially local, almost personal character of 19th century corruption. Even when a tiny margin of victory heightened the importance of this kind of corruption, it joined numerous other small-scale influences that affected a close election— no more or less a cause than rained out roads in some rural county or a flu epidemic in some city neighborhood.

Sleazy as they were, the Gilded Age scandals that surfaced during the 1870s projected much the same qualities of petty corruption on a slightly larger screen, and the prolonged sense of outrage that they roused was evidence of a certain innocence, a widespread assumption that American democracy simply would not tolerate bribery and graft of any scope. Even at the end of the century, when Matthew Quay and Mark Hanna raised the stakes of political influence by many millions of dollars, these entrepreneurs still lacked the means to do much more than spot some money here, some money there, hoping it would do the work. The driving force behind 19th century democracy was thousands of people spurring thousands of other people to act. Many little favors, many personal connections, wound a host of little springs to make the mechanism work. By and large over the course of the century, those with money could not get much political power for it, and those with political power could not get much money for it.

In the 19th century, then, democracy was rooted in local America. What characterized it and what it accomplished began with this particularity, this self-conscious separation of small group from small group. It ended somewhere entirely different, however. Nothing about 19th century democracy was more striking than its expansive capacity, an opening outward that gathered great mixes of these local pieces into a whole People and made the People, in turn, integral to building an

American nation. Viewed one way, democracy was an agglomeration of innumerable self-protective groups of white men who restricted membership, suspected outsiders, and defended the status quo. Viewed another way, it formed widening circles of connection that linked citizens over vast distances, invited collaboration across class and ethnic divides, and served as a beacon of self-respect for millions here and abroad. How 19th century democracy stretched from exclusive provincialism to inclusive nationalism completes the outline of its basic qualities: leveling, diffusing, uniting.

Democratic energies poured into this community life through fraternal channels: fraternity not in the sense of universal oneness but in the sense of lodge brotherhoods, sports clubs, or army platoons that depended on close bonds of trust among essentially equal members. Though a fraternity might confederate with others of its kind, as men did in a state conclave of lodges, for example, or a city sports league or an army division, its essential meaning lay embedded in the home club. The first rule of this lodge democracy was loyalty—inturning, unqualified—and to clear the way for this fraternal bonding, white Americans constructed a narrative of benign family dissolution.

As Europeans heard it, it was a tale of precocious boys simply walking out the family door. "From the earliest period of his life, a young American is accustomed to rely upon himself . . . ," Francis Grund reported. "By the time he is able to read and write, he is already forming the plan of his future independence." "[American children] seem born with all the responsibility of citizenship and wear it with great gravity," another wrote. Hence, as Tocqueville described it, "at the close of boyhood the man appears and begins to trace out his own path." The father "surrenders [his authority] without a struggle"; the son takes it "as a possession which is his own." [19]

The evidence on whether changes in family life early in the 19th century actually triggered this process is too mixed to be persuasive. But the need to believe it, which is not in doubt, certainly must have encouraged it to happen. In one sense, this was the indispensable tale of the new democrat's arrival: each white man automatically a free, self-directed citizen as he came of age. In another sense, the simple, peaceful parting of son and father expressed an effortless sweeping away of all patriarchal values. Where a tradition of town meetings existed, the new democracy needed to break down the customary concept of voting as the family-based community's coming together and replace it with one of voting as an individual's act, a shift that in Ohio, for example, came during the transition years after 1815. Although the prospect of cutting loose might stir considerable anxiety, in this storied democratic version it represented a natural, a painless repudiation of

any other inhibiting loyalties. In the tale of leaving home, those mo-
mentarily atomized young men almost at once cemented new connections of equal intensity. As they broke their old ties of dependence, in
other words, they bonded themselves into communities of self-
determining adults.

In these fraternities, brothers pledged to stand by one another whatever the provocation. Andrew Jackson introduced the values of lodge
democracy into the White House with his notorious demand that those
loyal to him show it through courtesy to a cabinet member's unpol-
ished wife, Peggy Eaton, a resourceful survivor in the rough games of
sex and marriage who was being ostracized by some haughty members of the president's circle. Jackson did Peggy Eaton no service by
championing her; he simply used her as a device to enforce standards
of personal loyalty on the men around him. One of those who had no
trouble understanding and passing Jackson's test, Martin Van Buren,
constructed his autobiography around lodge values: a political career
understood as a string of personal relations, each a case study either
in mutual loyalty, respect, and assistance, or in their opposites. Lincoln
expressed similar commitments. A competitor within his Whig lodge
he could always forgive—he named a son after one of them—but a
renegade never. Of one traitor Lincoln only recalled how "in my greatest need of friends he was against me"; of another that "he *lied* in
his *heart*."[20]

As these sentiments suggest, fraternity members joined at a deep
emotional level. Although lodge brothers referred to one another as
"friends," that term rang very different overtones than it had in the
republican 18th century, when friends associated people with abstractions: the friends of liberty, perhaps, or the friends of order. In the
democratic 19th, friends bound brother to brother, often in the name
of the lodge's favorite candidate: friends of Clay, friends of Blaine. A
new language of affection forged these ties, man to man. "I loved him
with the love that Jonathan had for David—'a love that passeth the
love of woman,'" General Usher Linder recalled of Stephen Douglas.
In a tug of war that many lodge leaders experienced, Robert M. T.
Hunter could not extricate himself from the tangled jealousies of two
other Virginia Democrats: "When and how come you so fond of
Hunter," one of them complained to the other. "You always loved
Hunter better than you love me."[21]

Political lodges had leaders, who took pride in their place and, following the army platoon model, often acted the captain to others who
called themselves lieutenants, foot soldiers, and the like. By a circular
logic that sets leaders in a category by themselves, it is possible to
conclude that an elite ran these lodges. Nevertheless, in a democratic

club, leaders were made and unmade by their brothers, and all parties in the process assumed an underlying equality. Public exchanges in particular mandated an egalitarian style. "I have seen the clerk of a steam-boat, and a grocer in a small village on the Missouri, sit down to take grog or play at cards with a member of Congress and an officer in the army; laughing together, swearing together, and the names of Bill, Dick, and Harry, passing familiarly between them!" the Englishman Charles Murray exclaimed.[22]

Nicknames for faraway favorites—Harry of the West, Old Hickory, Young Hickory, Old Abe—did not simply level them into the party's ranks; in effect, they assimilated these distant leaders into the local lodge. Jackson belonged to all Democrats. When he traveled, he helped citizens who may never have seen his likeness to identify him and enter into conversation. "Are you General Jackson?" "Yes, sir, I am." Of course some exchanges were more welcome than others. "Mr. Buren," a Tennessee farmer was reported as offering the fastidious eighth president, "the next time you come down here I want you to come out my way and ra'r around some with us boys."[23] Egalitarian procedures that applied in travel prevailed as well in church, even in the White House. Measured against these norms of openness, it was a democratic embarrassment of the first order when president-elect Lincoln slipped into Washington for his inauguration by special, secret train.

Presenting themselves in public, the democratic fraternities revealed great variety. Some, such as the revived Masons and the agrarian lodges of the late 19th century, stressed their respectability. Others, such as the fire companies and sports clubs, flaunted their streetcorner styles. Still others straddled the gap: militia companies torn between their uniformed order and their rank-and-file camaraderie, labor unions cultivating their reputations and acting out their demands. Despite Protestantism's extraordinary multiplication of ancillary groups, the churches themselves did not maintain sharp enough lines between male-public and female-private worlds to fit comfortably into democracy's fraternalism. Catholics, who divided men from women more easily than Protestants did, more naturally incorporated the church into their lodge life.

Political parties, the lodges of choice, also tried to bridge the distance between proper styles and rough-and-ready ones. On the one hand, party orators spoke a rhetoric of respectability; on the other, partisan bands bawled their political preferences and cursed their opposition in public. Formal rules, with at least a minimum courtesy, regulated debates between candidates. On the streets, however, lodge brothers let loose. After James K. Polk's election as Speaker of the

House of Representatives over John Bell, his archrival in Tennessee politics, one happy Democrat recounted:

> a goodly number of the good and true Jackson boys . . . re-paired to Vauxhall, where we screwed the necks off of a few dozen of champagne, under the roar of 48 rounds of cannon. After the 48 rounds and an immense deal of first rate enjoy-ment, the drum and fife arrived and soon collected several hundred men, who marched down town in regular order and after having passed round the square under constant dis-charges of muskets, the bells commenced ringing simultane-ously at eleven o'clock [P.M.] . . . Such shouting . . . I never heard; the good people of [Nashville] who were not in the se-cret, supposed the whole town was on fire. Every body was assured, some vexed to distraction . . . but it all passed off glo-riously.

From another town, a Polk partisan reported: "no lives lost and only a few wounded (not mortally) by the kicking of their pistols."[24]

One foot in respectability was not enough for the keepers of moral order. "But above all things," Baltimore's Reverend George Burnap ad-vised, "the young man has need to be warned against turning politi-cian as a business and profession. Of all employments this is one of the most wretched." The transcendental George Ripley associated democratic politics with "mire." "Pontius Pilate," the minister Horace Bushnell acidly remarked, "was a politician." In Charles Sheldon's popular novel *In His Steps* (1897), where the politics and saloons of Topeka, Kansas, went hand in glove, the prospect of competing for office—the ultimate civic sacrifice—made the genteel president of the local college physically ill. "'Politician,'" James Bryce summarized for 19th century American respectability, "is a term of reproach . . . among the better sort of citizens over the whole Union." When politicians re-taliated, they did nothing to improve their proper image. Leaning back toward the rough-and-ready side of the divide, they attacked their crit-ics as "man-milliners," "namby-pamby, goody-goody" reformers too delicate to fight the good fight.[25]

On the respectable side of the gap, the inherent coarseness of demo-cratic politics found expression in a string of fables, endlessly re-peated, that communicated a single message of decent citizens over-whelmed by the crude common herd. Appropriately, the most notorious of these stories originated in the shock of democracy's ar-rival. One told of a nationwide multitude stupefied by liquor and de-ceived by demagogues in the log-cabin-and-hard-cider presidential

election of 1840. Another, even more famous, described the disaster of
Jackson's first inaugural.

Gathering in great numbers to cheer their hero, the inaugural fable
began, people of all descriptions clogged the route to the Capitol,
forced the ceremonies outdoors, then rushed the new president as
soon as he finished his oath. Jackson, escaping from the back of the
Capitol, still had to fight past a wall of people to ride off to the White
House, only to be swamped there by vast waves of celebrants—someone estimated 20,000—who spread filth, smashed glassware, vaulted
through windows to get at the tubs of whiskey on the lawn, and even
obliged a makeshift ring of guards to escort the president himself to
safety.

Although various people, mostly enemies of Jackson and the popular government he represented, contributed bits and pieces, especially
about the White House riot, the crucial source was Margaret Bayard
Smith, a longtime eminence in Washington society and a close friend
of the Clays, who combined the relatively little she saw with the great
deal she heard in a long letter a week after the event.

In code words, it was a story composed of a mob, a rabble, dirt, and
liquor. To begin with the mob. No doubt an unusually large number
of people were about the capital on this inaugural day. In 1829, March
4 fell on Sunday, and the holiday encouraged all kinds of people, particularly the district residents themselves, to come out and enjoy themselves. How many of these unenfranchised Washingtonians saw Jackson as their hero or even cared about his election, how many of them
only craned a neck when there was something to see, and how many
were just going their own way on a Sunday we will never know.

We do have some evidence, however, that only modest numbers followed the inauguration itself. They did not block traffic; in fact, there
was enough space as Jackson rode to the Capitol for one carriage simply to hold a place alongside the general so that its occupants could
get a good long look at him. Nor did much of a crowd gather on the
Capitol grounds. Arriving there at the last minute, the group with Margaret Bayard Smith, who was over 50 and encumbered by party dress,
executed a simple walking maneuver around the entire assemblage to
"a clear space . . . [with] a clear, full view of the whole scene."[26] Did a
crowd block Jackson's departure from the rear of the Capitol? Probably
not. Smith herself saw nothing. Short of an Olympian sprint, she could
not have circled the building while Jackson was walking through it.
Even her borrowed account admitted that once Jackson chose to mount
his horse, he had no difficulty riding away.

We are left with the mob in the White House. Smith missed that one
too. After attending a parallel party at Senator Thomas Hart Benton's,

she arrived at a White House largely emptied but not yet cleaned, never a charming moment in the life of any party. Nonetheless, other accounts make it clear that the White House was very crowded. Apparently the party remained in full swing about three hours, and certainly many more people came than were expected. Moreover, it required an effort for people to get to the White House, and once there, they probably stayed awhile—say, between a half-hour and an hour on average. If at any one time around 700 could pack themselves into Jackson's White House and if at the peak another 200 were having their party on the lawn, a total of 3,000 is a reasonable estimate.

Facing 3,000 guests when you had anticipated perhaps 1,000 would throw any party into crisis. Little wonder that witnesses remembered overwhelming numbers, cramped spaces, and the inevitable spilled drinks and broken glassware. At the White House party as at the Capitol ceremonies, nobody was in charge of numbers. There were absolutely no provisions for what would later be known as crowd control: no boundary markers, no guards, no directions of any sort. Under the circumstances, people managed themselves quite well. Jackson, ostensibly at risk from a mob throughout the celebration, thought the day went well. And what could anyone make of jaundiced observers who complained that the rabble had "trampled over the lawns and newly planted flowerbeds"?[27] Why not walk on the lawn? Even assuming someone resolved the mystery of what flowers to plant on the first of March in Washington, could a gathering of people be expected to spot them and steer clear? At the White House, of course, a timely use of the lawn saved the day: setting refreshments there was a beleaguered staff's smartest move.

As anyone might have expected in unpaved Washington early in March, "the streets were muddy" on the 4th, and most visitors brought the mess with them into the White House.[28] At a party that absorbed every minute of the staff's energy, men arriving on horseback tied up their own animals, and hence they, like the pedestrians, got mud on their boots. Only those with carriages to bring them directly to the entrance—a tiny elite by any count—came into the building clean.

If tracking dirt condemned all but a very wealthy handful, so did drinking whiskey, the spike in the White House punch. Jackson's inaugural roughly coincided with the pinnacle of the nation's alcohol consumption at levels that almost defy the imagination. It was routine in the 1820s, various observers reported, for conscientious, industrious white men in America to spend the entire day downing one drink of hard liquor after another after another—while they worked, while they ate, while they relaxed. Only later generations, with far lower alcoholic intakes, turned the simple fact of its abundance into evidence of a mob out of control at the inaugural. In 1829, most Americans took liquor's omnipresence for granted.

What separated one group of imbibers from another were the details. Whiskey in buckets attracted Margaret Bayard Smith's attention, for her drinking tastes ran in the direction of Senator Benton's competing party—"a perfect levee," she thought—where she found "wine . . . in profusion," no doubt served to her by the glass.[29] In almost all other circles, however, whiskey was the popular choice, and fortunately for the White House staff, they found barrels of it for their large, all-American crowd. In summary, an unusually large number of people from a Sunday crowd celebrated Jackson's inauguration, generally in good spirits and quite well-behaved. Angry just to see those people, elite commentators transformed who they were—their ordinary behavior—into America's most enduring fable of democratic vulgarity.

As local agencies, political parties energized the community. Their work never ceased: "directly the acrimony of the last election is over," Dickens moaned, "the acrimony of the next one begins." As a continuing celebration of the ability of citizens to govern themselves, politics was affirmation, instruction, diversion, entertainment, and inspiration. In a nation of mobile people, parties called out to the community's shifting population with "a steady drumbeat" of appeals, "identifying new voters, keeping the issues before them, winning their involvement, and . . . bringing them out to the polls on election day." Before as much as after the Civil War, the most common metaphor among partisans was the party as an army, ready to move out again and again in an endless round of battles.[30]

People responded because each party's "insistent and morally peremptory demands on its members . . . [were], at the same time, deeply linked to these members' own identities."[31] By no means were parties the only source of identity. Nevertheless, during the devoutly partisan half-century between 1840 and 1890 in particular, they wove themselves around a strikingly wide variety of other, important ones. As fathers passed partisan commitments to their sons, those names— Democrat, Whig, Republican—were assimilated into the family's identity. Both religious convictions and national origins functioned reciprocally with party loyalties. To the frustration of those 20th century historians who wished that workers would stick to class business, 19th century wage earners now merged, now separated, now exchanged their attachments to a labor organization and a major party. These many intersecting lines formed networks of peculiarly intense connection in the 19th century. In 1908, when the philosopher Josiah Royce, nearing the end of his life, pleaded with his countrymen to make loyalty to loyalty itself their highest ethical value, he was actually marking the end of America's century of loyalties.

Party ranks were remarkably inclusive. No other white fraternity came close to matching their reach. Through laws covering twenty-two states at some time in the 19th century, aliens as well as citizens participated. Although residency and even literacy provisions for voting gained some currency over the century, communities made their own decisions about eligibility, and liberality proved to be an expedient bipartisan rule. In a fluid society, representation generally kept pace with migration. By the 1840s, the principle prevailed everywhere that a legislator represented the district, not the state, in which he was elected, and districts with a swelling population invariably fought for a place in this scheme of things. By no means, of course, did fairness always triumph. Sometimes polling places closed too early or opened too late. Bullies blocked access, money passed hands, ballots got destroyed. Nevertheless, these passionate partisans made dedicated poll-watchers, quick to suspect and hard to deter. Moreover, one person–one vote was not a 19th century fetish. Though it mattered a great deal who voted in local elections, it mattered much less whether one local district matched the others in size. Gerrymandering was more likely to cause outrage because it broke the accepted boundaries of community than because it violated an exact equality in representation.

In one sense, therefore, lodge politics created innumerable little worlds with lives of their own. A fraternity's vitality depended on its local sustenance. Even in the city, an individual's political authority could normally expect to reach no farther "than a neighborhood or at most a ward." [32] Elections were local loyalties mobilized, collective expressions of attachment that sometimes were made collectively as lodge brothers marched to the polls in groups waving their party's colored ballots. Even where one side's victory was foreordained, every vote still counted. Voters rarely chose between candidates; they rallied behind one or the other candidate, and the precise margin of defeat or victory—5, 500, or 5,000—spoke to a fraternity's pride in doing absolutely the best it could.

Yet even at its most inturning, lodge politics stretched outward as well. Where voting expressed partisan attachments, the winner represented his party far more than his district, and members of the losing party, in effect, now lived in occupied territory. Although a substantial local majority for a defeated gubernatorial candidate might inspire claims that this territory, at least, had never been occupied by the victor, most on the losing side in an election simply looked elsewhere in their party's network for representation. It was this version of virtual representation that kept the peace in 19th century politics.

The elastic consciousness of these democratic lodges suggested how marvelously expandable 19th century parties were. Large loose leagues of loyalty, they were held together by pride in a common name, shared heroes and memories, a few deeply felt party truths, occasional puffs of news about lodge victories elsewhere, and the quadrennial mobilization for a national campaign. These requirements, conveniently light baggage in a highly mobile society, allowed parties to spread as rapidly and dramatically as the United States. Local branches behaved much the same wherever they appeared. It did not require transcontinental railroads to integrate mid-19th century California and Oregon into the American party system. Well before they drove the golden spike in Ogden, Utah, a spreading uniformity had already given nominating conventions, partisan newspapers, long ballots, polling procedures, and the like a common look across the country. Beginning on November 7, 1848, the United States had a standard presidential election day.

Other loosely linked organizational chains, relying on similar elementary truths, enabled churches, professions, reforms, and schools to expand along with the nation and shape an institutional context for the major parties. Common schools, for instance, taught the kind of accessible rhetoric, malleable Protestantism, and simplified virtues that underwrote the parties' expansive political networks. In Lee Soltow's and Edward Stevens'apt phrase, they transmitted America's "ideology of literacy," an ideology that without mentioning parties prepared new generations to enter 19th century partisan life: internalize a handful of basic values, read to reinforce them, and be prepared to fight for them wherever the enemy might appear.[33] Common schools taught the children of native whites what they already knew to be true and the children of immigrants what they needed to know in order to compete on equal terms.

Because standards for creating new lodges were quite flexible and traditions of local autonomy very strong, almost no group of white men was denied a place in the 19th century party system. Where it felt natural, Germans, Swedes, and other clusters of immigrants maintained native languages inside their party lodges. Even conducting public education in English was not a sharply focused issue until late in the century. Countertendencies, of course, always existed. Once in awhile they coalesced in a political movement, most notoriously the anti-immigrant, anti-Catholic surge that rose in northeastern cities during the late 1840s and early 1850s, then crested between 1854 and

1856 as the American or Know Nothing party. Still, if its nativism reflected a long American tradition, so did the quick failure of its politics, which found legislative power of little use, lost its edge, and soon
disappeared inside the new, diverse Republican party. Protestants
might still fight Catholics, but they also leagued with them to create
Republican majorities in such states as New York and Missouri.

In 1844, when the Mormons, after teetering for years on the edge of
acceptability, actually were driven from Illinois public life, their violent
exclusion stood in sharp contrast to the 19th century norm among
white men of an angry competition and a sullen toleration. All major
parties had to reckon with ethnic heterogeneity; none could push too
hard against the other's diversity. Whether there was any truth to the
story that in 1884 a single Republican minister's harangue against
"Rum, Romanism, and Rebellion" alienated enough of his own party's
Catholic voters to cost James G. Blaine New York—and by losing New
York, the presidency itself—it was a cautionary tale that every contemporary politician understood.

A grudging acceptance of differences sufficed to give 19th century
lodge politics its distinctive form of equality. It was an equality that
had nothing to do with a belief in everybody's worth or in everybody's
right to his own habits, customs, and faith. It implied no willingness
whatsoever to rub elbows with strange people. Political fraternities
banned unwelcome outsiders without a qualm, and outsiders, forming
their own fraternities, were free to do the same. Nor was civility at
issue. Hate—compressed in stereotypes, hardened in discrimination,
and paraded in public—played an important role in defining the culture of lodge politics.

This equality was strictly procedural: preparing for elections, voting,
participating in the results, and on round again. By 1840, at the beginning of America's half century of high partisanship, customs about
using public space and containing political conflict, along with reasonably stable rules about nominating, balloting, challenging, and other
aspects of the electoral process, pushed violence to the edges of an
increasingly regularized party competition, one that civil war interrupted but by no means destroyed. Democracy's cardinal principle of
getting into politics by getting into it was also a way of expressing how
a hostile tolerance worked in this world of diverse lodges: asking, the
answer to outsiders would have been no; doing, the result was yes.
Despite the massive bloodletting of the Civil War, southern rebels
worked wonders for themselves by pushing their way back into the
political system and, once there, demanding to be treated as equals.
Nor did varied immigrant backgrounds interfere with the process. Prospective voters were not expected to pass through stages of civic readi-

ness. Just as the franchise defined the citizen, so the citizen defined the franchise. There was very little to tell the neophyte. Participation trained citizens—in effect, it made people citizens.

Decentralization was crucial to this process. So was the general leveling of authority that generated a sense of all groups holding some for themselves and no group holding a great deal for any purpose. It was a curious validation of James Madison's faith that in an extensive republic, suspicious, fragmented factions would police one another's power. No doubt the scheme benefited immensely from the widespread scattering of America's white nationalities. Whatever clusterings occurred here and there, they produced no balkanization—no German state or Irish region—and hence no territorial solidity of any consequence to America's ethnic conflicts.

Only procedure united these countless pieces. Yet in those terms the results were stunning: equal but separate, separate but joined. Behind the Reverend Thomas Starr King's ripe Victorian rhetoric in 1852 lay an astonishing and distinctively American scene: "We have become so accustomed to the facts that we are not startled by the marvel which the facts reveal . . . those mighty living tides of English, Germans, Irish, and Scandinavian emigration flowing westward and crystallizing as they flow into beautiful social order." A few years earlier, watching from the gallery of the House of Representatives, the normally dismissive British visitor Alexander Mackay caught a glimpse of the same vision: "In one sense, truly, you have a congress of nations in this Congress of the United States." You have an extraordinary sample of human types, he continued, "with all their diversified habits, predilections, histories, creeds, and traditions; you have the representatives of almost every country in Europe living together, not a paralytic life, but a life of constant industry and active competition, and regulating their [own] political existence." [34]

But what held all this together? The political parties themselves fell short because they mobilized only to divide into warring camps. What gave heterogeneity its wholeness in the 19th century, what created unity, pure and simple, out of this diversity, was the single moment of a general election. Here democratic culture came full circle. At the beginning it was the franchise that defined each white man as the equal of every other, validated his right to self-determination, and invested him with public authority. At the end it was using those same badges of sovereignty that transformed otherwise scattered, suspicious men of every type and persuasion into one governing People. Approaching the polls, they carried a full panoply of insular loyalties. In the act of voting, however, it was as if citizens entered a peculiar state of nature, where as they cast their ballots they were stripped of any identity other than that of sovereign citizens deciding collectively. For that instant, they were the American People. Then the moment passed; they left as they had come, with all their divisive attachments intact. Far less mystical than they were practical, these beliefs more or less took the world as they found it. Unity in the instant of an act required no drastic change in people's characters or cultures, no fusing of intractable pieces into an American *Volk*. An intense consciousness of differences still served as the hallmark of this democracy. Additive rather than holistic, it relied on the Bancroftean sense of an electoral whole that rose in quality and importance as more and more voters participated. In the creation of this additive People, it mattered profoundly that American traditions from deep into the 18th century already assumed an additive citizenship, one that enable newcomers to enter an endlessly expandable body politic fully, equally, indistinguishably. It also mattered that 19th century democracy acknowledged no significant contradictions between individual self-interest and collective action. The People sacrificed no individuality. Moreover, it was a concept that for all intents and purposes reflected white men's experiences. In election after election, subtracting those who were sick, decrepit, disabled, or somewhere on the move, just about everyone who could have voted did. From a white man's point of view, those turnouts, especially in presidential elections, looked just like the People deciding.

This democracy was essential to America's complex 19th century process of nation-building. As modern Western nationalism rose out of the crucible of the Napoleonic Wars, democracy was on the verge of sweeping the United States. Where European cultures invoked ancient traditions and folk spirits to unite their nations, American culture called on democracy, which occupied the heart of America's romantic nationalism. By midcentury, popular understanding made America and democracy synonymous. When European commentators tried to quarantine the virus by arguing that democracy only suited America, white Americans heartily concurred. Democracy defined their nation; they claimed it as distinctively and exclusively theirs. What visitors mistook for a hopeless vanity was really a matter of identity. Americans boasted about precisely those democratic characteristics that made them feel American, including a sovereign People who incorporated the very mix of nationalities that most European commentators cited to prove no American nation could exist.

Americans, in other words, merged People and nation. One of Lincoln's great Civil War accomplishments was his imaginative integration of the two: a war in behalf of the American nation, with its government of, by, and for the People. Conflicts over constitutional union had deadly implications, and preserving that kind of wholeness released

powerful emotions of punishment and destruction. But the more benign concepts of the nation and its People lay loosely enough over the
slaughter of war that whites north and south could construct regional
versions of a People's decision to fight a People's war for America's
highest values and eventually combine them in a single national story
of fraternal valor and collective judgment.

"How wisely . . . has the American people made up its mind upon
public questions of supreme difficulty and importance?" the conservative Charles W. Eliot of Harvard asked in 1888. He specified three:
"first, the question of independence of Great Britain; secondly, the
question of forming a firm federal union; and thirdly, the question of
maintaining that union at whatever cost . . . Everybody can now see
that in each case the only wise decision was arrived at by the multitude, in spite of difficulties and dangers which many contemporary
statesmen . . . thought insuperable . . . No government . . . could possibly have made wiser decisions or executed them more resolutely."
"The country," William Dean Howells wrote that same year, "belongs
to the people"; their decisions alone square policies with public needs.
Did the process of making these basic national decisions seem chaotic?
Thank heavens, the usually sedate Frederick Grimke declared, for "it
is that very freedom of thought and action, unbounded as it may be
supposed to be, which gives being to public opinion; and without the
influence of public opinion society would be a mere waste." Even skep-
tics had to give the democratic devil its due in America. "There may
be some mistake," the jaundiced Henry Adams said through a character in his novel *Democracy* (1880), "about a doctrine which makes the
wicked, when a majority, the mouthpiece of God against the virtuous,
but the hopes of mankind are staked on it."[35]

From Bancroft to Whitman, the tribunes of 19th century American
democracy highlighted very similar attributes: dynamism and stability,
individuality and unity, instinct and judgment, diversity and wholeness. Hence in 1893 when Frederick Jackson Turner offered a new interpretive synthesis of American democracy, he could assume an audience already attuned to these qualities as he explained their frontier
origins. Turner's young white men, cut off from their families but by
no means bereft, work out a new egalitarian society by living it: by
hunting, fighting, farming, building. Abilities, not credentials, matter.
Nobody plans the new order; nobody asks to join it. Newcomers enter
this evolving democracy simply by entering it. Both sturdy individualists and natural collaborators, generations of pioneers determine their
destinies one by one and they determine them collectively. As the frontier thrusts its challenges on them, it is not the wisdom of the ages but
their instinctive judgment that sustains them. In a manner of speaking,

they carry their diverse cultural baggage to the very edge of the frontier; then at the critical moment of encounter, of decision, they jettison it. Suddenly their cultural past is irrelevant. By that act they are transformed: they lose all identities other than American democrat. They comprise a single white fraternity. On the far side of that experience once again they reclaim various baggage and become Swedish or Irish, farmer or professor. But when they are face to face with the nation's crucial decisions, at those points where democracy must be renewed or it will atrophy, they are the American People.

‖‖‖‖

CHAPTER 4

IN OR OUT

‖‖‖‖ The 19th century People included some Americans and excluded others. How were the lines drawn? Getting inside the circle of lodge democracy required above all else acting as full, free participants acted, that is, as citizens who were in charge of their working lives and their public lives. It was rarely a nuanced matter. The proof, by and large, stood open to public view. Those who behaved like self-directed workers and independent citizens established their claims and took their places. Hence another way of phrasing the question of inclusion and exclusion: what groups were able to present themselves as self-determining citizens and what groups were stopped from acting free?

The answers lay scattered throughout 19th century America. No authoritative national gatekeeper decided who did and did not belong. Although the wording of the Constitution and the actions of the national government certainly mattered in this regard, a persisting decentralization, even after the Civil War, ensured an unevenness, an uncertainty to all decisions about inclusion and exclusion. Nor did the fraternities by themselves clarify the issue. By embodying white men's hostilities, they expressed a great diversity of differences without revealing how to sort among them. Simply listing a fraternity's enemies did not distinguish which of those hostilities fell within the boundaries of lodge democracy's roughly egalitarian competition and which ones, pitting insiders against outsiders, were inherently unequal. In fact, a procession of claimants kept those boundaries in doubt throughout the 19th century, and tension between these assertions and the resistance to them became in its own right a defining component of democratic public life.

Some tensions over entry lost their force during the century. Roman

Catholics, whose hierarchical church stood at odds with 19th century democratic values, roused spurts of furious opposition from Protestant Americans, especially before the Civil War, and suffered generally from discrimination and rejection throughout the century. Nevertheless, even at the height of attack, both Irish and German Catholics lived out the principle of getting into democratic life by getting into it—acting as independent workers, leaguing together in various fraternities, and inserting themselves into local politics. It helped that as the Catholic church spread across the continent, so did lay influence and local control in its affairs. With few exceptions the church hierarchy kept a step removed from party politics. Inside America's decentralized democracy, in other words, Protestants and Catholics fought one another as equals.

At the other end of the spectrum, some tensions disappeared because with the slightest tug from the outside they simply snapped. Native Americans, it seems clear, never had a chance to participate. Instead, they lived out a deadly inversion of white men's democracy. From time to time America's 18th century hierarchies provided a modicum of shelter for Native Americans who adopted the status of wards in exchange for a white government's protection. Destroying those hierarchies, democracy eliminated the assumption of reciprocal obligations between superior and inferior and left the hopelessly outnumbered Native Americans to defend themselves. Indian reservations, always a cruel hoax on the theme of separate but equal places in America, now became a cruel irony as well, for white men reserved only the right to take back whatever they had once granted: *Indian giving* was the whites' ambiguous phrase for the practice. As democrats took the lands they needed for white men's self-directed work, Native Americans lost the indispensable resources for theirs.

The ultimate inversion involved the meaning of development in 19th century America. As white democrats understood it, development enabled them to look beyond their immediate failures to future prospects, justifying today's means in the name of tomorrow's progress. What allowed whites figuratively to vault over life's limitations, however, caught Native Americans literally in a death trap. Whites, requiring Native American land to fulfill their own development, demolished Indian nations that stood in the way. In the white mind's eye, which saw the future in the present, Native Americans slipped out of focus. "Yet they have vanished from the face of the earth," one eastern gentleman signed as early as 1825, "—their very names are blotted from the pages of history."[1] Fated to die, dying, soon to die, already dead blurred into a single vision of Native American elimination not just as inevitable but as natural. Like other wild creatures made extinct

by civilization, a commentator on democracy concluded, Native
Americans were "essentially untamable. They find what we call freedom a fatal slavery."[2] Appropriately, democratic governments mustered power sufficient to destroy their nations but never sufficient to
protect them. Make way for progress, and let the dead bury the dead.

Perhaps no basis existed in the 19th century for Native Americans
and whites to come together in a democratic polity. Certainly white
men had no interest in exploring the possibility. The highly varied and
complex changes that Native American cultures underwent rarely affected the policies imposed on them. As legislators in Michigan decided without a hint of irony, Indians could never be genuine citizens
because they did not belong to the "great North American Family."[3]

Between the extremes of a tension absorbed and a tension broken lay
a range of indeterminate interactions between lodge equality and everyday inequalities that had no simple resolution in the 19th century.
The most important of these—the ones with a shaping influence on
the meaning of democracy—involved white men who earned wages,
African Americans, and white women.

Where individual autonomy defined the democratic citizen, wage
earners suffered from a number of disadvantages. A long European
tradition, more or less equating wage earners with servants, denied
even the possibility of their independence: servants had masters, masters controlled servants. The 17th century English Levellers, though
radicals on the extension of the franchise, still excluded "servants or
wage earners," whom they categorized along with "beggars." John
Locke left no place for them in his social contract, nor a century later
did Adam Smith picture them as a sentient part of public life. In the
same Enlightenment spirit, Cesare di Beccaria assigned employers,
courts, legislators, and police the responsibility to set and enforce rules
for society's wage earners, who, he claimed, did not have the resources
to decide their own course.

Those rules from above belonged to an even more ominous tradition: that society had a right to the labor of its working classes. English
statutes dating from 1350 ordered those not already bound in a dependent relationship to accept work at whatever wages were offered in
their neighborhood. If their wages did not provide a subsistence, workers had to hope that local governments would fulfill an obligation to
add a relief supplement. Although by the 16th century more and more
people escaped this impossible situation by moving about in search of
better wages—and breaking other restrictive laws as they did—the
principle that they did not have a choice about working stuck tenaciously to them wherever they went. What had originated as a personal

or status right of superiors to the labor of inferiors became in time society's right to the labor of its citizens, a right that European governments were still bent on enforcing early in the 19th century.

As onerous as these conditions were, the wage-labor market drew in hundreds of thousands whose alternatives were various forms of unpaid rural dependence. One of wage labor's attractions was its margin of personal latitude—however slender a margin—in settings where a local elite could not keep an eye on them. Cities even allowed the option of not working for hire. Where the market alone no longer held people to their jobs, the champions of compulsory work fell back on other principles. Ministers and priests enthusiastically enlisted Christianity to the cause. The British Parliament revised the poor laws so that they would corral impoverished people of all ages into the labor market. In the machine age, some privileged Europeans took an almost aesthetic pleasure in envisaging "the peaceful hum of an industrial population whose movements are regulated like clockwork." [4] Even Friedrich Engels felt obliged to warn a fellow radical that under communism comrades would still be compelled to put in a hard day's work at the factories.

Americans shared in these traditions. Despite a widespread commodification of work relations, master-servant principles held fast into the 19th century in a variety of indentured, apprenticing, and paid-work settings. Americans as well as Europeans demeaned wage earners as "hireling" labor. Early in the 19th century, workers' bargaining organizations were still prosecuted under laws that made a withdrawal of their labor a criminal conspiracy against society's interests. With the establishment of democracy's crucial norms—self-directed work and self-defined authority—the meaning of these disabilities sharpened. Wage earners no longer represented just one form of dependency in a hierarchy of dependencies. Among white men they seemed to stand alone, uniquely subject to superior direction at work and higher authority at law. Their first challenge, therefore, was to break with tradition, a process that spread widely between 1828 and 1842.

Appropriate to the spirit of the new democracy, wage earners asserted their rights. After 1828, workingmen's political parties cropped up in cities and towns in the northeast. Numerous trade unions organized between 1834 and 1836. Sundry newspapers claimed to speak for these workers, and various reform movements claimed to represent their best interests. Though particular protests came and went rapidly, as a whole the outbursts changed public agendas wherever wage earners congregated. Economic hardship was not its driving force. In fact, wage earners were much more aggressive during the generally prosperous years before 1837 than during the hard times afterward. What stirred these men was the sudden rush of a democracy that threatened to leave them behind. They were demanding the wherewithal for independence.

Independence required opportunity. In the city, labor activitists targeted obvious inequalities in privilege and power as the great obstacle. Break the merchant capitalist monopolies. Reward only those who produced. Eliminate the lawyers. Workingmen's movements rarely advocated a new system, just an honest version of the existing one, where wage earners would have a reasonable chance of setting up for themselves. Before the Civil War, the standard meaning for *free labor* was self-employment. The independent farmer, of course, was the standard model of self-employment, of self-directed work generally, and hence cheap land served as a staple in almost all democratic reforms. "Vote Yourself a Farm," the labor reformer George Henry Evans told working men in the 1840s. Immigrants such as the wage earners in New York City's Kleindeutschland also took up the cry.

Another democratic attack on the tradition of dependence was simply to take charge of one's own life. By 1840, self-help, always an option, became a movement. A self-help strategy, by its nature, rejected radical confrontation. Radicalism rested on the premise that something terrible had gone wrong in the world. In a standard European version, it contrasted the hopes of rural migrants for a better life as wage earners with the realities of their industrial lives: families packed into health-sapping slums, wealth stolen by the owners, wages squeezed to starvation levels, bodies chewed up by factory machines. In an intolerable context of broken promises, the logical solution was total change. In America's democratic context, on the contrary, workers already knew that a wage-earning dependence left them inherently worse off than other white men: no promise here, only problems. Their task was not to explain otherwise inexplicable losses but to take one more step, to stretch for the ring of independence that seemed just out of reach. Instead of turning everything upside down, the better choice might well seem a summoning of inner resources to make the final push for autonomy.

If self-help was not radical, it was certainly not conservative. It required exceptional courage to push out of the violent, destructive environment that surrounded many wage earners' lives. Saloons housed drunks who diseased themselves, brutalized their families, and maimed one another. Fights broke bones, gouged eyes, and stripped men of their livelihood. Gambling sucked up the resources that held workers precariously at the margin. In this setting, buying a home, joining a church, and taking the pledge were profound personal and cultural statements. By the 1840s, foreign observers were routinely noting how many more American than European wage earners had some church attachment. Even in a society that exalted individual choice, the extraordinary drop in the consumption of hard liquor between 1830 and 1850 gave evidence of a powerful urge for self-determination: nothing was harder to escape than an addiction. In this general environment of self-improvement, the Washingtonians, total abstinence associations that flourished among workers early in the 1840s, were merely the tip of the iceberg. Experiences in Providence, Rhode Island, where "self-discipline," not "external restraint," was already driving workingmen's temperance by 1828, were more indicative of how the self-help movement was gathering momentum decade by decade. Especially in "that indeterminate territory of skilled workers and small employers," which abounded in cautionary tales of sobriety and frugality succeeding and drunkenness and dissipation failing, why not believe the individual could choose between the wages of sin and the blessings of independence?[5]

At least as important as declaring their independence in the community was claiming it on the job. There workers stood head to head with the devil itself: that a wage earner was some master's servant. To establish their democratic credentials they acted in democratic ways. Travelers' accounts routinely contrasted European and American wage earners' presentations of themselves. Unlike the beaten mill hands in England, according to a typical report in 1840 from James Silk Buckingham, factory workers in Dover, New Hampshire, were strikingly ambitious, optimistic, and industrious—and very prickly about their social equality. Visitors found personal service, doubly damned as the antithesis of self-determination, in utter shambles in America: Irish maids putting on airs and walking off the job, housekeepers sitting down to chat with their employers, valets abusing their superiors. "I heard, myself, an American servant tell of the gentlemann 'he lived with,' " gossiped Francis Grund, *"that he liked him very well; but always crossed him in politics. His master knew this; but kept him in his employ."* In contrast with the British, a cosmopolitan hairdresser observed, many Americans "dare not engage a servant, unless he or she happens to suit all the other servants in the house." It was assumed as a matter of course that American workers would never wear livery: uniforms made men look "like prize cattle," one newspaper sneered. Changes in language reflected these democratic feelings: *help* for *servant, boss* for *master.*[6]

A more complex approach to gaining independence on the job traded safety for autonomy. One of the crucial concomitants to democratic individualism early in the 19th century was a new sense of owning one's body. Its origins lay in various Enlightenment propositions

about the body's integrity—in philosophy, in science, in criminal punishment. For ordinary citizens in the 18th century, however, these
might have humanitarian, but rarely empowering, consequences: elites
still monopolized the authority both to heal and to harm their bodies.
No *philosophe* opposed beating discipline into soldiers, and Jefferson,
for one, considered castration the appropriate punishment for buggery.
Starting in the 1820s, the right of control over one's body was democratized. Popular medicine gave Americans the resources to care for
themselves. Campaigns against all forms of damaging punishment
gained support, not as protests against pain or even violence but as
the rejection of any outsider's claim to inflict harm. The abolition of
flogging in the navy capped this movement at midcentury, by which
time the right of each white man to dispose of his own body was a
well-established democratic principle.

Creating a right did not make life any safer. Age-old dangers still
blanketed the 19th century. Poisonings and infections crept in and stole
lives indiscriminately: here today and gone tomorrow indeed. With
few useful diagnostic tools, lives ended as mysteriously as they did
abruptly. In the working world, disabilities were routine. Harry Crews'
description of a later time applied as well to this one: everybody, it
seemed, "had something missing, a finger cut off, a toe split, an ear
half-chewed away, an eye clouded with blindness from a glancing
fence staple. And if they didn't have something missing, they were
carrying scars."[7] What changed was the locus of choice. Within the
leeway that life allowed, democracy decreed that each white man
would make his own decisions about the disposal of his own body.

The intimate linkage between democratic standing and the ownership of one's body gave wage earners their own perspective on 19th
century labor law, anchored on Massachusetts Chief Justice Lemuel
Shaw's notorious decision in *Farwell v. Boston & Worcester Railroad*
(1842), which placed almost all responsibility for industrial accidents
on employees. In one sense, *Farwell* was a chilling triumph for entre-
preneurial capitalism: employers take the profits, workers take the
risks. No doubt Shaw, like the justices of the United States Supreme
Court, wanted to remove inhibitions to business enterprise and recognized the rising costs of industrial injury as a significant factor in the
cause. Nevertheless, there are reasons why no prominent labor spokes-
man or organization mounted a campaign against *Farwell* during the
19th century.

In retrospect, of course, comprehensive social insurance and safety
laws look much better than *Farwell*. In the 1840s, however, law and
custom set entirely different standards. Publicly financed workers
compensation was never a consideration. At law, few people in any

circumstances recovered losses through tort cases. As one historian put it, the courts operated in a "no-liability" environment.[8] In addition, whatever made the United States a Christian nation in the 19th century, it was certainly not a commitment to the gentle virtues. No one cited sympathy for the crippled as a salient American trait. The most likely alternative to *Farwell* was a Massachusetts court settlement from three years before, *Barnes v. Boston & Worcester Railroad*, in which an injured worker did win compensation. *Barnes*, however, spoke in the idiom of traditional Massachusetts patriarchy, not in the new language of democracy. It situated the worker in a company hierarchy and re-warded him for his good character—his loyalty, his honesty, his relia-bility. It established no wage-earner rights of any sort. By substituting the court's good graces for the employer's good graces, *Barnes* reaf-firmed the very kind of dependence on authority that democratic wage earners needed to escape.

In democratic terms, *Farwell* was a trade-off. On one side, work crews held responsibility for their own safety. As Shaw declared, coldly but not illogically, that placed the management of risk "upon those who could best guard against it." Often these crews constituted small lodges, where approximate equals monitored one another and the work place alike. If they did not, no one did. In exchange, *Farwell* ac-knowledged a substantial measure of wage-earner freedom. In the de-centralized working world of 19th century America, many of these crews were left more or less to their own devices, training newcomers, managing their own work days, and watching out for themselves. It was a high-stakes gamble: those who won functioned on the job as free men; those who lost—a slip, a serious injury—fell into destitution. Nobody knows how many workers willingly chose to gamble, or how many of those lived to regret it. But as hard a bargain as it was, it made democratic as well as capitalist sense in the 1840s.

A final strategy for independence confronted the devil's other face: society's right to its workers' labor. As the flat denial of workers' auton-omy, it declassed them as democrats. In the new dispensation, wher-ever wage earning implied compulsory work, it became *wage slavery*: a free man could make his own decisions to work or not. Moreover, common law conspiracy doctrine continued to raise the specter of compulsory work. Although the legal scope of labor conspiracy had narrowed considerably early in the 19th century, Chief Justice Edward Savage of New York still applied the doctrine vigorously to strikers who, he ruled in 1835, had deprived "industrious" men of the right to work and hence injured "the community, by diminishing the quantity of productive labor"—precisely the time-honored logic behind man-dated work.[9] As it turned out, Savage's ruling was a last gasp. Once again, it was Lemuel Shaw, the Massachusetts chief justice, who pointed a new direction. *Commonwealth v. Hunt* (1842) shifted society's stake in productive labor to employers, whose contracts with employees replaced worker's obligations to society as the operative legal doctrine. If only in theory, wage earners emerged as free bargaining agents, not society's drudges.

Farwell and *Hunt* both appeared in 1842. With land reform, labor pride, and workingmen's temperance in full voice by then, the campaign to win equal standing for white wage earners reached its limits. These themes—of self-definition, self-help, job independence, and job action—dominated the balance of the century. At the heart of the movements for restricted hours—first the ten-hour day before the Civil War, then the eight-hour day after—lay arguments that more free time would enable wage earners to fulfill their role as full-fledged, informed citizens. Charges of land monopoly, ringing across the century, appealed as much to wage earners as to farmers. Through a "single tax" to reclaim the value that social progress had added to land, Henry George demonstrated as late as the 1880s how land reform still bridged agrarian and industrial America. On the one side, his insight into the way control over land destroyed equal opportunity came in California, the symbol of western openness. On the other side, his crucial illustrations came from the big cities, and his primary supporters clustered there. Terence Powderly, Grand Master Workman of the Knights of Labor who considered land reform central to the union's program, was one of George's admirers. When George ran for mayor of New York City, white wage earners formed his major constituency.

If anything, the wage earners' urge for independence on the job, including the willingness to take the high personal risks commonly associated with the greatest independence, increased over the century. Unusually dangerous skilled jobs in railroading, iron and steel, and coal mining ranked among America's most coveted wage-earning positions. In none of these industries did organizations of workers leave a record of pressing for safer jobs. On the contrary, in each case "a skilled craftsman [was] responsible for his own work and safety," and the carnage was appalling.[10]

Even in the absence of systematic government data, pieces of evidence suggest the horrendous price that risk-taking exacted in the American work place. In the late 19th century, 40 percent of the crew members on Santa Fe trains annually suffered some injury. Although the least skilled workers probably had even more accidents, one seven-year study of the Illinois Central Railroad concluded that among the most skilled, job-related injuries completely disabled 1 in 20. Comparative studies sharpen the picture. American railroad companies were last among industrial nations to install even those safety devices, such as Westinghouse brakes, that Americans had invented. Despite a significant underreporting of accidents in the United States data, a study in 1910 still concluded that American railroads had 3 times the annual death rate and 5 times the injury rate of the British, and 2 1/2 and 5 times the rates of the Germans. Early in the 20th century, a spot check in American coal mining revealed a death rate more than 3 times higher than Belgium's and almost 3 times higher than Britain's.

Extra efforts and high risks did not resolve the problem of the wage earner's citizenship. No breakdown in wage-earning relations opened the way to an industrial era in self-directed work and self-determined authority. Much of what wage earners gained was secured piecemeal from a grudging judiciary. In standard 19th century democratic rhetoric, white wage earners continued to be regarded as more dependent than their brothers: Frederick Grimke called them an "inferior" class to their employers' "superior" class. How workers used public spaces—to strike, to protest, to educate—was subject to special restrictions, always a signal of second-class citizenship in 19th century democracy. Making a similar point, many public leaders clung to the notion that poor men owed labor to society. From the wage earner's angle of vision, the Civil War draft was this bitter old enemy in flimsy disguise, functioning much like the old press gangs as it swept workers into the military. After the Great Fire of 1871, Chicago businessmen wanted to refuse relief to those who were not rebuilding the city. Vagrancy laws late in the century criminalized idleness—that is, for the poor.

To the degree that wage earning seemed only a temporary situation, a way station toward self-employment, these disabilities weighed less heavily. But as the years passed, a larger proportion of the labor force worked for wages, and a larger proportion of them, in turn, were wage earners for life. If wage earners could not move up, at least they could move away. It was a commonplace to equate physical mobility with a wage earner's freedom: leave the bad jobs, find the better ones. It resolved no problems, however, to keep a step ahead of discrimination by staying on the run.

What did alter the wage earner's democratic standing was to change identities, then reenter public life through lodges that affirmed their members' independence: now no longer wage earners but Irish Democrats or Iowa Grangers or Civil War veterans. By making themselves invisible as wage earners, their citizenship lost its ambiguity. Sometimes, of course, these lodges were merely labor unions with a new sign over the doorway. More often, however, wage earners recast themselves in work-neutral terms, shifting among the multiple identities

that the fraternal networks provided for white men and acquiring public equality as they did. A democratic problem that could not be resolved in the working world, in other words, found its most effective
answer in the political world: switching democratic means changed
democratic ends.

It was precisely this kind of invisibility that whites denied African
Americans. They were allowed no second public identity. Before 1860,
blackness and slavery bounded their niche, and whites had no difficulty recognizing it as the antithesis of democracy. Democrats poured
into public spaces; African Americans dodged the slave patrols and
filled the slave auctions. If self-directed work defined the democrat,
slavery established its opposite. Where owning one's body and risking
it by choice were essential corollaries of democratic labor, beatings defined as they punished the slave. He would turn them into "Negro
slaves," the lash-wielding captain in Dana's *Two Years before the Mast*
bawled at his white seamen. These were black degradations. Even the
last lingering forms of involuntary servitude early in the 19th century
involved northern blacks, caught in the toils of their states' gradual
emancipation laws, who in increments of freedom were edging their
way out of slavery.

Slavery was also the antithesis of post-Enlightenment values about
essential human rights, which already prevailed in the bourgeois circles of western Europe as democracy triumphed in the United States.
Southern slaveholders, as a consequence, faced the threat of double
ostracism. Europeans condemned them as uniquely barbaric, northern
whites as uniquely aristocratic, a privileged few who broke the democratic code and lived from other people's labor. In response, leading
southern whites turned inward to mobilize their own resources. As
the historian Drew Faust writes, "The significance of the proslavery
argument [that developed after 1830] . . . lay within ante-bellum Southern society itself." [11] Building a wall of silence around discussions that
might challenge slavery, southern white men shrank the scope of their
own public affairs and tried to do the same nationally.

Although slavery contradicted democracy, the two did not necessarily clash. Southern slavery hardened as American democracy arrived,
and an expansive white democracy gave new impetus to demands for
the extension of black slavery. Jacksonians, championing democracy on
one hand, collaborated in suppressing national debate over slavery on
the other. Even such important voices of democracy as George Bancroft
of Boston and William Leggett of New York, both repelled by slavery,
made no special effort to fight it. In fact, its most prominent enemies
concentrated in areas of New England where democracy was devel-

oping sluggishly, and the most powerful appeals against slavery—images of chained men and grieving mothers and hunted runaways—primarily tapped the sentiments of evangelical Christianity and the Enlightenment, not democracy. Slavery and democracy lived side by side for decades, and northern complicity with the institution showed everywhere. If southern whites beat their slaves, one observer wryly noted, northern whites sold them the whips. Moreover, while democracy in the midst of slavery did take on distinctive qualities, inflating the power of community sovereignty, reconstruing the role of manual labor, and limiting the public agenda, white fraternalism and conclaves of the People flourished in the south, too. It was in the southern states, after all, that the secession conventions of 1860–61 provided the world's closest approximation to a popular referendum on war.

As long as slavery existed, it walled in all African Americans, including free blacks, who numbered about half a million on the eve of the Civil War. Their freedom was measured by its distance from black slavery, rather than by its nearness to white freedom. Southern states denied free blacks most of the civil rights that whites enjoyed and imposed many of the same legal penalties that slaves faced. In a number of states, south and north, free blacks could not be legal residents. In no northern state could free blacks count on the law to defend them against white violence; in only a few did they have protections, other than their own, against reenslavement through kidnapping. The civic definition of an African American, in other words, began with slavery.

Although American democracy certainly did not create white racism—nor did white racism produce American democracy—the two blended in volatile ways. One part of that mix generated a new emotional charge for the meaning of community membership. In the 18th century hierarchy, free black men, finding places at or near the bottom of society one by one, rarely seemed a general threat to whites. The great danger then was an uprising, epitomized by the slave revolt of the 1790s in Saint-Dominigue that destroyed the whole social scaffolding. In the lodge democracy of the early 19th century, however, individual black men did pose an immediate threat, one that whites expressed through the scare term *amalgamation*.

In theory, all barriers fell to anyone entering a democratic fraternity. Where the difference between slavery and freedom was as clear as black from white, this kind of mingling conjured images of imminent degradation. The racist chestnut warning white fathers about the marriage of their daughters to black men, a way of thinking that would have been incomprehensible to the Revolutionary generation, came directly out of this democratic soil. By the same logic, nothing blocked a full-fledged citizen from rising to any office in the land. In areas of unusually high mobility and social flux, such as New York City and the states of the old northwest, with their heavy flows of diverse people through and around local lodges, racist cartoons made the most of these amalgamation fantasies by depicting apelike blacks who sat in judgment over helpless white men and propositioned vulnerable white women.

The second part of that potent mix blended racism with nation-building. As democracy defined the nation in the making, so did democracy's whiteness. If the nation itself was white, blacks were not simply marginalized, they were eliminated entirely from the real America. In the language of the 19th century, their exclusion became *natural*. Perhaps their slavery was also.

Before the Civil War, these burdens sank the prospects of free blacks in all three areas critical to democratic participation: the franchise, the ability to organize around its use, and the public space to act out their decisions. As white fraternal democracy triumphed, free blacks progressively lost voting rights: Maryland in 1810, New York in 1821, Tennessee in 1834, North Carolina in 1835, Pennsylvania in 1838. New western states denied African Americans the ballot from the outset. By the Civil War, only the tiny number of free blacks in those sometime-reluctant democracies, the five New England states, could vote. In the early 1830s, moreover, a wave of restrictive laws spread through the southern states, banning the group activities and public gatherings of free blacks. In the north, white men produced similar results through violence. During the early and mid-1830s literally hundreds of incidents in which northern blacks were beaten or killed intimidated the rest and drove them out of public life. The churches, centers of African American organization, were favorite targets of attack. No society in history, Orlando Patterson concludes, treated the free segment of its enslaved population more oppressively.

Almost all northern blacks, in other words, were driven into democracy's shadowland of inversions where racism replaced egalitarianism, assault competition, and silence participation. Although they still gathered together, their public spaces lay hidden indoors: the streets belonged to the whites. In an effort to step out of this shadowland, African Americans were caught in a politics of indirection that asked whites who had no need to hear them to hear them and officials who did not represent them to represent them. The time-honored means of requesting something in this context was the petition, and free blacks employed it persistently.

How under the circumstances could blacks give enough of an edge to a petition to compensate for its ritual language of dependence: we humbly pray, we most respectfully present? Petitioning the government of Ohio in 1858, one African American convention denied the democratic credentials of "a State which Taxes a portion of its inhabitants without allowing them a representative, excludes them from offices of honor and trust, refuses them an impartial trial by Jury, refuses an equal education to their youth, disparages their patriotism by refusing to enroll them in her militia, allows them to be hunted through her cities, confined in her jails, and dragged thence to hopeless slavery," before politely requesting the elimination of "white" from the Ohio Constitution. The tension in such efforts crackled. Be courteous but not obsequeous: "We submit, therefore, that there is neither necessity for, nor disposition on our part to assume a tone of excessive humility." Protect the argument from the servility of its language: "Sir—My reasons—I will not say my apology, for addressing you this letter." [12]

Nevertheless, in a culture where petitioning represented "a retreat from the rights of the franchise towards the submissions of slaves," theirs was a self-defeating exercise.[13] By definition, democrats had a direct voice in the governing process and an unimpeded access to the governing officials. Denying African Americans those privileges, whites obliged them to use procedures the very execution of which reaffirmed their exclusion. To the white democrats in power, the mere act of petitioning ratified the petitioners' inferior status. Squirm and twist as they might, free blacks were still kept on bended knees. When they did talk as equals, they were invariably called "insolent."

Yet they had few choices. Once in a long while African American rage exploded in public. The mysterious maverick David Walker's *Appeal* of 1829 heaping scorn on "this *Republican Land of Liberty!!!!*" was a particularly stunning example. Otherwise, free blacks could only vent their anger among friends, as Robert Purvis did in the company of fellow abolitionists decrying America's "base and contemptible" system, its "piebald and rotten Democracy, that talks loudly about equal rights, and at the same time tramps one-sixth of the population of the country in the dust." Exhorting a wider audience, they played upon white sensibilities to publicize black grievances. Walker sought to arouse Christian consciences. Other African Americans tried to turn the themes of freedom in the Fourth of July to their cause. As whites celebrated, one editor declared, it was "the bleakest day of the year" for blacks. "What to the American slave is your Fourth of July?" Frederick Douglass asked whites in a mixed gathering at Rochester in 1852. "This Fourth of July is *yours*, not *mine*. *You* may rejoice, *I* must mourn." Although some free blacks declared August 10th, the date of the British emancipation of slaves, their independence day, the standard protests drew on the traditions of America's Fourth. By selecting the fifth of July as a day of dissent, for example, New Haven church members in effect stood next to white America's heritage and requested room for themselves: "The Declaration of Independence has declared . . . that all men are born free and equal. Has it not declared this freedom and equality for us too?" [14]

In a smashing of continuity more profound than anything in white history, the destruction of slavery revolutionized the lives of all African Americans. By removing the incubus of black slavery, the Civil War redefined the meaning of black freedom. The Thirteenth Amendment made self-directed work the norm for all men; the Fourteenth Amendment promised all men their public rights. Through these amendments, in other words, an African American man ceased to be the child/slave that even white antislavery rhetoric made of him and became an adult/citizen. In the decade following the war, those race-specific legal disabilities that had once held free blacks precariously close to slavery disappeared in northern state after state. Even in the lower south governments recast the basic rights of free people, black as well as white, in a postslavery context. With the very shape of society at issue, there were moments in the 1860s when the sense of a new day, of a nation born again, swept through America. Great changes came through sudden, dramatic conversions, evangelical Americans believed. Could democracy itself experience such a conversion?

In those crucial democratic areas where antebellum blacks had lost out—voting, using public space, organizing—there was some cause for optimism. Franchise laws, soon embedded in the Constitution, offered the breathtaking spectacle of men only recently bound in slavery now voting their officials up or down. Following democracy's cardinal rule, African American men poured into public life, milling, talking, and balloting as 19th century citizens were expected to do. Illiteracy was no bar to participation, especially among people who had long mastered the talents of quick, efficient communication among scattered groups. Organizing meant a proliferation of black lodges, separate but equal fraternities through which freedmen could act in their own behalf. To a striking degree, African American leaders in the Reconstruction South made the same interchangeable moves from politics to other careers and back to politics again that had characterized members of the white fraternal networks from democracy's beginning. These lodge patterns required neither an end to white racism nor a general commitment to black equality. Whites might despise blacks, even consider them dangerous, yet still accept their presence in the loose agglomeration of groups forming the People. The additive nature of 19th century democracy invited just such an outcome.

What destroyed these prospects was the special meaning that white racism gave to the sheer number of blacks in the south. Of course by contrast with the smattering of blacks in the northern states, millions of freed people did bunch densely in sections of the south, particularly in eastern South Carolina and across the lower south's so-called black belt. Nevertheless, the critical issues were conceptual, not numerical. Only African Americans were denied a second identification. Unlike white immigrants, whose opportunities for chameleonlike shifts among an array of lodges allowed them to blur the faces they presented to other Americans, whites saw blacks just as blacks, whatever variety of church or fraternal or occupational associations they might form. Congregated in portions of the south where white economics had originally put them and the economics of their own poverty still held them, African Americans, now and forever black, had the look of a nation within the nation.

If whites defined blackness, blacks also defined whiteness. Measuring one dimension of a free society by its distance from black slavery, white men colored their freedom. With identities inextricably bound into slavery, African Americans might be pitied, but they could not be genuine democratic participants. Moreover, as interpreters from Thomas Jefferson to Horace Greeley explained it, the crucial meaning of slavery lay not in the lives of the slaves themselves but in its shaping effects on white personality and white society. Hence if in retrospect the Civil War had been about slavery, many white men could still construe it as a white experience—first of victorious and vanquished whites, eventually of white brothers reunited. And just as slavery intensified one kind of white consciousness, so its abolition sharpened another kind. A postwar wave of miscegenation laws spread even among those northern states most inclined to expand blacks' civil rights.

As those laws suggested, African Americans became repositories for a tangle of white men's most dangerous emotions: as their object, as their subject. In fantasy, whites transformed their own actions into black intentions. When whites pictured emancipation bringing "the Horrors of all the Rapes, Robberies, Murders, and Outrages," they used their own record to conjure up a hypothetical black revenge: rapes, robberies, murders, and outrages were daily occurrences in slavery.[15] It was this pattern of projection and denial that generated the images of black men lording it over the white men who were actually lording it over them, and sexually assaulting white women as white men actually assaulted black women. For at least a century before the Civil War, southern white leaders warned that freeing the slaves would trigger a race war. Slavery, of course, was the real race war. What whites remembered as years of peace, African Americans recalled as "a war that has been waged on us for more than two centuries."[16] Only after 1861, when whites warred on whites, did blacks sight prospects of peace.

It was against this backdrop that southern whites set out to drive African Americans from public life. Once again, white vigilantes attacked black leaders and their organizational headquarters; once again, the risks for blacks acting collectively rose sharply. These were preemptive moves, the proponents of violence argued: strike now or fall beneath the black hordes. The standard democratic logic of separate but equal lodges was simply not able to match these fearful messages of race-nation against race-nation. Not all southern whites agreed; not all freedmen lost their democratic rights. Nevertheless, wherever intimidation loomed, the old shadowland of dependence threatened again to envelop African Americans.

Increasingly southern blacks had to rely on their own resources. By the early 1870s, it required violence at the insurrectionary levels of the Ku Klux Klan to prompt a significant national response. By the end of the decade, few elected officials anywhere still claimed to represent black voters. Even at the height of Reconstruction, northern Republicans tended to treat African Americans as fledgling lodge members, much in need of tutelage and hence not really democratic adults. Now freed people slipped back into the more demeaning role of petitioners, whose very appeals declared them inferior. In 1890 a group of Republicans, headed by the aristocratic Bostonian Henry Cabot Lodge, made the century's final legislative attempt to secure southern black men's democratic rights. Labeled the Force Bill by its opponents, their effort succeeded only in publicizing African Americans' marginalization in southern public life.

Throughout these struggles for collective self-governance, democracy's second strand, individual self-determination, remained an attractive alternative. Even during the years of slavery a sprinkling of blacks north and south managed to punch holes here and there in the wall around them and achieve economic success. In fact, the new 19th century principles of labor supplied the one democratic argument against slavery as persuasive as those from Christian morality and humanitarian ethics. Whatever else, black slaves certainly had worked, and however many circles of irony the reasoning contained, constant labor gave slaves a powerful justification for freedom. Lincoln's views were exemplary. Sharing the white fraternity's social aversion to blacks, he still found it unconscionable to deny slaves the product of their labor. If the antebellum slogan *free soil* made promises to whites only, its companion *free labor* drew on values that touched blacks and whites alike.

Little wonder, then, many Americans saw the Thirteenth Amendment, universalizing the right of self-directed work, as a full-blown, nationally mandated revolution in citizenship all by itself. Certainly African Americans exalted that right. Resisting gang labor, carving out farms and shops of whatever size wherever they could, and cherishing the freedom to operate them, black families sacrificed almost anything else in order to preserve their independence at work. Nevertheless, in 19th century democracy, collective self-governance and individual self-determination inextricably merged. It was simply impossible to lose in one realm and hope to compensate with success in the other. Credit, already critical in every white man's prospects for success, became the lever by which merchants and landowners subordinated black workers. The weaker black voices grew in public affairs, the tighter the legal system squeezed those workers. As long as black men and their white allies remained competitors in southern politics, lien laws, for example, protected a reasonable share of the crop for the African American workers who grew it; but just as soon as that political power declined, so did the sharecroppers' protections.

In the first generation after slavery, African Americans made extraordinary progress: civil rights widened, choices expanded, and accumulations of education, skills, and property grew at strikingly steady rates. Into the 1890s southern black voters retained power in a number of local and state settings. But withal, they held a precarious perch in American democracy, a situation that the Supreme Court's ambiguous decision in *Plessy v. Ferguson* captured in 1896. On the one hand, the Court's acceptance of separate but equal public facilities for whites and blacks derived from one of the underlying principles in 19th century lodge democracy, a formula that in fact served some African American needs reasonably well in the postbellum south. Where common practice shunted blacks into the worst facilities—freight cars on trains, for instance—separate but equal represented a concession to black demands for decent treatment. On the other hand, it required no genius to realize that the more African American power flagged, the less equal separate would become.

How could they avoid getting lost entirely in democracy's shadowland? Frederick Douglass never wavered from his commitment to full political equality. Why? "We answer, Because . . . personal liberty . . . and all other rights, become mere privileges, held at the option of others, where we are excepted from the general political liberty." In the 1880s and 1890s, it seemed far less simple to a younger leader, Booker T. Washington. Blacks had no choice, he decided, but to work through southern whites: "They control government and own the property."[17] Applying the standard of separate but equal, he soothed white fears of amalgamation with his famous image of socially distinct fingers on an economically united hand. Democracy's strand of individual self-determination had a good deal of elasticity to it, he realized. Resource-ful blacks always used it to their advantage. Setting politics to one side, Washington sought to empower as many black men as possible through self-directed work. By showing the world what African Amer-ican industry could accomplish, he would also give the lie to the whites' latest charge: that the lazy freedman had neither desire nor capacity for self-directed work and hence did not even qualify as a democratic adult. It was a complicated strategy, a gamble that by tak-ing one step backward—by proving worthy of the rights of an in-dependent citizen rather than simply asserting them as whites did—African Americans could husband the resources for a long march for-ward. Although Washington understood a great deal about 19th cen-tury democracy, he still slipped into an old, familiar snare: dependent outsiders were petitioners, and petitioning, even for a master at the art such as Washington himself, kept them outside.

At a glance, white women and black men seemed to occupy compar-able places in 19th century democracy. For the black man's segregation there was the white woman's sphere, both democratic traps camou-flaged as nature's mandate. White men's violence that drove black men out of public spaces also held white women at bay, that is, left them dependent on men either to relent or to protect them. Neither white women nor black men could find ways of making their democratic rights issues of continuing importance inside the white men's political world. Both, therefore, were drawn into patterns of petitioning for white men's good graces.

Beneath those similarities, however, lay differences as basic as their different relations with white men. Free black and white men met in public, white women and white men in private, and in each case their disabilities began there. African American men's most pressing demo-cratic need was acceptance as a group, white women's acceptance as individuals. The men, subordinated in public life, made the most of their opportunities for individual self-determination. The women, sub-ordinated in private life, sought democratic outlets in public. In the process, aspiring black men made the most of their family resources—though seldom acknowledging them—while aspiring white women separated themselves as best they could from family life—though sel-dom failing to talk about it. Self-directed work, often a black man's most promising prospect, simply blocked the way for white women. Although Catharine Beecher, among others, tried to legitimize house-hold management as self-regulated work, and wage-earning women sometimes scandalized employers with their declarations of indepen-dence, very few white women in the 19th century could escape the stigma of dependence. Little wonder that despite white women's abolitionist contributions, the two causes touched without effectively joining. Little wonder, too, that African American women suffered double jeopardy: one set of disabilities for race, another for gender.

Early in the 19th century, families swallowed women's lives. There men held centuries-old rights to women's labor, women's property, women's wages. Kept economically marginal inside the family, women had a far more difficult time than men avoiding abject, desperate poverty outside of it. If wage-earning in an urban-industrial context later in the century had a tendency to atomize families, pursuing market opportunities in a commercial-agrarian world tended to tighten family cohesion. In all kinds of early 19th century economic settings—merchandising as well as farming—what passed for individual self-determination in the white men's scheme of things only succeeded through the combined efforts of immediate family and kin networks. A white man's standard use of the possessive for his shadowland supports—my wife, my slaves—indicated how thoroughly the independence of the one subsumed the dependence of the others.

Possessive rights revealed themselves in white men's everyday phrases. "Free love," an expletive of horror that men flung at reforms of all sorts, not only associated women's sexual satisfaction with chaos and immorality; it also made women's freedom and their sexuality oxymoronic, equated love with sex rather than affection or mutual support, and even implied better solutions through bargain and sale. The polite phrase "women and children first" was equally revealing: its company of dependence, their common status below genuine adulthood, the going when they were told to go, perhaps even a reminder that "the first shall be last." Nothing underlined women's subordinance more tellingly than men's freedom to use violence against them. Even the antebellum campaign against corporal punishment laid a veil over wife-battering. Until the late 19th century, a woman's standard appeal from an intolerable marriage, outside of Pennsylvania, remained a personal petition for divorce to a legislature of men. As tough a competitor as the writer and abolitionist Lydia Maria Child, who faced her family's bankruptcy with a ringing promise "to start afresh in the race," still knew how to flatter a bumbling husband with helpless-me big-strong-you baby talk.[18] Where there was no other recourse, women's passionate crusade for temperance confronted quite literally a matter of life or death.

With the arrival of democracy came a fully articulated doctrine of spheres that stamped the woman's world as domestic and private. In one sense these 19th century formulations raised the social value of tasks, especially child care, that over the centuries had always been

women's responsibility. Nevertheless, as the range of American public
affairs broadened and the connection between these activities and
white men's identities solidified, democratic fraternities drew protective lines around their own sphere and tried to sharpen its separation
from women's. In its original form, in other words, white men's democracy accentuated the isolation of private life.

European after European commented on the exaggeration of these
spheres in America. American women had greater authority running
the household, visitors concluded, but less recognition beyond it. European women whose class position in their home country drew them
into discussions of public life deeply resented their exclusion in
America: here women lived in a hot house of trivialities, Harriet Martineau complained. American men were obsessively courteous.
"Women may travel alone . . . with less risk of encountering disagree-
able behavior, or of hearing coarse and unpleasant conversation, than
in any country I have ever visited," the urbane Charles Lyell reported.[19]
Manners, of course, were forms of control. Where egalitarian democracy's critical distinction was in or out, men's elaborate courtesies reminded women daily that they were out. Appropriately, the less white
men used social forms among themselves, the more social niceties
structured relations between white men and women. Women, the standard argument went, were too gentle for the rough and tumble of public life: they needed men to insulate them from its harshness. When
women with a different sense of boundaries such as Martineau and
Frances Trollope intruded into what the lodge brothers considered
their space, men splattered their skirts with tobacco juice. For white
women as well as for blacks, it paid to know one's place in a white
man's world.

What some white men saw as a clean, impenetrable division, however, others made no concerted effort to police, and venturesome
groups of white women moved through the gaps, muddying the lines
between public and private, men and women. For one thing, the leveling of traditional authority which cleared the way for white men's democracy during the first decades of the 19th century was empowering
women too, especially where custom already gave them a foothold of
authority. If men maintained control over self-government and economic opportunity, women often took charge of their families' salvation and health. From there it was a short though profound step for
women to share in the new sense that individuals owned their own
bodies and disposed of them as they saw fit. Democracy heightened
women's eagerness to learn about their own physiology and regulate
their reproduction. The fact that childbirth in women's lore remained
"the valley of death" made these moves toward self-determination all

the more significant. As new possibilities beckoned, white women's literacy rate—an important index to democratic ambition—rose fast enough to catch up with white men's, at least in the cities. Moreover, white middle-class girls were now reared to be democrats. Numerous visitors expressed surprise at the assertiveness and self-sufficiency among boys and girls alike. "There are no children, in our sense of the term, in America," one Scot observed, "—only little men and women." [20] An Englishman reported with astonishment how a choir of teenage girls settled their own affairs through majority vote. Although it was equally commonplace to contrast the outgoing, self-possessed qualities of unmarried women with restrictions on the married ones, the lessons from those early years were never erased.

In the 1830s, as white men, still forming their democracy, drove free blacks from public life, white women began to explore possibilities of getting into it. Initially in a stretch from New England through New York across the old northwestern states, then in towns and cities generally in the north, and by the late 19th century throughout the nation, groups of white women changed the agenda for public discussion by mobilizing behind issues of their own choosing. Middle-class women dominated the century-long process, despite a few occasions when wage-earning women managed their own strikes. Women's sphere was conceptualized less in terms of space—inside the house—than in terms of activities: child rearing, homemaking, and the like. This understanding opened the way for middle-class women to expand into public life. Under domestic banners of family, morality, and charity, they attacked prostitution and slavery, promoted education and sanitation, tended the sick and the poor, and above all organized behind temperance. In sensibility as well as in values, evangelical Protestantism served as an approximate common denominator among them. Usually white women enacted their public lives indoors: meeting halls, publication offices, church auxiliaries. Nevertheless, in the winter of 1873–74, when thousands of women poured into the streets of Ohio to revive the temperance movement, they staked a new claim to the outdoors that their successors never relinquished.

There from the outset, white women participated in shaping both the style and the substance of democracy's public life. Their presence forced greater decorum in public discussion. In a nice twist, they turned some of the politeness that men employed to control their behavior into a means for regulating men's behavior. Even as women grew more confrontational by the 1870s, they bent every effort to avoid violence. Only their persistence kept a range of issues involving health and morals in public view. When some men pulled away from evangelical politics, dismissing it as merely private, women filled the vacuum, recruited other men to join them, and revitalized the campaigns: one historian has called the process a feminization of evangelical Protestantism. What would be labeled social housekeeping early in the 20th century was already an established women's strategy decades before. To promote their causes white women learned early to form corporations that gave them a gender-free legal standing. Late in the century, they relied more and more on associations exclusively of their own: such rock-solid, freestanding organizations as the National Woman's Suffrage Association and the Woman's Christian Temperance Union.

In its mix of universality and particularity, 19th century democracy specified equal public rights for many distinct groups, and ambitious women, led by Elizabeth Cady Stanton, expected precisely that for themselves. All men and women are created equal, her ringing declaration at Seneca Falls read in 1848, inaugurating the first organized women's movement in the Western world. At the same time, she, no more than the white men around her, expected everybody to dissolve into a common civic whole. Women would be women, forming a sorority, as it were, to parallel the existing fraternity. Even if some causes crossed gender lines, many people would not. Like the white fraternity, the sorority too would have many groupings of its own. Irish working women would combine with other Irish working women, not with Stanton. At critical moments of decision, however, all these groups, lower class and middle class, men and women, would share equally in creating a comprehensive, a truly democratic People.

This vision had no meaning without the franchise. A daring demand when Stanton first announced it in 1848, it emerged from the Civil War as the natural one, with black suffrage in the air and the universalization of citizenship a reasonable hope. The ballot was democracy's talisman. It brought self-respect: voting validated citizenship. It promised power: newspapers, politicians, even husbands would pay closer attention to voting women. "Never have the disfranchised classes had equal chances with the enfranchised," stated Susan B. Anthony, condensing the same sentiments that Frederick Douglass expressed in behalf of the freedmen.[21]

For women who felt themselves equal, the right was already theirs: "every citizen in a republic (and a woman is a citizen) has a natural right to vote, which no human law can abrogate," the reformer Elizabeth Jones declared in 1852.[22] But in the so-called new departure of 1870, when Anthony, Virginia Minor, and a few others, following the 19th century democratic precept of Don't Ask, Act, took those feelings directly to the ballot box, they lost twice, once at the polls and again before the Supreme Court in *Minor v. Happersett* (1874). Hence they remained outsiders who had to request their rights. Requesting meant petitioning; petitioning reaffirmed their standing as outsiders.

In fact petitioning carried double jeopardy for women. Not only did they reenact their public inferiority; they also restated their private subordinance in public. Women learned their rituals of dependence in the family. Entering public life offered the prospect of transcending those limitations through a self-created collective independence. Petitioning, in effect, kept them home. Women had no difficulty making a domestic translation of John Quincy Adams' defense of women's petitions as "a prayer—a supplication—that which you address to the Almighty Being above you."[23] What followed was the familiar story of squirming in the embrace of subordinance. Some petitions were less humbling than others. "As our chivalrous knight," read Stanton's biting version to the New York Legislature in 1853, ". . . we only ask, that in your leisure hours, you will duly consider the unjust laws that now disgrace your statute books."[24] Perhaps the least degrading form was petitioning by acting or witnessing—temperance women's confrontational prayer meetings right in the face of their late 19th century opponents, for example. Nevertheless, even an assertive bow was not a democratic gesture.

The figurative journey home reminded some reformers that in the end their battle would have to be won there. Stanton called it a campaign for "self-sovereignty": extend women's property rights and expand their work opportunities, renegotiate marriage contracts and liberalize divorce laws, remove the special constraints on public behavior and legitimize independent living arrangements. The strategy was to turn whatever collective power women mustered in public to the relief of their individual disabilities in private. In the first half of the 19th century, they pushed married women's issues into public discussion; in the second half, some version of a married women's property rights law passed in most states, and laws giving women control over wages succeeded in some. By no means were these inconsequential accomplishments: simply the emergence of a distinguishable woman at law marked a giant step.

But these reformers moved in a foreshortened circle, limitation playing on limitation. The insertion of "male" in the franchise clause of the Fourteenth Amendment (1868), probably necessary to its passage, had chilling consequences for women's suffrage, which for the balance of the century achieved only a few minor victories. No vote, no equality. The prospect that women might use the power they acquired in public to redress private disabilities led white men, repeating a pattern already familiar in race relations, to project their own actions onto white women's intentions: give women civil rights, they cried, and they will make men their domestic drudges. Men were digging in. Late in the century, as wage earning loosened restrictions in more women's domestic lives, white men tried to limit white women's choices elsewhere: the Comstock Law banned birth control information, new legislation reinforced the norms of monogamous marriage, and the number of sexually charged, ritual lynchings of black men rose sharply.

The persistent pressure that white wage earners, African Americans, and white women applied at the margins of 19th century democracy arose from their assumption of its extendability. Democracy's easy multiplication of lodges and its universalistic language fed that expectation. The advocates of extension declared over and over again that they were asking for nothing new, only more of the same. Stanton's inspiration to frame women's rights in a paraphrase of the Declaration of Independence came instinctively, she claimed. "We are Americans," the African American leader Alexander Crummell cried. As members of a single nation, both blacks and whites lived by a single code of values—"the eternal truths for which Jefferson wrote, and Attucks and Warren bled," in one black editor's language—and as a matter of course they should share the same democracy.[25]

These were not utopian expectations. Their vision of an all-inclusive People derived reasonably from the possibilities around them. White wage earners by the legions did become full-fledged participants in democracy's public life; so did some black men, especially in the north, and some white women, especially in the west. Nevertheless, limits were as intrinsic to 19th century democracy as expansion. Beneath its universalistic covering lay a multitude of particularistic groupings whose values set boundaries and whose behavior policed them. The meaning of democracy flowed as much from these everyday urges toward exclusiveness as it did from an overarching spirit of inclusiveness, and the results, scarcely a celebration of universalism, showed it.

White fraternity defined the scope of free movement. What enabled white wage earners to assimilate into its operations far more successfully than African Americans or white women was their far greater mobility—from place to place, from opportunity to opportunity, from lodge to lodge. That gave the dependence of employees on employers an entirely different democratic meaning than the dependence of blacks on whites or wives on husbands. The fraternity accentuated its separateness by cultivating exclusive democratic memories: the Daniel Boone pioneer, the Abraham Lincoln rise from poverty, most tellingly the fraternal Civil War. As first white women and then African Americans were shunted to bit parts, this focal American experience was transformed into a public glorification of white heroes exemplifying the white man's courage. Emotional reunions of Billy Yank and Johnny Reb at the end of the century more or less marked the boundary of democratic openness.

Exclusiveness bred exclusiveness. As the fraternity separated itself from outsiders, outsiders separated themselves from one another. Black men rarely gave a hint of support for women's rights, suffrage or otherwise. After the war the most aggressive advocates of women's suffrage, in turn, contrasted their white middle-class virtues with the vices of the lower class, black and white alike. Stanton, who once scorned Confederate women's "mere pride of race and class," sounded notes similar to theirs late in her life.[26] Of course white men were not simply bystanders to these fights. With superior power, they commonly set the terms of public debate. Stanton's circle was probably correct, for example, in claiming that white men had consciously chosen black men over them. In that context, disparaging blacks continued a dialogue that white men had commenced: the women said, *choose again.*

These prolonged struggles at the margin also italicized the proposition that 19th century democracy's collective and individual strands were inextricably bound together. Each attempt to treat them separately, to balance out weaknesses in one with strengths in the other, failed. Full citizenship required a firm grip on both. White women who tried to use public authority as compensation for their private dependence were no more successful than African Americans who tried to use private accomplishments as compensation for their public disabilities. Even white wage earners, who moved farthest from the margins into public life, still limped toward the 20th century under handicap of dependency, a deficiency as employees that politics enabled them to bypass but not overcome. For all three groups, these democratic problems had dug deep grooves by the late 19th century. It would require another large-scale breakdown, comparable to the collapse of hierarchical authority and the rise of self-directed work at the beginning of the century, to shake them loose, give them new definitions, and open the possibility for fresh solutions.

PART TWO

METAMORPHOSIS
1890s–1920s

‖‖‖‖‖ **A**s the second great wave of the industrial revolution, with its characteristic concentration of capital, systematized factory production, and transnational flow of labor, reoriented economies on both sides of the Atlantic between the late 19th and the early 20th century, it gave cities a new centrality. Focusing on cities heightened a middle-class sense of crowdedness, and feelings of crowdedness, in turn, sharpened a sense of human differences—of distinctive cultures and talents and proclivities among various people, including their proclivities toward disorder and violence. In the United States, the result was an apparent paradox: the more white Americans saw themselves bound into a single society, the more divided that society grew. The diffuse 19th century sustained their faith in the People; the centralized 20th century destroyed it.

In explaining these changes, Americans commonly started with their expanse of land. Even in the face of "the compulsions toward conformity that have periodically swept like tides over the nation," one apostle of cultural pluralism declared early in the 20th century, "the spacious continent has permitted the spontaneous self-rooting and automatic growth of differentiated communities . . . in the spaces of the continent democracy could not but prevail, and the lives of cultural groups retain their integrities."[1] By such Turnerian logic, it was the disappearance of America's open spaces that eliminated its special source of elasticity and tolerance. But a strictly American explanation ignored how generally new social divisions and conflicts were spreading elsewhere during these same years. Layers of white-collar employees complicated the structure of urban societies throughout Europe. Working-class cultures first materialized there between the 1870s and the 1910s—even in Britain, Eric Hobsbawm has argued, where earlier outbursts of class sentiment had failed to jell.

The heart of the matter in both Europe and the United States was an interrelated set of changes in the meaning of work and the sources of authority. With what was customarily called industrialization came hierarchies that sharpened invidious distinctions, especially by differentiating people's work, and sought out ways to regiment subordinance, sometimes through government and sometimes outside of it: more differences to measure, more rules to issue, more rules to follow. Everybody belonged, everybody had a place. Whose rules determined whose prospects in these hierarchies expressed the broadest of all changes accompanying industrialization: changes in class structure.

Class is a way of connecting people's economic circumstances and social power—power in their range of life chances and in their ability to affect or control one another. Long-term conflicts over these issues generate classes, which in turn set frameworks of opportunity and power around people's lives. Lesser fissures and inequalities and hatreds, including big puffs of anger during strikes and riots, may reveal next to nothing about class relations. Moreover, the critical components in class relations vary dramatically. Governments may or may not play a crucial role. Sometimes control over tools and trades matters a great deal, sometimes very little. Some conflicts are centralized, others diffused. What never changes is the dynamic quality of these relations, a perpetual shifting both in the way conflicts express themselves and in the allegiance of people whose situation along a permeable boundary between classes leaves them vulnerable to sudden changes. *Displaced artisans, tenant farmers, labor aristocrats,* and even *lower middle class* are terms commonly used to identify groups in this fluctuating borderland. It is the dynamic quality of class that distinguishes it from caste. Caste is a box; class is pressure. Though they may blend where their ends touch, they essentially describe very different situations: to encase and be encased on one side; to push and be pushed on the other.

The chief beneficiaries in the distribution of society's rewards develop class ideologies to justify their good fortune. Otherwise, a patently unequal division would be robbery, even if the current winners leave other people more than another set of winners would. Class ideologies, in other words, explain the justice in inequalities: not only why some merit the lion's share but also why others merit very little. These explanations change. During the 19th century, for example, capitalism's winners stressed how individual worth determined rewards: people got from the system just what they deserved. In the 20th century, more and more explanations have depersonalized the process: the success of the system itself has come to justify the inequalities accompanying it. How those at the bottom of the scale view inequalities rarely finds systematic expression.

Nobody offered a more piercing commentary on this process than Karl Marx, who flipped the 19th century bourgeoisie's pretentions to respectability and leadership on their back and exposed how brutally self-serving the primary beneficiaries of industrialization were. Property, rather than the foundation of virtue, became the source of vice in Marx's version, and property holders, rather than moral exemplars, became savage hypocrites, who instead of protecting society from violence and chaos, perpetrated them. "Only theft can still save property," Marx had the bourgeoisie scream in crisis; "only . . . disorder, order!"[2]

Read from the bottom up, however, those neat reversals were considerably less illuminating. Progress came not from the propertied but from the propertyless, Marx claimed. Only the dangerous classes were safe, only social disintegration promised social cohesion. Rather than peace standing guard against revolution, revolution pointed the way to peace. This prescription not only mistook powerlessness for innocence; it also miscalculated the trend toward revolution. War sometimes triggered domestic revolution, but industrialization did not. Part of the Marxian problem lay in assuming that mechanization, by inexorably draining workers of their skills, progressively immiserated them. Although technological changes beginning at least with the invention of the wheel did radically rearrange the priority for skills, the consequences were by no means uniformly demeaning. Sequence after sequence of mechanization in transportation, manufacturing, and mining brought mixed results, elevating new skills and undercutting old ones, easing burdens on some and piling them on others. Certainly many of those who used steel hardware or mechanical reapers or chain saws would not have abandoned them for a preexisting order of skills.

What emerged with industrialization in the United States was a three-class system, conflictual but not revolutionary: one class geared to national institutions and policies, one dominating local affairs, and one sunk beneath both of those in the least rewarding jobs and least stable environments—in the terminology of my account, a national class, a local middle class, and a lower class. New hierarchies ordered relations inside both the national and the local middle class; both of those classes, in turn, counted on hierarchies to control the lower class. This modern class system retained distinguishably American characteristics. It still mattered that no leisured aristocracy took root: all three classes worked. It also mattered that within the increasingly elaborate work hierarchies of the 20th century, skilled laborers, always at a premium in America, acquired additional standing through additional responsibilities—above all, for keeping the crucial machinery in operation—and hence a renewed claim to middle-class membership. At the same time, the stigma of race, penalizing not only people of color but everybody in the lower class, was just as characteristic. Democracy in the 20th century accommodated to these distinctions.

CHAPTER 5

SINKING THE LOWER CLASS

_____ The two-class system in 19th century America was as distinctive as the democracy that thrived alongside it. Three characteristics set it apart: the absence of an aristocracy, the general acceptability of manual labor, and above all else the broad base of white men's self-directed work. By consensus if not by logic, the more privileged of the two classes was known as the middle class. The crucial line of division between the two ran right through the ranks of what Europeans called the working classes.

Because the independent farmers and skilled workers who comprised the bulk of America's middle class were themselves manual laborers, no stigma was attached to calloused hands and stained clothes outside the high-bourgeois circles in a few cities. Even there, the fastidious around midcentury rarely disparaged all manual work, only drudge labor. Later in the century, some native-born white-collar workers, especially in New York City, did try to distance themselves from blue collars. But in nearby Paterson, New Jersey, across the state in Buffalo, north in Rutland, Vermont, west along the railroad lines, and in thousands of other towns and small cities, skilled workers, clerks, and small shopkeepers continued to live side by side, with similar patterns of home ownership and similar habits of farming their backyards, repairing their buildings, and hiring domestic help when they could.

White men's prospects for self-directed manual work in an expansive commercial-agrarian economy confounded European class schemes. Karl Marx, for one, threw up his hands and waxed mystical about a United States where classes continually change and interchange their elements in constant flux, where the modern means of production, instead of coinciding with a stagnant surplus population, rather compensate for the relative deficiency of heads and hands, and where, finally, the feverish, youthful movement of material production, which has to make a new world its own, has left neither time nor opportunity for abolishing the old spirit world.[1]

It was not that economic inequalities lessened with the arrival of democracy; on the contrary, they increased early in the 19th century, especially through concentrations of wealth at the very top of the scale. But so did the possibilities of self-directed work in society's middle ranges. Those enticements were difficult to price. Although investing an adult's working life to clear new farm land on the gamble of distant payoffs in a chancy world might make little economic sense, hundreds of thousands of antebellum migrants left a more profitable agricultural economy east of the Appalachians to "work for nothing" in the greater independence of the west. Opportunity, not redistribution, obsessed these people. In George Sidney Camp's smooth explanation, "The distinction of wealth"—equally open to every man—"is a peculiarly democratic distinction."[2]

Access to credit divided America's classes. In the world's most highly developed commercial-agrarian capitalism, producing and exchanging goods of a wider variety over longer distances with greater efficiency than any other 19th century economy, credit sustained the smallest and largest participants alike. There was no secret about its centrality. The credit enabling the farmer to live through harvest season, the merchant to stock the store, and the wage earner to bridge hard times defined the terms of independent citizenship. From the chartering of the Second Bank of the United States in 1816 to the establishment of the Federal Reserve system a century later, credit was never far from the heart of democratic politics. Cries to liberalize credit rose wherever the democratic spirit surged. During the 1830s, legislators in such states as Georgia and Missouri tried to mandate its popular distribution; early in the 1890s, the Populist Subtreasury Plan promised farmers credit on demand.

From this general need came a nationwide culture of credit that by midcentury set 6 percent as the just rate of interest, more or less universally applicable. On this one matter at least, Abraham Lincoln, William Fitzhugh, and Lewis Tappan agreed. At the end of the 19th century some state laws still specified that rate. What in a scrambling capitalist society with widely varying rates seemed quixotic at first glance was neither reactionary nor perverse. The 6 percent standard was a cultural declaration asserting the indispensability of regular, dependable credit to make it in democratic America. Without credit who could even try? In the midwest, where around midcentury a farm laborer's annual wages were around $200 and start-up costs for a modest farm in excess of $1,000, it required the strictest discipline for much of his adult life expectancy to take the first step toward independence on cash alone. Orestes Brownson captured the essential truth about working life in 19th century America: "no man born poor has ever, by his wages, as a simple laborer, risen to the class of the wealthy."[3] Even Horatio Alger's heroes needed someone to stake them.

Creditworthiness, though associated with property ownership, was by no means interchangeable with it. In a sprawling, developing country, those with credit to dispense were themselves dependent on their debtors. Through the middle decades of the 19th century, people at work paying their debts were precious assets whom creditors expended considerable effort not just to attract but to hold. In an economy where all risks were high, a substantial number of propertyless white men benefited from these calculations, both in starting out on their own and in staying there during hard times. At these margins of creditworthiness, intangibles—reputation, appearance, personal habits, and local prejudices—mattered a great deal.

From the 1830s to the end of the century, the middle and lower classes were roughly equal in size, with perpetual shiftings between them. Volatility, however, did not destabilize the classes themselves, which actually grew firmer around midcentury. By then, heavy Irish immigration placed a clear ethnic stamp on an expanding base of propertyless wage earners whose option was now less likely to be owning a farm than simply laboring on one. After the depression of the 1840s, short-term agricultural credit remained available, but long-term farm mortgages became more difficult to command. Middle-class desires to consume and display, to tighten police protection and judicial procedures, helped to consolidate a full-fledged culture of respectability.

The more elaborate the culture of respectability grew, the more pronounced its distance from the disreputable lower class. Disreputability, in turn, came wrapped in ethnic, gender, and racial biases that held most Catholics, most white women on their own, and almost all African Americans, American Indians, East Asians, and Latins in the lower class. Beginning in Jacksonian times both skilled workers and clerks developed their own adjuncts of respectability, including self-improvement clubs, mutual aid societies, sanitized fraternal orders, temperance groups, and nativist organizations. Even while hanging by a thread—perhaps especially then—they swore fealty to middle-class values. Men at the class margin, for instance, placed an unusually high premium on removing the women under their control from the labor market and maintaining them in a home.

The borderland between the middle and lower classes was crowded with people who struggled for a foothold of respectability, then got one, only to lose it. Every economic downturn, every bankrupt company or defaulting merchant broke crucial chains of personal credit and pitched more marginal members out of the middle class. Above all, manual workers reckoned constantly with the terrible threat of their bodies giving way. The errant fall of a tree, the loose sleeve in a machine, the kick of a horse, the slip of a saw could instantly destroy a family's livelihood. Or the hodcarrier, the cabinetmaker who milled his own lumber, the farmer who cleared land, sold it, then cleared more, simply gave out from years of life-sapping effort. Little wonder that the manual workers most likely to make it in 19th century America were those who could spread costs and risks across family networks.

What kept the tensions along this slippery borderland within tolerable limits defies a simple explanation. The critical indices on either side of the breaking point were the experiences of skilled workers and marginally independent farmers. Despite repeated downturns between the 1820s and the 1850s, skilled workers generally fared well by standards appropriate to antebellum America. After the depression of 1839–42, no prolonged slide occurred for them before the war, as the increasing success of the ten-hour movement and the general assertiveness of artisans in public life illustrated. Though the percentage of the highly skilled in the work force shrank, the lot of those who stayed in the ranks improved over the decades. New machinery expanded as often as it undercut the range and demand for skilled workers. Transportation in particular—from building the bridges to running the trains—created whole new areas of skill. The third quarter of the 19th century were bonanza years, with a steep rise in real wages that not only widened the gap between skilled and unskilled but in many trades set the income of American skilled workers on a plane well above their European counterparts. About one-fourth of them crossed the line into self-employment, roughly the record that salaried clerks, their close companions in the middle class, compiled during those same years. Meanwhile, buoyant markets, combined with war-related labor shortages, gave white farmers considerable leverage in the credit market around midcentury. As long as the credit materialized and real incomes kept rising, in other words, this labile class system continued to work.

Crisis at the class margin occurred when those economic feeders dried up. Even in a capitalist scheme always beset by ups and downs, the bust-boom-bust years after 1873 were particularly turbulent, and they struck independent farmers and skilled workers with particular force. As crop prices slid and a long-term deflation increased the debtor's real interest rates, mortgage payments became more difficult to meet, prospects for agricultural credit shrank, and the terms for working other people's land grew more onerous. Tenant farmers, once considered a step away from owners, were more often a step away from ordinary laborers. At law, late 19th century sharecroppers became wage earners who no longer ran their own farms and whose returns through delayed annual payments resembled the worst kinds of wage-earning arrangements from predemocratic times. As real wages among skilled workers stagnated or slipped, the gap that had been widening between them and the less skilled narrowed. In such major industries as clothing and iron, technological changes were especially severe on traditional crafts. Gyrations in the business cycle, moreover, heightened the possibility that layoffs would devour a wage earner's savings. One historian, in a telling oxymoron, reports that in the railroad industry, "even for those steadily employed, employment was irregular and uncertain."[4]

It was as if a giant slide were pushing more and more people into the class borderland, then threatening to carry them the full distance into the lower class. Seemingly overnight, one skilled worker lamented in 1883, he and his fellow craftsmen had fallen all the way from respectability into "the lower class."[5] Marx, of course, had predicted just that in the *Communist Manifesto*—"The lower strata of the middle class . . . sink gradually into the proletariat"—and during these late 19th century years, Marxism found a place in this American discourse. In 1890 the census made its first formal division between people who earned salaries and people who earned wages. As the century wound down, Americans and Europeans alike pictured too many workers and too little fresh farm land closing out opportunities for the common man.

Twice toward the end of the century it looked as if a new class would be formed by these pressures. The first of these times, occurring between 1883 and 1886, appeared to be the moment when an American working class—a self-conscious and separate wage-earning class— would materialize. In that short span clustered a great variety of class-charged job actions: extensive boycotts, biracial protests, contagion strikes where workers walked out spontaneously in support of their fellows somewhere else. The peak of the curve brought extraordinary displays of comradeship, such as the May Day strike of 1886 in Cincinnati, when over a third of the city's wage earners joined in a common protest. By then, new members were flooding so fast into the Knights of Labor, a nationwide organization fresh from its victorious confrontation with the corporate giant, the Union Pacific Railroad, that no one could keep count: perhaps there were 3 million Knights, perhaps 4 million.

The second moment extended from the late 1880s to the mid-1890s, as farmers alliances in the south and the west rallied hundreds of thousands of recruits to protests that quickly spilled into political action and, between 1890 and 1892, the creation of the Populist party. Contemporaries called it a revolution. The party's Omaha Platform of 1892 represented the century's most ambitious popular agenda for democratic revival and economic justice, including a union of all workers, democratized credit, direct popular decision-making, a single-term president, and public ownership of railroads, telegraph, and telephone. As their anger mounted, some white agrarian rebels made inviting gestures toward southern blacks and urban wage earners, thereby threatening wholesale changes in the nation's social system.

Both labor and farm leaders aimed their fire at the same small privileged group of Americans. If they overestimated how closely their enemies cooperated, they still grasped the main lines of late 19th century capitalist development and expressed a similar outrage in response. Preambles to the constitution of the Knights of Labor and to the Populist's Omaha Platform sketched a deepening class conflict that was plunging the nation toward catastrophe. (In 1886, even the constitution of the much more cautious American Federation of Labor opened with reference to "a struggle between the capitalist and the laborer, which grows in intensity from year to year.") Morally indignant voices in both camps described the degradation of ordinary Americans at the hands of organized wealth. The honest worker, George McNeill of the Knights cried, lies under "the iron heel of a soulless monopoly, crushing the manhood out of sovereign citizens." The Populist William Peffer concurred: "He is now at the mercy of combinations which are in effect conspiracies against the common rights of the people." "We believe that the time has come," read a famous sentence in the Omaha Platform, "when the railroad corporations will either own the people or the people must own the railroads."[6]

Both movements drew on natural law theories about just prices and the intrinsic worth of goods and services. Bloated capitalist profits were a crime against the laboring people whose sweat generated them. "Wealth belongs to him who creates it," the Omaha Platform declared. Or as McNeill phrased it: "wealth should be distributed in the process

of production." "Ought not the producer be the first paid?" Peffer
asked rhetorically. After all, "Money produces nothing; labor produces
all that is produced." Yet creditors held the workers in bondage: "This
dangerous power . . . is fast undermining the liberties of the people."
Major branches of both the Knights and the farmers alliances pursued
the logic of their analysis into producer, distributor, and consumer cooperatives.[7]

It was a fighting creed with radical overtones: all honest workers
marching shoulder to shoulder against the capitalist foe. Yet those
movements passed with scarcely a trace. By 1887, the Knights of Labor
was in rapid, irreversible decline, with nothing broad-based to replace
it. After the Populist party merged with the Democrats in 1896, the
radicalism of its platform disappeared in a cloud of campaign rhetoric.
In each case a seemingly fatal event marked the turning point: in 1886
a lethal bomb exploding in Chicago's Haymarket Square triggered
widespread repression of labor radicals; in 1896 the Populist acceptance of the moderate William Jennings Bryan as its presidential candidate and his campaign's obsession with free silver signaled the end
of agrarian militancy. What really mattered, however, was the general
fizzling of a late 19th century ferment wherever it had appeared. The
eruptions among wage earners and farmers alike were played out before the turn of the century.

One explanation was the insistent pull of middle-class respectability.
Early in the 19th century the new democratic norms of self-directed
work and self-defined authority gave a grand boost of pride to craftsmen and farmers, many of whom continued to draw energy from those
feelings, to define themselves at the heart of American society, even
after their autonomy was seriously eroded. They were not being nos-
talgic; they were fighting to keep a precious tradition alive. Reflecting
middle-class fears of lower-class disruptions, the Grand Master Workman of the Knights, Terence Powderly, and his Populist counterparts
made full public display of their pacific intentions. Only their enemies
threatened violence, never they. None of them endorsed the principle
of strikes. Indeed, Powderly's abandonment of various groups of
Knights who did choose to strike hastened the organization's collapse.
Decorum mattered. As Powderly declared, "If the [Knights'] assembly
is a bad place for a woman to go, it is a bad place for a man to go."[8]
To emphasize their respectability, leaders in both movements addressed the nation in the orotund, moralistic style of the Victorian
evangelical.

In the same spirit, both causes appealed to wholeness, not to divisions. Their enemies, they assured their fellow Americans, were small,
aberrant minorities in a population overwhelmingly dedicated to hard

work and honest rewards. The Knights did not speak just for wage earners or the Populists just for farmers. Each invited all respectable citizens to join in the national revival. Both envisaged sweeping social changes from simple, peaceful mechanisms: cooperatives, land reform, the subtreasury, bimetalism. Correcting the crucial errors would bring all Americans together again. If they often opened their arguments with battle metaphors, they tended to close them with medicinal ones: they had the cure for an ailing body politic. Wholeness was natural. As Edward Bellamy, a fellow traveler to both movements, had his voice of rationality in *Looking Backward* say about late 19th century America: "Now nothing about your age is, at first sight, more astounding . . . than the fact that men engaged in the same industry, instead of fraternizing as comrades and co-laborers to a common end, should have regarded each other as rivals and enemies to be throttled and overthrown." [9]

Behind these expectations of wholeness lay the vision of the People, the American citizenry deciding in the common interest. Nobody in the 19th century invoked them more fervently than the Populists. After all, the People *were* the government. To rule, they had only to activate themselves. In the end, the Knights did not behave like declassed wage earners or the Populists like proletarianized farmers; they strode into public as angry lodge brothers rallying support in America's fraternal democracy. Some of those lodges gave a class edge to their assertions; many did not; and many more sent a mix of indeterminate messages. Who knew whether an association built around ethnic identity would serve as a bridge to radicalism or as an alternative to it? In this fluid, diffuse world of particular loyalties, not many broad connections of any kind held for very long. Even at the borders, an array of lodges offered enough white men sufficient dignity—as residents of a town or a neighborhood, as Norwegians or Sicilians, as Southern Baptists or Roman Catholics, as Republicans or Democrats—to suspend basic changes in America's class system for a few more years.

When those fundamental shifts occurred, they did not draw skilled workers and beleaguered farmers into an expanded working class. On the contrary, they isolated the bottom level of America's wage earners in a multiracial, multiethnic, unskilled lower class. Economically, legally, physically, and ideologically, other Americans created categories that set this layer apart, restricted its power, and maintained it as a pool of surplus labor. Lasting changes took time: it required the first quarter of the 20th century to sink the modern lower class.

The critical economic turn came as the depression of the 1890s was lifting. Over the next twenty years the differential in real wages between skilled and unskilled workers, which had been narrowing late in the 19th century, spread to a record gap by 1916, and after an interlude of wartime labor shortages all around, it widened again to match that record by 1929. In fact, during prewar years that were generally prosperous ones for Americans, real wages for the unskilled more or less stagnated. Opportunities to rise from an unskilled to a skilled job shrank, and unemployment stayed high, not uncommonly over 10 percent. Although periodic unemployment was the lot of all kinds of wage earners, skilled workers were more likely to be laid off from jobs to which they could return, while the unskilled were more likely to be dumped into the pool of job seekers. Perhaps nothing underscored the economic precariousness of these workers more starkly than the fact that their wage levels failed to rise as incidence of child labor dropped sharply in the prewar years. Whatever the variation industry by industry, adults overall now did the work that children had done for roughly the children's old rate of return.

Trends were even more dismal for unskilled laborers in the south, where wage rates remained significantly lower and their distance from skilled wages that much greater. What defined the difference was the regionwide system of Jim Crow, an elaborate construction of laws and rules, more or less completed by the 1920s, that boxed African Americans inside segregated facilities in virtually every aspect of public life, from cradle to grave. The concept of separate but equal was not itself the culprit. Not only did that concept have deep roots in America's democratic tradition; it had sometimes served southern blacks insisting upon decent treatment. By the turn of the century, however, separated facilities lost all of their associations with contested terrain, where blacks pressed and whites responded, and became universally the seat of coercion and degradation.

The 20th century system of Jim Crow, adapting the principles of regimented lives and allocated spaces from slavery, operated—also like slavery—as a labor system, a way to regulate workers and their wages throughout the south. Of course much had changed since the Civil War, and the new racial segregation addressed those differences. With slavery, whites controlled labor in order to control land. After slavery, whites relied on the converse: use land to control labor. Trying to control labor through land, however, turned out to be a chancier, sloppier scheme of things in the late 19th century. As they moved about, African Americans kept their choices alive. Caste, by closing the public channels of redress to black workers, maximized the supply of ready labor at the cheapest price.

White votes elected white officials who manned the white courts and the white police to enforce all work contracts, and they squeezed the racial vice as necessary. The legal rights of southern tenants, once more or less autonomous farmers, deteriorated to the point where by 1900 tenants were simply another class of wage earners, no better off at law than sharecroppers. During the first decade of the century, tough new peonage laws in the Gulf states made a white employer's word sufficient to turn a black laborer into a debt slave. Under Jim Crow, vagrancy laws ceased to be minor matters. They threw a loop around African American men that white judges through arbitrary sentencing powers could tighten at will, pulling blacks from the streets into the chain gangs that white employers leased at rates substantially lower than those for free labor. Convict labor, thriving in the lower south after the 1890s, completed the circle: remove black men from the labor market, then reinsert them as prisoners to depress the wage level.

The quasi-slavery of peonage and convict labor stood as an intimidating reminder of the possibilities, cautioning a far wider circle of blacks and even poor whites not to push hard against the limitations on lower-class work. Out west, the white men's legal system, functioning in roughly similar ways, sent a comparable message to East Asians. Some of these legal instruments had general coverage. Old common law principles involving the responsibilities of masters and servants, the enticement of wage earners from their places of work, and the malicious intent of economic actions—doctrines more or less set aside as the process of industrialization buried their original meanings—were dramatically revived around the turn of the century, now with the very different purpose of blocking workers' cooperative efforts to help themselves by striking, picketing, and boycotting. Court injunctions against those actions, more than tripling in frequency between 1900 and 1920, had a particularly devastating effect on wage earners without the resources to regroup after a defeat and fight again, that is, on laborers in the lower class. With no particular ideology in mind, a Hungarian immigrant offered a baleful summary of the situation in 1907: "there was law in America, but its benefits to the poor were accidental." [10]

Uniformed police, increasingly trained for lower-class control, spanned the short gap between legal coercion and informal violence. Around places of work, moreover, the official police force often blended with the employer's private enforcers in ways that made it hard to distinguish between them. In isolated mining and lumbering towns, which were proliferating around the turn of the century, employees might never escape the shadow of the company's guns. During 1910 and 1911, in a story repeated from coast to coast, company deputies at what was appropriately called one of United States Steel's captive coal mines, in addition to beating workers, evicting them from their homes, and smashing their belongings, killed miners at the rate of one for every five days they were on strike. The fact that the state government in Pennsylvania legalized all of these actions only underlined the company's right to use force as it chose.

Visible minorities were particularly vulnerable. Varieties of white neighbors and competitors routinely attacked East Asians before the turn of the century. After 1910, Chicanos too faced escalating violence in the southwest, as their numbers rose rapidly and peonage spread among them. African American workers above all others functioned day by day in an environment of unpredictable and unregulated violence. The incidence of southern lynchings soared during the 1890s and stayed high until the mid-1920s. On the basis of impressionistic evidence, beatings and threats also appear to have increased during these same years. Blacks migrating north had to reckon with the possibility of violence at both ends of the journey. It required a modern underground railroad, the Atlanta branch of the new National Association for the Advancement of Colored People reported, to slip victimized blacks out of the south. Even if they succeeded, threats against family members who remained behind were a common worry. Race riots trailed the migrants as they moved northward; ghetto boundaries hardened around them in city after city following the First World War. As lower-class blacks felt the lid close on their opportunities, the perpetual prospect of violence locked the clasp.

Along with these economic, legal, and physical forces of separation came an ideology of difference to explain why ordinary human standards simply did not apply to this sinking lower class. What has been called the discovery of poverty between the 1890s and the First World War was fundamentally the spreading perception of social distances so vast that middle-class Americans saw no prospect of bridging them. The ambitious proposals for public welfare that accompanied this discovery expressed the sense that a human connection across classes was no longer possible. Hence the riveting attraction of the settlement house movement, exemplified by Jane Addams and Hull House in Chicago, for risking a cheek-by-jowl proximity to the lower class. Addams became "Saint Jane" not because she modeled what middle-class Americans could picture themselves doing but because she dared what all but a handful of her admirers considered utterly beyond them.

An ideology of difference spread to cover members of the lower class wherever they lived. The reputation of southern "poor whites" or "poor white trash," both in the fields and in the mills, took a sharp turn for the worse around 1900, and philanthropists described their living conditions and health problems—hookworm, pellagra, rickets—as if these existed not in everyday America but in an exotic other world of lower-class degradation. The ideology of difference concentrated, however, on the cities, especially centers of 100,000 or more where by 1900 about 20 percent of the population lived, in contrast to a mere 5 percent in 1850. Not simply poverty, which was at least as prevalent outside the big cities, but what middle-class commentators saw as a culture of poverty attracted most of the attention.

The slum, a new concept redolent with suffocating closeness, crushing deprivation, and degenerating morality, captured the messages of viciousness and alienness at the heart of this ideology. Choked apartments and teeming streets coarsened daily life. What chance did the simple virtues have? No privacy, no decency, went the standard middle-class logic. Slums killed. To the evident hazards of polluted air, contaminated food, and untreated sewage, investigators added appalling statistics on disease mortality, as if the slums themselves were breeding death. Photographs of spindly children suggested relentlessly recapitulating life cycles. What began as a concept acquired more and more geographical specificity until slums came to have an arbitrary exactness that implied literally a world apart. Urban geographers mapped the slums, police departments patrolled their borders.

Social scientists widened the ideological distance with a term that implied a kind of human blankness on the far side of the class gap: *unskilled*. Although skill distinctions had always been crucial in the working world and pride in superior skills their invariable companion, those wage earners toward the bottom of the scale had traditionally been known for what they did: they were laborers, common laborers, or more precariously, day laborers. The new term, there late in the 19th century but widely adopted only after 1900, stripped them of any dignity by defining them as a nullity, a nothing. Indeed, short of a Three Stooges skit, who could even conceive of a human being unskilled—without any skill?

The stereotypical slum dweller—strange, stunted, unskilled—was an immigrant, and a shift in the primary sources of European immigration to the United States provided a critical component in the emerging ideology. By the 1890s the main flow was clearly coming from southern and eastern Europe, in particular from Italy, Poland, Russia, and the Balkans. Moreover, immigrants came in record numbers, averaging around a million a year after the turn of the century. In an earlier immigration from northern and western Europe, the popular argument went, families had pooled resources and incurred great risks in order to cross the Atlantic, and they came ready to enter into American life. Now steamships shuttled passive hordes of southern and eastern Europeans across the Atlantic simply to take jobs. They had no affinity for democracy, no connection to American culture, and no inclination to change. Many of them, especially the mass of single men on the loose, did not even intend to stay: birds of passage, they were called. The ideology of difference, in other words, created new categories of cultural compatibility and incompatibility, acceptable and unacceptable foreignness. Those from southern and eastern Europe became the utterly alien new immigrants, by contrast to the familiar, assimilable old immigrants from northern and western Europe. The one had proved they belonged: they fit in. The other proved they did not: they fell to the bottom. Around the turn of the century many Protestant ministers lamented losing touch with people whose names, family customs, or even religious affiliations they did not know, and many reformers pictured the most ordinary exchanges between middle and lower classes as dramatic moments when someone leaped the divide. Humanitarian efforts, it was assumed, fell on deaf ears. Looking layer after layer downward, as if he were on another planet, the progressive Walter Weyl wrote that reconnecting society would require "a raising of the lowest elements of the population to the level of the mass." [11]

By the First World War, it was common to explain the inferiority of the new immigration through racial categories. By contrast to the good old immigrants, who were "Anglo-Saxon" and "Nordic," the bad new ones were "Mediterranean," "Latin," and "Semitic," purportedly scientific designations far down the scale of biologically distinctive peoples. Southern and eastern Europeans, widely circulated hereditarian ideas proclaimed, arrived inherently inferior: weaker, duller, lazier, dumber. Worries about a "mongrelized" America, while reflecting a general tendency to barbarize the lower class, carried special impact because they really had no resolution: race created permanent pariahs.

Racism worked best in color. Unlike the race theories denigrating European immigrants, race and color had centuries-deep roots in American culture. Nevertheless, a certain ambiguity softened that connection late in the 19th century. It was during the 1880s and 1890s that white middle-class optimism about the prospects for Native American assimilation and uplift peaked. However arrogant those attitudes, they were a striking improvement over the murderous norms of earlier decades. And however slowly, African American rights in the northern states did expand decade by decade late in the century. If blacks and whites formed separate labor and farmer organizations in the 1880s and 1890s, their parallel associations still found ways to collaborate on common objectives.

Then around the turn of the century, one nonwhite group after another was isolated by a combination of scientific claims and social aversions. Imperialism in the Pacific and the Caribbean not only fed the popularity of racial thinking but also rationalized the use of violence against discredited people of color. After 1900, optimism about assimilating American Indians soured, and middle-class whites pictured Native Americans as permanent dependents, a backyard version of the White Man's Burden. There had been no late 19th century reprieve for East Asians; now fresh waves of racism swept up the Japanese along the West Coast as well as Chicanos in the southwest.

In the south a virulent new racism branding African Americans as wild beasts rose in the 1890s to prepare the way for the systematic repressions of the early 20th century. Following the old practice of turning white men's actions into black men's intentions, African Americans were punished for harboring thoughts that matched white behavior. As white men raped black women, they said black men lusted after white women—and lynched them for it. Stealing from blacks at every turn, whites called blacks inherently larcenous—and jailed them for it. Scientists contributed their bit by declaring the "Negroid" race biologically prone to various contemptible "social diseases," for which African Americans commonly could not get treatment in a white-controlled medical system.

During and after the First World War, these several trends sinking the lower class flowed together toward a climax. Among the most important aspects of this accelerating process were the drives to eliminate any possibility of concerted action among lower-class workers. War let loose a whirlwind of vigilante violence against lower-class groups that threatened action in the work place. A general wartime hostility against "slackers" gave renewed force to the old argument that society had a right to the labor of its poorest members. It was not happenchance that middle-class publicists changed the name of the IWW, the union most scornful of their values and most open to the lower class, from Industrial Workers of the World to "I Won't Work," as cooperating courts and posses proceeded to destroy it.

Withdrawing work always had a revolutionary potential; with the Bolshevik Revolution in 1917, that potential seemed to become reality. "Labor is not striking against the employer alone," the reformer Frederic C. Howe declared in the midst of these new fears. "Labor is striking against society." [12] The ultimate horror was the ultimate withdrawal of work, the general strike. Labor injunctions, which shot up in frequency right after the war, struck with particular harshness at strikers' attempts to connect their cause to wider circles of support—through pickets, leaflets, boycotts, and the like.

Wartime also brought army-related tests that claimed to give scientific proof of the mental inferiority of young lower-class men, and by implication the entire class behind them. What a striking contrast between the ways in which the Civil War was experienced as bonding

across classes and the First World War as validation of the chasm between classes. Early in the 1920s, as whites were plugging the last holes
in the southern wall of segregation and drawing battle lines around
the northern urban ghettoes, Congress was fashioning racial quotas
for European immigration and racist exclusions of Asians, policies that
came together in the comprehensive immigration laws of 1924.

Early in the 20th century, while the boundaries around this lower class
were not yet firm, three sometimes overlapping groups hovered in the
vicinity: skilled wage earners, the Socialist party, and an immigrant
petty bourgeoisie. The choices they made had a direct bearing both on
the nature of the emerging lower class and on its eventual isolation.

Skilled workers, potential allies of the unskilled since the late 19th
century, brought mixed impulses to this relationship early in the 20th.
On the one hand, their long tradition of independence included proud
distinctions between their own respectability and the precarious,
rough-and-tumble world of ordinary laborers—"whose conduct and
votes endanger the republic," the Gilded Age labor reformer Ira Stew-
ard declared. A quarter century later, with recent immigration on his
mind, the labor publicist John Swinton called the mass of the unskilled
"Alien Starvelings."[13] On the other hand, rapid changes in the value of
various skills between the late 19th and early 20th centuries spread
turmoil throughout American industry. Around the turn of the century
unprecedented numbers of wage earners poured into unions and out
on strike. How would these energies get channeled?

In general, loyalties followed the reallocation of skills. In the transition, such groups as shoemakers, glassblowers, cigar makers, and traditional craftsmen in textiles, iron, and steel lost out. Even where they
maintained unions, these were usually shells, just reminders of the
good old days. Big winners came out of such modernized industries
as automobile and munitions production—tool and die makers, ma-
chinists, and an assortment of troubleshooting maintenance personnel—and in large-scale construction, including new crafts in steamfit-
ting and structural iron and steel. Centralized factories and city
skyscrapers put some skilled workers in a rarefied category of indispensable men: the entire operation stopped without them. Men in
these pivotal roles commanded privileges. Early in the 20th century,
American skilled workers enjoyed substantially more leverage on the
job than their German counterparts and earned wages sufficiently
higher than their British counterparts to discourage comparison. The
best situated of these labor aristocrats—perhaps one in every seven
American wage earners—had annual incomes comparable to ordinary
white-collar workers in the same industries.

What happened at work mattered even more during the first quarter of the 20th century because neighborhood life was contributing less to the craftsmen's sense of importance. In some cases, as in Paterson, New Jersey, once integrated, respectable blue- and white-collar communities dissolved. In other cases, as in Detroit, cohesive blue-collar neighborhoods near the work place, where skilled wage earners had reaffirmed their standing off the job, disintegrated. Urban mass transit scattered ethnic communities, such as Chicago's Italians, who had once honored their skilled wage-earning compatriots. With more modern choices came greater anonymity. The standardization of prefitted clothing, the spread of tract housing, and the popularization of mass-produced consumer durables meant that by the 1920s more and more well-paid craftsmen blended off-hours into a general middle-class culture, with its tangible but impersonal rewards.

For a good many skilled workers, what prestige they had drawn from where they lived now had to come from where they worked. In broad terms, between the late 19th century and the 1920s, skilled workers exchanged community respect and sagging wages in small-unit production for work place respect and rising wages in large-scale production. These trade-offs often made skilled workers more demanding at the bargaining table but almost never more rebellious in the streets. They certainly widened the gap between skilled and unskilled.

The fate of the Socialist Party of America, which rose and fell in an arc between 1901 and 1925, depended on America's skilled workers. Although votes for the fiery Eugene Debs, the party's perennial presidential candidate, revealed hundreds of thousands of loyalists in occupations ranging from the arts in New York to the farms in Oklahoma, skilled workers were the party's organizational core. What these skilled workers were becoming, give or take some local peculiarities, the Socialist party became. That included a heightening sense of difference between their respectability and an alien lower class. Polish Socialists in Chicago felt it was simply impossible to make common cause with the Polish unskilled. In Milwaukee, the toughest kernel of the Socialist party, a significantly smaller percentage of the city's black population was allowed access to industrial jobs than in neighboring Chicago, and German skilled laborers, the backbone of Milwaukee Socialism, enforced those race values. Although some Socialists mounted sweeping attacks on American capitalism, Socialist radicalism and class-crossing radicalism were quite distinct phenomena. Such ideologically serious Socialists as Morris Hillquit and Victor Berger were particularly harsh on the lower class. It was the ideologically vague Western Federation of Miners and its successor, the IWW, which moved easily across class lines as they recruited for revolution, and for their deviance the Socialist party expelled them.

Other Socialists had little encouragement to resist these trends. The dedicated party campaigner Kate Richards O'Hare declared that "the great slum population" was "the greatest menace to humanity—and civilization." In *The Jungle* (1906), the most popular socialist appeal of the early 20th century, Upton Sinclair poured venom on ignorant, passion-driven "Negroes and the lowest foreigners—Greeks, Roumanians, Sicilians, and Slovaks." In the veteran editor J. A. Wayland's socialism, blacks and Asians would be segregated; Charlotte Perkins Gilman's socialist utopia was pure Aryan. In the real world, however, Gilman worried about inundation. Everyone recognized "The common fact," she wrote, "that the women of the lower social grades . . . bear [children] more easily than the women of higher classes." Not surprisingly, as the party collapsed after the First World War, its leaders generally disappeared into the middle class.[14]

Milwaukee's successful mating of socialism and ethnicity highlighted a third group along the class boundary, a stratum of small businessmen, neighborhood professionals, and local politicians who functioned at critical junctures in an immigrant community's operations. For individuals who fell on hard times, their help could be crucial: provide a little credit, send news of a job, navigate through the city bureaucracy. They controlled the native-language press. They gave voice to community causes and pressured city government in behalf of community needs. In brief, they were indispensable in making ethnic assertions formidable. During several strikes early in the 20th century—in Paterson and Bayonne, New Jersey, and in the Chicago stockyards, for example—assistance from these community leaders kept lower-class fights alive. In the southwest, a cross-class Mexican Protective Society supported Chicano workers both in their strikes and in the courts.

With the First World War, however, a confluence of pressures began to squeeze out that support. In the demographic turmoil of those years, some ethnic communities simply disappeared, leaving undifferentiated lower-class residences in their wake. Even the sturdiest of the remaining communities had very limited economic reserves. Wartime involvements, especially with their home countries, absorbed much of those resources. From outside the communities, there were always the demands to assimilate, characteristically posed as either-or propositions: either come out of the neighborhoods to pursue America's middle-class opportunities or stay behind as just another suspicious alien.

By the early 1920s, the social costs of mobilizing ethnic or racial consciousness for public purposes had risen sharply. White middle-class leaders across the nation branded such powerful expressions of the spirit as Zionism and Garveyism extremist, disruptive, even un-American. And white-collar opportunities did beckon to enterprising members of America's ethnic communities. Early in the 1920s when another round of strikes occurred in Bayonne and in the Chicago stock-yards, no immigrant bourgeoisie appeared to underwrite them.

America's boosters cited this drift toward respectability as proof of the nation's classlessness. Yet as the families of ethnic leaders blended into the middle class, as the families of craftsmen saved for better homes and better schools, and as former Socialists cheered them on, a lower class was sinking beneath them. Radicals attacked those same trends as class desertion, as an exposure of the traitors who gave away the battle. In fact, skilled workers, Socialists, and petty bourgeois immigrants did not have the power to change America's course. Operating near the margin themselves, their most notable contribution was to disappear from the borderland and complete the isolation of the lower class.

What distinguished this process was the way people in many walks of life collaborated in the sinking of the lower class. The drives for conformity and control expressing themselves in wartime patriotism, the Red Scare, and the Tribal Twenties doubled as an unsystematic but general attempt nationwide to regiment the lower class. By 1924, that loose campaign more or less disbanded. The Red Scare dissolved, the open-shop drive against labor unions subsided, and the most virulent forms of tribalism, such as the Ku Klux Klan and Henry Ford's anti-Semitism, fell on the defensive. In the south the number of African American lynchings dropped abruptly; in the north race rioting almost ceased. It was the quiet of victory. At the bottom of American society, class realignment had run its course.

During these same years, between the 1890s and the 1920s, the lights dimmed in the great showcase of 19th century democracy: the extraordinary public outpourings to electioneer and to elect. In national contests, turnouts declined from around 80 percent of the eligible voters in 1896 to under 50 percent in 1924. Sudden, severe drops came first in the south. In South Carolina, where prospects of a turnout in excess of 80 percent had been realistic in the 1880s, 18 percent voted in 1900. By 1904 the level in the eleven former Confederate states fell below 30 percent. "It was gratifying to see the voting booths free from noisy crowds," thought one Augusta editor.[15] More gradually, voters disappeared everywhere else: in Indiana, for example, from approximately

92 percent of the eligible voters in 1900 to 72 percent in 1920, in New York from approximately 88 percent to 55 percent. Although turnouts in national elections recovered somewhat after the mid-1920s, they remained on average about 20 percentage points below 19th century norms.

Evidence indicates that as turnouts shrank, the least powerful were the least likely to vote. In the baldest cases, members of the lower class were simply denied the right to participate. As national law banned Asian immigrants from becoming citizens, it sealed the exclusion of this fast-growing minority from west coast democracy. Even more egregiously, state legislation throughout the south, following some tentative precedents in the 1880s, disfranchised African American men around the turn of the century. Many poor whites were no more able than blacks to pay the poll taxes or answer the arbitrary questions about the state constitution or produce the ancestral records that these restrictive southern laws imposed on them. Even if fellow whites winked at the rules and informally qualified them, they lost standing as independent voters. Now they participated at other people's discretion. This practice of majorities turning democracy on itself by adding more and more exclusionary rules to the electoral process spread well beyond the south. By the 1920s a dozen states elsewhere adopted literacy tests, all but three states tightened their provisions governing registration, and about half of America's counties required personal registration before voting.

At their worst these restrictions—particularly the disfranchisement of southern black men—violated democracy's fundamental principle that electoral majorities cannot eliminate minorities from future contests. Such heavy-handed tactics made some of the lines between new legal barriers and turnout levels short and straight. Disfranchising procedures in Houston, for example, cut registered voters from 76 percent of those eligible in 1900 to 32 percent in 1904 and as a consequence enabled the local leaders who sponsored the laws to consolidate their control over the city. More often, however, these connections remained elusive. In Tennessee, for instance, neither new registration and poll tax laws nor a recent gerrymandering of its voting districts kept turnout in 1896 from soaring to one of its 19th century peaks. Poll taxes in Vermont and New Hampshire and literacy tests in New York and Oregon had no demonstrable effect on turnouts there. Some measures associated with a restrictive democracy were already in place before nationwide downturns began. Others, such as the provisions for personal registration, arrived on a long curve from the late 19th to the mid-20th century, with no unusual bulge during the years when the sharp decline in turnouts occurred. The mechanics of exclusion, in other words, made a contribution, but only a contribution, to shrinking the pool of voters.

What disempowered the largest number of voters between the 1890s and the 1920s was the sinking of the lower class, the fundamental change to which restrictive political procedures simply added weight. Two interrelated trends had the greatest nationwide impact on lower-class participation: closing off public spaces and atomizing the electorate. In America's loosely policed 19th century society, neither a middle-class obsession with property rights nor sundry local ordinances to preserve the public peace kept white fraternal politics from a remarkably free use of available spaces. For many public purposes, squatters' rights expressed a political philosophy as much as a land policy. Demonstrations of popular opinion that in Europe belonged exclusively to a revolutionary tradition were built into 19th century America's democratic one.

Just as a multiplication in the popular uses of public spaces had marked the arrival of democracy early in the century, so new limitations on those choices signaled its transformation. Even before the end of the century, tighter regulation and stricter enforcement were taking elasticity out of that tradition. With the churnings of class activity in the mid-1880s came redefinitions of public space that affected all kinds of poor Americans in a variety of ways. Hard-scrabble Georgia farmers, for instance, lost access to spaces that traditionally they had been free to use for grazing, hunting, or just socializing. Vagrancy laws multiplied. Especially after the Haymarket bombing in 1886, urban police expanded their surveillance over the street life of the poor, and more private police cordoned off more company property. To use what had once been open to them, lower-class men found themselves increasingly at odds with the law. In the process, the acceptable ways of making political statements in public were dwindling.

These changes accelerated after 1900, most significantly in the southern caste system's barring of African Americans from a common public. City ordinances outlawed the ad hoc demonstrations and eliminated the marches to the polls that had once vitalized urban politics. Groups at the margin of the middle class, such as craft unions, found that to preserve their reputation for respectability they had to abandon an array of open-air tactics. The sharp rise in antilabor injunctions had its own dampening effect on public expressiveness. As the regulations for public parading tightened, fraternal associations in town after town—the Elks of Litchfield, Illinois, the Moose of Bangor, Maine—built little castles for themselves at the beginning of the 20th century and took their activities indoors. By the 1920s, a high proportion of these lodges identified themselves by their civic services—charitable works no more public than the modern United Way. The parades that did survive showed an eerie resemblance to the structured, orderly processions of predemocratic America.

Clearing the streets had a deadening effect on lower-class men, who counted on collective, fraternal strength to secure their places in democratic politics. Now scattered in public, they were further atomized by the new electoral rules. Short of outright exclusion, nothing disfranchised lower-class men more effectively than the introduction of the so-called Australian ballot, a government-prepared form that each person used in secret. Voting, once a loyalty-affirming public action, became an individualized private act. Instead of crowding to the polls and waving the party's ballot as they went to vote, lower-class men, one by one, ran a gauntlet of electoral officials, perhaps only to discover that they could not decipher the procedures. New, technically abstruse initiative and recall elections were no compensation for lower-class citizens. Nor were the primary elections that several states adopted early in the 20th century. For a party's public gathering to nominate its candidates, they substituted a solitary voting booth. In the 19th century, electoral politics above all else enabled lower-class white men to fend off disorganization; in the 20th, electoral politics became one more part of the fragmenting process.

By the 1920s almost no voices spoke up for the old collective, hurly-burly democracy. Public discussion took an individualized electorate for granted. The cohesive political community, once a democratic ideal, now looked downright ominous in the form of an impenetrable immigrant neighborhood. Even the public philosopher John Dewey, one of the few to retain faith in community-based democracy, scorned the marching and huzzahing, the banners and the ballyhoo that had been integral to the class-bridging politics of the 19th century. But how democracy expressed itself was always critical to its meaning. Those who took delight in stripping electoral politics of its gaudy 19th century attire rarely acknowledged how many poor people had disappeared with the trappings.

||||||
CHAPTER 6

RAISING HIERARCHIES

|||||| Severe tensions in the 19th century middle class also triggered a second realignment, this one at the top of American society. The trajectory of change looked strikingly similar to the companion process at the bottom: first, a hustle and bustle of activity late in the 19th century that produced no permanent restructuring; then a gradual, deeply etched reconfiguration that by the 1920s formed America's modern three-class system. In this case, the sound and fury of the 1880s and the 1890s came from groups of wealthy urbanites who made gestures toward separating themselves as a distinctive upper class.

There had always been Americans with aristocratic pretensions, of course. When elites lost much of their authority at the beginning of the 19th century, they gave up none of their wealth. By midcentury every major city had its ostentatious social life, and throughout the south, slave-owning planters surrounded themselves with the accoutrements of grandeur. Nevertheless, the trappings of wealth did not bind up a class. Although the rich and wellborn in major coastal centers from Boston to Charleston created the semblance of city-specific upper classes, these neither interconnected one with another nor impressed European visitors one by one. By most accounts they were working elites. Tocqueville pictured them as "expelled from political society," then taking "refuge in certain departments of productive industry."[1]

When successful businessmen tried to strike a pose of leisured wealth by announcing their retirement, they often just shifted to more discreet ways of making money. The British consul Thomas Grattan caught the contradiction in his sneer at those expressing "the loftiest pretensions to 'aristocracy' yet descending to very low methods of

money-making." They acquired "only the raw material of elegance—
handsome houses, fine furniture, expensive dress—money, in short, in
its various modes of disbursement . . . There is nothing more absurd
than to hear the wealthy classes in the North American cities boast of
their 'fashionable society.'" The closest antebellum approximation of
an upper class was the interwoven cluster of planter families at the
head of South Carolina's society and government: "the miserable aristocracy of a false republic," Charles Dickens exploded. Nevertheless,
other planters—perhaps 1 percent of the white south, thinly dispersed
among the region's agricultural states—had no luck matching the
South Carolinians' success. The Civil War then demolished all of
their prospects.[2]

Against this background of false starts, the efforts to create a monied
aristocracy late in the century had the look of a formidable enterprise.
Some of the leading beneficiaries of America's urban-industrial growth
built exclusive winter homes in the cities and summer homes in such
thriving resorts as Newport and Bar Harbor; they insulated their
churches and their clubs; and they invested substantially in a ladder
of education running from private preparatory schools through elite
colleges. Where they could, they elaborated a paraphernalia of privacy
in public life: curtained carriages, exclusive ballrooms, detached orchestra boxes, and, in the case of the new Madison Square Garden in
1890, even a separate palace for society events. This metropolitan vision of rising in splendid isolation out of the hurly-burly of democratic
America attracted followers across the nation. Late in the century,
Worcester, Massachusetts, boasted its own society magazine; numerous small cities claimed their local Four Hundreds. "Until recently, a
leisure class has scarcely been known" in the United States, Andrew
Carnegie wrote in 1886. "I must not fail to note, however, the signs of
change."[3] A literature of nostalgia for the gracious life of the slavehold-
ing planter made its appearance at about this same time.

As the design for an upper class, however, these attempts failed.
Fragmented city by city, America's plutocrats never achieved critical
mass. Each small cluster had its own Social Register, its own Four Hundred; none could sustain a systematic effort at class formation. Even
New York City's wealthy, the richest of the rich but seriously divided
within their own ranks, could not meet the challenge. In the early
1890s opera boxes went begging, and the hard-pressed proprietor of
Madison Square Garden had to look beyond the millionaires for a
wider, more reliable clientele. Nor did the commitment seem to penetrate very deep. If the nabobs of Pittsburgh relied on as common a
vehicle as a newspaper to shore up "the spirit of the socially elite,"
could collapse be far away? The itch to accumulate ever more wealth

rarely left America's richest 19th century capitalists. As a frustrated socialite in Manhattan complained: "There are no men of leisure; consequently, when a man of fortune in New York is not in business, there is nothing for him to do, and he has no companions to do nothing with."[4]

Public responses pushed the aspiring plutocrats further on the defensive. An increasingly self-conscious urban middle class, still loyal to traditional values, distanced itself from squandered wealth and unproductive leisure. Cartoons lampooned the haughty matrons of society and their stuffed-shirted husbands. Foreign ridicule was particularly damaging to these fragile class structures. The British commentator James Bryce could barely suppress his disdain: "The upper class in America (if one may use such an expression) has not in [any important] respect differentiated itself from the character of the nation at large."[5] When beleaguered plutocrats boarded up the Waldorf Hotel in 1897 so that outsiders could not see their fancy ball, they slipped into self-ridicule. It showed more wit than has generally been realized for rich Americans with serious aristocratic ambitions to migrate abroad and marry into European nobility.

In 1899, Thorstein Veblen's *The Theory of the Leisure Class*, scrutinizing America's plutocrats like insects in a bottle, served as the requiem for their class aspirations. A certain amount of the class apparatus just disappeared. After George and Hattie Pullman, whose upper-class vision included presiding over an industrial fiefdom just outside of Chicago, lost control of their workers during the great strike of 1894, for instance, no other employer tried to fit a modern-day feudalism into the big city. When they operated in the isolation of a mining camp or a rural factory, despots were merely despots.

Much more of this class terrain was simply overrun by a vigorous capitalism. Privileges were always difficult to protect in 19th century America. As new waves of the wealthy poured into the plutocrats' fledgling suburbs and schools and resorts, they transformed them from class outposts into institutions for a mongrel rich. Early in the 20th century, as their own ranks became increasingly porous, self-styled social elites acted more and more like rich customers in a general urban market: their money purchased outstanding goods but not class position. In the new century, those with sufficient wealth displayed their elegance from the best seats at the symphony and the opera; those with a little less wealth bought the next-best seats and looked at them.

The abortive upper class of the late 19th century, like the abortive working class of those same years, fell victim to the powerful pulls of middle-class respectability, with the values of individual hard work and fraternal inclusion as its gravitational center. As a way of affirming the values that triumphed, the attacks against upper-class pretensions grew even stronger after their defeat. A few people of great wealth repudiating democratic values for themselves were made to sound like a malevolent plutocracy trying to destroy those values for everybody. After the turn of the century, prominent members in both major parties ran masterful campaigns against those fading aristocrats. Where the agents of plutocracy could make no lasting changes by fiat in the 1880s and 1890s, however, a significantly broader layer of successful middle-class Americans managed more gradually, more sinuously, between 1900 and 1925 to alter America's entire class dynamics. The critical innovation was the creation of a new national class, thereby reshaping the 19th century two-class scheme into a radically different three-class system for the 20th century.

The new national class emerged to lead America's transformation from a commercial-agrarian to an urban-industrial society. It was certainly not a story of the collapse of a creaky old agrarian economy and its replacement with a vital new industrial one. As industries flourished in the United States late in the 19th century, so did the world's most sophisticated capitalist agriculture, a system that at the end of the century still set the pace in mechanization, still relied on a broad foundation of landowning farmers, and still sustained a universally praised transportation network. Indeed, commerce continued to dominate almost all aspects of America's late 19th century economy, from the market its railroad network provided for the iron and steel industries to the commercial orientation of its banking system. The booming cities of the American interior acted as funnels through which agricultural and industrial products passed into regional, national, and international markets. After the depression of the 1890s, staple-crop agriculture entered its golden age of profitability.

New enterprises built on that success. As commercial cities thrived, they generated their own needs in construction, services, and finance. Business networks formed specifically to connect this nation of cities, which still prospered as headquarters for a commercial-agrarian economy but increasingly geared its activities to the needs of the urban market. Early in the 20th century these diverse, flourishing nationwide interests materialized in a new corporate economy with offshoots in finance and agriculture itself, in entertainment and news services, in advertising and government offices.

By the 1920s common values and interlaced institutions drew the people who were contributing to this broad process into a national class: national both in the sense of transcending local attachments or boundaries and in the sense of holding central, strategic positions in American society. Although members of the new class might care very deeply about their geographical roots, particular places no longer defined them. They fulfilled roles that could be played out just as well in hundreds of alternative locations: public commentator, CPA, physical chemist, movie star, labor economist, roles that only made sense as interrelated sets of skills in a rationalized society. Charles Beard and Ruth Benedict, Henry Luce and Harold Ross, Jane Addams and Margaret Sanger, Herbert Hoover and Bernard Baruch, Walter Lippmann and Henry L. Mencken, W. E. B. DuBois and Norman Thomas, John D. Rockefeller, Jr., and Harvey Firestone, Martha Graham and Eugene O'Neill, J. Walter Thompson and Cecil B. DeMille, all belonged in this interdependent national scheme of things, and each in turn modeled a life for countless others who saw themselves as participants or at least aspirants in some comparable arena.

By and large the members of the new national class were urban, both because their skills fit neatly into city life and because they took America's urban future for granted. In the 1880s and 1890s, it had been common to picture city and country contesting the nation's future, as Josiah Strong's *Our Country* (1884) did in its vision of the alien, immoral forces of industrialism chasing upright Protestants across the continent to a final battle in the west. By the 1920s, as a century of America's greatest urban growth was ending, those Protestants seemed uptight rather than upright, and the new class's spokesmen saw the cultural war in a very different light. "Intolerance," the commentator Horace Kallen flatly declared, "is . . . an attribute of the country and tolerance of the city." The frontier, the economist John B. Andrews decided in 1922, was just "a dream."[6]

Although a great deal of wealth and prestige concentrated in the national class, it was by no means the same old grandees making their second try at a plutocracy. The erstwhile aristocrats of the late 19th century had done nothing to soften their local identities: they were Chicago merchants, Philadelphia lawyers, Boston Brahmins, with art museums and symphonies honoring their names in their cities. Leaders of the new national class, not those local nabobs, rode to power after 1897 on a crest of corporate consolidations and the expansive financial arrangements that accompanied them. Unlike high society's preoccupations with leisure in the 1880s and 1890s, the new national class broadcast its commitment to old-fashioned work values, even as it was reshaping those values to suit their scheme of interlocking specializations.

Rather than buy their way into a highly restricted culture of leisure, members of the new class took it over. Elite northeastern colleges be-

came preparatory universities for modern capitalism. Telephones con-
nected the fancy resorts with the world of business. Where the spirit
of the aspiring aristocrats did survive was in those pockets of immobi-
lized high status that in the 1940s the social anthropologist W. Lloyd
Warner and his associates breathlessly called "upper-upper class": inbred, inturning families of local prestige, diametrically at odds with
the national class in their scope and sensibilities. From the new class's
angle of vision, those insular elites were epitomized in Tom and Daisy
Buchanan, whom F. Scott Fitzgerald in *The Great Gatsby* (1925) spun
inside a sterile little cocoon of privilege.

In the 19th century, the middle class justified itself with concepts of
Character; in the 20th, the national class used concepts of Knowledge.
Experts—and behind the experts, science—carried the burden of
hopes for a new era of specialized parts and systematized wholes
where nothing worked without carefully mastered bodies of knowledge. Critics as different as Frederick Jackson Turner, Thorstein Veblen,
John Dewey, Lewis Mumford, and John Dos Passos agreed that scientific disinterestedness with a practical bent, often encoded as *the engineer,* held the key to the good society. Although once in a long time
expertise might come through a magical mix of genius and experience—the popular image of Thomas Edison, for instance—increasingly it required years of training. The more elevated the leadership,
the more disciplined the mind needed to be. Herbert Hoover, the Great
Engineer, rode those expectations to the White House.

These values, as the national class construed them, did not simply
refurbish the 19th century concept of Character for a modern age.
Character in the 19th century drew upon attributes of everyday life,
universal traits that ordinary people could find in themselves and see
in their neighbors; any sensible adult could judge both its qualities and
its consequences. The training that produced scientific detachment in
the 20th century, on the other hand, separated its beneficiaries from
ordinary minds; only experts were qualified to evaluate other experts.
In the 19th century, science, like nature, held answers for everybody.
Even some scientists shared in the belief that American science was
peculiarly democratic. In the 20th century science, as the national class
used the term, almost always implied a specialist's method—or meta-
phorically a specialist's way of thinking—that a few were capable of
turning to the benefit of the many.

Ordinary people were expected to pay attention and to stay abreast
of an ever-changing world as best they could. *Cultural lag,* the sociologist William Ogburn's extraordinarily influential formulation, expressed how members of the national class understood this process.
As science, technology, and the broad economic forces accompanying

them changed, it was culture's challenge to adapt, to make a rational fit with reality. But popular values could not keep pace with those changes in the objective world, national-class publicists believed. Without firm moorings, ordinary people were confused, resentful, generally ill-equipped for modern life. Effective public leadership, by giving citizens a sense of direction, at least kept culture on track in its chase after reality. Even then, the best outcome was never more than a diminished gap: "There is always a certain lag," as Lippmann put it.[7]

As a new national class peeled off the top of the traditional middle class, it left behind a far larger number whose identities were still grounded in their localities. In the face of a dramatically different scheme of national-class values, the local middle class declared itself the one authentically American voice in a cacophony of competitors. In the 19th century, widely shared truths about a personally rooted system of moral justice meting rewards and punishments for good and bad Character had daily verification in the only setting that really mattered—local life. In the 20th, competing with a blare of national-class publicity for efficiency at work and live-and-let-live tolerance at leisure, those traditional values tended to acquire a defensive, suspicious tone from people who sensed that they were losing authority to a distant, powerful enemy. To the degree that America's local middle class did stand still, it found itself in a fundamentally altered position.

The new national class and the reconstituted local middle class built lives around different economic cores. By no means was it a division between rich and poor. There was a lot of money to be made in local America, and a good deal of genteel poverty in the national class. The primary distinction lay between the extensive connections of the national class and the intensive orientation of the local middle class. Real estate, yielding profits only to those who mastered the details of its immediate environment, sat at the center of most local economies: dealing in land, zoning land, farming land, mortgaging land, building on land. Modern America's fixation on tangible property drew its greatest strength from the local middle-class economy. The sources of its credit, always crucial to class identity in America, were overwhelmingly local. Around the local land economy circulated a wide variety of retailers, service providers, officials, and professionals whose livelihood depended on carefully wrought, personally sustained local networks. These webbings did not transfer from place to place; each was built to local specifications.

Substantial corporations with national markets, such as Endicott Johnson Shoes in Binghamton, New York, Buckeye Steel in Columbus, Ohio, and Ball Glass in Muncie, Indiana, belonged to these local networks because they burrowed their affairs deep into their towns. Appropriately, Endicott Johnson's president played a major role in Binghamton real estate. The managers for Buckeye Steel, who "worked their way up through the ranks" and generally stayed until "their death or retirement," supported Columbus charities, joined its Chamber of Commerce, and wove themselves into its politics.[8] The head of the firm, Samuel P. Bush, sat tight on the lid to Columbus and rose to leadership among other locally rooted, open-shop employers in the Ohio Manufacturers' Association.

While Buckeye's local logic relied on a base in Columbus, U.S. Steel's national logic spread its interests generally. In fact, U.S. Steel's biggest plant grew out of no city at all: the city grew out of it, with an imported name—Gary—that had no connection to the people of northwestern Indiana. In the same spirit of imposed creation, Gary's instant school system served briefly as a national laboratory for educational reform, again with no essential links to its Indiana locality. U.S. Steel had no social, cultural, or moral commitments in Gary that it did not feel free to abandon at any time.

It was pure conceit, of course, for spokesmen from the national class to lay exclusive claim to efficiency and science. In fact, these were universal code words for the progressive ways of doing things, as much the property of local as of national firms. No persuasive evidence argued that General Motors, a model national-class corporation, was more efficient in the 1930s than locally grounded Caterpillar Tractor, or DuPont more scientific in the 1940s than Rochester-rooted Xerox. Nevertheless, local businesses had to make a case that they were up to date, whereas the big corporations behaved as if their case was already made.

During the transitional years of class formation early in the 20th century, scarcely any significant public issue escaped the pulling and hauling between these classes as they carved out their domains. Appropriately, many of these conflicts involved business practices and business values. Did the price-cutting national retail chains represent progress or, as the advocates for local business argued, "Competition That Kills"? In local America, competition continued to be parallel, pitting little monopolies against the fates of the market but not against one another. According to one account, the golden rule for a businessman in Topeka, Kansas, was: "He would never . . . try in any remotest way to get the advantage of any one else in the same business."[9] In the national scheme of things, on the other hand, businesses did indeed chase and swallow their competitors: the alternative was declining efficiency and rising prices. Those interests promoted a parcel post law to nationalize marketing; local business opposition held it up for years.

What constituted a legitimate business asset? More and more intangibles, from name recognition to great expectations, qualified in national-class circles. In behalf of the local middle class, by contrast, Senator Robert LaFollette demanded that railroad rates be based on a "physical valuation" of the company's assets, an assessment that rested on natural law premises of an intrinsic, or real, value in goods. Assets no one could see or feel did not exist. By the same token, Andrew Frame, country banker from Waukesha, Wisconsin, predicted wholesale catastrophe if the rapidly multiplying paper instruments in national-class finance acquired the same legal standing as precious metals and government bonds to underwrite the United States currency. In general, national-class interests sought the leeway to make up the rules for their major corporations as they went along: their favorite device was the regulatory commission. Local middle-class interests, on the other hand, favored specific legislative rules to govern what they called "big business": the antitrust laws that spread from thirteen states in the 1890s to forty by the 1920s embodied their values. Although most of America's prominent professionals argued the national-class case, Louis D. Brandeis, premier lawyer and Supreme Court justice, was an eloquent champion of local business integrity against corporate predators.

Politically, the local middle class did better at the state than at the national level, in the House of Representatives than in the Senate, with Congress than with the executive branch, with the federal executive than with the federal judiciary. Its base was local; numbers of people and square miles of territory were on its side. Through large portions of the south, where county seat cliques ran affairs, no national-class voice even penetrated, and men such as the editor and later ambassador Walter Hines Page who found it a narrow, constraining environment had no chance of changing it, only leaving it. Most urban politics, too, revolved around the local middle class.

It took time to clarify these distinctions. At the beginning of the 20th century the several trends toward consolidated power and systematized procedures—strengthened political bosses, organized special interests, rationalized municipal government—seemed as congenial to a national as to a local class. Businessmen split. As Lincoln Steffens revealed in his arresting magazine series "The Shame of the Cities," many of them supported the bosses; others vowed to replace political machines with managerial city government. By the 1920s the meaning of these alliances and conflicts more or less worked itself out. Urban politics triangulated a particular, locally bounded set of these new centralizing forces: business-minded leaders of the local middle class, political bosses, and city bureaucracies. By then the emerging national class, to whom Steffens had addressed his exposés and from whom the municipal efficiency movement had drawn its inspiration, largely disappeared into other activities.

Only sets of locally focused interests answered an unequivocal and consistent yes to the crucial question: was city government really worth the fight? Even where a giant corporation dominated the city's economy, as U.S. Steel's affiliate the Tennessee Coal and Iron Company did in Birmingham, Alabama, the company's tiny national-class coterie discreetly protected corporate interests from the sidelines, while a far larger contingent of prosperous local leaders competed for Birmingham's offices, plunged into real estate, and generally governed the city as their preserve. It was much less of a contradiction than many commentators thought when two branches of the local middle class—big city bosses and county courthouse barons—joined in the 1920s to control the Democratic party's "politics of provincialism."

National and local middle classes wove distinctive social fabrics. While the national class was underwriting the American Bar Association, the American Bankers Association, and an abundance of comparable organizations, special field by special field, local middle-class fraternal orders, ranging from such old favorites as the Elks and the Moose to those shaped for the Swedish bourgeoisie in Chicago and the black bourgeoisie in Harlem, also flourished. Rotary, an ideal type of 20th century local middle-class leadership, established over seven hundred local branches during its first twenty years. Kiwanis, founded in 1915, boasted more than half a million members by the 1930s. The Lions, another success story, originated in 1917. That quintessentially local middle-class politician Warren G. Harding never tired of promoting the Masons, which also thrived during his presidency.

Thousands of professionals sorted themselves out between classes. Did doctors identify with the new laboratory medicine of the professional hospitals and elite medical schools, or with a loosely regulated, locally geared family practice? Was the superintendent of schools a native who climbed the local ladder or a member of the National Association of School Superintendents who made career steps from city to city? Did academics think of themselves as faculty members of a college or university with local students and local support, or as mathematicians and political scientists with peers in nationwide professional circles? In general, higher education provided each class with a separate mobility track: Fordham and DePaul for the local middle class, Columbia and the University of Chicago for the national class.

As the two classes fought for position, the national class appropriated *urban* for itself and rhetorically consigned the local middle class to the sticks. In fact, in no city was the national class more than a small minority, and in only a few of the largest did national-class voices predominate. By the 1920s Hollywood qualified. So, above all, did New York, which, as William Taylor has written, now "produced commercial culture for a national rather than a local market."[10] From theater to architecture to photography it defined artistic norms. The smart ideas and brash styles in such slick new journals as *Time*, *American Mercury*, and the *New Yorker* set standards of sophistication from Dubuque to Portland. Although the *New York Times* held a monopoly in no one market comparable to the monopolies that innumerable local newspapers enjoyed in theirs, it was on its way to becoming the paper of record in national-class circles everywhere. Collectively, these voices passed judgment on everybody else's values. They praised their special version of urban ways. Their idea of a healthy city neighborhood was Greenwich Village. Towns fared poorly in the writings of their favorite authors: Sinclair Lewis, Sherwood Anderson, Thomas Wolfe. Rural life smacked of outhouse sanitation, *Tobacco Road* morality, and H. L. Mencken's "anthropoid rabble" from Dayton, Tennessee.

As they wrapped their own values in a mantel of science, national-class spokesmen equated local America with an oppressive Protestantism. The *Scopes* trial of 1924, pitting Darwinian biology against Tennessee law, brought such howls of national-class protest in part because it fit so neatly into the preconceptions of a long-suffering science forever beset by reactionary religion. The very meaning of science was freedom of thought, national-class voices insisted. Traditional moralists "think they are dealing with a generation that refuses to believe in ancient authority," Walter Lippmann wrote. "They are, in fact, dealing with a generation that cannot believe in it." In one of the most revealing propositions of the new culture, Lippmann recommended two gods, one for the national class and another for everybody else. Away from "the centers of modern civilization," let the old persecuting, irrational religion run its course. But in the cities, where simple truths no longer sufficed and god was obliged to be a pragmatist, educated Americans should be allowed to shape a sensible religion for the modern age.[11]

As the 19th century middle class was sliced in two, a number of public agencies that tried their hand at compromise could manage nothing better than a thin veneer. In the course of softening the rigid, abstract categories of 19th century law, the judiciary, for example, opened contract law to more and more implicit economic arrangements, largely in response to national-class needs, and simultaneously laid over them the kind of "good faith" moral principles that cemented local middle-class business life. Popular media, in their effort to paper the gap, gave with one hand what they took away with the other. Widely circulated magazines such as the *Saturday Evening Post* and,

after 1919, *True Stories* offered their readers a titilating look into expansive new worlds of personal leeway before slamming the door with an
old-fashioned moral climax. Cinema perfected the formula: exciting
lives and exotic thoughts, packaged at the end in traditional judgments. Soon radio programs were exploiting the same combination.
Politicians offered their own blends: Harding's local-class affability
and national-class cabinet leaders, Calvin Coolidge's homespun apho-
risms and big business policies, Hoover's traditional individualism
and creative system-building. None mated these contradictions more
effectively than three public heroes of the 1920s—Charles Lindbergh,
Henry Ford, and Thomas Edison—each championing tomorrow's
technology in the guise of yesterday's virtues. It was a characteristic
of the 1920s, in other words, to generate signals that could be read
simultaneously as affirming messages in opposing camps.

Beneath this slick surface raged a ferocious battle for cultural control
in which the local middle class, its monopoly over respectable values
broken, tried one maneuver after another to recoup its losses. When
members of the national class declared religion the great separator,
they helped to make it so. Modern and fundamentalist strands of Protestantism, emerging during these transition years, managed to live together until class conflict set them at each other's throat. Theology and
ideology followed class lines. The antievolutionary laws that spread in
the 1910s and 1920s were local middle-class responses to a threat first
of all and statements of a belief only after the fact. In a roughly similar
way, the revived Ku Klux Klan's mix of racism, nativism, prudery, and
xenophobia expressed no coherent philosophy; it supplied a grab bag
of enemies from which the local middle-class leaders of various Klav-
erns could take their pick. What was chosen mattered, of course. Each
of these movements promoted certain beliefs at the expense of others:
class anger did forge a set of class values.

What did not change in the fires of class hostility was the essentially
decentralized nature of local middle-class America. Prohibition, its
most national cause, illustrated that proposition. Bedded in Protestant
congregations throughout the country, mobilized by the Anti-Saloon
League, and blessed by the high hopes for social change around the
First World War, the campaign for Prohibition closed down entire industries, amended the Constitution, and enlisted national law to enforce local mores—a phenomenal range of accomplishments by any
standards. Yet in its moment of triumph the movement could only
return home where it belonged. It had no feel for national management, no affinity for national government, no voice in the new national
discourse. Prohibition disintegrated as much from national inattention
as from local resistance. During those same years, the KKK's appalling

record of schisms, defections, corruption, and scandal cast in a particularly lurid light the drift of a locally geared organization as it got
caught up in ambitions for state and national power.

As the confusions surrounding Prohibition demonstrated, the
breakup of the 19th century middle class threw wide open a range of
questions about how best to affect public policy: hunker down locally
or spread out nationally? resist the central government's power or ride
with it? stress tradition or innovation? Making these choices was
chancy business, particularly for those whose own class position, like
that of their cause, was confused by the flux around them. The careers
of three leaders in the transition—Samuel Gompers, Booker T. Washington, and Carrie Chapman Catt—illustrate these special challenges.

At first glance they made an odd trio: the Jewish Gompers, born in
1850, who was already an apprentice when he emigrated at thirteen
from the London tenements to a German workingpeople's neighborhood of New York City; the African American Washington, born a
slave in 1856, who named himself as he carved out a life in the Reconstruction south; and the white middle-class Catt, born in 1859 in small-
town Wisconsin and raised in rural Iowa, who used a solid education
to make herself independent before she was thirty. Even if all three
championed self-reliance for their followers, each construed it very differently: collective strength for white wage earners, personal self-
sufficiency for black men, public rights for white women. Neither
Washington nor Gompers had any interest in women's rights. Catt and
Gompers accommodated easily to white racism. Washington opposed
the unions that Gompers directed, and Catt despised the workers' culture that sustained them.

Yet as leaders—Catt as organizer behind the successful drive for
the Nineteenth or Woman's Suffrage Amendment, Washington as the
renowned champion of African American self-help, Gompers as virtually lifetime president of the American Federation of Labor—they
adopted strikingly similar styles and strategies. First of all, they were
representative figures, immersed in the groups they led. As Catt's National American Woman's Suffrage Association shifted toward the end
of the 19th century from a universalist feminism to a tight focus on
voting rights, Catt helped articulate the change. As NAWSA's racism
deepened at the turn of the century, Catt followed along. African
American, Asian American, and Hispanic American patriarchies made
those cultures highly resistant to women's rights. With no encouragement to recruit there and not much more to recruit among wage-
earning women, Catt did neither.

Washington represented a small black bourgeoisie who dotted cities

north and south, associated primarily through churches, then expanded the range of their organizations after the depression of the
1890s. Both the growing black lodges and the National Urban League,
founded in 1910, expressed its spirit, as did Marcus Garvey's Universal
Negro Improvement Association early in the 1920s. As W. E. B. DuBois
described the bourgeois blacks in Philadelphia, they self-consciously
pulled away from lower-class African Americans, even as they sought
some way of helping their impoverished brethren. Increased migration
of destitute African Americans from the countryside to these cities,
greatly enlarging the scope of black needs, sharpened the bourgeoisie's
sense of difference. Washington appealed to their pride in success and
their faith in self-help with an optimistic, work-oriented program that,
more than any of his competitors', also reckoned with the day-to-day
situation of the African American poor.

The unions in Gompers' AFL flourished around the turn of the century along with the job-conscious, male-conscious, blue-collar-
conscious trends in white skilled workers' lives. From a skeleton force
of a few hundred thousand after the depression of the 1890s, the AFL
grew to over 2 million by 1904. As social visionaries such as P. J. Mc-
Guire of the carpenters were pushed aside in favor of hard-nosed conservatives, Gompers narrowed his own attitudes. Mixing races, sexes,
or ethnic groups in the shop did disrupt unionization, and Gompers
joined in the nativism, racism, and sexism that spread among craft
unions in the new century. But he took the initiative in none of this.
His AFL was only adapting to member unions that excluded blacks in
their bylaws, shunned new immigrants, and ignored wage-earning
women.

All three leaders participated in the sinking of the lower class below
them. Washington's famous Atlanta address of 1895, accepting racial
inequalities as a given with which he had to work, and the exclusionary turns in NAWSA and the AFL that occurred just a few years later,
belonged to the beginnings of that process. As a corollary, they shared
doubts about a popular political process. Gompers, who wanted to
join the statesmen, not the politicians, complained that it was the enemies of the AFL who dragged it into partisan elections and legislative
conflicts; and his inflated claims to the AFL's success at the polls only
highlighted his discomfort. Washington became famous for his willingness to set politics aside until blacks made greater economic gains.
Years in the suffrage campaign left Catt with a mugwumpish disdain
for the entire democratic process, which she repeatedly described as a
dirty (male) affair of private deals and purchased votes. One word, she
declared, explains why the United States was a disgraceful twenty-
seventh to adopt women's suffrage: "politics."[12]

To emphasize their distance from lower-class life, they shaped their appeals to fit traditional values. Catt, cutting America cleanly into respectable and disreputable parts, held out prospects of a far greater respectability in public life through the elevating effects of white women's character and simple moral truths. Gompers cultivated the role of a businessman ready to deal with other businessmen, always as good as his word. Washington promoted equally familiar 19th century values: blacks, given the opportunity, would rise by dint of good habits and honest labor. The three of them wrapped their causes in attractive promises: civic virtue, economic rewards, social harmony.

All of them cultivated reputations as moderates who were fending off the radicals just next to them: Washington the upstarts in the Niagara Movement and the National Association for the Advancement of Colored People; Catt the militant suffragists behind Alice Paul; Gompers the strike-minded expansionists in and around of the AFL. Sublimating their anger at more obvious enemies—employers, whites, men—they bent every effort, and at least some values, to make the enemies of these enemies their enemies: Gompers the stalwart antagonist of socialism; Washington the earnest opponent of amalgamation; Catt the implacable foe of urban riffraff. The most telling moment in this record of accommodation came with the First World War, when Catt and Gompers, once pacifists, charged to the head of the military parade.

They presented themselves with a similar scrupulousness: the impeccable dress of Gompers and Washington, the impeccable address of Washington and Catt. In effect, they were highly skilled petitioners, experts in a politics of indirection who tried to draw powerful people to their causes without sacrificing respect for their constituents. Each concentrated on overcoming the stereotype most damaging to the cause: Washington's passion for personal industry countering the image of the shiftless black; Catt's relentless organizational drive the image of the impulsive woman; Gompers' glorification of negotiated contracts the image of the bomb-throwing radical. That same passion for controlling the situation characterized their leadership. Catt, an opponent concluded in 1916, drove a "well-oiled steam roller [that] has ironed this convention flat!" [13] The longer Gompers remained as president of the AFL, the more he stifled any member who dared stand up to him. Washington was notoriously unscrupulous in silencing critics.

Their sensitivity to reputation and power prepared them for their most imaginative leap—a recognition in the fluid class world of the early 20th century that a new kind of national authority with its own mechanisms and voices was taking shape around them. Specifically, they spotted the new national class as it emerged, grasped at least some of its profound implications, and schemed to use its leverage to catapult their causes. By no means were these insights thrust upon them. All three thought naturally in decentralized, local terms. Washington opened Tuskegee Institute in 1881 with southern funds and burrowed himself into southern life. He had to learn all over again about the potential of national power. When she first assumed NAWSA's presidency, Catt, the child of the rural midwest, had no trouble orienting herself to its state-by-state strategy. The AFL that Gompers led initially in the 19th century was a confederation with less power over its member unions than many city centrals exercised.

Washington was the first of the three to sense that a new overarching pattern of communication was developing. National media created national figures who might engage an entire public in dialogues. Dramatic statements, focal encounters, symbolic gestures, he realized, rose above the places where they occurred, spoke to a whole nation, and invited responses to him as a new kind of national individual. Through an extensive network of black newspapers, he jacked himself to a national plane addressing African Americans everywhere, and through selective, staged dealings with important white men—almost all members of an incipient national class—he sought to secure a place for himself where their national power lay. What he might have built from that base was lost with his death in 1915.

Catt, the least experimental, came last to the new national level when she returned for a second term as president of NAWSA and in 1916 redirected its energies from the states to the president and Congress. It was her special insight to understand how separated, yet how interdependent, the modern versions of national and state/local politics were. Attacking on both levels simultaneously, she realized, would confuse and distract her opponents. At the same time, she calculated, good national publicity—endorsements from national officials, publicized successes in a few state legislatures—might give the Nineteenth Amendment momentum and hurry it on to victory, precisely the way events did transpire. Meanwhile, her combination of ardent wartime patriotism and international sophistication struck just the right note among national-class men.

Gompers saw the deepest into national trends and gambled the most on them. In the mammoth corporations materializing at the turn of the century, he recognized something more than just bigger businesses, and he set out to find ways of matching, neutralizing, or cooperating with that new kind of power. At every opportunity he drew more authority into AFL headquarters. He invested scarce resources in facilitating industry-wide national contracts, and he tried to extricate unions from their local disasters by shifting to national tactics: boy-

cotts, publicity, mediation, whatever might work. Eventually those issues—more accurately, the government's willingness to outlaw those
tactics—drew him into national politics. Before that, however, with the
AFL growing and forming beneath him, Gompers risked collaborating
with the new corporate powers and their allies inside the National
Civic Federation, an organization that claimed to be seeking a higher
level of industrial peace for the 20th century.

It was always a case of using and being used. Who gained more
when Washington had dinner with Theodore Roosevelt at the White
House? when Gompers eschewed strikes during wartime? when Catt
flattered the eleventh-hour convert to woman's suffrage, Woodrow Wilson? In fact, following the will-'o-the-wisp of national-class power may
not have improved any of their records. Only in the imaginary world
of public relations—itself a national-class creation—did the giant corporations have more enlightened union policies than their smaller
counterparts. Association with union busters in the National Civic
Federation became a downright embarrassment to Gompers. In the
decade before the First World War, the crafts netted no important
industry-wide contracts, and labor law gave no advantage to national
unionization. After a final, futile effort in 1924 behind Robert LaFollette's presidential campaign, Gompers' national policy lay in shambles. Even though Catt came away with something concrete, the Nineteenth Amendment, her national-class alliance seemed irrelevant to
victory. The same applied to Washington's accomplishments, occurring
as they did against a raging backdrop of Jim Crow restrictions which
nobody was halting.

Nevertheless, Gompers, Washington, and Catt were neither fools nor
sellouts. If their hopes of capitalizing on the big changes around them
were premature, they had the imagination to recognize them. As the
founding of the CIO in the 1930s, the movement for civil rights in the
1960s, and the campaign for the ERA in the 1970s illustrated, the essence of their experiments—using national power to overcome ensconced local powers—became standard strategy among marginal
people. Even in Washington's lifetime his enemies in the NAACP
might have given him a bow for pioneering the national publicity on
which they depended.

What the three of them failed to realize was how little other people
cared about their causes. The issues that mattered deeply to them simply did not stir much interest in the national class. Although national
and local businesses certainly had basic differences early in the 20th
century, union policy was not one of them. Liberals in the national
class who styled themselves friends of labor by demanding equality
for unions before the law did not really mean that, of course. None of

them suggested that the injunctions paralyzing unions also be applied to management. Workers who did not like the company's terms were expected to look elsewhere for jobs, but managers who rejected a union's terms were not asked to vacate for new management. Companies might hire "guards," but unions could not use "thugs." Quite rationally, Gompers wanted most of all to keep friends like these, and their government, as far away from the unions as possible.

With women's suffrage the law, no national-class leaders looked to Catt for advice. It was at least prudent and perhaps wise of NAWSA, despite its vague promises to elevate public morals, to remain officially a one-issue organization and hence to make suffrage more or less an end in itself. National-class men were delighted by the prospect of women just disappearing in the pool of voters. On matters of African American rights, national-class leaders preferred to deal in appearances: repudiate lynching, express dismay over race riots, praise the movie *Intolerance* as a balance to the outrageous racism in *Birth of a Nation*. If, as the best white wisdom argued, race relations were matters of basic human nature and ingrained local custom, then the hard issues, the sources for exclusion and segregation, lay beyond the ken of national policy. Washington, too, had excellent reasons for expecting no help from a national-class government.

Out of sight, out of mind. Invisible in national affairs, the people these three represented turned their attention locally. After Catt herself left the movement, NAWSA's successor, the League of Women Voters, reverted to state and local politics, where its precise knowledge and persistent work were more likely to command respect. Washington's personal network dissolved with his death, and its many northern components collaborated with other local interests to make the most out of urban politics. Bargains with the white bosses, such as the one in Chicago between Oscar DePriest and Big Bill Thompson, were the wave of the future. Muted in national affairs, the craft unions turned inward. Some, especially in the buildings trades, had never really been anything but local. Others, such as the unions in the coal and clothing industries, presumably national, actually derived their power from bargains with a multitude of local companies. By the mid-1920s, in some towns and cities, but not in the nation, unions still mattered a lot.

The modern three-class system placed hierarchy at the center of American public life. Fundamentally at odds with America's original democracy, hierarchy largely survived during the 19th century in white men's dealings with the people they excluded from the fraternity. Now in much more elaborate forms hierarchy emerged to organize 20th century society. The new model was the large business firm, rationally structured and centrally controlled. Just as the triumph of self-directed work at the beginning of the 19th century undermined the old 18th century hierarchies, so the undermining of self-directed work prepared the way for new hierarchies at the beginning of the 20th.

Systematizing the work of industrial wage earners attracted the most attention early in the 20th century. Before the turn of the century, America's decentralized work culture accommodated great variations. Small establishments with a handful of wage earners remained the norm. Even in the exceptional large plant late in the 19th century, authority over work was commonly parceled among many autonomous groups. In some industries such as textiles and coal mining, foremen acted as little dictators over hiring, firing, and much of what happened to employees in between. Petty labor brokers often controlled access to jobs in construction. Elsewhere many skilled workers presided over their own fiefdoms. Unionized hatters neutralized the foremen in their shops, and skilled cigar workers blocked intruding employers from theirs. Although railroad managers issued sets of formal work rules as early as the 1850s, an elite of craftsmen continued to run their own little baronies, including power over hiring and firing, that generally served family, friends, and ethnic brethren. Against the grain of these customs, counterpressures to regularize factory work operated throughout the 19th century: to inculcate obedience to the clock, to exclude liquor, to sharpen precision, and to extend interchangeability of parts. Nevertheless, what went on inside the shops of Poughkeepsie, New York, in the Gilded Age applied broadly to American industry: "the rhythms and control of work were much closer to earlier artisan production than to twentieth-century mass production."[14]

With the new century, disciplinarians set about rationalizing these work processes with schemes that managers, not wage earners, controlled. In railroading, for example, central administrators not only destroyed the craftsmen's baronies; they also subjected all employees to the company's regular job evaluations. A few years later, coal operators harnessed their employees to new work rules as they mechanized the mines. Subordinating the old-style, freewheeling foremen to these management-directed production programs was a critical element in the transformation. Moreover, after 1900, increasing numbers of large firms operated as coordinated factories rather than merely as shells over a collection of separate work units. The assembly line was one logical expression of these impulses to integrate industrial work. Early in the 19th century visitors came from Europe to witness America's astonishing ant hill of self-directed work; by the 1920s they traveled from around the world to study its pioneering ventures in systematized factory production.

Firms drew in their white-collar employees just as tightly. On some railroads, in fact, the disciplining process affected middle managers before it reached skilled workers. During the first two decades of the 20th century, other company hierarchies were extended to cover previously scattered, autonomous sales forces. Integrating telegraph with telephones in 1909 established the kind of quick, extensive communication network that headquarters needed to direct a far-flung distribution system. Farther down the ladder, sales clerks found their work increasingly regimented as the widespread adoption of single-price policies for retailing goods eliminated their latitude in bargaining with the customers. Supervision also tightened around telephone operators at the beginning of the 20th century. In these areas, as in the swelling ranks of office employment generally, the feminization of almost all routine work confirmed the faith among the men in charge that they had virtually a god-given right to dictate rules to their staff.

Hierarchies fanned out in all directions. Some looked directly to the corporations for a model. Agribusinessmen, for example, hoped to profit from the same rationalizing principles that were being applied in industry. School systems, with countless analogies to productive efficiency, consolidated rural districts, integrated the rapidly expanding junior and senior highs into an educational ladder that ran from kindergarten into the university, toughened attendance laws, and promised a flow of responsible citizens coming out at the end of the line. Even criminal gangs, once perceived as a pack of neighborhood toughs, emerged in the 1920s with a reputation for systematic, businesslike organization.

More important still, hierarchy was a way of thinking about American society. How attractive a way became clear during the First World War, with its widespread depiction of military discipline as a social ideal and its burst of interest in coercing labor from lower-class men. "Work or Fight," they were told. Although there were sharp debates over the kind of army to create—the local middle class favoring the National Guard, which it dominated, and the national class favoring full-time professionals, who best reflected its values—both sides formed a chorus to glorify the military hierarchy. Professionalism itself strengthened the hierarchical cast of mind in several ways. Each of the professions, many just firming early in the 20th century, strained to enhance its social standing. Oddly, low-salaried college teachers ranked quite well, perhaps because they seemed to keep alive the old dream of self-directed work. Within professions, hierarchical sensitivities also sharpened, usually elevating those with longer training and greater specialization over more general practitioners. Ultimately, Americans were expected to internalize hierarchical values for use in all aspects of their lives. The new American Home Economics Association, for example, told housewives to grade their own work according to a hierarchy of skills: from bumbling amateur to efficient professional, with expert homemaking as the association defined it crowning the peak.

Inevitably professions appeared to smooth the functioning of the social hierarchy itself. Occupational guidance, a specialty within the educational system that flourished after the war, sought to channel students into the levels of work most appropriate to their skills and personalities. The passion for maximizing every worker's productivity in a corporate enterprise inspired the new profession of personnel management. Employers in the 19th century seemed satisfied with a few general rules of thumb: praise the industrious and berate the laggard, pay the least and demand the most, hire young and fire old. Now professionals promised astonishing improvements in efficiency from a three-part agenda: select the right person for each job, eliminate the losses from turnover, and organize work into step-by-step systems.

Nobody had more than impressionistic grounds for matching people with jobs or determining an optimum duration of employment. Viewed one way, turnover corrected against mismatching people and jobs. The close regulation of work patterns, familiarly known as scientific management, was just as much a matter of trial and error, despite the efforts of Frederick W. Taylor and his zealous followers to formulate a set of unvarying rules. Scientific management was no more than an inclination, an orientation toward imposing order in the work place in an unsettling time of major industrial changes. Nevertheless, by striking all the right chords, it raised capitalist expectations around the nation. Workers also understood its essential message: more work, less rest.

Managing workers involved motivating them; motivating workers required humanizing them. Take the issue of turnover, for instance. In the 19th century, not much inhibited the individual white man's right to walk out the door in search of another job. Why he moved on was his own business. In those days turnover was self-directed work. In the 20th century, as employers sought to control more and more factors in production, they recast old matters of individual choice in new psychological terms. Employees' interiors mattered. What were they thinking? What made them want to work? What made them stay at work? It was a domestic version of what William Howard Taft expressed about the Filipinos early in the century after a stint as their governor-general: "What we have to do is in a sense to change [their] nature; it is to furnish . . . a motive for doing work which does not exist under present conditions."[15] Sometimes the formulations were chilling.

Hugo Münsterberg, a pioneer industrial psychologist, recommended organizing the shop floor so that workers would be unable to talk with one another. Shades of the old Auburn prison system. At other times the preoccupation with motivation held out possibilities for a new collaboration. By 1928 even the hard-boiled National Association of Manufacturers talked about wage earners as "partners" in the plant.

Hierarchies made success social and visible. Winners did not just defeat the odds, as they presumably had in the parallel competition of the 19th century; they defeated other people—losers—who often remained on view in the firm. The greater the importance of prestige at work, the more winners warmed to the new schemes. Prominent in these ranks were elite wage earners who reskilled to become the indispensable men inside the new factories. During the 19th century, the best-paid among them tended to have multiple skills suitable to a variety of tasks. It was an American tradition to keep investments in machinery low enough to stop and start production in response to changing market conditions. Operating in an economy where human power continued to be the primary source of energy, employers prized adaptable craftsmen who could solve all kinds of problems in a technologically straightforward shop.

Trends changed rapidly around the turn of the century when a combination of the centralizing potential of electric power, the consolidating implications of corporate mergers, and the escalating costs of machinery caused a sharp growth in capital-intensive production. In 1900 electricity contributed only a tiny fraction of the motive power in American industry; by 1930, 80 percent. Manufacturing boomed. The size of its labor force, after remaining stagnant between 1870 and 1890, leaped by 50 percent between 1890 and 1920. Capital invested in manufacturing almost doubled between 1899 and 1909, then doubled again during the next two decades. More than any other single factor, it was these investments that transformed the nation's capital markets and the financial institutions serving them. As railroad managers had long known, high fixed costs with insistent and impersonal creditors made a shutdown catastrophic. In the big 20th century firms, victory no longer went to the agile capitalist who slipped in and out of production; it required continuous output. Now the most precious workers kept those costly machines in use.

These labor aristocrats stood atop the shop floor hierarchy. Studies of turnover and talk about partners referred above all to them. To maintain steady, systematic production, therefore, their contributions were often the least systematized, the most open to the skilled workers' own interpretation of what needed to be done. If they remained loyal, the argument went, the rest would fall into place. By the First World

War, welfare programs targeting skilled workers who stayed with the firm spread to about 2,000 companies, many of them leaders in the new capital-intensive industries. Even where these programs reso-nated with an old-time paternalism, they applied modern tech-niques—company bulletins, recreation programs, clean toilets, stock purchases—to a modern objective: stabilizing the company hierarchy. It seemed to be a winning strategy. Each year more evidence accumu-lated that these workers were identifying themselves inside the com-pany hierarchy. By the mid-1920s company unions, with well over a million members, were growing much faster than the AFL's indepen-dent variety.

Some at the bottom of the wage-earning pool also benefited from hierarchy. African Americans unquestionably fared better in a stream-lined new industry such as automobiles than in the tradition-weighted ones dominating the American Federation of Labor: the building, metal, or printing trades, for example. Even in those few instances where 19th century separate-but-equal principles led whites and blacks to divide the jobs, as in the case of the half-and-half arrange-ments on the New Orleans docks, opportunities for blacks actually increased under the employers' rationalized system of the 1920s. The modern factories offered women wage earners better hours and wages, greater chances for advancement, fewer hazards, and less sex-ual harassment than did traditional shops or putting out work at home. In some cases, women first gained legal control over their own wages through factory work. Employers, on their part, had good rea-sons to welcome women, who generally accepted the going wage, used their families as backup, and rarely sustained union membership. Bet-ter received by their bosses than by their fellow workers, an impressive number of these wage earners, white and black alike, held fast to their company loyalties even in the Great Depression.

As mobility within and among hierarchies sharpened competitive-ness and encouraged ambition, it filled the borderland between classes with people on the edge. Nevertheless, 20th century America had only three classes: half national and half local, half middle and half lower, were transitional moments, not cultural options. When Preston, son of Columbus's local-middle-class patriarch Samuel Bush, moved east and became a United States senator from Connecticut, he joined the na-tional class. Despite a spreading impulse among those employees with clean hands to sort classes by collar color, families in the skilled-labor aristocracy by and large kept the middle-class faith: their children stayed in school, their savings bought and furnished homes, and their daughters took respectable, if low-paying white-collar jobs. "In health morbidity, adult mortality, infant mortality, nutrition and material conditions generally . . . ," a comparative study of European and American industrial class systems around midcentury concluded, "[the] important divide [in the United States lies] between the upper-working class, and the unskilled and casual workers . . . with the racial minorities being a substantial component of those on the wrong side of it."[16]

On this grillwork of classes modern American democracy emerged. The 19th century fraternity sought to divide the nation cleanly between those who joined as equals in the governing process and those who were excluded altogether. White women and people of color seldom passed that threshold. The new democracy, on the contrary, expected citizens to enact the meaning of their inequalities in public life. By the 1920s democracy expressed hierarchy. At the same time, this hierarchical democracy held out the prospect of growing into a more inclusive system. In the 20th century, newcomers did not have to prove themselves somebody's equal; they only needed to find their proper level. Simple exclusion by gender no longer worked. Although race and class could be made compatible with modern democracy, it generated increasing resistance to purely color-based exclusions. Appropriately, those most enthusiastic about the new hierarchies pointed the direction toward a more inclusive scheme of inequalities, while those whom the hierarchies displaced held out for variations on the traditional in-out, white men's egalitarianism. In this context of fundamental changes and crosscurrents, Americans set about redesigning their democracy.

‖‖‖‖

CHAPTER 7

DISSOLVING THE PEOPLE

‖‖‖‖ **D**uring the 1890s, as class alignments began a thirty-year transformation, the plates beneath American political life shifted. Profound if elusive changes in popular perception— a cultural reorientation, a new consumer consciousness, a psychic crisis, historians have called it—redefined the terms of public discussion. At a time when partisan attachments were important sources of personal identification, extensive shuffling among Democrats, Republicans, and Populists laid the foundation for a new Republican majority that lasted until the Great Depression of the 1930s. In general, a wholesale shaking out of American political life released energies and opened up issues that early in the 20th century developed into the progressive movement.

Progressive reforms set new criteria for evaluating government policies. In contrast to the 19th century, the state acquired broad responsibilities to further social justice. Children had the right to a childhood; juveniles need not suffer a lifetime for their mistakes; women deserved protection against the impersonal pressures of the labor market. Injured workers warranted compensation; diseased bodies required treatment. Indignation over the flaunting of great wealth and the power it brought fueled demands for the state to step in and ensure economic fairness. Increasingly, government was expected to arbitrate major economic conflicts. By their very existence large corporations challenged deeply felt traditions of equity: "the struggle of democracy [is] the struggle of the small man against the overpowering influence of the big," announced Louis D. Brandeis.[1] Radical inequalities in the distribution of wealth raised questions of whether civil society could even function. Poverty, no longer viewed as an incentive to improvement, became a great destroyer: "He is not a free man," the progressives' favorite labor leader John Mitchell declared in behalf of a new "industrial liberty," "whose family must buy food today with the money that is earned tomorrow."[2]

As much to invigorate their society as to reform it, progressives declared a democratic revival, a renewal of the spirit that made America, in Jane Addams' words, the "most daring experiment in democratic government which the world has ever seen."[3] Their objective was close, continuous communication between government and citizenry. One reform strategy called for new means of direct democracy: popular initiative in legislation, a referendum on a significant law or issue, and ways to recall public officials, perhaps even judicial decisions. By the First World War, twenty states had versions of the initiative, twenty-three some form of the referendum. Even more instituted popular primary elections. In 1913 the Seventeenth Amendment empowered the voters, not their legislatures, to elect United States senators.

If the people did not rule, went the reformers' refrain, the interests would. The interests thrived on secrecy, the people on information. No word carried more progressive freight than *publicity*: expose the backroom deals in government, scrutinize the balance sheets of corporations, attend the public hearings on city services, study the effects of low wages on family life. Mayor Tom Johnson of Cleveland held tent meetings to educate its citizens. Senator Robert LaFollette of Wisconsin heaped statistics on his constituents from the back of a campaign wagon. Once the public knew, it would act: knowledge produced solutions. "To right any wrong in the United States is after all a simple process," the sometime socialist Charles Edward Russell declared. "You have only to exhibit it where all the people can see it plainly."[4] With evenhanded justice an informed public could resolve the bitterest conflicts, including industrial wars between capital and labor.

These reformers, in other words, made sustained efforts to adapt the 19th century tradition of community self-government for 20th century urban-industrial society. They took citizens seriously. It required knowledge to act on these enlarged reform agendas, and progressives assumed the responsibility of preparing the voters to act. In place of a community's common knowledge, they substituted extensive documentation, then did their best to spread it before the public. They explored basic questions about how to prepare youth as citizens in the modern world, and they redesigned the old model of community education to serve the children of immigrants and native-born alike. Moreover, they understood their enemies quite well. Corporate wealth did distort the governing system they prized, and attacking its influence was crucial to their reforms. City machines did prosper out of the hides of the poor; only the romantic fantasies of later scholars likened them to Sweet Charity prostitutes dispensing favors from their hearts of gold. In the progressive scheme of things, ward bosses corralling otherwise oblivious voters were no better than employers herding compliant employees to the polls. Finally, reformers competed for public favor among an unusually wide range of electoral choices, broadened especially by a vigorous Socialist party.

Phrased another way, progressives favored quality, not quantity: better informed, more alert, less gullible citizens. Their model voter was an individual who approached political problems as scientific issues to be resolved objectively in the public interest, then cast his secret ballot accordingly. All of those adjuncts to the high 19th century turnouts—color-coded ballots, party insignia, group voting—violated progressive principles of sound citizenship. Implicit in these standards was a line somewhere toward the bottom of society where inadequate qualifications became disqualifications, where people were simply not capable of functioning as citizens of a democracy.

For years middle-class commentators had identified the voting power of the lower class as democracy's great challenge. Almost all 19th century solutions took the white fraternity as given and sought ways to improve its performance: neutralize the Catholic church, ban liquor, enact civil service. In that spirit, when Jacob Riis reported in *How the Other Half Lives* (1891) that "The rumshop turns the political crank in New York," he assumed that his readers would be spurred to do something about the saloons and the slums; "our theory of government," he reminded them, establishes majority rule, and "More than a working majority of our voters now register from the tenements."[5] After 1900, however, the prospect of simply eliminating incompetent voters was at least as attractive. What more efficient solution than allowing a bottom layer or two, already distant and suspect, to drop out of the electorate?

If most progressives did not set out to keep the poor from the polls, they had little invested in bringing them there. The reformers preached to those who already understood their language. The rest had to ready themselves by breaking with the bosses or the slums or the immigrant cultures and joining the audience one by one. Entering the progressives' civic life, in other words, meant leaving the lower class behind. Whatever its merits in logic, this understanding of citizenship was disastrous in context, for it defined lower-class life itself as antagonistic to democracy. The critical point was not that progressives were classbound—who was not?—but that their version tolerated lower-class exclusion.

In the end, what mattered most to the progressives was not getting out the vote but getting things done, priorities that produced a good deal of impatience with unresponsive citizens, hostility toward locally oriented political parties, and praise for streamlined administrative solutions to broad public issues. The more specialized the groups or boards that managed progressive reforms, the more specialized the language obscuring these issues from ordinary citizens. The weaker the public grasp of issues, the more reformers relied on administrative solutions. Drawn down this spiral, reforms that originated in a desire to make governments more responsive to people's needs ended up making them less responsive to people's voices.

Time and again, progressives found it quite compatible to propose improving lower-class lives without soliciting lower-class votes. Reformers first advocated citywide nonpartisan politics to circumvent self-serving, self-perpetuating city councils and force governments to listen to their constituents' needs. In practice, however, such techniques silenced minorities and insulated city government from public discussion. Progressives proceeded to change the rationale: now consolidated governments were praised for their efficiency, often explicitly for their ability to accomplish more with less public fuss. If the citywide ballots for these consolidated governments contained too many choices for citizens to make intelligently, the reformers called for shorter ballots, that is, fewer choices. The mature progressive formula featured responsible government and empowered officials.

Yet if numbers alone told the tale, the progressive years were an epiphany. The Nineteenth Amendment mandating women's suffrage meant an instant doubling of the electorate, by far the grandest increase in American democratic history. As Anna Howard Shaw declared in 1910, who could talk about the state of democracy in America when it had not been given a chance: "We have never tried universal suffrage." [6] By rights, a flood of new voters should have vitalized the entire process. For millions of women who now had the ballot, of course, the consequences were direct and dramatic. What was puzzling, however, was how little else women's suffrage changed, how isolated this great moment remained in a democratic transformation that otherwise rolled on as if it had not happened.

At the beginning of these transition years, in the 1890s, suffrage advocates were mobilizing all over again after the effective collapse of their 19th century campaign. The reorganized National American Woman's Suffrage Association with around 13,000 members in 1893—by contrast with over 200,000 in the Woman's Christian Temperance Union and its affiliates—represented little more than a reform cadre. Even under new leaders who beat the drums persistently and expanded NAWSA's base impressively, the movement accomplished little until a sweep of victories between 1910 and 1914 brought women's suffrage to six western states, plus Kansas and Illinois. Then in 1915, with stunning defeats in four important states—New York, Pennsylvania, Massachusetts, and New Jersey—the campaign stalled once more. Conflict between those who wanted to continue state-by-state campaigning and those who insisted on a new departure threatened to disrupt the organization.

During this long drive, none of the progressive causes that men dominated gave priority to women's suffrage; very few even mentioned it. A number of men certainly favored women's suffrage, as the considerable attention given to it by the Progressive party in 1912 illustrated, but they provided no ongoing, organizational support. One explanation lay in the contrast between the American campaign and campaigns for women's suffrage elsewhere. In western Europe and in Australia, where workingmen's movements gathered momentum during these years, women's suffrage appeared to be a way of augmenting their strength—the masses versus the classes—especially in those countries where the workingmen themselves were denied ballots. On the eve of the First World War, the women's suffrage campaign in Britain, where 40 percent of the men still could not vote, was allied with the Labour party; in France, with the Socialist party. Throughout western Europe, as the American suffragist Rheta Childe Dorr shrewdly noted, "not *woman* suffrage, but *universal* suffrage is being struggled for."[7] Enfranchised white men in America, on the other hand, had little incentive to break their own monopoly. At best, women's suffrage tended to float by as a good cause.

NAWSA operated at the edges of progressive reform in a fashion similar to the Anti-Saloon League, the power behind the drive for Prohibition and in many ways a model for the suffrage organization. There was a natural affinity: the call for women's suffrage originated in the mid-19th century during a prohibition campaign, and the two causes remained close for the balance of the century. Early in the 20th century the leaders of NAWSA, like their counterparts in the Anti-Saloon League, initially placed their hopes on intensive lobbying and pivotal elections in the many state legislatures. Three years after the Anti-Saloon League in frustration turned from state-by-state campaigning to a constitutional amendment, NAWSA made the same shift. The suffrage amendment arrived two years after the Eighteenth Amendment established Prohibition. Both causes appealed to the same camp of social and settlement workers; both organizations borrowed those women's prestige without giving them a share in the leadership. Indicatively, NASWA's official account of the suffrage campaign singled out the Anti-Saloon League's opponents as its own primary enemies: an "Invisible Empire" of liquor interests and the alien, boozing voters who supported them.

In the end, the suffrage movement made the most of its weakness. Instead of challenging the world that white men made, NAWSA affirmed virtually all of it. As hierarchies appeared, its leaders spoke hierarchically, burying the lower class in a scornful rhetoric that contrasted women's virtues with African American and immigrant men's vices. NAWSA had its reasons. Very rarely did a man's voice from the African American or immigrant communities support women's suffrage. Nevertheless, NAWSA's attacks on "dirty hands and degenerate faces" in the lower class had a particularly hard edge.[8] Moreover, despite routine mention of workingwomen's special need for the ballot and the more than routine efforts of suffrage leader Harriet Stanton Blatch in New York to recruit them, NAWSA developed almost no connection with women wage earners. Not even the radical activists in the International Ladies Garment Workers Union expressed an interest. Finally, NAWSA's own aversion to a federally imposed black franchise circumscribed its campaign. It was not mere chance that as victory approached, NAWSA headquarters marked each additional state triumph on a large map of the United States under the heading "Make the Map White."

One important consequence of NAWSA's acceptance of hierarchy was the clear break it represented from the universalist arguments of 19th century suffragists. By the old logic, the common humanity of men and women led inexorably to universal suffrage, and universal suffrage ratified the common humanity of men and women: make all humans equal in civic life. Hierarchy disrupted this 19th century equation. Now the act of voting canceled no other inequalities: women who voted in the 20th century gained only the vote. In this regard, the suffrage movement in the United States resembled its counterparts in Europe. Nothing in British Labour or French Socialist support for women's suffrage implied sympathy for a larger feminist agenda. During the final drive for the suffrage in the United States, American men could make the same claim. What women gained from the Nineteenth Amendment, in other words, was less a depreciated vote (though it was that too) than a dissociated vote, a legal right that carried no other promises.

The hardest lesson of the suffrage campaign was the relatively little it accomplished. How was it even conceivable, exploded NAWSA's leader Carrie Chapman Catt, that the United States, first in the field with an organized women's movement and mobilized from sea to sea behind the suffrage, had limped in twenty-seventh among the nations to legalize it? Although no one would have given women the vote if they had not demanded it, how they demanded it or how many of them demanded it did not seem to make much difference. Whether women spoke patiently or impatiently, whether they used the orderly tactics of Catt's NAWSA or the disorderly tactics of Alice Paul's Congressional Union, men responded largely with platitudes until, in the grand march to victory after 1917, officeholders changed their minds for other reasons.

The immediate cause was the war. A widespread conviction that men and women mobilized together for war gained inestimable support for suffrage. The home front—the women's front—was not simply backup, as it had been in the lore of the Civil War; it was integral to waging the war itself. When Woodrow Wilson argued the case to the Senate in 1918, he used precisely that logic: "This war could not have been fought . . . if it had not been for the services of the women"; now women's suffrage was "vitally essential to the successful prosecution of the great war."⁹ By accepting auxiliary places in the patriotic hierarchies and by publicizing their contributions, suffragists extracted the most from the moment. They claimed to have earned not equality but a right.

Catt in particular shone in the role of loyal American. In 1916, as a preliminary to NAWSA's drive for a constitutional amendment, she committed the association to national preparedness. When war came, she quickly upstaged the antisuffrage National League of Women's Service, which also identified itself with the war, shunned the suspect Socialists, and cheered on the troops. When Wilson belatedly endorsed women's suffrage, Catt responded by promising an even greater war effort. At some level, all of this must have hurt deeply. In her initial address as president of NAWSA, Catt ranked militarism first among the enemies of women's suffrage. After the amendment passed, she devoted years of her life to the international peace movement. For these critical months, however, she accepted the fact that war was what the men were doing and she made them pay the camp follower.

If it was a painful twist of fate for Catt to ride a war to victory, the ultimate irony of the campaign was the link between its success and the fact that the United States *was* twenty-seventh. Enfranchising women as an acknowledgment of their importance in the war was an international movement. Until 1914, only 3 countries had equal suffrage. Then the gates opened: 2 more in 1915, 3 more in 1917, 11 more in 1918, 4 more in 1919. As Wilson stated late in 1918, "There seems to be growing a great voice in the world" that insists upon women's suffrage. That general cry accounted for his own "conversion," he admitted. "Are we alone to refuse to learn the lesson?"¹⁰ When Wilson spoke,

it looked as if women's suffrage as a war measure was about to triumph in France. By 1920, Belgium and Ireland joined the ranks, which
already included all the predominantly Protestant nations. The great
question, in other words, was whether, in the face of what appeared
to be a universal sweep for women's suffrage, the nation claiming to
make the world safe for democracy would be the sole holdout. Even
then, conservatives in the United States Senate and in southern legislatures made a contest of it. As Catt recognized, it was a shabby victory.
Little wonder it did not release a great outpouring of democratic energies elsewhere in America.

The arrival of suffrage also marked a fundamental change in how
women affected public policy. During the progressive years a cluster
of extraordinary women, including Jane Addams, Florence Kelley, Julia
Lathrop, Alice Hamilton, Lillian Wald, and Margaret Dreier Robins,
reached peaks of influence in public affairs far higher than any other
cohort achieved until late in the 20th century. The key to their success
was learning how to draw maximum power from the old politics of
indirection which presumed basic differences between the sexes and
expected to reflect those differences in public life. Out of the urban-
industrial dislocations and class confusions around the turn of the century, men and women together compiled the progressive agenda for
social justice. But it was these reforming women who gave it shape,
who explained it in language sufficiently traditional yet sufficiently
immediate to win widespread public acceptance.

They took the initiative by construing social justice as interrelated
matters of family well-being and community morality, long the specialty of public-minded women. Issues of factory safety and public
health, a living wage and a decent home, prostitution and prohibition,
child labor and juvenile court, all lent themselves nicely to arguments
about protecting the vulnerable, nurturing the next generation, preserving the family's cohesion, and surrounding it with respectability.
At the same time, they presented themselves as purely dispassionate
witnesses: they alone had no ambitions other than the public good.
Accumulating quantities of facts and turning them into the studies,
statistics, and charts that denoted scientific accuracy early in the century added further gloss to the image of impartiality. By framing their
appeals in this fashion, women got men's attention on these issues
much more effectively than men got men's attention.

From this base, progressive women mounted numerous, creative explorations across class boundaries, establishing city playgrounds and
day care centers, facilitating the formation of labor unions, spreading
information about health and welfare to the rural poor, and publicizing
the skills and insights that immigrants brought to America. In a fluid

time of multiplying options, they made superb use of their opportunities. Above all, they excelled in communication. Addams in particular became famous for the exceptional range of her public conversations: with the rich about the effects of poverty, with the lower class about the values of the middle class, with the native-born about the culture of immigrants, with townspeople about the needs of city dwellers. Only when Addams talked about peace to a nation at war did they shoot the messenger.

As Catt understood, women who opposed the war were trespassing on men's territory. Nevertheless, the essence of the reforming process was to probe those boundaries, always at the risk of outrage. Playing it safe got nothing done. One of the most persistent of these chancy ventures involved assistance for wage-earning women. The settlement houses and community centers that middle-class women operated became their meeting grounds. If they could begin organizing on their own, Margaret Dreier Robins' Women's Trade Union League might back them up. In some states reformers convinced legislators to set minimum wages, hours, and other working conditions for women, on the grounds that their special nature—their physical limitations, their family responsibilities, even their delicate sensibilities—generated a special need for protection. As women fanned out into new areas of employment early in the 20th century, the gendering of jobs—one aspect of a deepening hierarchical consciousness—followed them to work, and protective legislation for women capitalized on these increasingly elaborate distinctions about paid work appropriate for each sex. At the same time, gendering was highly restrictive. In both white- and blue-collar work, it segregated women in jobs with the lowest pay and least opportunity: "light work" requiring little "mechanical skill" in clothing manufacture, for example, or routine clerical tasks in the office.[11] Even successful reforms, it turned out, had their risks.

Progressive women offered politicians an exceptionally fine bargain. Officials still held all the choices. They might listen to what these women told them about social injustice or they might not. Through what one historian has called a "judicial patriarchy," they defined the legal boundaries around women's lives. The protective legislation they issued, for example, they could also take away. When reforming women lost, they usually persisted but they rarely crowded the men in charge: relations in the politics of indirection were quite formal. By no means did these women advocate the entire spectrum of progressive reforms. They dispensed their resources carefully. Without the franchise, they gained nothing from direct democracy and a good deal from discreet negotiation with legislators. Suffrage was only a secondary cause, and among some of their associates—the General Federation of Women's Clubs, for instance—it scarcely mattered at all. In brief, these reforming women made ideal allies. They did not compete for offices, they contributed an abundance of knowledge, and they laid a unique sheen of virtue over common causes. Where interests coincided, therefore, women and men regularized a strikingly effective political process: women educating the public, men proposing the law, women arguing the case, men claiming the credit.

After 1920, women's suffrage broke up this arrangement. Now neither sex was impartial or even necessarily virtuous. Everybody competed, everybody took her chances. Reforming women lost their claims to a superior knowledge of social justice. Wage-earning women lost their claims to a special protection in the labor market. As justice George Sutherland coolly remarked in *Atkins v. Children's Hospital* (1923), overturning a minimum wage law for women, "It cannot be shown that well paid women safeguard their morals more carefully than those who are poorly paid." People varied: let the hierarchies sort them out. Politically, progressive women had little luck transferring power from the old to the new context. A politics of indirection, for example, did not sharpen their skills in partisan mobilization or legislative horse trading. In fact for decades to come, those institutions that dominated politics as women entered it remained overwhelmingly male preserves—men's clubs, as commentators called such crucial centers as the United States Senate and the Democratic and Republican National Committees.

Hence in the 1920s, when branches of the League of Women Voters tried to play the traditional women's game of promoting high-minded causes to the legislature, they lost; and when the United States Children's Bureau tried to play the men's game of Washington infighting, they lost. The old rules no longer applied, and the new ones did not work. Once assimilated inside the existing hierarchies, almost all politically active women found themselves slotted too low to have much of an effect.

The decade from 1914 to 1924, the public philosopher Horace Kallen realized, was "one of the most critical ten-year periods that the Republic has ever passed through."[12] There was the Great War, of course, snapping old certainties like rotten boards. But Kallen had domestic even more than international affairs in mind, and here also he caught the timing just right. A final wave of changes solidifying new classes, designing modern hierarchies, institutionalizing caste divisions, redefining women's authority, and reconstructing the electorate came together in a rush during precisely those years to set the course for 20th century American democracy.

Nothing better measured the decade's significance than the disappearance of the People, the ultimate expression of 19th century self-government that in the culture of America's original democracy spoke through general elections to make broad policy determinations. As many Americans saw their society take a dangerous turn late in the century, reformers reaffirmed the ability of the People to set it right. Contrasting the promise of his program with the troubled nation of the 1880s, Edward Bellamy in *Looking Backward* (1886) had his man of the future, Dr. Leete, invoke a revitalized People: "the solidarity of the race and the brotherhood of man, which to you were but fine phrases, are, to our thinking and feeling, ties as real and as vital as physical fraternity." [13] The many versions of a social gospel or a Christian socialism around the turn of the century shared a similar vision of a healing, reconciling People, as—with more fire and brimstone—did both sides in the Battle of the Standards in 1896, pitting William Jennings Bryan against William McKinley.

There were signs of the People's fragmenting after 1896, notably in the sinking of the lower class and the increasing atomization of voters through standardized secret balloting. Nevertheless, a basic faith held firm. Those advocating new provisions for direct democracy, such as the initiative, the referendum, and the popular primary, justified their reforms as a way of letting the People decide. Time and again, progressives spoke glowingly of the People's power. It "sweeps over opposition, brushes aside legal technicalities . . . ," Walter Weyl declared in 1912. "No overt opposition can withstand it. It cannot be bribed. It cannot be stifled." [14] As Weyl implied, faith in the People and faith in the irresistible progress of civilization were close companions.

It was in this spirit that Americans two years later blamed the horror of wholesale war in Europe on a handful of rulers who dragooned their citizens into battle. "It seemed literally impossible," the critic Harold Stearns recalled, "that we should ever get into the war ourselves." An old American axiom stated that autocracies generated wars and democracies kept the peace. Ordinary people never wanted war. Frederick Grimke thought democracies would "throw away military pursuits. For war is the most effectual instrument which can be employed to undermine public liberty." Hence the more democracy spread in Europe, American commentators argued at the beginning of the 20th century, the more remote the prospects of war became. Unfortunately, it seemed, change had not come fast enough. With general war a reality, only a complete "democratization of Europe" would eliminate "the spreading cancer of militarism" and ensure "a world disarmed." [15]

The evidence, however, simply could not be made to fit. By all accounts, war—relentless, plough-'em-under war—emerged a popular cause everywhere, except perhaps in czarist Russia. Then in 1917 the United States, with its own patriotism whipped to a froth, joined the pack. Following the war, the Versailles Treaty, which seemed to be shaped far more by a popular selfishness than by an impartial justice, completed the mockery of those old assumptions about democratic influences guaranteeing a decent, peaceful world order. This was the first great war, moreover, to occur against a backdrop of expectations about modern medicine ensuring healthy young adults a long, rewarding life. A war that scaled new heights of slaughter—a million and a quarter dead just in the stalemated battle along the Somme in 1916—also raised new questions of senseless dying, of battle casualties as the cold-blooded execution of the young. Democracy stopped none of this.

Cumulatively, this crisis did in the People, and attitudes toward public opinion—the People in action—traced its demise. Before the war, even as conservative a commentator as A. Lawrence Lowell, president of Harvard, affirmed that the very definition of American democracy was "the control of political affairs by public opinion." To assuage doubts about the People's competence, Lowell wanted to add a new category of governors: a permanent, well-paid civil service of experts to manage technical problems in public policy. "There is a limit to the total amount of labor the whole people can expend on public affairs," he concluded. The People should set the government's general course; its supporting staff of experts should handle the complicated matters of implementation. How these spheres interrelated Lowell did not explain. He left them operating side by side, each with responsibilities, each with a watchful eye on the other.[16]

As war swamped the People with propaganda and swept them up in the passions of jingoism, Lowell's vision of apportionment and balance dissolved. Conceptually the People lost coherence and deteriorated into a mass of people, myopic and gullible. Sometime reformers issued particularly scathing denunciations of "the human herd," in Randolph Bourne's phrase. "We think as we are directed to think," a disillusioned Frederic Howe wrote. "We believe the things we are told to believe."[17] Among these overnight cynics, the person who best made sense out of the anger—who not only discarded the fallen People but also sketched a persuasive, modern alternative—was Walter Lippmann.

As a precocious publicist fresh out of Lowell's Harvard, Lippmann struck notes similar to his before the war: the "chaos" that ordinary citizens experienced in modern society, the force of emotions in public life, and the importance of "the scientific mind" to an effective democratic government.[18] Yet Lippmann, even more than Lowell, expressed great confidence in a public who debated differences, made decisions, and on the big issues transcended the selfishness of individuals and groups. Through the war years he supported Woodrow Wilson, the golden voice of a whole, moral democracy. Then as the president, declaring the election of 1920 a "solemn referendum" on the League of Nations, made a final gesture toward the sovereign People, Lippmann veered off. Two years later he demolished the notion of the People in one of the most influential books ever written about American democracy, *Public Opinion*, which he supplemented with further commentary in *The Phantom Public* (1925) and *A Preface to Morals* (1929).

As if he were an archeologist picking among the ruins, he examined one "mystical notion" after another from democracy's lost past. " 'The people' were regarded as a person; their wills as a will; their ideas as a mind." "The naively democratic theory was . . . that the opinion of masses of persons somehow became the opinion of a corporate person called The People and that this corporate person then directed human affairs like a monarch. But that is not what happens." Countless individuals made countless decisions in countless concrete situations: nothing more existed until an enterprising politician made something more out of it. At the heart of the old theory stood the conscientious, rational citizen. "It was believed that if only he could be taught more facts, if only he would take more interest, if only he would listen to more lectures and read more reports, he would gradually be trained to direct public affairs. The whole assumption is false." "The discovery of prejudice in all particular men gave the [old-fashioned democrat] a shock from which he never recovered." So much for George Bancroft's transcendent public judgment. Human failings, not human wisdom, were additive.[19]

In "the isolated rural township," a democracy of simple problems and definite solutions might still work, Lippmann granted, but in the "wide and unpredictable environment" of modern America the electorate became dupes: "the number of mice and monkeys known to have been deceived in laboratories is surpassed only by the hopeful citizens of a democracy," each one a gull in a behaviorist trap who "responds quite readily to a glass egg, a decoy duck, a stuffed shirt or a political platform." Hence "an inner circle"—a self-appointed clique of ambitious, often unscrupulous men—took control of the institutions basic to the governing process. Reformers responded with the "absurdity" of "various proposals such as the initiative, referendum and direct primary," all premised on the misconception that majorities had special merit. "The justification of majority rule in politics . . . [lies solely] in the sheer necessity of finding a place in civilized society for the force which resides in numbers." Properly understood, the ballot was a safety valve, a method for sublimating violence and sustaining social order.[20]

Like Lowell, Lippmann advocated a staff of highly trained specialists with life tenure to administer complex modern government. But where Lowell had pictured the experts supplementing electoral democracy, Lippmann pictured them substituting for it. Because sound decisions were "inevitably the concern of comparatively few people," this handful of qualified officials—Lippmann's experts—must not be badgered by popular demands. In any case, ordinary citizens cared very little about the process of government. America's "democratic fallacy" hid the central truth that "men do not long desire self-government for its own sake. They desire it for the sake of results." Indeed, the whole apparatus of self-government had been blown far out of proportion. "Mankind was interested in all kinds of other things, in order, in its rights, in prosperity, in sights and sounds and in not being bored."[21]

Lippmann's themes dominated the lively postwar discussion of democracy. With a bow to his former student, Lowell converted in 1923. The "atrophy" of democracy's traditional, holistic "public opinion on large questions" marked the end of an age, he acknowledged. Liberty Hyde Bailey, once the tribune of rural America, now spoke the sophisticated language of national-class disillusionment: "reforms can be brought about only if they are forced on the masses by superior intelligence." "It is no more to our credit to 'pass around' [government] offices," Bailey argued in behalf of the new expert leadership, "than to ask first one neighbor and then another to serve as the family physician." Forty years later, when V. O. Key, Jr., wrote his generation's authoritative work on public opinion, he could do no better than paraphrase Lippmann's account of the 19th century's "weird conceptions": "In an earlier day public opinion seemed to be pictured as a mysterious vapor that emanated from the undifferentiated citizenry and in some way or another enveloped the apparatus of government to bring it into conformity with the public will."[22]

The most important dissent to this new consensus came from John Dewey, already a prominent reformer for a quarter of a century before Lippmann's attack on the People. Stung by his own misplaced enthusiasm for the world war's democratic potential, Dewey returned in the 1920s to his first love, the vital community, and issued as urgent an appeal to energize democracy locally as Lippmann's to rationalize it nationally. "The local," Dewey intoned, "is the ultimate universal, and as near an absolute as exists."[23] There individuals acquired both a definition and a direction in society: they remained actors, and their actions meant something. Sensitive to the many powerful forces impinging on local life, Dewey sought ways of strengthening a traditional action-oriented community democracy with modern scientific techniques. Like Lippmann, he valued expert knowledge; unlike Lippmann, he rejected expert government. Use the experts' information, Dewey insisted, but never let them rule. In a democracy, citizens interacting one with another made the decisions.

Nevertheless, by granting so much of Lippmann's argument, Dewey cut away the basis for a separate approach to modern democracy. Great economic and social forces had in fact disabled the old communities, he conceded, and left the public "inchoate and unorganized." There was no longer a People's government, only "too many publics and too much of public concern for our existing resources to cope with." In rather cranky language, he deplored the gaudy distractions of consumer life, feared people's vulnerability to propaganda, and bemoaned the standardization in their thought and behavior. Like Lippmann, he disparaged electoral democracy—"not the most inspiriting of the different meanings of democracy"—and allowed it a place largely because "some form" of it was "inevitable." But he had no alternative method for implementing his democratic vision. Vaguely, hopefully, he looked forward to "a kind of knowledge and insight which does not yet exist." [24]

For the time being, therefore, Dewey became just another voice in the chorus declaring a crisis in democracy. As if it scarcely needed to be said, he noted in 1927 that "democracy is today under a cloud." "In great measure our democracy has been ineffectual," the liberal young journalist Frederick Lewis Allen acknowledged. Lippmann wrote a second book on public opinion, he explained, "to account for the disenchantment of democracy." How should Americans respond to "the failure of democratic government," the publicist T. V. Smith wanted to know. Did it "justify such deep despair"? Only ridicule, Henry L. Mencken decided, as he christened ordinary Americans the "booboisie." [25]

Along with the crisis in democracy went a crisis in citizenship, one that had been gathering throughout the progressive years and weakening the props beneath the People. In the People's heyday, citizenship came inherent in the vote. "The ballot in the hands of the citizen is the badge of his sovereignty," a Gilded Age senator declaimed, and using it certified his citizenship. [26] There was no special preparation, only an act. Early in the 20th century, progressives raised the stakes considerably. Instead of a self-defining act, voting was now the outcome of a carefully calculated process. The reformers' ideal-type citizen subsisted on a regimen of facts, scientifically digested. By absorbing increasing amounts of information on a multiplying array of issues, he usually, she occasionally, would bring democracy and public policy into the modern age.

Democracy in the 19th century had no counterpart to this new citizen. Whether they were viewing citizens collectively or individually, 19th century democrats counted on character, not expertise, on bedrock values, not accumulated information, on innate good sense, not scientific reasoning. Hence what various commentators, including such erstwhile progressives as Lippmann and Dewey, singled out as the nub of 19th century democracy's failure—that the citizen who needed to be a rationally equipped individual had turned out instead to be an emotionally confused member of the crowd—was a blow to very recent progressive demands but not to 19th century traditions. Imposing their own frustrated hopes on a more distant past, 20th century reformers declared 19th century democracy a failure for reasons irrelevant to 19th century democracy.

These same critics created a second problem for themselves, one closely related to the first. The demanding public role they set for the modern citizen required preparation; preparation involved a set of standards common to disparate Americans; common standards meant imposing qualities of sameness where they did not otherwise exist. The 19th century People was the grand muffler of differences. In the face of a multitude of antagonisms dividing the democratic lodges, voting froze America's hostilities in place. The act of citizenship was itself neutral. All kinds of people in all kinds of clothes saying all kinds of things in all kinds of languages joined as an electorate—as the People—without needing to join in any other way. Wholeness of this sort did not require wholeness of any other sort: cultural diversity among white men simply did not threaten it. Rather than Lippmann's "mystical notion," the 19th century People accommodated remarkably well to the everyday reality of America's sharp-toothed heterogeneity.

The sinking of the lower class and the process of alienation accompanying it were already straining this scheme in the first years of the 20th century. Middle-class images of the lower class that accentuated its strangeness also emphasized its ignorance, and elections did little to mediate those divisions, not even in the moment of decision. Early 20th century commentators measured the strength of the electorate by the intelligence of its majority rather than by the total, incremental contributions of all members, as in the 19th century understanding. With the weakening of the middle-class sense of fraternity, in other words, lower-class men lost the buffer of an enveloping, compensating People. It was no longer a matter of how elections affected cultural differences but how cultural differences affected elections. Were the increasingly isolated members of the lower class even qualified to vote? The atmosphere of the early 20th century was ready-made to justify excluding people of color.

Inside this framework of assumptions, middle-class Americans faced a monumental challenge of their own creation. Even as the old cement of the People was giving way, they insisted on a much tighter degree of cohesion. The sheer number of nationalities bedeviling some early 20th century commentators was not the issue. Heterogeneity always lay in the eye of the beholder, as a social worker illustrated with her description in 1913 of the reactions of an immigrant just off the boat to those who had preceded her: "The very things which strike the native born as foreign seem to [the newest arrival] as distinctly American: the pretentiousness of signs and advertisements, the gaudy crowded shop windows . . . her own countrymen in American clothing . . . she sums it all up as 'America.'"[27] In the late 19th century, when as compulsive a systematizer as Edward Bellamy sought greater "public spirit," he envisaged little more than a naturally emerging civic commitment. By the early 20th century, however, even modest versions of civic unity seemed to require complicated schemes of direction.

As the meaning of citizenship spread diffusely beyond the act of voting, it gathered in all kinds of middle-class concerns about social disorders. Citizenship did not simply happen; it had to be made to happen. Nobody would learn about citizenship unless they were taught—taught the customs, taught the language. In middle-class circles, the immigrants' use of such public institutions as the schools, the press, and the theater to preserve their language of birth was no longer just an object of disdain but a problem to resolve. Indicatively, Frederick Jackson Turner, the eloquent theorist of traditional democracy's natural unity in the 1890s, worried about immigrant diversity after 1900. What emerged was a new set of key words: *hyphenate Americans, assimilation, Americanization,* connoting a complex combination of behavior, attitudes, identity, and values that required conscientious policies and careful measurement.

The term *Americanize,* which dated back to the arrival of democracy, referred throughout the 19th century to helping greenhorns learn the rudiments and find their way. Native-born and newcomers alike expected the immigrants' more experienced compatriots to assume much of that work. Even as the sense of a natural process disappeared around the turn of the 20th century, the first gestures toward more organized alternatives were relatively gentle. Some middle-class groups expected well-publicized information about economic opportunities to distribute immigrants nationwide, that is, scatter them thinly enough to get lost in the majority. Hull House and other settlements counted on dialogue to sway immigrants toward their middle-class models—models that the rapid multiplication of routine white-collar jobs made eminently practical. Even Israel Zangwill's more aggressive metaphor of a melting pot—strictly a 20th century creation that expressed the new, not the 19th century vision of unity from diversity—pictured an inclusive People as the happy outcome of this homogeneous middle-class brew.

More coercive variations on Americanization gained favor around 1910. Left to themselves, the educator Ellwood Cubberly warned, immigrant enclaves would perpetuate "their own national manners, customs, and observances. Our task is to break up these [clusters] . . . to assimilate and amalgamate these people as part of our American race." Now the prospect of ethnic groups managing their own assimilation suggested subversion. "Americanizing America is the task and responsibility of Americans," declared one champion of the cause to an appreciative business audience.[28] Some companies made courses in Americanization a condition of employment. Recently mandated public behavior—saluting the flag, pledging allegiance—infused martinet qualities into the process, and wartime gave these rituals a great lift: social discipline meant cultural discipline, loyalty meant uniformity, and the need to mobilize meant the right to enforce. After the war, racially shaped immigration restriction embedded many of these values in law.

To the culturally oppressive side of these nativist movements the critics Randolph Bourne and Horace Kallen issued the most impressive dissents. Both scorned the Americanizers' narrow Anglo-Saxonism; both gloried in the effects of ethnic pluralism. Bourne likened America to "a federation of cultures," one that in the midst of Europe's wartime slaughter offered the peaceful alternative of an "intellectual battleground of the nations" generating a unique "trans-nationalism." The "cooperative harmonies" among these many cultures, as Kallen pictured America, carried the potential for "an orchestration of mankind." Maintain English as the common language, both of them argued, and create in the public schools an arena for interaction and growth; then let immigrants adapt their cultures naturally—"acclimatize," Bourne called the process. Kallen's awareness of how a great variety of occupational, religious, and social groups fit into an American tradition gave his vision the look of a still-vital People: "Democracy has meant the multiplication of [voluntary] relations; it has consisted in the formation, clash, integration, dissolution and reformation of ever more and more associations wherewith the individual may give his life purpose, import, color and direction."[29]

Two silences, however, marked the limits beyond which these pluralists did not go. There were no people of color in their cultural orchestra, and there was no politics in their civic life. To preserve what they could from a tradition at risk, they created another world for it, a world of white diversity that had nothing to do with governance or with any sort of collective decision-making. Willy-nilly, Bourne and Kallen also belonged to a new time. Like its predecessor, modern democracy arose from the ruins of the arrangement preceding it: breakdown, then atomization, finally reconstruction. Early in the 19th century, to express how individual citizens just released from hierarchical authority should recombine, white men devised the democratic People. Early in the 20th, to manage citizens now scattered by the collapse of the People, they created new hierarchies. The power to govern resided in these hierarchies.

The new citizenship, self-consciously shaped to its tasks, was perfectly compatible with hierarchy. Everything now came in scaled differences and graded ladders: levels of education, seriousness of crimes, degrees of skill. Sorting citizens according to their political qualifications—to decide, to implement, to vote, to watch—followed naturally. The ones judged least capable were, in fact, the ones least likely to participate at all. Some of these—recently enfranchised voters or people on the move—19th century democracy, acculturating through publicly visible example and loosely regulated access, would have drawn into the electorate right away. The People renewed themselves. Only in the 20th century, for instance, were members of the youngest cohort less likely to vote than their elders. As if to draw an official line demarcating the new from the old democracy, federal legislation in 1925 denied the ballot to anyone who was not formally a citizen of the United States.

Class above all else determined participation. Although 19th century democracy certainly did not eliminate classes, it pulled against many of their effects, and in the process it opened public life to a cacophony of voices, a jostling of competitors, a mixture of styles. Politics countered at least some of the restraints from on high: lower-class white men needed no permit to take to the streets and raise a little political hell. In the new century, that elasticity disappeared. If in the 19th century race and gender drew the hardest lines of separation, in the 20th century class divisions fixed them. Modern hierarchies hardened those divisions, and electoral politics reflected the outcome. One authority on 20th century politics has called "the class skew in American voting participation . . . greater by a very wide margin than it is in any other Western country," perhaps excepting Switzerland.[30] Now politics functioned in an entirely different atmosphere. Early in the 19th century, soaring turnouts among white men reinforced the impression of the People governing; early in the 20th, falling turnouts reinforced the impression of people being governed.

PART THREE

MODERN DEMOCRACY
1920s-1990s

||||||| As industrialization spread, so did democracy. Envisaging a world made safe for democracy was no mere Wilsonian conceit. By the time of the Great War, democracy gave all the appearances of being the favored child of progress. Yet as more and more countries joined them, Americans still considered themselves the pacesetters, with an intuitive understanding of how democracy really functioned and what it really meant. Theirs, they believed, was the measure of all other democracies. European champions of a welfare state, however, laid out a different standard, one where nations with the most comprehensive programs for social insurance and public service set the pace and the United States lagged behind.

In fact, the world's democracies did not form a line with leaders and followers. Europe was not catching up with the United States, nor was the United States now dragging in the rear. The timing and context of democracy's arrival, including the elementary fact that around the turn of the 20th century America had a democratic past to accommodate and European nations did not, gave the versions on either side of the Atlantic distinctive stamps. In particular, they divided over issues of national unity, race, the role of the state, and the relative importance of majorities and individuals.

In the 19th century, democracy was so crucial to America's nation-building process that rhetorically America and democracy became inseparable, almost interchangeable. That nation-defining linkage never broke: throughout the 20th century a great many Americans continued to think of democracy simply as what they were. When democracy slipped into harness with class, therefore, it was almost impossible to implicate democracy in America's social rifts: democracy united. In the

United States the overpowering conceptual strength of democracy-as-cohesion turned evidence of democracy-as-division into an anomaly, an aberration that would surely pass.

In Europe, on the other hand, nationhood and democracy had separate origins. Even where they arrived together, as they did in Norway, Finland, Czechoslovakia, and by a stretch of the imagination Germany, only the chronologies coincided: they did not define one another. European democracy was woven into the formation of classes, not nations, and it emerged in conflict. For Europe's reactionaries and revolutionaries alike, a class-based democracy expressed the very divisions they vowed to close: national wholeness meant eliminating democracy. Because, on the contrary, democracy expressed America's wholeness, it threw up powerful defenses against an assortment of authoritarian movements that from time to time in the 20th century crushed democratic governments almost everywhere else in the world. Except for a handful of people at the fringes, fascism and communism simply fell off the scale of American considerations. Their popularity in other countries seemed literally beyond belief, evidence of some strange, deep cultural rot.

Viewed from a different angle, however, the white people of Europe, by exporting their racism through imperialism, maintained other possibilities for unity at home that whites in America did not have. No persuasive evidence indicates that color prejudice among Belgians in the Congo or the British in India was any less thorough or vicious than among whites in the American south. Nevertheless, externalizing the one and domesticating the other had profound effects on how the public—the whole citizenry—was understood in these settings. Indeed, country by country, European democracies held almost all of their harshest ethnic and nationality prejudices at bay. If American theories of Nordic supremacy collapsed in part from their sheer absurdity in a multicultural society, parallel German beliefs in Slavic *untermenschen* survived in part as a luxury of Europe's many, separated nations. How European nations dealt with the major exception to this rule of externalization—Jewish fellow citizens—defined their democracies as tellingly as race relations did America's. Later, Japanese democracy followed the European model of exporting prejudices against other Asian peoples as a way of highlighting racial unity at home.

White men in America, spreading themselves thin early in the 19th century, assumed they could create a democracy without the state. Europeans, congregating in cities late in the century, needed the state to create their democracy. Those opposing visions had their origins in opposing quests for personal independence. Americans went to the land in search of theirs; Europeans left the land looking for theirs.

Customary privileges clung to rural Europe, and the grip of poverty squeezed it mercilessly. The escape routes ran to the towns and cities, whose 19th century inhabitants came to be as distinct from the villagers, a French commentator noted, as "two different peoples."[1] As democracy arrived in America, in other words, freedom of movement and liberty went with agriculture; as it arrived in Europe, they fused with city life.

Unlike white men in America, who acquired the franchise gradually and easily enough to think of it as a natural right, Europeans won their ballots as the spoils of war. Commonly, the franchise belonged to a combination of goals. Acquiring the right to vote and the right to unionize together, one historian has written of Sweden, "the worker had become a free subject, a citizen."[2] There and in Finland, Belgium, and Austria, workers between 1896 and 1913 mounted general strikes in an effort to broaden the franchise. Europeans in all walks of life came out of these conflicts defining the ballot along firm social coordinates—by class, by group, by public policy—and assuming it would be used to enact social programs. Everything hinged on controlling the state, which became invested with all kinds of conflicting hopes for security, order, and justice. American democracy, thriving on suspicion of the state, invested far fewer hopes in it. Not only did American policymakers early in the 20th century think less grandly about state-sponsored programs; what they did propose in such areas as pensions, public health, and unemployment compensation was usually borrowed from Europe.

Ballots won in conflict had a high value: Europeans used them. As Americans cast them less often, they watched one of their oldest democratic traditions migrate across the Atlantic. In 1889, James Bryce could still declare quite accurately, "The vote of a majority has a sacredness in America not yet reached in Europe."[3] By the 1920s a majority of eligible citizens no longer even voted in many American elections; by midcentury a pattern of turnout percentages one-third again larger than America's was standard in Europe. While American experts were busy explaining how well their system worked with low levels of participation, some European countries established legal penalties for not voting.

As majorities rose in importance in Europe, the individual replaced them at the heart of American democracy. Always significant in the American scheme, the individual now became central. Initially that meant multiplying the choices available to individuals, whether in consumer markets, occupations, or lifestyles. Increasingly, however, choices came to be swallowed up in large concepts of rights. Unlike Europeans, many of whom continued to think of their rights as collectively based, almost all Americans saw them inhering in individuals, one by one, in infinite series. In fact, America's individuals seemed to live apart from its communities. To charges of failure in America's social record—the effects of racism, for example, or the distribution of medical services—cold war patriots often countered with the triumph of individual freedom in America. In some circles the argument worked well enough. America's individualism sparked envy around the world late in the 20th century, and commentators in a global range of countries pictured it on the verge of sweeping across their own cultures.

The worldwide attractions of American individualism suggested how democracies were converging after midcentury. The big state now thrived in the United States too. Here as elsewhere, the national government concentrated on matters of economic and military policy, leaving most cultural and ethnic issues to regional or local jurisdictions. This arrangement, one version of which was already underwriting democratic public policy in America before the Second World War, unraveled everywhere between the 1960s and 1990s, as a resurgence of tribalistic values among peoples as varied as Protestant fundamentalists and French Canadians, Sikhs and Basques, challenged the rule of centralized democracies. During the 1980s and 1990s, as racism settled into class-carved grooves in the United States, it was spreading rapidly through Europe. By the 1980s, social agendas were shrinking in Europe, and so-called market solutions to public issues, long a favorite in America, were gaining favor instead. On its part, the United States took steps in the 1990s to bring public health policy in line with that in comparable democracies.

The difference that did not disappear was the far lower levels of voting in the United States than in Europe. At the end of the 20th century, America's greatest single contribution to world history, the concept of inclusive popular self-government, could draw little comfort from the record in its home of origin.

CHAPTER 8

THE INDIVIDUAL

||||||| During the very years that the People dissolved, a new individualism flowered. They went together: what weakened democracy's community component in the transition from the 19th to the 20th century strengthened its individual component. Between 1914 and 1924, in the final stage of that process, as popular energies were draining fast from the collective side of democracy, they flowed just as rapidly into its individual side. The expressiveness that had more or less disappeared from America's political life resurfaced in people's personal lives.

Two fundamental changes fueled the new individualism. One of them cracked the unitary Character of the 19th century and distributed pieces of it among the many activities of modern life. What had been a whole individual became "a play of many characters within a single body." "The modern man," Walter Lippmann announced, "is unable any longer to think of himself as a single personality."[1] He wore many "hats," it was said, not only in public but also with his family, at leisure, or alone. John Dewey, Lippmann's sometime adversary, echoed his judgment. The most profound consequence of this decentered character was the disappearance of a single, fixed standard of conduct. In the 19th century, the same moral codes stuck with middle-class Americans wherever they went. If a man cheated on his partner in a business deal or on his wife in a back alley, it communicated a uniformly applicable message about the whole person. A man was what he was: there were no excuses. Nor, if a woman wilted under the stress of Victorian saintliness, was there any place to hide. Now those rock-solid values fragmented: "Right and Wrong," the liberal editor Freda Kirchwey cheerfully noted in the mid-1920s, "finally followed the other absolute monarchs to an empty, nominal existence somewhere in exile."[2]

The heart of the matter, however, was not relativism but segmentation, not a chaos of personal values but a multiplication of the settings that determined those values. The basic divide separated work from leisure. Now free time had its own logic: it would be as unacceptable to slip leisure values into the work place as it would be self-defeating to impose work values on a night out. Work values also splintered. In the national-class world where specialization defined status, each professional or business group claimed to have its own needs and experiences and hence its own code of conduct. Values "differed in different occupations," Lincoln Steffens concluded around 1930. "And an ethical practitioner formed and fitted into one occupation . . . is apt to be disqualified thereby for another occupation, morally as well as technically." Or as the publicist T. V. Smith put it more generally, "If ethical values are not in current work, they are for most men nowhere."[3] Only those inside the work group could comprehend its rules well enough to judge one another. By this logic, the perfect defense against an outsider's challenge was the collective agreement among insiders that the challenger was wrong.

The second fundamental change accompanying the new individualism opened up—and legitimized—a vast interior life. In the 19th century, middle-class Americans visualized character as architecture. It might have strange closets and hidden crannies, but it was a bounded whole. In that scheme of things, dangerous interior forces once let loose might never be contained again. In the 20th century those impulses were reconstrued as boundless sources of energy through which individuals discovered who they were: personality flourished only through exploration and growth. The external person, character's bulwark in the 19th century, was now little more than a facade.

Self-determination, the key word in the male-oriented democratic individualism of the 19th century, looked outward to the world and commonly found expression in economic terms. Individuals got ahead; they proved their worth. The most prominent exceptions, from transcendentalists to religious seekers, almost always distanced themselves from democratic culture. Although wealth obviously mattered a great deal in the 20th century, it could no longer measure democratic individualism. Where its meaning unfolded through endless discoveries, who could even decide what to measure? Achievement depended on how a person felt about it. In ways utterly alien to the 19th century, the modern individual spent a lifetime searching for her real self, perhaps also for his real relationships with other people. The relatively concrete considerations in 19th century democracy's self-determination, in other words, expanded grandly and indeterminately into an entirely different psychic enterprise: *fulfillment.*

Self-directed work and democratic self-determination arrived together early in the 19th century, each drawing reciprocally from the other. In this context, work was not simply a virtue in life that promised future rewards. Controlling one's work was its own reward. It did not lead to democratic individualism; it expressed that individualism. Radical visions of a just society, rather than looking for alternatives to hard work, sought ways of removing the encumbrances on it—the tyranny of bosses, the artificially low returns, the ceiling on opportunities. Early in the 20th century, the multiplication of work hierarchies gave more and more people the sense of being slotted in somebody else's system under somebody else's control. Hierarchical consciousness was as intimately associated with the rise of the new individualism as self-directed work was with the old. If some people took pride in their jobs, not many associated personal fulfillment with an impersonally structured working world. One of the reasons for the continuing popularity of Edward Bellamy's *Looking Backward* far into the 20th century was its precocious anticipation of this change. Where earlier utopias promised people freedom in their work, Bellamy's promised them freedom from their work—how, in effect, to devote the least number of years to life's most suspect activity. In 19th century dreams, the west was a place where any individual might turn hard work into economic success. In 20th century dreams, the west became a sunny paradise of glamour and ease.

Under the best of circumstances, in other words, realizing one's full humanity required some escape from work. By the 1920s the annual vacation, previously a privilege of the comfortable middle class, became a national norm. Time apart from work in the 19th century was an occasion for self-improvement, for renewal, and for important social obligations, all uses that reflected character and augured even greater success back on the job. The 20th century freed strictly personal time and in the process set it at odds with life's everyday obligations, especially at work. By the standards of the 19th century, time was no more free than work was ever done: evading life's responsibilities only squandered it. Respectable men might take time from work to stretch themselves to the limit—the end-of-the-century vogue of a roughrider manliness was a case in point—but eventually a limit was there. Fulfillment, implying the continuing creation of a new self, yearned for time away from work to break past whatever restrictions kept the new self unborn.

Democracy's individual and collective components, after moving in tandem through the 19th century, uncoupled early in the 20th. As each came to operate in its own context, with a distinct calculus of rights and responsibilities, majoritarian and individual democracy did not necessarily clash with one another. They simply parted company to follow quite separate paths for about half a century.

The 20th century proposition that individuals had a right to serve themselves one by one had little precedent. Democracy in the 19th century held individuals within bounds—family, community, universal law—with a promise that groups and individuals benefited one another through mutual reinforcement. When the European visitor Adam Gurowski described the core of American democracy as a "union of the utmost individual independence with a well-regulated social and political organization," he was reflecting his hosts' sense of a harmony, not a tension. Even critics who might have had reason to dissent agreed. Genuine individual and community "rights never clash or interfere," Elizabeth Cady Stanton declared in 1860; "The progress of social organization has produced a corresponding degree of individualization . . . the fullest individualization that the world has ever seen," Charlotte Perkins Gilman boasted four decades later.[4] In 19th century culture, apparent exceptions, such as the visionary inventor or the lonely abolitionist, were not actually disconnected from the community, only well ahead of it along the path of progress. Their glory came when Americans en masse finally caught up and collectively validated their truths: Fulton's folly as a transportation revolution, sinful slavery as the Civil War.

Despite a progressive tendency to think of citizens as separable, rational beings, each one listening, learning, and judging, democratic theory held individual and community together through the First World War. By the 1920s, however, the new individualism broke open the package and fundamentally altered the nature of public discussion. On the one hand, by redefining a number of reform issues as strictly individual concerns, it contracted the social end of the postwar agenda. On the other hand, by redefining as public matters once considered exclusively private, it expanded the personal end of the postwar agenda.

The rise of psychology as a talisman in all kinds of public affairs marked the arrival of the new age. Nothing made the idea of the People seem more ridiculous than popular theories of behaviorism that pictured humans responding mindlessly to the stimuli around them, or popular versions of Freudianism that pictured them captives of their inborn, unconscious drives. What could 19th century character possibly mean in the face of these forces? Now the human personality

was a battleground where each individual marshaled her own resources in the struggle for fulfillment. Former stalwarts of reform
adapted to modern times. The publication of Mary Richmond's *What
Is Social Case Work* (1922), for instance, signaled the shift in that progressive stronghold from socially shaped goals to psychologically oriented services. Now the individual defined the field.

The fate of public health after the First World War also illustrated
this shift from forest to trees, from society to the individuals compris-
ing it. Between the 1890s and the world war, the formulation of professional standards for medical practice and medical education, the transformation of hospitals from neighborhood charities to rationalized
health providers, the campaigns to eradicate a broad range of dread
disease, the emergence of modern dentistry, the use of public schools
to routinize health habits, the spread of clinics to deliver health services, and the experiments in preventive physical and mental health
combined to produce a sea change in the connections between health
professionals and other Americans. Public health was a field of tremendous promise, with aspirations to instruct the nation in life-
preserving hygiene and to spread its benefits as people's needs required them. If public health suffered from the middle-class urge to
impose its ways on the world, it also expressed a powerful reform
impulse to improve life chances among the poorest Americans. Certainly it was one of progressivism's best responses to the sinking of
the lower class—blacks, immigrants, and native whites alike. As Dr.
Josephine Baker, a leader in the drive to lower infant mortality, declared, "Well-baby clinics should be as free as the public schools."[5]

But America was not kind to its Josephine Bakers. Early in the 1920s,
the field of public health atrophied, as men who were committed to the
private practice of medicine for profit swamped the service-minded
reformers. Major medical schools ignored the field, and the American
Medical Association, once a supporter, abandoned it at about the same
time as it reversed judgment on Prohibition, originally a close companion of the public health movement. What remained were educational
carryovers, voluntary distributions of health information that rarely
fell into the hands of poor people and certainly did nothing for those
who read another language or no language at all. Social insurance, a
staple of public health throughout western Europe, never materialized.
Instead, Americans fended for themselves, family by family, one by
one, and the health care they received reflected their places along a
hierarchy of privileges. Forging ahead in the science of medicine, the
United States dropped to the absolute bottom among industrial nations in combined maternity and infant mortality rates. In many areas,
African Americans had no access at all to modern medicine. "There is

no short road to Justice and Mercy in this Republic," a weary Florence Kelley concluded in 1923.[6]

As issues previously public slipped into a private realm, matters previously private rushed into public view. Beginning around the First World War, in fact, what constituted private became a subject of continual public negotiation. Cinema, raising voyeurism to a national pastime, gave crowds of people the impression that safely in the dark they could peek into the intimate affairs of an almost infinite variety of fascinating people. Magazines exposing the lives of the actresses and actors themselves proliferated. In a host of ways, the lines between private and public fantasies blurred. As official monitors of obscenity such as the old Comstock Law fell in retreat, public debate took their place. Unlike the situation in the 19th century, local values no longer simply determined the matter. Now local differences and national standards interacted to influence one another. Being banned in Boston boosted sales across the country. If it played in New York, why not in Peoria?

The diversity in points of reference for public discussion would have bewildered prewar Americans: Pablo Picasso and Norman Rockwell, the Chicago school of sociology and the Federal Bureau of Investigation, the oedipal drama and the chorus line, the NAACP and the KKK, the American Legion and the American Civil Liberties Union, Hollywood by day and Harlem by night. Little on the extended public agenda of the 1920s had a political outcome, however. Private lives and personal choices were not easy to politicize. Even new subjects with extraordinary potential in public policy usually remained matters for discussion only, options in belief rather than sources for action. Franz Boas's relativistic anthropology, for example, demolished the premises behind Jim Crow without generating a drive among whites to change the laws. If, as Walter Lippmann argued, "the most momentous question of government" was "how to validate our private versions of the political scene," social movements had simply lost all standing.[7]

The abruptness of these changes, a great many of them spreading nationally between 1914 and 1924, cast the new individualism as a generational conflict. Modern ways came in the trappings of youth, and their champions, in Gilman Ostrander's clever term, bowed to the values of "filiarchy." They adopted its fads, spoke its slang, and danced to its tune. Against the reign of youth were arrayed the aging forces of bigotry and repression. In Rollin Kirby's famous cartoons, a gaunt, wizened old Prohibition hovered about to destroy all pleasures. "Sour old women," in Lippmann's phrase, gave virtue a bad name among the young. From the earliest grades, proponents of the new child-centered education insisted, it was imperative to protect pupils

from the deadening effects of aging authority. In this climate, mental
hospitals adopted policies that dumped chronically ill old people into
society's worst custodial bins. The patients of choice were the young
ones, presumably with some prospect of cures.

Many older adults did balk at a leap into the new individualism. At
one extreme, Richard Washburn Child, a prominent American admirer
of Mussolini, deplored youth's new "philosophy of freedom at any
price and irresponsibility at any cost."[8] At another extreme, earnest
progressives who were dedicated to the virtues of hard work, not the
potentialities of creative leisure, showed little sympathy for an expressive individualism. Even reformers as exemplary as Frederic Howe
and Jane Addams participated in film censorship. What possible benefit could Samuel Gompers or Booker T. Washington derive from these
new values? Although Gompers took a young bride at seventy and
Washington got tangled in scandal at a white woman's door, both knew
exactly how to draw maximum advantage from standing behind the
familiar Victorian wall of silence.

How deep a divide the new individualism drove between generations was revealed with particular clarity in women's responses to the
call for sexual freedom: a woman's right to sexual pleasure and her
right to regulate reproduction. Women prominent in public life before
the war turned a cold eye on both causes. Shaping their careers required unwavering self-discipline, a tight emotional control that they
then turned into a crucial political tactic. They presented their causes
as well as themselves in the garb of science, not emotion: factual, dispassionate, anything other than expressive. Although such leaders in
women's causes as Anna Howard Shaw and Charlotte Perkins Gilman
spoke eloquently about the importance of the individual, theirs was
a 19th century version stressing economic independence and social
obligations. They took 19th century democracy's measure of individual
self-determination as their own. Carrie Chapman Catt recalled vowing
as she came of age never to rely on a man for her everyday expenses.
"No self-respecting American woman of the middle classes," the social
reformer Edith Abbott wrote in 1905, "is any longer willing to be supported by her masculine relatives." Moreover, their individual still
functioned symbiotically with society, the two prospering together. Everyone, in Gilman's language, was expected to contribute to "the ever-
nobler forms of life toward which social evolution tends." Specifically,
the woman's responsibility, in Julia Lathrop's phrase, was "carrying on
the life of the race."[9]

These women addressed the subject of sex only under pressure.
Strictly speaking, they believed, it was a man's issue. Gilman, the most
outspoken, judged men's "morbid excess" in sexual activity a curse on

192   CHAPTER EIGHT

humankind, and reformers of both sexes, led by the crusader with the
fairy-tale name, Prince Morrow, adopted that general point of view in
attacking problems of prostitution and recently discovered venereal
diseases. A special session on these topics at the National American
Woman's Suffrage Association annual meeting of 1908 demanded the
suffrage so that women could impose on men the controls that men
did not impose on themselves. If women's sexual instincts homed in
on perpetuating the human race, only coercion turned them into prostitutes. Operating from the assumption of prostitutes as passive vic-
tims, even objects of kidnapping, the major antivice law of the prewar
years, the Mann Act of 1910, penalized the interstate transport of
women for immoral purposes. The White Slavery Act, it was called. A
number of veteran reformers, including Jane Addams and Belle
Moskowitz, contributed to the campaign.

Around wartime, the world turned. The New Woman and the Flap-
per put a fresh emotional openness and sexual interest on display in
movies and theater, literature and the fine arts, photography and advertising, and in public life at large. Indicatively, later studies would
identify a sharp rise in sexual experimentation in the cohort of middle-
class women coming of age between 1915 and 1930. Writings on sex
by the Europeans Ellen Key and Havelock Ellis, which had been
stopped at the gates earlier in the century, now found a ready American audience. As jolting as these new values were on arrival, they were
already absorbed by the mid-1920s. Tracing the transition, Margaret
Sanger, the tenacious crusader for birth control, began it in jail on obscenity charges, only to emerge in the 1920s as the widely admired
founding mother of what eventually became Planned Parenthood. In
both her radical and her respectable phases, Sanger held to the same
objectives: women deserved a full sexual life, not just a well-managed
one, and women should take charge of it. By the 1920s those views
were no longer considered the ravings of a revolutionary; they were
mainstream ideals. Running parallel to Sanger's campaign, another effort to increase women's control over their reproductive lives sought to
relieve the pain in childbirth.

Veterans of an earlier women's movement endorsed none of this.
Among suffragists, one of their leaders recalled, Ellen Key's "very
name was anathema." [10] More than Addams' wartime pacifism eroded
her authority in the 1920s. Hull House, with its citizenship training
and its sedate dancing, stood on the far side of a generation gap from
which she essentially never spoke to the likes of Sanger, Isadora Duncan, or Amelia Earhart. These new feminists understood autonomy not
as a self-denying discipline but as a self-fulfilling quest: the right, in
Crystal Eastman's declaration, to "exercise their infinitely varied gifts

in infinitely varied ways."[11] Sexual expression, in other words, belonged to a larger strategy, one with sweeping implications if for no
other reason than its vision of each woman's separability. She was not
a homemaker for the family or a keeper of the morals or a mother of
the race; she was a distinctive human being. The new individualism,
with its expanding public presence, its deepening emotional reach,
and its automobility, was that strategy.

Looking across the divide, even as generous a spirit as Addams resented what she saw as young women's willingness to sacrifice their
social conscience to selfishness. To the degree this conflict took institutional form, it pitted the handful of officials in Washington and a number of state capitals who continued to push the standard reform programs upstream in a resisting era against the tiny National Woman's
Party, whose hallmark, the Equal Rights Amendment, challenged the
premises beneath those efforts to legislate specific protections for
women. Unquestionably the progressive veterans had greater sensitivity to class differences than the National Woman's Party, which promoted the virtue of occupational hierarchies and refused to acknowledge how much social change came out of the hides of the poor. The
ERA's simple ban on discrimination by sex, however, had other goals
that arose out of the modern ambitions for personal fulfillment: open
up the world and let each woman try what she liked. With the iron-
willed Alice Paul in charge, no one mistook the NWP as a front for the
wild life: it provided a serious, sustained examination of how women's
needs and the new individualism interrelated. Nor did its small size
and meager record make it a failure. The NWP was a weather vane, a
proponent of timely values whose legitimacy, in the spirit of the new
individualism, depended neither on organization nor on politics.

By winding itself through the primary tensions, rifts, and conflicts in
modern society, the new individualism contributed to defining all of
them. Its class origins mattered most of all. Just as surely as the decline
in majoritarian democracy went with the sinking of the lower class, so
the rise of individual democracy went with the emergence of the national class, relying initially on its rationale and authority. Champions
of the new values in the 1920s pictured them functioning hierarchically. Americans were scaled according to their degree of sympathy
with the new freedoms, even their ability to make use of them. As
such harbingers of the new individualism as Van Wyck Brooks and
Sherwood Anderson depicted popular culture, it was the sensitive
soul's ultimate trap: spring it or die in its grip. For a time, a class-
generated aura of escapism hung around the values of personal fulfillment. Artists who wanted to express them and movie stars who

wanted to live them felt impelled to flee into a European exile, an urban bohemia, or a Hollywood castle.

As spokesmen for the national class belittled the sensibilities of people down the hierarchy, they were belittling other people's work. Jobs outside their own class appeared to fall somewhere between dull and deadly dull. Only a fraction of men would continue to work if they could get income some other way, T. V. Smith concluded. "And the proportion would certainly be far less for . . . housewives."[12] For those who had no experience whatsoever inside one, the modern factory epitomized dreary, dehumanizing work, a view immortalized by Fritz Lang's *Metropolis* and Charlie Chaplin's *Modern Times*.

Looking back a few decades to William Morris and the crafts movement, a circle of national critics created an image of what genuinely rewarding manual work entailed. It was a modernized version of 19th century democracy's self-directed work—now, for the modern age, fulfilling work—that could satisfy the inner man through its intimate, personally mediated connections among raw materials, tools, and products. What greater violence to this vision—to Thorstein Veblen's imagined instinct for workmanship, for instance—than the assembly line. Down the years charges of this nature echoed in repeated national-class attacks on the "de-skilling" of employees. It was a problem more easily deplored than defined, one that critics rarely tried to see from the point of view of the workers. Sometimes the sheer scale of factory machinery seemed its greatest sin.

Dull people went with dull jobs. National-class critics embedded their pictures of demeaning work in cultures of futility. In Elmer Rice's *The Adding Machine* (1923) Mr. Zero, a routine white-collar functionary, was still Mr. Zero in afterlife. The white-collar world looked much the same in Kenneth Fearing's account:

> And wow he died as wow he lived,
> Going whop to the office and blooie
>   home to sleep and biff got married
>   and bam had children and off got fired,
> Zowie did he live and zowie did he die.[13]

Salesmen fared no better. Sinclair Lewis's *Babbitt* (1922) provided a byword for lives lost in verbal vacuity. A quarter of a century later in *Death of a Salesman* (1949), Arthur Miller's caricature of local middle-class aspirations, Willy Loman's destructive individualism desolated everyone he loved.

It required no special wit for local Americans to recognize what was being done to them. It was equally clear that they were engaged in real conflict: middle-class and national-class values were sharply different.

Nevertheless, few middle-class Americans cared to deny themselves all the pleasures of the new: *modern* had a happy, hopeful ring in almost all of local America. Theirs was a challenge in management. Even as middle-class Americans pursued their own dreams of fulfillment, they continued to build lives around their reputation in a human-scale environment of family, friends, church, and work—the elements of old-fashioned character. How might they import what they wanted without losing control inside those personal worlds?

The usual answers lay in endlessly adjusted, locally regulated compromises. Cosmetics, one useful index to the new individualism, offered a case in point. Between the 19th century norms, where bad women painted their cheeks and good ones pinched them, and the modern standards of personal experiment and expression, local-class families created an array of middle grounds: they would decide when a daughter first tried a cosmetic, how much a nice woman used and how much made her a tramp. It mattered less that these rules tossed in the seas of subjectivity—from family to family, community to community, and time to time—than that rules were always there and regularly articulated as reminders of control.

The new individualism offered people in the lower class modern democracy's best promise, and they took what they could get from it. By and large, nationally sponsored leisure activities, in movies or retail chains or print media, imposed fewer restrictions on lower-class choices than the locally controlled alternatives, whether in small towns or city neighborhoods. Cars and radios added critical range to lower-class lives. Poor families did not refuse rural electrification. If the national class imagined factory jobs as individualism lost, countless wage earners decided otherwise. Less enervating than a fruit harvest, less dangerous than a coal mine, less body-breaking than a timber run, the modern factory was good work for anybody in the lower class who could get it.

Though severely restricted by caste and poverty, African Americans, too, drew what they could from the new individualism. As public aspiration, however, it made little headway among a black bourgeoisie. A wife respectably at home remained the mark of the successful African American family, and collective rights the persistent national demand of the most prominent black organizations. In the 20th as in the 19th century, black men had compelling reasons for seeing public oppression as the crux of their problems and a unified response as the indispensable first step to justice. The fact that Marcus Garvey drew inspiration for his vision of black pride from Booker T. Washington's narrative of self-help suggested how intimately the collective and the personal were interlaced. Nevertheless, in the racial self-determination of Garveyism or in the legal equality of the NAACP, individuals continued to find their meaning inside the African American community.

For women, on the other hand, whose immediate and highest hurdles were their private disabilities, the new individualism was irresistible. Simply to have the stature of an autonomous person in those realms where the new individualism spread—choices in sex and reproduction, appearance and entertainment, the world's vices as well as its virtues—was a revolutionary step. It offered vast and enticing answers to the perennial question of women's movements: what enabled a woman to stand on her own two feet, fully upright? Despite impressive progress in opening new areas of work early in the century, paying her own bills was not enough. Whatever her social class, on the job she was second class. Nor was the vote sufficient. As such superb petitioners as Jane Addams and Florence Kelley lost their authority, politics became even more a man's game after the war than it had been before. What made the new individualism so radical was that ultimately each person defined it and sought it on her own. At work and in politics, the bosses were men. Fulfillment, however, would be hers, not his.

Early in the century men were sensing the danger. After each advance in her rights, the perceptive Frances Squire Potter observed, men in authority roused themselves with "the vague feeling that [woman] has been allowed to get on too fast ... while the good man slept."[14] The White Slavery Act of 1910 expressed concerns not just about too many loose women but about too many women on the loose, too many divorcées and single wage earners, too many women fashioning their own lives. Where women struck out on their own, men followed with advice. Had women grown obsessed with sex? Were they snaring their sons in oedipal complexes? Nothing was more suspect than a woman's natural impulses, male experts warned. Drawing on an accumulation of such advice, *Infant Care,* the immensely popular guide distributed by the United States Children's Bureau, provided a step-by-step corrective to natural motherhood.

As sexual freedoms expanded, men always seemed a step or two ahead. National-class animus toward Victorian prudery—the successful campaign against Prohibition, for example, or the enlightened view that slum living held no special dangers for women—actually infused new life into the rights of men at the expense of women, including greater freedom to batter them. In this modern age, wives learned that if they wanted their husbands' affection, the sexual game never ended. The new values arrived along with a gigantic cosmetics industry, including beauty parlors to apply them. Nor could the modern woman escape the commandment to remain forever youthful. By solidifying

20th century norms of female slimness as well as the dieting to maintain it, the 1920s set in motion what became a familiar whipsaw of enticement and derision. As older women tried to be young, biology undermined them, dress styles exposed them, and the new dances positively popped their joints. They had no better luck if they acted their age. The men shaping Hollywood images ridiculed older women who expressed sexual interests and stereotyped as vamps the younger ones who took the sexual initiative. It was as if women's every move elicited a countermove. In 1921, as the Equal Rights Amendment was unveiled, the first Miss America was crowned.

Here was the new individualism as hegemony, with millions of ordinary Americans participating in their own subjugation—or at least their own marginalization—as they internalized the values of the atomized consumer. As an activity common to all, modern consumerism offered a new understanding of citizenship, one that gathered people into a society without demanding anything in particular either of them or of their society. It acculturated and equalized without affecting differences and inequalities. In fact, much about the new individualism denied the legitimacy of posing questions as social problems, and those means of general communication most characteristic of the new era commonly played to that tendency, validating existing hierarchies in the process. Advertising spread benign images of wage earners and office workers smiling in neat rows by their machines. As movies, radio, and everyday national slang demeaned African Americans, they were made to seem fit for exactly the places they filled. Outside the Native American nations, the most familiar Indian was a dead Indian.

In some ways, the new consumerism was not that new. Even though household electrification and a combination of inexpensive cars and paved roadways did give the 1920s special qualities, the patterns of modern consumerism had been forming since the late 19th century. What did make the war years a dividing line was the reconception of the consumer world as a highly personal domain, equipped to deal with an indeterminately expanding range of human needs. At the beginning of the 20th century, even advertisers treated consumers as social beings whose community values their products exemplified. As progressives used the term, consumers helped to shape economic and social policy: Louis Brandeis's consumer demanded lower tariffs and railroad rates; Florence Kelley's employed boycotts in the cause of social justice. In a rough sense, these consumers were the People, adapting themselves to the marketplace and serving the whole society much as patriotic tea boycotters had before the American Revolution.

Around the First World War, advertisers consciously shifted their attention from the careful buyer seeking information to the unfulfilled buyer seeking realization. By the 1920s, these new values of inner satisfaction informed a national consumer culture that issued increasingly standard messages from a few central places. Quite suddenly, hegemony was a plausible charge. Consumers were encouraged to believe not in rational choices but in infinite choices, not in good and bad products but in a vast array of products through which individuals, selection by selection, crafted themselves. Consuming to create selves located the reasons for a decision in the purchaser, not in the product. People did not use products as much as products transformed people. Surely, an uncomfortable Joseph Wood Krutch grumbled, someone is not "twice as happy when moving at the rate of fifty miles an hour as he would be if he were proceeding at only half that speed."[15] Why not? Who knew? The scheme had enormous potential for manipulation.

At the same time, the new individualism was 20th century democracy's wild card. If products transformed people, just as certainly people transformed products. On the loose in the marketplace, consumer goods were what people made of them As a matter of course, women combined the standardized clothing, cosmetics, and decorations around them into personal statements. As long as changing styles suited expressiveness, they responded. No advertising campaign on the face of the earth, however, could have forced them back into those billowing prewar folds of cloth. Whatever the origins of a rather hazy, essentially deracinated ideal in the African American beauty industry, black women made it serve African American ends—an expensive and painful beauty culture, perhaps, but strictly their own. Only whites saw it as off-white. Most striking of all, once industries performed the miracle of lighting the nighttime city, users took charge, releasing imaginations to play in the glitter and greed of a genuinely new world, creating and re-creating their own cultures of the street, their own purposes for commercial establishments, their own communities in side street bohemias. *Nightlife* really was the people's choice.

The subversive qualities of the new individualism might seem utterly innocuous at first, as they did when it sidled gingerly into alliance with the national government. Who could have expected those traditional antagonists to generate much of anything? Since the time of the American Revolution, free citizens had looked upon distant governments as natural predators and thrown up bills of rights as a defense against them. Even as the sense of threat weakened in the 19th century— how could the People's own government abuse them?—overweening authorities remained the most likely enemy of individual liberties and political decentralization every white man's best protection against it.

Authoritarianism raised these stakes dramatically in the 1920s and 1930s. In Italy and Germany, as well as in many smaller nations, dictators overpowered the democrats and used the government to snuff out freedoms. Not only did visions of goose-stepping soldiers and saluting masses violate a traditional American individualism; companion images struck directly at the new individualism's sensitivity to private pleasures and personal choices: officials boarding up theaters, crowds burning books, stormtroopers smashing into homes. If in the broadest sense Adolf Hitler and Josef Stalin demonstrated the irrelevance of the individual by ruling entire populations expendable, in the narrowest sense their governments seemed to leave no place for the lone dissenter to survive: *Darkness at Noon*, in Arthur Koestler's terrifying metaphor. To replace the traditional nightmare of a tyrant taking away the people's liberty came the modern one of a totalitarian government crushing each citizen's individuality. It was the simple stark antithesis of individual fulfillment: the destruction of people's inner lives.

Meanwhile, white Americans were accumulating a body of evidence about official oppressions at home. In the formative years of 20th century democracy—and the Bolshevik Revolution—during and just after the First World War, national and state governments alike swung wildly at all kinds of deviants. These repressions shocked some progressives sufficiently that they later opposed aggressive government under the New Deal as the same old wolf gussied up in reform clothing. Many liberals as well as conservatives experienced Prohibition as a contest between ham-handed government and free citizens, and the red tape of the Second World War as a behemoth bureaucracy's violations of personal liberty.

The standard recourse in the 19th century was a decentralized federalism, setting state and local against national power. For the new national class, however, that strategy no longer worked. By definition their national problems required national solutions. Instead of turning away from Washington, modern defenders of the individual looked within it for a more sympathetic center of power—a balance—and they found their answer in the federal courts. Despite precedents from Reconstruction, the thought of the least popular branch of the most distant government functioning as a bastion of democratic rights would have boggled minds in the old white fraternity. For similar reasons, however, it suited the national class quite well. It promised uniformity, it honored a hierarchy of power, and it presumed that the best trained minds would resolve issues free from popular pressures. Using the courts as a brake on elective government went nicely with the growing concerns about majoritarian dangers to democratic rights, an oxymoron in the 19th century that became national-class dogma in the 20th.

Nobody rushed to revolutionize judicial policies in behalf of the democratic individual. During the 1920s and 1930s the courts were no more than cautiously responsive. Nevertheless, in various combinations moderates and conservatives collaborated, first, to protest the national executive's expansive use of wartime emergency powers and, second, to explore ways of stretching the Bill of Rights across state and local affairs by tucking it into the Fourteenth Amendment, which could conceivably cover all arbitrary assaults on an individual's life and liberty. No better evidence of the greatness of Justice Oliver Wendell Holmes, Jr., exists than his ability in his eighties to reckon with these modern needs. Just after the war he was still working from standard 19th century premises: majorities had a "natural right" to silence opinions they found abhorrent.[16] Then under prodding from the precocious law professor Felix Frankfurter and Judge Learned Hand—exemplary representatives of the new national class both—he reconsidered. The upshot was his pivotal pronouncement in *Gitlow v. New York* (1925) drawing First Amendment rights into the Fourteenth and thereby placing federal courts between individuals and oppressive government at any level. Two years later, a safely conservative Supreme Court based its first decision on the Holmes principle.

Still, not much happened. In *Palko v. Connecticut* (1937), Justice Benjamin Cardozo laid down the broad principle that would go unchallenged for another decade: under the Fourteenth Amendment, federal courts would protect those guarantees in the Bill of Rights that were essential to "a scheme of ordered liberty." A year later, in a footnote to an otherwise routine decision in *U.S. v. Carolene Products,* another of the moderates, Justice Harlan Fiske Stone, suggested that in the future the Bill of Rights, along with the political rights of minorities, might receive the Court's special attention. But most footnotes, after all, remain buried. Only the swelling importance of individual democracy could float this one into the mainstream.

What the judiciary contributed from the start—what gave even these bits and pieces of precedent a subversive potential—was the universality of court-made law. Whatever the class bias of their origins, the flatness, the indiscriminate coverage of these constitutional rulings on a citizen's rights kept open the possibility of demanding that public policy abide by a uniform law, that in a social system designed to distribute benefits hierarchically, public policy actually protect the rights of all individuals equally. If the term *general welfare* were ever to achieve comprehensive coverage, by far its most promising prospects in

America lay with those principles that rested on the inviolable rights of every citizen, that is, with assumptions about fairness and justice that drew their strength not from the collective conscience of the community but from 20th century democracy's vibrant side, its search for individual fulfillment.

||||||

CHAPTER 9

THE STATE

|||||| The modern individual's growing reliance on government marked a shift with momentous consequences: the state replaced the People as democracy's last resort. According to the assumptions behind 19th century democracy, not only did the People come together to decide basic questions through elections; popular decision-making in its many varieties simultaneously provided a loose, welcoming context for individual achievement. The benefits taken from government back into private life—land, above all—had a powerful influence on individual opportunity, but the operations of the government itself did not. With governments small and pliable, it was not unreasonable to think of them as the People acting, and if the People themselves were the government, no state worthy of the name existed.

Even the government expansion dating from the Civil War did not seriously affect this sense of plasticity. At the national level certain activities that had been left to the discretion of states and localities were now regularized. For example, wartime laws set rules for a new class of national banks on such matters as reserve holdings and currency issuing. But regularizing, as a host of 19th century institutions ranging from Protestant revivals to elementary education illustrated, had no necessary connection with centralizing or bureaucratizing public policy. Hence as late as 1891 the Populist William Peffer could still invoke the standard image of a government waiting for its citizens' instructions. Government—even one that owned important means of transportation and exchange—was not "some foreign entity," he argued; "in truth it is simply the agent of the people . . . Now, then, let the people, through their agent the Government, build such railroads as they need for their own use."[1]

As the People dissolved, the state thrived. The same early 20th century reformers who thought of citizens as individuals under their tutelage and who promoted ways for them to vote one by one in private also advocated dramatic extensions of state power. Unlike the Civil War banking acts, for instance, the Federal Reserve Act of 1913 did create the mechanism for a national financial policy, even if its headquarters shifted from time to time between New York and Washington. Riding a momentum of centralization that spread everywhere during the First World War, governments at all levels with substantially larger budgets institutionalized new centers of power to cover more and more aspects of public policy—nationally in new areas of agriculture and forestry, communication and transportation, mining and manufacturing, domestic retailing and foreign trade, and much more as well. As the modern state solidified, it filled the spaces that a disintegrating People vacated, then rolled on to create empires of its own.

The new state not only adapted to the hierarchies developing in the society around it; it devised a hierarchical universe of its own. A significant part of progressive politics was a sorting out of ambitious groups in search of their most advantageous positions in the government's tiers. To the extent anything in 20th century democracy replaced the 19th century sense of the People in action—the old policymaking public opinion—it was a proliferation of lobbies and pressure groups that by the 1920s were configured in a recognizably modern way throughout the governing process.

Some of the pulling and hauling of the progressive years separated interest groups between national and local politics: the NAACP committed itself to a national presence, for example, while the misnamed National Urban League stuck to local alliances. Synthetic national identities—Italian, Polish, Swedish, or the like, all of them creations of American life—experienced a surge in popularity, partly because those groupings were already there when the People dissolved and partly because of the passions generated by a world war. After the frenzy over the Versailles Treaty, however, they diffused throughout local America, even spilling into lower-class life. Organizations such as the Anti-Saloon League and the National Association of Manufacturers served prominent local constituents who continued to find national affairs alien even as they stuck stubbornly to beliefs about what national government should do. Some groups gave specific issues such single-minded attention that they laid claim to pieces of public policy as their property rights. The American Farm Bureau Federation and other more specialized agricultural associations sedulously promoted that impression in farm politics. Other groups only existed in the imagination—following the passage of the Nineteenth Amendment, a women's bloc, for example.

The unorganized fell to the bottom of these hierarchies: no group, no voice. At best, atomized citizens became the political cartoonist's beleaguered, befuddled John Q. Public, honest enough but utterly lost in the intricacies of modern government. Whatever inhibited association undermined power. By making American Indians citizens of the United States, for example, a law in 1924 encouraged them to abandon their tribes and scatter. At the same time, government officials were strongly discouraging sign language among the deaf—a distinctive, bonding connection—in favor of ostensibly normal means of oral communication that would disperse them into the crowd.

The vote alone seemed insignificant, creating the apparent paradox of a single vote's greater importance in the collective democracy of the 19th century than in its individualistic 20th century counterpart. The ultimate value of a person's vote, some modern pundits seriously argued, lay in the possibility that it might, after all, make the critical difference in a hairbreadth election—a chance so remote it disappeared into sheer fantasy. Certainly large numbers found no incentive at all to vote. Beginning in the 1920s, the electorate separated very roughly into thirds: one-third voted regularly; one-third moved in and out of the electorate; one-third never voted. The approximate third who cast ballots in the pivotal election of 1946, when conservatives amassed sufficiently large majorities to override President Harry Truman's veto and thereby to reshape public policy, constituted the committed core. The 63 percent turnout in the presidential election of 1960, when John Kennedy slipped past Richard Nixon, included perhaps the highest proportion of in-and-outers since 1920.

By all accounts, the third who did not participate tended to be poor, the youngest and oldest adult cohorts, and, less predictably, women. During the heart of the 20th century the combined weight of these factors had a remarkably consistent effect on turnouts. With the mean turnout in all presidential elections 1900–1988 at 59.2 percent, the comparable percentage for 1928–40 was 59.4 and 1944–60 59.6. Some shifting from year to year did nothing to shake the steady long-term trend.

The movements toward centralization and hierarchy swept up political parties in their course. Turnouts drastically lower than their 19th century counterparts reflected no weakening of the parties, only their adaptation to a scheme of things where lower turnouts made sense. Until after midcentury, party loyalties remained quite strong among those who still participated in the electoral process. Party organization tightened. Changes in electoral procedures around the turn of the century—the Australian ballot, direct primaries, and the like—came through the major parties, not at odds with them, and did no damage to the new concentration of power in central party headquarters. State-controlled ballots, for instance, eliminated the aggravation of last minute, local challenges to the party ticket.

In the 20th century, American democracy changed from labor-intensive to capital-intensive. Big government contained big prizes. If great wealth exhausted itself chasing all but a few objectives in the diffuse 19th century, it had less and less trouble finding its targets in the centralizing 20th. The wider the range and the larger the scale of government activities, the more money could buy, and the size of the favors purchased through bribery, direct or indirect, grew exponentially from the corruption in Grant's administration during the 1870s to the Harding scandals of the 1920s to influence-peddling in the Truman years after the Second World War. The major parties reoriented to fit a capital-intensive system. Rather than haphazardly tapping a few business nabobs, as even the most famous of the late 19th century campaign managers, Matthew Quay and Mark Hanna, had done, full-time national committees, products of the transition years early in the 20th century, systematically gathered in money on a national scale. Though Republicans led the way in modern fund-raising, the Democrats, inspired particularly by John J. Raskob of General Motors, more or less caught up by 1928.

Campaigning and financing changed together. In the 19th century it required extraordinary efforts, year after year, to energize such a decentralized political process. With so much dependent on the self-starting behavior of countless, scattered voters, nobody's money carried influence very far. Lucky strikes—buying just the right group of Indiana voters to turn an election—occurred rarely. A number of astute commentators noted these severe limitations on transferring economic into political power; in a particularly telling image, Alexander Mackay pictured the democratic politician and the successful businessman meeting in the mid-19th century on "neutral ground."[2]

Instead of thousands upon thousands of personal arrangements, nickel-and-dime bargains, and voluntary labors, 20th century politics came increasingly to rely on strategic investments. An advertising style in electoral politics, where central messages served in lieu of a small army of block captains, first appeared around the First World War, then spread more and more generally with each decade. Implicit in the new campaigning was an assumption that votes could now be purchased on an unprecedented scale. In the 19th as in the 18th century, the greatest single danger of corruption lay in bribing officials by the score; in the 20th, buying voters by the millions. In two ways the New Deal focused these modern concerns. First, enemies charged that through public relief programs, particularly the Works Progress Administration, liberal Democrats were paying for the votes to perpetuate themselves in power. Second, the astonishing success of Franklin Roosevelt's radio addresses conjured images of a party cozying up to the voters and manipulating minds in the comfort of their own living rooms. In the emerging age of television around midcentury, Republicans even more quickly than Democrats recognized the huge potential for capital-intensive campaigning in this new medium.

Citizens made quite different attachments to these centralized parties than voters had to the decentralized 19th century version. For one thing, modern parties were more distinct and separated. They no longer sprawled across America's social spaces, interacting with whatever voluntary associations they encountered: 20th century parties were usually here; other organizations, lodges, and clubs there. By the same token, they functioned less often as a citizen's primary source of personal identification, merging as they had in the 19th century with church, ethnicity, work, and public service into a composite meaning of a man's life.

One reason for these narrower and shallower party loyalties in the 20th century was their more private, atomizing characteristics. Unlike the social politics of the 19th century, the new advertising styles of campaigning tended to reach people one by one: no group connectedness, no collective reinforcement. Fragmentation primarily affected those most in need of encouragement to join the political process. The lower class, as Maurice Duverger pointed out years ago, always has greater need than the well-to-do for a mobilizing political party. By and large, America's 20th century parties simply shaped their operations to the disappearance of the bottom third.

In very broad terms, the national bureaucracy acquired its modern form in the 1920s: a layer of offices where public officials and private interests negotiated problems of mutual concern, economic area by economic area; and a higher administrative circle where competing policy areas thrashed out their differences. Ordinary citizens, one by one, had no access to these offices, no legitimate business with their government, and increasingly elaborate security procedures barred them from the premises. Citizens were cast in the role of tourists. As early as the 1930s, the Federal Bureau of Investigation enjoyed unusual popularity for the first-class show it offered its streams of visitors.

Herbert Hoover, with a passion for simple, functional bureaucracy, was spiritual father in the 1920s to America's first integrated national governing arrangement, one that encouraged business groups, collaborating with an array of specialized Washington offices, to systematize segments of the economy. What Hoover's New Era modeled, Roosevelt's New Deal expanded and refined. It would be absurd to minimize the differences in policy, mood, and leadership between the two administrations: millions of Americans understood. But popular participation in government was not one of them. Despite the image of an approachable president and his open government, New Deal decisions occurred even more commonly than ever behind Washington's closed doors. Indicatively, no important study of democracy appeared in the 1930s; Thurman Arnold's *Folklore of American Capitalism* (1937), often cited as the New Deal's most significant commentary on government, derisively dismissed the very thought of popular rule.

The number of specialized government agencies, growing substantially in the 1930s, exploded during the Second World War. Overall coordination was no longer a possibility. Policy itself fragmented into a multitude of exclusive dialogues among administrative officials, congressional committees, and powerful citizens. By the 1940s it was quite common for the same cluster of officials and citizens to write a law in private, then execute it in private, with just a quick public peek into the process as it was enacted. Few laws were designed for more than a tiny minority to comprehend. In the 19th century, democracy measured public policy against a universalist standard, an ideal of one land policy or one corporate policy for all. Separate laws for separate groups automatically suggested corruption. The model for the mid-20th century was the diametric opposite, a constellation of specific policies tailored to suit each of innumerable group needs: a policy for cotton, for instance, another for wheat, another for dairying, and so on. In this scheme uniformity, by definition, meant inequity.

As a national bureaucracy insulated domestic affairs from popular influence, basic foreign policy issues slipped even farther away from the public. Early in the 20th century the common wisdom assigned popular pressure a shaping influence—especially a limiting one—on the nation's international involvements. In 1916, Woodrow Wilson's reelection was widely attributed to the responsiveness of his neutrality policy to popular sentiment. The defeat of his League of Nations four years later, many said, marked one of those moments when public opinion—disillusioned, cautious, selfish—determined a critical turn in the nation's history. The many attempts during the 1920s and 1930s to insulate the United States from future wars—by outlawing them through treaty, by disarming, by tightening the nation's neutrality laws—all were understood as indices to the way popular attitudes set a general course in foreign policy.

By 1938, however, with war already blazing in Asia and now threatening in Europe, that long-running interplay between public participation and private decision-making broke down. The pivotal event of that year was the close defeat in Congress of the so-called Ludlow Amendment to subject a declaration of war abroad to popular vote. Drawing on a plan first broached in 1914 and once identified with William Jennings Bryan and Robert LaFollette, Sr., it stayed on the fringes of public discussion until 1936, when a fresh campaign for it produced a rush of popular support. One poll registered almost three out of four adults in its favor. Opposition to the Ludlow Amendment centered in the executive branch, which successfully lobbied to block it in Congress and which within a year began weaving a pattern of secret international decisions leading into war. The executive's clandestine maneuvering simply grew much more elaborate after December 1941.

Franklin Roosevelt had ample precedent, of course: Lincoln and Wilson also suspended democratic rules in the face of war. This time, however, the wartime moratorium in foreign affairs became permanent. After 1945, the cold war evolved in the midst of much anger and recrimination but with only scattered and abbreviated public debates over policy. As the United States revolutionized its international commitments with a global band of treaties, public discussion played almost no role in the process. Appropriately, the cadre of unelected officials who defined national security policy during these years expressed disdain for politicians as a breed and distrust of anyone in the governing process who was responsive to popular sentiment. Their crucial document, NSC 68, explained how to secure the United States by nondemocratic means. As these changes unfolded, the executive branch monopolized the information that was crucial in understanding international affairs, chose between supporting or overturning foreign governments, and deployed military forces in response to international challenges. Decisions to produce thermonuclear weapons—decisions, that is, with the potential to destroy life on earth—were state secrets.

At midcentury the Korean War institutionalized both the nation's cold war policies and the government apparatus to implement them. Entering it on Truman's orders, which Congress never officially ratified, completed what Arthur Schlesinger, Jr., has called "the capture by the Presidency of the most vital of national decisions, the decision to go to war."[3] The tunneling among the government's public-private decision-making nodes crisscrossed into what President Dwight Eisenhower, then everyone else, called a military-industrial complex. To ordinary citizens these centers of power became a bunkered state, impassably remote. As Samuel Huntington, political scientist and government adviser, put it, "hierarchy, coercion, secrecy, and decep-

tion" joined the "inescapable attributes" of a great power.[4] Appropriately, that key term—*great power*—denoted only what the state could
do in world affairs, never how it was decided to do it. As recompense,
the modern state offered *security*, a goal sufficiently elusive that it fueled an ever-greater demand for itself and for the means to achieve it.
The vastness of the problem deepened the sense of public helplessness
and dependence. It became the state's charge to save democracy—if
necessary, to save it from itself. In Lincoln's day, the government was
expected to enact the People's will; now it was supposed to look after
the people's needs.

Explaining the modern state as it evolved fell largely to spokesmen
for the national class, who felt comfortable with large-scale managerial
government and who spread before the public the policies to achieve
it. During the 1920s the very meaning of public policy changed to take
on broad responsibilities for a smooth running, comprehensive economy. Here Hoover was the class prophet, drumming incessantly on the
importance of rationalized manufacturing and distributing systems
and the need for reliable support from financiers, professionals, and
employees. Alert Americans learned a new language: national income,
the federal budget, coordinated marketing, national trade associations.
Because Hoover and his associates seemed to be working from the
fundamental principles of scientific efficiency, their economic predictions carried a new authority. Instead of mere flights of rhetoric, they
became determinate promises of prosperity.

To concentrate on what they considered important—economic policies—national-class leaders set about eliminating from the federal
agenda what they considered distracting: moral and cultural policies.
Before the First World War, Americans with a more integrated sense
of their society used the growing power of the state to influence a wide
spectrum of public issues. In a number of southern states, for example,
new laws early in the 20th century banned from public spaces various
forms of rowdiness—drunkenness, swearing, cockfighting, and the
like. The sentiment for national prohibition grew with the expansion
of governments. In the world of the national class, however, moral and
cultural matters belonged to the private realm of the individual by
the 1920s. The intrusion of public policy into those areas impinged on
personal rights, its spokesmen argued, just as the intrusion of private
issues into public policy disrupted good government.

Prostitution, only recently the nub of a nationwide debate over white
slavery and uncontrolled lust, was filed away as a subsection under
political boodle, organized crime, and infectious diseases. A decline
in "country life," the lament of a presidential commission before the

war, no longer had resonance in national circles; now farmers had mar-keting problems. National journals excoriated the cultural politics of the Ku Klux Klan and deplored attacks on the Catholicism of the Dem-ocratic presidential aspirant, Al Smith. "It is old-fashioned in these days, isn't it, to mention religion," a veteran of the settlement move-ment realized in 1930.[5] To battle the Eighteenth Amendment, the most disruptive of all these issues, corporate leaders founded the Associa-tion against the Prohibition Amendment, which then rallied support from an urban network of professionals, businessmen, and parallel women's organizations. The American Medical Association, once an advocate of Prohibition, retreated in embarrassment. When the Twenty-first Amendment cancelled the Eighteenth in 1933, national-class voices everywhere cried good riddance.

As national-class leaders defined the boundaries of legitimate policy, they made everything else in public life dependent on overarching eco-nomic programs. The Great Depression only sharpened these priorit-ies. If traditional moral and cultural criteria had no place in setting policies, for instance, they had no place in selecting policymakers ei-ther. What distinguished the next generation of Washington insiders, an unprecedented mixture of Protestant, Jewish, and Catholic New Dealers, was their professional training, their economic conception of public issues, and their easy acceptance of the government's responsi-bility for national management.

But the managers did not bring back prosperity. Staking everything on recovery, they risked losing everything—including their right to govern—in an unrelieved depression. There was always an alternative to national-class management, a commonsense economics that drew on 19th century traditions of antimonopoly, land, and currency reform, expressed local American values, and bubbled invitingly around the edges of national policy. In 1934 and 1935, a half decade after the Great Crash, these economic formulas with their readily grasped solutions soared in popularity: in particular, Huey Long's Share Your Wealth, with a flat tax on the rich and homesteads for all; Francis Townsend's revolving old-age pensions with promises to restart the entire econ-omy; Father Charles Coughlin's inflationary panaceas; and Upton Sin-clair's EPIC—End Poverty in California—campaign.

The pivot in the contest over economic policy lay with America's local middle class, whose representatives governed almost everywhere below the national level and whose votes dominated elections at all levels. No doubt the prolonged failure of national-class management gave popular economics considerable appeal in their ranks. Neverthe-less, as Republican and Democratic politicians alike made the case for them, local Americans had little taste for high-risk policies. Instead, they sought assurances of two kinds. First, they wanted a sufficiently steady flow of economic help—in different forms to different ends for different groups of them, but still consistent help—to sustain local economies that no longer functioned on their own. Second and equally important, they insisted on maintaining control over local life. How to combine the two was by no means self-evident. Little of anything might survive without national help, but national help with national rules might destroy much of what local leaders were trying to save, a fear especially strong among that significant proportion of the local middle class—some Republicans, some Democrats—who were deeply suspicious of Washington's high-powered, multiethnic New Dealers.

In a simple yet fundamental arrangement worked out in the middle of the decade—the compromise of the 1930s—national- and local-class leaders traded support and reaffirmed realms of authority. National government would increase its economic assistance for local America; local politicians would remain loyal to the existing national parties. Members of the national class would set broad economic policy; members of the local middle class would set the rules in their own localities, including many of the decisions about how federal monies would be allocated.

Major laws in 1935, including an expanded and consolidated Social Security and a Works Progress Administration that absorbed a third of the federal budget, provided symbol and substance of a fresh commitment to local American needs. After a brief experiment in nationally designed relief programs in the winter of 1934–35, which local leaders fought step by step to control, future administrators of relief rarely challenged local authority. By itself, WPA sent a rush of life-giving money into local America without disrupting local standards. The Tennessee Valley Authority, with a large, vague potential for multi-purpose planning in its region, looked initially like a bombshell of intrusions. By the late 1930s, however, TVA was safely attuned not to the wishes of the grass roots but, in Phillip Selznick's felicitous term, to those of the "grass tops"—the local elites. Some later commentators thought the heart of the matter was a bargain between the New Deal and the urban machines. In fact, the same basic approach covered farm supports as well as blue-collar relief, the south and the west as well as the north, and counties, towns, and small cities as well as major metropolitan areas.

These arrangements constituted one of the major political compromises in American history. In the short run, they translated into Roosevelt's triumphant reelection in 1936, with its sweeping repudiation of Long-Townsend popular economics in favor of the New Deal's ongoing economic leadership. But the compromise, which remained the norm in politics and government for the balance of the 20th century, soon became bipartisan: Republicans as well as Democrats had to reckon with the same tensions between national policy and local rule. In the 1930s and 1940s, as city governments across the country bureaucratized the modern range of services that outside support enabled them to provide, whichever party held office had a deep vested interest in turning national resources to local ends. Around midcentury, no political leader was more enthusiastic about the main lines of the compromise than the Republican Eisenhower.

Because many local middle-class leaders operated effectively at the state level and national-class leaders increasingly thought just in terms of Washington, the compromise sometimes looked like constitutional federalism in action: class politics doubling as federal politics. Time after time, class leaders set the boundaries of their domains in federal terms. In 1938, for example, when Roosevelt launched a national attack on Democratic opponents in Maryland, South Carolina, and Georgia, his enemies turned their state parties into impregnable fortresses that defeated the president's candidates without ever requiring a popular vote. It mattered not at all that the health of each of these state parties depended on benefits from Washington. State politics was local middle-class territory; there national-class New Dealers were intruders. The battle between Eisenhower and Senator Robert Taft of Ohio for the Republican nomination in 1952 drew a particularly clear line in a number of states between Eisenhower's national-class sponsors and the Taft organization's reliance on local middle-class support. After the general won the presidency, however, he either took those original Eisenhower Republicans to Washington with him or he dumped them in favor of Taft loyalists, because only the Taft Republicans had the local middle-class connections to make state politics work. Indeed, their state leadership was indispensable to the compromise.

Old and new policies alike came to nestle comfortably within the compromise. Farm organizations smoothed the edges of federal agricultural policy to fit local interests. TVA settled in for the long haul as a white southern institution, with its national-class technical corps instructed under the "partnership principle" to accommodate local leaders in Rotary and the chambers of commerce. The wartime draft, with enormous potential for conflict, generated remarkably little fuss: national criteria, local interpretation. The FBI concentrated on catching isolated gangsters and identifying possible subversives rather than attacking organized crime, which was tightly, painfully bound into local middle-class life.

From one angle of vision, the compromise leagued national and local middle classes against America's multiethnic, multiracial, unskilled lower class. By reinforcing local power, then leaving it to its own devices, the compromise helped to cap eruptions of protest from migratory workers in California, tenant farmers in the southwest, and other marginal laborers elsewhere. In the cities and the countryside alike, ethnic and racial distinctions remained critical to the distribution of federal benefits. In some cases, federal relief brought urban political machines back from the dead. At harvest time in the cotton south, when landowners needed an abundance of cheap black labor, the WPA ceased to function.

Under the compromise a familiar old alliance of Washington bureaucrats and local allies reasserted its dominance over Native American affairs and closed out the hopes of the enthusiastic New Dealer John Collier. For a time through the Indian Reorganization Act of 1934, Collier brought the freshest breeze of the century into this dank area of federal policy by championing the principles of Native American cultural integrity and tribal self-government. No doubt he remained a white paternalist. Nonetheless, his values stood sharply at odds even with such liberals as Henry A. Wallace, who—just down the hall, as it were—published this appalling statement in 1934: "The Indians, wild animals and disease of [America's next frontier] are the forces of prejudice, fear, greed and suspicion"; civilization would eradicate the new dangers as it had the old.[6] By the end of the decade, Collier's light was eclipsed, and Washington's policy slipped gradually into its old ways. Early in the 1940s, the most dramatic use of national power affecting people of color enforced white racial values along the West Coast by corralling Japanese Americans into concentration camps for the duration of the Second World War. Although some national-class voices deplored what was happening, none of those in power rose to challenge it.

In the 1930s and 1940s, organized labor posed the most immediate challenge to the compromise. With crucial support from the National Labor Relations Act of 1935, might unions, especially the new ones in the Congress of Industrial Organizations, scramble the allocations of local power, demand their independent place in national circles, and polarize politics into radical and conservative camps? Would unions empower African Americans, for example? Would they form labor parties to run local governments?

By a gauge of such hypothetical possibilities, the unions behaved very mildly indeed. Inheriting almost no superstructure of political connections, radical traditions, or leverage in industry, they were still struggling to survive at the end of the 1930s. The most personal context of the union leaders themselves—their churches, their families, their work experience—was almost always paternalistic and hierarchical; as soon as they could, they bureaucratized their own unions along those same lines. The price for bringing different skills into a single industrial union was usually a rigidification of the hierarchy among those skills, especially through tracking systems that left each layer of skills in charge of its own craft. By choice or necessity, unions accommodated to the powers around them. Only at a rare moment—Walter Reuther's postwar challenge to the automobile industry, for example—did a union official demand a say in company management.

In its early vulnerable years the CIO tucked itself under the wing of the national government and generally avoided political confrontations. It certainly required a fevered imagination to picture as loyal and obedient a party man as Sidney Hillman of the CIO's Political Action Committee dictating terms to the leaders of the Democratic party. When the most assertive of the new unionists, John L. Lewis, did seek a position of some authority in national politics, he discovered that he could take a back seat, or none at all.

In local affairs, however, organized labor did disrupt the seating order. Mixing voters in new coalitions, unions managed to challenge ensconced politicians at both local and state levels. Here the ability to draw on national support, if only in court, could make the critical difference. In the old-guard circles of local America, nothing made hatred for the New Deal glow hotter than its labor policy. When the Dixiecrat party broke with the Democrats and Harry Truman in 1948, a local middle-class antiunionism ranked right along with prosegregation as spurs to rebellion. Even at the peak of the compromise's effectiveness, in other words, class anger continued to swirl around it. The Republican counterpart to the Dixiecrat uprising was the bitter feuding between Illinois' Everett Dirksen, the sonorous voice of middle America's middle class, and New York's Thomas E. Dewey, the slicked-up champion of the national class's corporate establishment. At best, the compromise held these conflicts in tension.

Nobody rode those local passions farther into enemy territory than Wisconsin's Senator Joseph McCarthy, whose slashing attacks on national-class values, loyalties, and motives attracted tens of millions of admirers, especially in a belt of towns and small cities across America's heartland and among a neighborhood-rooted white urban middle class. Cowing members of the Washington establishment or fingering big shots in the publishing world made him an authentic local hero. Although McCarthy erred critically in 1954 by attacking the army, shining emblem of patriotism in local America, his communist-hunting campaign and the many others similar to his had already sent their essential message, reaffirming the compromise as a two-way bargain.

National policy relied on local power; local power demanded national restraint.

As the state's responsibilities for its citizens' well-being expanded grandly, national-class interpreters altered their understanding of democracy to suit these new roles. At a basic level, the meaning of democracy shifted from process to results. In the 19th century, democracy shaped the state; in the 20th the state shaped democracy. Now the crucial question was what came out of the state rather than what went into it. Nineteenth century democracy concentrated on how things were done and who did them. It meant communities turning out to vote. What made the myth of log cabin to White House democratic was the activity it identified: ordinary white men competing for all the stakes. In the 20th century what counted was who got what when, not who did what when. The meaning of the community's votes lay in what the community received in return; the meaning of rags-to-riches lay in how many got rich. Democracy's health was a matter of record. Charts traced its vital signs.

By far the most common measures were economic. Whatever else democratic governments might provide, they were expected to pay. Hence during the Great Depression, with dictatorships thriving elsewhere, the historian Carl Becker worried about the survival of a democracy, "in some sense an economic luxury," that had "betrayed" the industrial poor.[7] Applying economic criteria was certainly not new. In 1886 Andrew Carnegie defined America's *Triumphant Democracy* with production statistics. Economics underlay the progressive Walter Weyl's "new democracy." Nevertheless, only by the 1920s did it become an article of popular faith that the American economy could generate an abundance for everybody. Even prolonged depression was visualized as want in the midst of plenty, a problem in distributing a natural surplus. Presidents had little choice but to promise prosperity. "Economic Democracy," as Henry Wallace asserted, determined a modern government's agenda: "The political democracy of a hundred years ago adequately took care of the decentralized economic forces of that day. But it is not equal to the task of balancing highly centralized economic forces." "The ideal democracy," he believed, "would, of course, arrange a job for every able-bodied citizen."[8]

Advocates who felt obliged to argue the profitability of their favorite democratic measures filled the air with unprovable promises: a minimum wage would pay in lower crime rates; Prohibition would pay in higher productivity. Many of these claims simply lacked plausibility. Who in the 1920s really believed that generous national pensions, as one earnest proponent guaranteed, would bring the United States "in-estimable" economic gains? Smart labeling was safer: David Lilienthal called each TVA project a "People's Dividend."[9] Lilienthal's use of a corporate analogy followed an old American habit. But when George Bancroft in 1826 likened government to a corporation, he did so to emphasize its limited, contractual powers; and when Mugwumps in the Gilded Age followed suit, they meant to highlight able, conserva-tive leadership. Only the 20th century version focused on the payout.

Assessments of the new democracy involved not simply how citi-zens were doing but how they fared relative to other citizens, where they fell, that is, along a scale of returns. A modernized version of an old concept, *status*, became a favorite way of expressing these emotion-ally charged preoccupations with hierarchical placement. With each succeeding decade, apportionment defined more and more of the big battles in public policy. Psychologically as well as managerially, the modern innovation of formal government budgets offered a way of interpreting any one benefit relative to the rest. How, Mary Anderson of the United States Women's Bureau wanted to know, could congress-men appropriate $1.5 million in relief of animal tuberculosis and refuse to vote $75,000 in behalf of wage-earning women? In the past, taxes, inherently inequitable and eternally disputed, had been judged either tolerable or intolerable, one by one. Now political leaders combined them into complicated, comprehensive taxing policies, with promises that together these many particular inequities would cancel one an-other out and produce a general justice for all. If 19th century democ-racy was America's way of conducting affairs, the public side of 20th century democracy was America's state of affairs, its panoramic picture of relative returns.

By midcentury the most common means of filling out that picture was a nation of people consuming goods and services. Not only did consumerism neatly combine the crucial modern themes of individual fulfillment and social apportionment; it also seemed to mute many of the conflicts around them. While registering economic inequalities, the consumer market diffused attention into countless byways of private difference and projected a general prospect of everybody's betterment. Robert Taft, along with such cautious journals as *Fortune* and *House Beautiful*, picked up on these conservative qualities right after the Sec-ond World War as they declared adequate housing for all citizens es-sential to a "sound and stable democracy." In perhaps the most popu-lar moment of his long career, Vice President Richard Nixon drew cheers back home in 1959 when, in the so-called kitchen debate with Soviet Premier Nikita Khrushchev, he used the American consumer durables at a Moscow trade fair as the very definition of democracy.

Around midcentury the historian David Potter, probing for bedrock beneath American culture, struck upon abundance as his answer and advertising as this culture's representative institution. Some years later, the cultural critic Daniel Boorstin described the shared experiences of consuming as modern America's peculiarly democratic source of "community."

This democracy of results rose or fell on the qualities of its leadership. To some degree that emphasis simply extended Walter Lippmann's insistence on the expert few directing the unqualified many. The academic entrepreneur Charles Merriam tirelessly promoted Lippmannesque government. "What particular measures are best adapted to [achieve economic justice] I am incompetent to say," the normally skeptical Carl Becker decided. "It is for the experts" to determine. After coauthoring the famous studies of Middletown, Robert Lynd concluded that ordinary citizens had no way of comprehending the world they lived in. "The people are in no position to evaluate experts," echoed B. F. Skinner's alter ego in *Walden Two* (1948). "And elected experts are never able to act as they think best."[10] According to Richard Hofstadter, ordinary citizens who disputed the experts' recommendations for fluoridated water qualified as paranoid.

A growing sense that only the state stood between its citizens and impending disaster lent new urgency to the need for decisive leadership. As national-class critics viewed it, the challenges of the modern world left no margin for hemming and hawing. High time to abandon the ridiculous American "quest for safety in weakness," the philosopher Joseph Tussman counseled.[11] Presidents above all had to seize the moment and act. Whatever his deficiencies as chief executive, Truman enjoyed a veritable cult following for his ability to make the big decisions, then never look back. Whatever his charms as a presidential candidate, Adlai Stevenson was forever plagued by a reputation for contemplativeness. In retrospect a president such as William McKinley who listened closely for public sentiments seemed spineless. By midcentury the very definition of a strong president included an imperviousness to the distractions of popular opinion. History validated contemporary wisdom, the pundit Max Lerner concluded in his lengthy survey of the nation's record. "In time of crisis," Americans always had the wit to give their leaders "the necessary power for meeting it." The title of a popular book at midcentury captured this contemporary wisdom: *You and Your Leaders.*[12]

With these considerations very much in mind, commentators ran an axis between leaders and followers that anchored their definitions of democracy. It began with the proposition that democracy simply could not function without—in V. O. Key's approving phrase—its "ruling classes." If by 19th century values the People decided for themselves what was best, in the 20th leaders had to decide for them. Not surprisingly, Plato's *Republic* with its philosopher-kings enjoyed quite a vogue around midcentury. Even public opinion, Key's subject, had no meaning until leaders gave it some kind of shape. The only proper role for the public, the influential public philosopher Joseph Schumpeter argued, was to vote in the good leaders and vote out the bad.

At the other end of the axis, ordinary citizens comprised democracy's weak link. National-class models of the world, filled as they were with highly complicated, interacting forces that only experts could comprehend and statesmen could manage, guaranteed an incompetent citizenry. What did they know about the issues? Scarcely anything reliable, ever, the historian Thomas Bailey concluded. Could they even distinguish WPA from PWA? How could they produce the desired outcomes in public policy? Could they increase GNP or counter Soviet aggression? To reach them at all on important matters, abstractions had to be personalized and complexities compressed into simple symbols. The most cynical critics treated them like the adult members of one advertiser's target family: "Mr. and Mrs. Moron and the Little Morons."[13]

Modern democracy deactivated these citizens. They were its recipients, not its creators. In Lilienthal's vision, TVA dams constituted "democracy on the march" and carried the inscription: "Built for the People of the United States."[14] Voters were construed as essentially passive consumers, waiting inertly to receive messages, then choosing between more or less trivial alternatives. As two prominent political scientists phrased it in 1956, "party and manufacturer alike . . . put the product over with the consumers."[15] A year later in his influential *An Economic Theory of Democracy*, Anthony Downs concluded that rational consumer-voters should know enough not to squander their resources trying to master the issues around them. Through cost-benefit analysis, commentators transformed the meaning of popular politics into the equivalent of a store filled with petty goods. As voters selected the counterparts to a razor or a refrigerator or a rollaway, nothing even resembling freedom or dignity appeared to be in stock.

By and large, national-class critics thanked their lucky stars for that. If their democracy worked best when strong leaders made the big decisions, it functioned absolutely at its worst when an ill-informed, volatile public made them. With the rise of authoritarian governments where democracies once existed came a standard account as early as the 1930s holding the citizens of these nations responsible for their own oppression. Even as circumspect a commentator as Eleanor Roosevelt located the sources of totalitarianism in the popular psyche:

widespread "discontent and insecurity" gave dictators "their hold on the people."[16] More baldly, Sinclair Lewis's *It Can't Happen Here* (1935) posited an omnipresent, populist potential for fascism that Buzz Windrip, his fictional variant on Huey Long and the nativist minister Gerald Winrod, tapped. In Archibald MacLeish's cautionary play *The Fall of the City* (1937), mass panic destroyed the ability to resist. Weren't these the same people whom Orson Welles duped into believing Martians had invaded the earth? In Frank Capra's popular movie *Meet John Doe* (1941), each planted rumor turned ordinary citizens into a club-wielding mob.

Judgments of the public psyche grew even harsher by midcentury. If in the 1930s people everywhere appeared vulnerable to a fascist coup, an ominously large proportion of them now seemed ready to welcome one. The widely praised social psychology of Erich Fromm's *Escape from Freedom* (1941) and Theodor Adorno's much-discussed concept of the authoritarian personality gave the experts' touch to explanations of why countless, anonymous people would actually embrace dictatorship. Arthur Schlesinger's benchmark for cold war liberalism, *The Vital Center* (1949), promoted this vision: "Most men prefer to flee choice, to flee anxiety, to flee freedom."[17] Around midcentury commentators were making casual reference to the ordinary citizen's state of mind as *brainwashed,* a term derived from psychological devastation inside totalitarian prisons. Little wonder, then, that majority rule acquired dark associations. A scholarly primer on American society linked "unlimited popular sovereignty, at first glance so pre-eminently democratic," with "absolutistic government."[18]

In light of a supine citizenry, strong leadership had its ambiguities. Some found it safer to rely on more impersonal aspects of their society. One set of commentators transformed a traditional enemy of democracy—interest groups—into the source of a healthy social equilibrium. David Truman, later president of Columbia University, pioneered these interpretations with an account of America's informal governance through competition among its organized interests. For the economist John Kenneth Galbraith, society's big competing blocs—business, labor, and government—interacted in a self-correcting scheme of "countervailing powers." The political scientist Robert Dahl called his arena of many competing groups a "polyarchy": government not by a minority but by minorities. In a similar spirit, popular Keynesianism pictured the need for only a fiscal nudge now and then to sustain balanced economic growth. As if to reify these midcentury formulas, a prominent city planner declared in 1960: "Freedom exists as a balanced condition . . . the maintaining of this balance is the principal function of government."[19]

Balance's near relation, stability, became American democracy's loudest boast to the world at large. In the wake of the Second World War, with such a high proportion of the world's population struggling to devise workable systems of government, the nation's most precious attribute seemed to be its institutional continuity: the longevity of its constitutions, the peaceful transfer of offices, the persistence of civil authority over the military, the uninterrupted vitality of a free press. When such practitioners in comparative politics as Seymour Martin Lipset and Gabriel Almond sought what American democracy had to offer other countries, almost always they found it in America's sources of stability. Continuity suggested bargain and trade, not the systematic political programming that many Americans associated with the modern world's bloody passions. In retrospect, America's record of piecemeal, cobbled reforms looked just right. Changes that many New Dealers found distressingly incomplete in the 1930s were considered pragmatic at midcentury.

In particular, the Constitution, object of withering attacks as an elitist document earlier in the century, was reclaimed as the very bulwark of democracy. A major revival of interest in the nation's founding generation focused on them not as popular revolutionaries but as closeted, stabilizing constitution-makers—the ultimate balancers. Sustaining the Constitution was a democratic virtue in its own right. "The Price of Union," one popular historian called the string of compromises accompanying it. Looking back, the crisis of 1860–61 stood out as the great exception. What 19th century northerners and southerners alike praised as a unique moment of democratic resolve now ranked as a unique democratic failure.

Voting had little to contribute to these formulations. Important books on democracy by Carl Becker and Harold Lasswell, for example, never mentioned elections. Dahl's did so only to disparage them. Nor were tears shed over the nonvoters. In the blunt summary of Morton Grodzins, a dean at the University of Chicago, "citizen participation in politics is not the hallmark of democracy." The widely admired social philosopher David Riesman argued that nonvoters were the least competent citizens, who helped to preserve democracy's health by screening themselves out. Many others agreed. From a slightly different angle, the political scientist Heinz Eulau, equating voters' indifference with their general satisfaction, interpreted nonvoting as "the politics of happiness." Making the most of that thought, Lipset called low turnouts "a reflection of the stability of the system" and only sudden increases a cause for concern, a signal of trouble on the way.[20]

By midcentury, it seemed, everybody believed in trickle-down politics. Whatever the favored democratic mechanisms, not many people

had access to them. In a particularly generous frame of mind, the political scientist E. E. Schattschneider estimated that perhaps 10 percent of
Americans had some connection to the groups actually forming public
policy and hence defining the public interest. Yet in Schattschneider's
most important contribution to his profession, his leadership in a campaign to reform political parties, he advocated greater centralization
of these traditional vehicles of popular influence, in the name of making them more "responsible." His group wanted parties that got things
done. Others praised them for what they did not do, for protecting
government against fads and extremes by delaying decisions and brokering compromises. Once the medium for expressing the people's
judgment, parties now served as a buffer against it. It was the obligation of political leaders not to respond to popular opinion but to create
the illusion that they did. In Key's formulation, "the belief must be
widespread that public opinion . . . affects the course of public action."
Or in Philip Converse's more grudging version: "it is the *perception* of
numbers" mattering that retains "some modest continuing importance
in democratic systems for the legitimacy they confer."[21]
    The most eloquent spokesman for these midcentury values was
Richard Hofstadter, historian and critic at Columbia University, with a
large, appreciative national-class audience. Hofstadter's greatest efforts went into exploring the narrow sectarian mentality, with its "disdain for authority and excellence and *expertise* of all kinds," that was
"founded in the democratic institutions and the egalitarian sentiments" of the 19th century and continued to draw its primary sustenance in the 20th from the midwest and south. As America "moved to
the city," this essentially rural "anti-intellectualism" acquired more
and more the characteristics of the nation's fanatical fringe. Hofstadter,
like Lippmann and Kallen before him, saw the city breeding tolerance
in America. Hofstadter's city, however, was no Tulsa or Sacramento; it
was an abstracted metropolis, a vast Madisonian arena for interacting
and self-canceling groups that supported democracy's "countertradi-
tion of cultural relativism—an enormously sophisticated and very
modern idea."[22]
    The historical precursors of this healthy mix of pluralism and prag-
matism, he came to believe, were America's bargain-and-trade political
parties, crucial solvents for a brittle 19th century provincialism and
still saving agents of democratic moderation in his own time. The very
definition of a political "paranoid" in Hofstadter's scheme was a person who "does not see social conflict as something to be mediated and
compromised, in the manner of the working politician." McCarthyism,
giving the nation's anti-intellectual tradition a particularly paranoid
twist, inspired Hofstadter's sharpest cultural criticism: it was the mob

spirit threatening everything of quality in American life. Against a politics of passion, he set the ideal of "comity," a civility in public life that would preserve the rights of citizens to find their own ways, their own truths. At root, democracy was a personal matter. As if it were a timeless truth rather than a modern innovation, Hofstadter and a colleague declared: "Freedom, if it is to be meaningful, must ultimately be exercised by individuals."[23]

As Hofstadter's appeal illustrated, values associated with tolerance mattered a great deal to these midcentury publicists. He agreed with his sometime collaborator Lipset that this kind of "democracy requires a high level of sophistication," uncommon in the lower class where "extremist and intolerant movements in modern society are more likely to be based."[24] It was also a democracy that placed a particularly high premium on society's stable, smooth functioning. If lower-class Americans themselves suffered the extremist and intolerant consequences of this system, they had only the system itself to help them.

The most striking example of this spirit of accommodation was an acceptance of southern politics as democratic—perhaps not American democracy's most attractive aspect but part of "the price of union." With the systematic exclusion of African American voters, the institutionalized self-perpetuation of local officeholders, and turnouts reminiscent of those in the days of President James Monroe, southern elections simply could not pass the minimum test for an electoral democracy. Yet those national-class voices crying outrage in 1952 at Eisenhower's meekness before McCarthyism said almost nothing about his Democratic opponent Adlai Stevenson's meekness before southern racism. The next round in defining American democracy confronted that discrepancy.

CHAPTER 10

INTERNAL WARS

||||||| **W**hen American democracy's two strands, individual and majoritarian, separated around 1920, they set off as if they would take entirely different journeys across the century. By the 1960s, however, their fortunes were intimately connected once again. This time, instead of combining forces as they had in the 19th century, they came to be pitted against one another: democracy at war with itself.

The halves of democracy turned on one another late in the 20th as they had not in the 19th because of the distinctive ways each evolved. What became the driving force in modern individualism was a vision of universalized rights. In the 19th century, those who talked of universalizing rights referred to a finite body of white men's civic rights: what qualified white men as full-fledged citizens would qualify others too. In the 20th century, however, rights were hooked to the urge for individual fulfillment, a process as open-ended as the imaginations feeding it. As the quest for fulfillment proceeded, rights multiplied.

Modern majoritarianism on its part concentrated on outcomes, on distributing benefits. Even in an expansive system with increasing rewards to distribute, their apportionment involved more for some, less for others, and an edge of unrequited ambitions all around. The more elaborate the agenda for universalizing rights, where in theory everybody got everything, the more niggardly and biased these distributions seemed to be. Nobody ever got everything; many got nothing worth mentioning. Viewed the other way, the sharper the competition over allocating benefits, the more burdensome any kind of mandated rights became.

The first major casualty of democracy's internal battle was the compromise of the 1930s: national-class economic management, local middle-class control over local life. As long as the compromise worked, it gave American democracy the look of a self-perpetuating system. Stripped of that illusion during the last quarter of the century, each of democracy's two strands came in for increasing scrutiny. It did not take long to discover how few putative rights enjoyed general approval and consequently how much coercion an insistence on universalizing a list of rights entailed. Contested rights inevitably spilled into competitive politics. Anyone seeking a political solution to complicated social questions soon learned how poorly a weakened electoral democracy served to resolve distributional issues of any sort—weighing rights and rules, allocating costs and benefits, redressing old imbalances and warding off new ones. Yet to take the remedial step and rehabilitate democracy's majoritarian side raised issues of class and power so fundamental to American society that they seemed all but intractable. Limits at every turn.

Long-term economic growth buoyed expectations for personal fulfillment. Despite the Great Depression, the first seven decades of the 20th century were the most prosperous broad sweep in the nation's history. Prospects soared most dramatically in the quarter century after the Second World War, as real income among wage earners doubled and the base from which Americans understood poverty shot upward. "The minimum subsistence budget that was used to determine welfare payments in New York City in 1960," one radical scholar has written, "specified a set of material conditions for family life that would have been regarded as fairly luxurious . . . in 1930."[1] Widely distributed rising incomes, in turn, powered an unprecedented consumption of goods and services, the hallmark of America's booming postwar years and a matter of global envy.

From a national-class perspective, America's consumer society was inexorably homogenizing. No image better captured this judgment than the one common around midcentury of smiling clean-cut men and women, white and black, young and old, with generic faces and generic clothes, shopping together in a large consumer mart. Commentators grew comfortable using such enveloping terms as "the American character" and "the American mood." Assuming that they knew essentially what was happening, social critics concentrated on what the new uniformity meant.

According to one line of analysis, associated with the sociologist Louis Wirth, major cities where barriers among diverse people fell and mutual acceptance grew in their place exemplified a tolerance that was extending nationwide as urban influences spread everywhere. Sexual taboos were lifting. A concerted postwar campaign against anti-

Semitism appeared to be succeeding. Presumably race prejudices would go next. As a stream of southerners flowed into national-class circles and wrote about their region, they made its distinctive qualities sound like echoes from a bygone day and furthered the illusion that this old bastion of difference, too, was on the edge of assimilation. Most local peculiarities of speech and manner seemed merely quaint. National loyalties were normal loyalties, intellectuals argued. If attachments extended in any direction, it should be outward. Around midcentury, *The Family of Man* (1955), a warmly praised, worldwide compilation of photographs, expressed a vague but important national-class concept.

A second, less cheery line of analysis about the meaning of cultural uniformity pointed up the deficiencies in the people being homogenized. Dulled by mass media and gulled by deceptive advertising, ordinary citizens were not so much contributors to modern public life as the results of it. The large majority lacked basic capacities of "conceptualization," an influential study of voters concluded. More bluntly, another specialist decided that most citizens "do not have meaningful [political] beliefs"—the equivalent in public affairs, apparently, of being without skills for work.[2]

In fact, the consequences were not necessarily bad. Leaders in the national class emerged from the Second World War with high confidence that they could quite literally move the world. Before the war the common wisdom argued that government policies succeeded in the long run only where they meshed with popular values: witness the failure of Prohibition. Now people's values seemed as plastic as their behavior: equally accessible, often indistinguishable. In the bureaucracies that the organizational theorist Herbert Simon designed, where otherwise irrational subordinates were programmed to be parts of a rational enterprise, behavior and beliefs merged. By the same token, societies could also be given direction. It was a case of putting the right people in charge.

In this spirit of managing America's almost-unity, well-situated members of the national class added authority and scope to their version of individual rights. Two lines of change in particular, each with great potential for expansion, pointed new paths toward the late 20th century. First, the meaning of individual rights was shifting from freedoms to claims, from what one individual shared with others in a common setting to what defined each of them as authentic human beings. During the Second World War, the much-publicized Four Freedoms— of speech and faith, from fear and want—provided the standard references for individual rights. Rights as freedoms relied on context, on the conditions that sustained them; limiting them impoverished the total environment. After the war, rights turned increasingly inward. They resembled private possessions, powers that the individual amassed and defended; limiting them violated the person. Rights in the older sense came and went in degrees. Settings might be less free or more free. Rights that defined the individual, on the other hand, had little use for increments. What would it mean to be partially human? By and large these rights came whole or not at all.

The second postwar trend changed rights from something to discover into something to create. People discovered what was there—obscured perhaps or unjustly denied but there to find. Creation was far more open-ended. Even though it dealt only with a restricted body of contract law, Lon Fuller's articles in the *Yale Law Journal* (1936–37), reversing the relation between rights and remedies, was a harbinger of this shift. Traditionally, discovering a right laid claim to a remedy. Fuller argued that legislating a remedy created a right, and, as Morton Horwitz has shown, his version became the new orthodoxy. Rising expectations in personal health illustrated a broader application of the proposition around midcentury. As doctors themselves painted the prospects, an improved surgical technology and an array of so-called wonder drugs promised miracles on a mass basis. Although a right to good health was not there to discover—the thought would have been incomprehensible in the 19th century—it could be said that scientific progress was creating one. From there, creating and acquiring went hand in hand: the right to a healthy atmosphere (the Clean Air Act of 1970), the right to a healthy work place (the Occupational Safety and Health Act of 1970), and so forth.

The Supreme Court's aggressive application of the Bill of Rights contributed to the expansion. Justice Hugo Black's dissent in *Adamson v. California* (1947), arguing that the Fourteenth Amendment gave federal courts the authority to protect the entire Bill of Rights in all jurisdictions, became constitutional law by the 1960s, and court-protected rights multiplied accordingly. As their range broadened, they revealed three interrelated characteristics. First, matters that had once been construed exclusively in collective terms were now atomized. Taxation without representation, for example, strictly a group concern when white men complained about it in the 18th century and free black men and white women protested against it in the 19th, was used in the mid-1960s to support each individual's right to an equality in representation—the principle of one person–one vote.

Second, new rights were adduced from the Constitution, most notably an elastic right to privacy. As Justice William O. Douglas described it, "The Right To Be Let Alone" covered everything that would "aid the fullest individual achievement of which each of [society's] members is

capable," including among a long list of particulars the right to personal dignity.[3] In *Mapp v. Ohio* (1961), the Supreme Court only took
responsibility for a right to privacy that stemmed more or less literally
from the Fourth Amendment's ban on illegal search and seizure; but
four years later in *Griswold v. Connecticut*, Douglas saw "emanations"
rising from the Bill of Rights as a whole that sustained his far more
expansive understanding of privacy.

Third, as the reach of individual rights stretched outward, the scope
of individual powers shrank. Continuing a theme that already had
wide currency in the 1930s and 1940s, national-class commentators of
all sorts stressed the helplessness of lone individuals before the impersonal forces of the modern world. Once individual privacy meant leaving public life and separating oneself from its authorities. Now individual privacy required entering public life and seeking guarantees
from its authorities. Here the ends met: weaker individuals claiming
more rights invited a stronger government to assert itself in securing
more rights for weaker individuals.

Weaknesses in the midst of strength also characterized the economy,
even in the postwar boom years. Prosperity had particularly mixed
effects in local America, where during the quarter century after the
Second World War a combination of chain stores, saturation advertising, diffused shopping centers, and head-to-head competition undermined the traditional retail establishments serving as one of the two
main pillars of these local economies. The Robinson-Patman Act of
1936, which legalized the price-fixing practices of local merchants, was
an integral part of the original compromise of the 1930s, with its sensitivity to realms of local autonomy, and the postwar disintegration of
fixed-price retailing traced one crucial element in the compromise's
decline. As the core of prime mercantile customers shriveled, local
banks found themselves more dependent on financial networks that
were run from metropolitan headquarters. A national market for credit
cards was just over the horizon. To the degree local bankers no longer
guarded the gates of personal credit, one of the critical determinants
of class standing slipped out of local hands. Although the second of
the main pillars, real estate, did not crack nationwide until the savings
and loan association debacle of the late 1980s, the economies in many
towns, small cities, and metropolitan neighborhoods were already
wobbling two decades earlier.

So was the integrity of local life, at least as important segments of
local middle-class leadership interpreted it. The 1940s and 1950s
brought an upsurge of state and national administrators into local affairs, often exceeding the ability of local lawyers to manage and local
governments to manipulate. In subtle ways, local America seemed

more and more culturally isolated. Radio once served as a powerful voice for the values underpinning local cultures. The very names of its perennially popular soap operas—"Ma Perkins," "Vic and Sade," "Just Plain Bill"—resonated with middle-class ideals. Despite occasional islands of tradition such as "Leave It to Beaver," television provided far less support, with its soap operas, for example, spinning out endless tales of sexual yearnings and smashed marriages. That sturdy champion of local American ways, the *Saturday Evening Post*, effectively ceased publishing. In the 1930s and 1940s, teams of sociologists discovered that the citizens in local American communities consistently placed their own inbred elites at the pinnacle of local prestige. By the 1960s and 1970s, national figures so dominated public attention that these citizens often could no longer identify a local elite. In 1975 the publisher of America's many social registers packed all of them into a single, comprehensive *Social Register*, burying the very distinctions, local society by local society, that justified those publications in the first place.

To experts looking in from the outside, local Americans appeared more confused than anything else. On the one hand, polls registered their approval of a national government that managed global affairs, maintained a healthy economy, and oversaw an equitable apportionment of its benefits—liberal, by national-class standards. On the other hand, by those same national standards local Americans were incorribly conservative in cultural matters. Their values had no coherence, analysts decided. Perhaps their cultural understanding lagged; perhaps, as some specialists concluded, they were downright "schizoid." No one thought to follow the wisdom of Mary Douglas and Aaron Wildavsky in the face of large numbers of people "choosing irrationally. Their odd behavior ought to suggest that the accepted model of rational decision making should be revised."[4]

Normal in local America meant distant management of distant affairs and community management of everyday affairs. A sense of control over choices—some individual, some collective—mattered immensely. Although material ambitions were usually modest in local America, personal initiative was a highly praised attribute, especially for men. Right divided clearly from wrong: vice was a sin, not a joke. However erratic their church attendance, most people in the local middle class thought of themselves as shaped by their god, not by the play of evolutionary forces. They sorted their world into ethnic and racial categories, calculating ancestry in percentages—so much German, so much Irish—as if each nation of origin had a separate genetic pool. Blood told. Children bore the moral as well as the physical marks of their parents: even the very young shared those benefits and bore those burdens. Any blending of white with black, yellow, or red was serious business. In the late 1960s, as Congress discarded the old racially based immigration quotas, "Thank God I'm Polish" or "Swedish" or "Italian" buttons sprouted to declare a quite different set of priorities in local America.

From the vantage point of the middle class, two enemy invasions struck local America during the 1960s. One was a battalion of national mandates, often associated with the Supreme Court under Chief Justice Earl Warren but by no means limited to it. Who controlled local schools? Courts ordered racial desegregation and banned prayers; Congress set a menu of special programs for special groups; the new textbooks exalted scientific truths and melted the world's people into a human race. Whose values had currency in the neighborhood? Restraints on the sale of pornography and the distribution of birth control information loosened. In 1968 the Supreme Court even overturned a statute penalizing public drunkenness. Who had priority, the law-abiding citizen or the criminal? A series of court decisions, most notoriously *Miranda v. Arizona* (1966), expanded the rights of those suspected of crimes; others set the death penalty in limbo. The humanitarian argument that death sentences led to nothing more than the ritual killings of marginal men doubled as the local American argument in their favor: there, death sentences were meant to serve as symbolic affirmation of middle-class values. In 1968, 70 percent in a nationwide poll considered the Supreme Court a major cause of crime.

An outpouring of national rules reshaped federal politics as well. Beginning with *Baker v. Carr* (1962), a set of Supreme Court decisions required states to approximate one person–one vote in their apportionment of legislative districts, and Congress enshrined that principle as the national measure of justice. Sundry local tests to screen out unwanted voters disappeared. The Voting Rights Act of 1965 authorized federal agents to register voters, and the Court invalidated all but a token residency requirement. As part of President Lyndon Johnson's War on Poverty, the Office of Economic Opportunity made gestures toward bypassing established local powers and dealing directly with groups of the nation's poor. New procedures in seeking public assistance swelled the welfare rolls nationally from under 8 million in 1965 to over 11 million by 1969. In general, much of Johnson's program for a Great Society was predicated on the assumption that local governments had no purpose higher than to mimic the national government, replicating its goals, supplementing its programs, and copying its taxing philosophy.

The pot-smoking, mantra-chanting, love-making hippies of the 1960s led a second column of invaders into local America. To parents who were trying to instill the rights and wrongs of respectability into their children, these vagabonds sent the youth of local America the most subversive message of all: if it feels good, do it. Popular media, linking the flower children with the excitement of the new rock scene and investing them with the special charm of a spacy innocence— loose, free, happy—only deepened the problems of local control. When challenged, these wandering youth, overwhelmingly from the national class, brought in their lawyers, put up bail, and threw a glare of publicity on heavy-handed local justice. Although local America eventually assimilated the music, the language, the clothes, and the hairstyles of the Woodstock Nation, it never downed the fear of losing authority, especially authority over the young. At the end of the 20th century, hippie was still a fighting word in local America. Always its force lay at least as much in what it suggested as in what it actually brought. Flag-burners and draft-dodgers, feminists and homosexuals, armed rioters for Black Power and armed militants for Indian power, whole armies of the Other seemed to rise just behind the hippies in the late 1960s and early 1970s.

As waves of middle-class anger poured over a weakened local base, the compromise collapsed. Beneath earlier outbursts of resentment— McCarthyism, for example—lay a safety net of popular faith that by and large the federal government served the public interest. Was it true that ordinary citizens could not count on their government to do the right thing? Only 1 in 4 adults reached that conclusion in 1958. Did the government really represent just the interests of a few? Less than 1 in 5 thought so the same year. Then came the sea change of the 1960s. By 1972, 2 out of 3 answered yes to both questions. Early in the 1960s, the reputation of each branch—Congress, executive offices, the federal judiciary—and of every related national-class institution—news media, major corporations, higher education, the leading professions— began its tumble down the same long, hard slide. The compromise rested on that bed of respect: no trust, no bargain.

As it collapsed, the political leader most alert to the implications was Richard Nixon. Courting a beleaguered local middle class as "forgotten Americans," he used his presidential authority from the moment he took office in 1969 to champion their values: stiffer law enforcement, an end to busing for school integration, tighter restrictions on obscenity, the right to pray in school. In the accents of personal conviction, Nixon condemned the national-class establishment as arrogant, spineless, and irresponsible, and he vowed to pack the Supreme Court with cultural conservatives. His administration gutted the controversial OEO and promoted instead federal block grants and revenue sharing that would flow through existing national-to-local channels. In an imaginative leap, his advisers even explored the possibility of a guaranteed minimum income. Meanwhile, the president sacrificed not a jot of control over general economic policy, which at times he made a secret personal domain. Nixon's smashing reelection victory in 1972 over George McGovern, an advocate of expansive national-class liberalism, gave the impression of a repaired compromise triumphant.

But the pieces no longer fit well. The most obvious immediate problem was a shortage of funds to sustain the compromise, especially in major cities. Even with its gigantic war machine, the United States in the 1970s fell to dead last place among Western industrial nations in the percentage of Gross National Product it turned into tax revenues. Further dampening efforts to strengthen the government's hand, opinions on public policy polarized. In the 1950s, polls on subject after subject approximated a bell curve: low at the extremes, bunched in the middle. Almost unanimously, social scientists came to regard that pattern as normal. On comparable subjects in the 1970s the curve of opinions formed a ripple: often no higher in the middle than at the two extremes. Despite a reluctance in many circles to admit it, that became the new norm: less margin for compromise, less interest in it. The unique aura of vitality, of common purpose, that clung in memory to President John Kennedy had some basis in fact. National connectedness of a certain kind was passing at his death.

The major parties showed the effects of these subterranean shifts. Around midcentury, Republicans and Democrats alike made the most of what one specialist called a "quilted pattern of opinion," in which groups with overlapping members entwined their interests to form reasonably stable conglomerates. As social scientists described the results—an almost boringly reliable "political culture of moderation"—it generated enough competition to define alternatives and maintain party loyalties, but not enough to disrupt the society around it.[5] What kept this system of cautious elite rule functioning was the anomalous politics of the south, where white people who might otherwise have joined the Republican party and made it a bastion of conservatism remained within the Democratic party—the traditional agency of southern white power—and thereby counterbalanced the party's aggressive liberal wing.

As American politics polarized, two-party competition spread through the south. Competitive politics in the south opened the way nationally for a conservative majority party, further polarizing politics. With less middle ground to share, interest groups less often overlapped, more often lined up one by one to trade their support for favors. These strains severely weakened the major parties. Before the 1960s, they drew their primary strength from brokering the central compromise in modern American politics. After the 1960s, instead of resolving its problems, the major parties expressed them. When the bell curves collapsed and interests fragmented, they fractured too. As national-class institutions slid into disrepute, so did the national leadership of the parties. Significantly smaller percentages in each new voting cohort assigned any importance at all to the parties. By the late 1970s, party-determined voting in Congress had fallen about 50 percent and ticket splitting in presidential election years more than doubled since the days of Franklin Roosevelt. Presidential aspirants did whatever they could to distance themselves from the Washington establishment. Once the label of outsider meant demagogue; now it gave a candidate the competitive edge.

For most of the century, local middle-class Americans looked to people with skills and insights quite different from their own to lead the nation. Although it was nice to hear those leaders express themselves from time to time in the familiar no-nonsense, I-know-right-from-wrong idiom that both Harry Truman and Dwight Eisenhower employed, fundamentally local Americans relied on members of another class operating in their own way to protect America's interests. By the 1970s, on the contrary, more and more local middle-class leaders were declaring that only they could protect America against those dangerous, distant national leaders. While local middle-class voices continued to talk in the language of a cultural wholeness where all real Americans shared their traditional values, their proud patriotism, and their common sense, they also expressed increasing doubts about the chances of this Americanism prevailing against the established powers. Even to preserve local control, growing numbers of them decided, they would have to set the national rules themselves.

Two movements with powerful influence on late 20th century democracy—expanding the rights of African Americans and empowering white women—came on either side of the compromise's breakdown and demonstrated how much difference a few critical years made. That phase of the drive for black rights led by Martin Luther King, Jr., rising out of the Montgomery bus boycott in 1955 and 1956 and culminating with the Civil Rights Act of 1964 and the Voting Rights Act of 1965, turned out to be the last chance to base major changes in public policy on the bell curve of moderate white inclinations. Appealing to national unity, shaming local middle-class whites with national-class values, relying on the mobilized authority of national-class institutions in government, media, and education—all crucial to the success of the civil rights movement—would look like historical curiosities a decade later.

Beginning early in the 20th century, most prominent African American leaders banked their hopes for breaking the grip of racism on the intervention of the national class. The offices of the NAACP were headquarters for this strategy, which included lobbying Congress, cultivating executive leaders, and challenging racial discrimination through the federal judiciary. To midcentury the approach brought uncertain results. Although President Truman's Committee on Civil Rights laid out a broad agenda for reform in 1947 and public discussion no longer contained crudely racist language, southern segregation held firm. Even in the north, recent laws specifying colorblind employment practices were understood to express an ideal, not what really happened on the job. The *Brown* decisions of 1954 and 1955, mandating school desegregation "with all deliberate speed," were the great triumph of this national strategy. Nevertheless, the Federal Housing Authority still refused to invest in racially mixed neighborhoods, most national-class institutions had only token black members, and no party leader in Washington made the speed of desegregation a primary concern during the 1950s.

It was the genius of King and his colleagues to combine the wherewithal available to them into a successful movement. Seeking public rights, African Americans had always been obliged to come from outside the system and petition in the white men's spaces. How to petition with dignity, how to show respect without losing self-respect, was the standing challenge in the politics of indirection, especially for former slaves and the descendants of slaves. King's legions—and after 1960 the young blacks who challenged segregated facilities throughout the south—transformed that potential humiliation into a brilliant set of tactics.

Through boycotts, demonstrations, marches, vigils, and sit-ins, they turned petitioning into a politics of protest; and by combining their public messages with an actual exercise of their rights, they raised the art of petitioning-through-witness to a new level. Rather than stand apart and pray as late 19th temperance advocates did, they incorporated their enemies into tableaux of justice that popular media then transformed into extraordinarily effective visual petitions to a national audience. Symbolically the civil rights movement merged petitioning with the activist axiom of 19th century democracy: get into the system by getting into it. Sit-ins in particular communicated that African Americans were not there simply to make a statement; they had come to stay. To petitioning as protest, King and his allies added protest as peace: an unwavering nonviolent discipline. But protest as peace, surrounded as it almost always was by white people's aggression, also flashed a message of danger, a glimpse into what would happen if African Americans, too, abandoned self-discipline. Hence the final twist: peace as the intimation of violence.

Making democracy work meant making America's three-class system work: democracy and class functioned together. The *Brown* decisions posed the issue of desegregation in white terms. A white national class told a white local class to change its ways, and through what was known as "massive resistance," white local powers balked. It was a debate over the law. Blacks would not win that debate. For one thing, whites were preoccupied with the effects of "all deliberate speed" on whites, not blacks. Basically, African Americans could not afford to depend solely on national-class power: that was the repeated lesson of the 20th century. They needed leverage in all classes.

By mobilizing broad support among African Americans, the civil rights movement automatically factored members of the lower class into the process, and as they did, they turned the question of white people's law into one of black people's rights. A considerable national-class audience listened and learned. Because national-class Americans defined their own privileges as rights and because in theory at least they universalized those rights, they had little difficulty understanding the conflict over segregation as a moral drama. Here King was the indispensable teacher. It remained to convert portions of the local middle class who still thought of rights as something earned, not given. King's Southern Christian Leadership Conference recruited support in those ranks by the flawless respectability, the unblinking self-control, the group solidity, with which its followers presented their case. These were white middle-class values at their best. The civil rights movement held church everyday in public. Local America's business leaders were particularly encouraged to strike a bargain with these orderly African Americans now in the hope of stabilizing prosperous race relations into the future.

In brief, King and his allies used national- and local-class leverage to raise lower-class rights, that is, the rights of Jim Crowed blacks. As if history had come full circle, what highlighted the radicalism of early 19th century democracy—white men taking over public spaces—also defined the most important reform in late 20th century democracy: opening public spaces to African Americans through the comprehensive Civil Rights Act of 1964, then the Voting Rights Act of 1965. The timing was crucial. King and his associates, riding the waves of an expansive national-class agenda, gained their legislative objectives before local middle-class morale ebbed too far. At a pivotal stage in the conflict between white classes, in other words, black rights were written into public policy.

The compromise came tumbling down just behind the civil rights laws, and race issues added force to the fall. A majority of whites, consistently concerned about race relations changing too fast, treated the new laws less as justice overdue than as justice overdone and, in the face of demands for further reforms, insisted on a halt to all of them. After 1965, King himself recognized that the possibilities for further reform were closing around him. Black attitudes, like white ones, polarized. Cracking the walls of discrimination opened up fathomless wells of rage and resentment that no reforms could appease. With government commitment to end discrimination at its peak, 7 of 10 African Americans in a national poll thought that whites would like to see them reenslaved. Looking into a white man's eyes, the black radical Eldridge Cleaver wrote, he saw himself being appraised along with the rest of the livestock.

As the bell curve crumpled in urban violence and nationwide anger, so did the faith that changing race relations had a direction, a goal. Whites overwhelmingly construed civil rights reform as a statement about democratic individualism: a black too should be able to compete for the benefits of American society. Policies that blocked off certain positions for African Americans or even gave them hiring preference met a powerful white opposition—in poll after poll during the 1970s, 8 or 9 to 1 against affirmative action. While national-class theorists worried about meritocratic standards and African American self-respect, at the job sites whites and blacks shared the local American preoccupation with "getting mine," especially as the economy weakened. The reforms of the mid-1960s could easily be interpreted as universal rights because the prolonged postwar economic expansion wrapped them in expectations of more for everybody. Stagnation in the 1970s redefined race relations as distributional issues, a very different matter. Any attempt to correct injustices at one place in a tight system of inequalities created problems of justice elsewhere in the system, problems that in a polarized public only generated bitterness.

African Americans on their part found little promise in a polarizing society. If during the late 1960s the rhetoric of Black Power was a variant on the language of personal fulfillment and the looting during a contagion of urban riots a variant on popular consumerism, neither enhanced individual opportunities in the long run. Nor did ghetto politics increase the African American share of society's common resources. Congregated in a metropolitan "colored nation" or a hardscrabble Mississippi county, poor blacks often received proportionately less in the 1970s and 1980s than they had earlier. The old reform agendas threw no light on these tenacious problems.

If the civil rights movement achieved the last major reforms on one side of a divide, women's campaign for the Equal Rights Amendment represented the first major effort on the other side. Superficially, the two shared almost everything except their timing. Like African Americans, reforming white women demanded their collective rights in the name of pursuing their individual goals. Adapting arguments and tactics from the civil rights movement, these women also dramatized their case with examples of outrageous discrimination, made similar claims to a self-evident truth from the same universal values—equality, opportunity, justice—and mobilized their own nationwide marches in behalf of the ERA.

That survey, accurate as far as it went, obscured deeper differences between the two causes. Women's problems in public were an extension of their disabilities in private: the poor pay and the constrained choices, the sexual harassment and the drumbeat of belittling remarks, the sheer invisibility in the eyes of those distributing rewards and determining advancement. From time-honored ways of thinking about domestic relations, a prominent political scientist concluded in 1964, for example, that "wives tend to double their husbands' votes."[6] If African Americans had to change public values in order to expand their individual opportunities, women had to change private values in order to expand their public opportunities. First break the crockery, then change society. Sensitive to that sequence, Betty Friedan's *The Feminine Mystique* (1963) stirred a new consciousness among women by personalizing their social issues: listen to your inner self and act on it. It required several more years for a substantial number to socialize those personal issues into a women's movement. The greater the potential for intimacy, opinion polls made clear, the stronger white resistance to African American rights grew. Whites accepted common jobs with blacks before common schools, schools before neighborhoods, neighborhoods before marriages. But in the lives of men, of course, every new right for women affected intimate relations.

Neither chance nor mimicry accounted for the timing of the two campaigns. Advocates of women's rights no more copied black leaders than King copied Gandhi. To get seriously underway, each campaign had to await at least a partial breakdown in those social relations blocking it. Following a pattern as old as American democracy, important changes never slid smoothly from the old into the new ways. For African American civil rights, the critical obstacle was the basic 20th century compromise in public policy, which left the rights of blacks everywhere at the disposal of local middle-class whites. Here the essential preliminary was early evidence that the compromise was in trouble: white arrangements in public policy sufficiently weakened to be exploited but not yet weak enough to trip a general white alarm. For women, on the other hand, the prerequisite was a shakeup in family authority: the initial round of what would be long-term challenges to the Dad-Mom-Dick-Jane-and-Spot model and a sharp increase in women's prospects for separating sex from conception and for regulating reproduction, primarily through new birth control methods and secondarily through abortions. As it happened, slipping the bonds of family occurred several years later for white women than slipping the constraints of class did for African Americans.

Numbers established the second major difference between the two movements. African Americans were a minority, women a majority. As a majority everywhere—in each state and city, in all classes—it was natural enough to consider majoritarian politics an ally, a way of stamping the elementary facts of demography into law. Almost as soon as an organized women's movement materialized, the idea of an Equal Rights Amendment was revived. Polls in 1971 indicated widespread, if vague, support. In 1972 a slightly modified version of Alice Paul's original ERA passed Congress and, with a rush of national endorsements and media attention, swept rapidly through a majority of state legislatures.

The general dispersal of women hid a final important difference between the two movements. From a constricted Jim Crow base, King and his colleagues succeeded only by mastering the complexities of class interaction throughout America. The women's movement and its campaign for the ERA, by contrast, originated in the national class, spoke the language of the national class, and relied fundamentally on the support of the national class. Only those values made public discrimination by sex unreasonable: where specialization and merit determined careers, gender was logically irrelevant. By the values of local middle-class America, on the other hand, gender differences, like those of race and ethnicity, were facts of life, rooted in biology, Bible, and timeless custom. Women's pride as well as men's power depended on the differences.

From their national prominence, champions of the ERA turned as a matter of course to tactics that were standard among publicly ambitious women in the 20th century: counting on class superiority to compensate for gender inferiority. Where other things were equal, men routinely cast women in secondary roles. To counterbalance that discrimination and achieve a rough parity, publicly minded women preferred dealing with men a step or two down the hierarchy. Long after national-class men turned their attention elsewhere, for example, national-class women remained active in the politics of their cities and

suburbs, relying on local-class officials, professionals, and businessmen to implement goals, often masked as public services or civic improvements, that these women set.

These national-class resources were almost enough to win the ERA.
Trying to coast from the top down, however, the campaign stalled in
1973, four states shy of the necessary three-fourths. Suddenly aggressive local middle-class voices, women's as well as men's, speaking
through the churches and clubs where they felt most comfortable and
organizing state networks where proponents of the ERA left vacuums,
snarled the cause in a tangle of fears about an intruding—a violating—
national power. Their images of shy girls humiliated in unisex toilets
and young women scarred in combat, of gray-haired mothers abandoned to poverty and their daughters forced into abortions, communicated in a coded moral idiom that had currency in towns and neighborhoods across the country. If advocates of the ERA hoped very much
to minimize the connection between their movement and the weakening of the traditional family, its local-class opponents would not let
them. In fact, a new hard-edged feminism, emerging in this polarized
environment, arrived just in time for local Americans to exploit it,
transforming the debate over the ERA into "a feminist issue instead of
a woman's issue."[7] A middle ground sufficiently broad—a bell curve
sufficiently high—no longer existed to amend the Constitution, and
the ERA's prospects disappeared in a clash and clang of holy rhetoric.

Nothing, however, could still the demands to extend individual rights.
In a process that seemed to feed on itself, more and more Americans
pressed forward with rights of their own. Small groups of gays and
lesbians early in the 1970s drew upon a general right to sexual choices
to campaign for their right to lives free from violence and discrimination. In a reform process that would climax with the comprehensive
Disabilities Act of 1990, the Rehabilitation Act of 1973 first set federal
standards of access for the physically handicapped. Members of the
national class championed the rights of a variety of dependents. In
1975 and 1976, for instance, the Supreme Court protected the mentally
ill from arbitrary confinement and treatment. Children's rights expanded rapidly during the 1980s. In 1985, as a patently absurd illustra-
tion of rights run riot, one legal scholar pictured offspring suing their
parents for a bad upbringing; in 1992, to a sympathetic national-class
audience, courts began granting children divorces from their parents.

The most explosive of these issues was the right to an abortion, established in Roe v. Wade (1973) and contested thereafter with increasing
bitterness. Soft-pedaled in law and policy until the late 1960s, abortions got caught in the swirl of America's polarizing attitudes and

emerged a central symbol of women's right to control their own lives. Among women it made excellent sense to think of such control as a matter of privacy: their disabilities originated in private; their autonomy had to be secured there. It was not clear, however, where in the law to root this right. Did it belong with protections against corporate surveillance and electronic file-keeping? Must it rely on Justice Douglas's elusive emanations from the Bill of Rights?

In a bull market of rights, precise answers could wait. During the 1980s, concepts of rights expanded far faster than the law allowed. As the commentator E. J. Dionne, Jr., has noted, all kinds of people from all walks of life kept current the famous formula from the 1960s: if it feels good, do it. With 5 percent of the world's population, Americans consumed 50 percent of its addictive drugs. Among their most enthusiastic publicists, rights changed as needs changed. The essence of democracy, one philosopher declared, was "not only 'one man, one vote' but also 'one man, one equal effective right to live as fully humanly as he may wish.'" A legal theorist identified rights with "the infinite quality of the personality . . . to transcend the limited imaginative and social worlds that it constructs." Translating grand propositions such as these into a bill of particulars had an almost arbitrary quality about it, as if the same person might well compile a different list on another day. "What I'm talking about now," Elaine Jones of the NAACP said in an interview, "is basic human rights, which include the right to a safe environment, health care, the right to participate in the electoral process fairly, to have employment, the right to some significant opportunity in training and education." [8]

Not only was individualism of this persuasion impatient with delays; it tended to see delays as denials, as barriers perversely blocking the individual's right to fulfillment. In this context, the meaning of family liquified, covering whatever living arrangements gave individuals satisfaction and, as a corollary, dissolving when those rewards disappeared. Attitudes toward health care reflected these values. A medical profession that inflated its authority by promising cures attracted patients who retaliated by demanding them. Malpractice law thrived on such expectations. So did activists in the cause of AIDS sufferers, who attacked official medicine for its sluggishness and insisted on immediate access to any pharmaceutical that might affect the disease. In fact, any interference with the individual's choice among cures, one advocate of alternative medicine declared in a revealing merger of Madisonian law with Jeffersonian rhetoric, "is a direct violation of our constitutional right to life, liberty, and the pursuit of happiness." [9] By the end of the 1980s more than 7 out of 10 adult Americans thought health care should be a constitutional guarantee; 4 out of 10 thought it already was. It required no unusual stretch of these values to accept the widely publicized vision of personal self-fashioning for the 21st century. As science mastered the human's DNA and brain functioning, individuals would make and remake themselves through genetic and chemical interventions according to their own evolving agendas.

Along with the growing appetite for personal rights on demand came a downright aversion to democratic constraints. Individual rights that traditionally were understood as the citizen's protection against arbitrary government were increasingly turned into the individual's protection against hostile majorities. Appropriately, Alexis de Tocqueville's early 19th century concerns about community pressure bottling up the superior individual enjoyed a revival after midcentury. Now it was individual fulfillment that popular values frustrated. Among conservatives, the writings of Ayn Rand, especially *The Fountainhead* (1943), inspired a cult of the self-validating superman that was still very much alive in the 1990s. Among liberals, the psychologist Abraham Maslow's elitist hierarchy of personality development, also still current in the 1990s, pictured an infinitessimal fraction of the population reaching the top of the pyramid and standing free as "self-actualized" individuals. Where the heart of democracy is "individual dignity," Thomas Dye and Harmon Ziegler argued, "elites, not masses, are most committed to . . . individual liberty, toleration of diversity, or freedom of expression"; "masses," on the contrary, manifest "antidemocratic tendencies." [10]

Among champions of the individual's immutable rights, the most dangerous masses were voting majorities. Majority rule, such national-class liberals as Ronald Dworkin and Ira Glasser decided, was a "fetish" and "democracy, properly understood . . . the protection of individual rights." Linking "crude majority rule" with the "great tyrannies of the past," they concentrated on ways of "curbing . . . majoritarian prejudice." With the utmost, if bewildering seriousness, the bulletin of the American Civil Liberties Union announced a "Historic Breakthrough in Voting Rights" in an article devoted to the replacement of elected judges with appointed ones and the consignment of voters to periodic yes-or-no decisions on their retention. Opinion polls supplied ammunition for this antimajoritarian bias: steady majorities opposed the individualists on such matters as the death penalty, the rights of criminal suspects, open homosexual preferences, and religious exercises in the public schools. An election affecting public policy on any of those issues was dismissively labeled a "plebiscite." [11]

Even before the 1970s, leaders in the fight for individual rights looked to the least responsive areas of government. Through the 1970s, those safe places included both judicial and administrative offices whose technical, sometimes hidden procedures screened out popular intrusions. In that spirit, Theodore Lowi sketched a model "juridical democracy" where overseers dispassionately made just decisions. Then in the 1980s, especially as environmentalism loomed larger and larger in human rights, the federal executive itself became too popular, and the judiciary alone stood guard. Among rights advocates, it was a matter of pride to convince judges that otherwise forgotten 19th century statutes could be used to circumvent contemporary majoritarian preferences. Much wiser to look for a friend at court, supporters of the right to die agreed in 1986, than depend on "volatile" state legislatures. In time, the courts came to be seen as the source of those rights. Ignoring how tenuous the tradition and how brief the history, Nadine Strossen, incoming president of the ACLU, called upon the Supreme Court in 1991 to fulfill "its traditional, historic role as the unique protector of [such] fundamental constitutional rights" as the individual's "privacy and freedom and autonomy." [12]

From one direction came the pursuit of individualist democracy by means hostile to majoritarian democracy; from the other, its converse: the use of majoritarian democracy for purposes hostile to individualist democracy. Just as national-class advocates of absolute rights shunned the electorate, so their local middle-class enemies, stretched across a much broader popular base, looked to the electorate for a judgment on those rights: let the voters decide. Although there were national-class echoes of encouragement for this opposition, including an impressive rally around Nixon in 1972, the vision of a populist retaliation, of real Americans standing up for their values, belonged to the local middle class. Rising with the polarized politics of the late 1960s and early 1970s, these newly activated citizens, like the young protestors who scorned them, cast themselves as keepers of the nation's soul. They mobilized most effectively by appealing to local America's religious sensibility: the elite enemy was morally empty—*permissive*—immorally alien—*radical*—but devilishly powerful. It was fight now or die: "our backs are against the wall . . . *The time has come for those who remain to band together.*" [13]

The battle included a struggle to control the key words of American democracy. White workers wrestled with the NAACP over the use of *equality*, conservatives with the ACLU over the use of *liberty*. In deference to the centrality of individualism in modern America, they fought above all over their claims to its language. Proponents of legalized abortion, for example, advocated rights that independent adults exercised for themselves; opponents promoted rights that superior powers mandated for inferior ones: a god's rules for humans, men's decisions for women. Nevertheless, both sides framed it as a contest over indi-

vidual rights. Whose choice qualified as pro-choice, whose life qualified for the right to life? Shouting the same words at one another did
nothing to lessen the chasm between them.

Local American majoritarianism was increasingly effective politics,
with more recruits year by year: southern whites, white wage earners,
businessmen, a curiously ecumenical mixture of Protestants, Catholics,
and Jews. Through their own characteristic fund-raising device, the
direct mail appeal, local middle-class activists marshaled impressive
sums of money, and their networks learned how to employ kinds of
politics that established powers usually dominated: the initiative, for
example, and political action committees (PACs). Local majoritarianism influenced legislation on a range of contentious cultural issues,
criminalizing some areas of the new individualism and restricting others. Then with Ronald Reagan's election as president in 1980, it seemed
to have won Washington itself.

Certainly nothing in Reagan's Hollywood gloss or in the Ivy League
polish of his successor George Bush reflected local-class life. Both administrations, however, fed on its anger. What followed was a cautionary tale for those who expected to maintain their version of individual
rights without political competition. Weeding liberals out of the executive and planting conservatives in the judiciary, the ascendant Republicans eliminated most of the quiet, hidden places where antimajoritarian individualists hoped to achieve their objectives. Greater leeway
for the police, harsher criminal penalties, weaker protections for free
speech, and less supervision to achieve racial balances followed. In the
most fiercely contested realm of all, courts and legislatures alike limited access to abortion.

As middle-class whites reclaimed control over local life, elements of
the old compromise of the 1930s were obviously in play. Nevertheless,
the Republicans in power made no effort to integrate those elements;
they simply made the most of polarization. Even more critical, they let
loose forces that were sapping local economies. National laws increasingly preempted state and local ones in "business regulation and
health and safety."[14] By easing restrictions in banking, the Reagan Republicans invited speculative investors anywhere in the world to treat
local real estate markets like so many nights at Monte Carlo. In the
wake of the nationwide collapse of the savings and loan associations
late in the 1980s, local builders relying on local credit suffered the
most, and national home-building corporations—Centrex, Toll Brothers, Ryland—supplanted them. Even funeral parlors, the quintessen-
tial neighborhood business, were gathered into national chains. Hence
just as the cultural politics of the local middle class was succeeding, its
economic underpinnings were eroding further. Whatever public policy

alternatives did exist in the 1990s, re-creating the old compromise with its identifiably local economies was not one of them.

Nevertheless, in the battle of democracies, majoritarianism was winning: individual rights not grounded in popular politics stood at risk of disappearing. What diehard champions of an imposed universalism called backlash was in policy terms the competitive pressure of contrary interests. When military leaders, refusing to "condone" homosexuality, kept gays and lesbians in service muzzled, they expended little effort in developing a reasonable case; their policy simply expressed where the political balance, and hence the balance in rights, lay. Majoritarian politics followed a distributional model. It apportioned rights.

A majority of whom? As the franchise became more accessible to more citizens in the 20th century, a smaller percentage of them voted. Some blamed women, the new voters who stayed away from the polls in disproportionate numbers for a time after 1920. But by midcentury their record evened out with the men's. Nor in any simple sense was competition the issue. When Harry Truman slipped past Thomas Dewey in the exciting four-way race of 1948, 51 percent participated. Four years later in the foregone conclusion between Dwight Eisenhower and Adlai Stevenson, 62 percent voted.

Then beginning in the 1960s, a whole range of obstacles to voting was swept away, and even some radical critics decided that the United States finally qualified as an electoral democracy. The Voting Rights Act of 1965 opened the polls to southern blacks. In the process, it outlawed literacy, educational, and character tests. A constitutional amendment barred poll taxes. More structural barriers fell in the 1970s, including residency requirements in excess of thirty days. With Republicans spreading through the south and Democrats expanding in New England, both parties had genuinely national scope. Yet for twenty years after 1960, as these deterrents to voting disappeared one after another, the turnout dropped a little at each presidential election until by 1988 it landed flat at 50 percent, 30 percentage points below the last outpouring of 19th century democracy, the election of 1896. During the 1980s, a composite of twenty other leading democracies had an average rate of participation in national elections 25 percent higher than America's.

Study after study repeated the same explanation: apathy and its near relation, powerlessness. Citizens with little to decide had less faith that it mattered. Apathy and powerlessness went hand in glove with atomization, an interconnectedness that revealed itself not only in the weakness of grassroots party organization of all sorts but also in the strength of democracy's individualist values. The same cultural characteristics that emancipated individuals seeking personal fulfillment trapped them seeking public power. Even the process of collective self-government was understood as millions of isolated acts: one person–one vote in infinite regression. Though Americans might be categorized by groups in the opinion polls, they were pictured going one by one to the voting polls. You arrive, the columnist Anna Quindlen told her readers, "draw the curtain closed on election day and are alone in your personal democracy." [15] Alone, that voter was helpless.

Politicians operated in a sea of atoms much as advertisers did. In theory, however, they were distributing information, not goods, and in the modern conception of citizenship, information about an array of difficult policy matters was critical to responsible voting. Dispensing information through popular media cost large amounts of money. Hence, when a law in 1971 capped both individual contributions and total expenditures for candidates in federal elections, the Supreme Court in *Buckley v. Valeo* (1976) disallowed the limit on total expenditures as inhibiting to the free flow of information. As costs rose, especially for television, so did contributions, now coming less through individuals than through political action committees—around 600 of them in 1974, over 4,000 in 1991. The breathtaking sums from PACs— $1 billion for campaigning as early as 1980—called forth brokers to serve as intermediaries between candidates and these proliferating groups, and especially to help incumbents draw off the lion's share. In the meantime, businessmen who openly sought profits from politics formed a sharply rising proportion of the PACs. What emerged was a world of big money operating light-years from the voters, now more than ever atoms in a distant sea, waiting for the most expensive information money could buy.

Perhaps everything was essentially all right: government did what it needed to do; parties functioned well enough; PACs kept the game in the open; and ordinary citizens accepted the results. A number of publicists and political scientists claimed as much. Or perhaps democracy worked when it was needed: apathy disappeared; atoms congealed; government responded. So it seemed in the fall of President Johnson over the Vietnam War and the resignation of President Nixon over the Watergate scandal.

Discussions of both affairs, however, confused popular disruption with popular self-governance, delegitimizing government with democratically conducting it. Although the antiwar movement did change American politics briefly, its democracy, as the expression went, was primarily in the streets, and its energies had little effect on the majoritarian process. The war, after all, dragged on for five more years after the peace movement peaked. Like the antiwar movement, the Watergate affair resembled crises in legitimacy that all kinds of governments encountered from time to time. These challenges contained roughly the same elements in dozens of other countries around the world as they did in the United States: marches, resistance to the law, hostile news reports, intragovernment conflict, charges of corruption, a run of defections, the call for resignations. However popular in a general sense, the process had no necessary association with political democracy. In 1974 President Nixon lost the Mandate of Heaven, resigned, and was replaced by a handpicked journeyman politician. Democratic self-determination was not at issue.

The upshot was neither an electorate with more faith in its officials nor officials with more faith in the electorate. After the initial shock of Watergate and revelations related to it, the government's devious, illegal actions increasingly came to seem normal. With the first news that Ronald Reagan's administration connived with Iran and violated the law to arm guerrillas in Nicaragua, polls showed a majority thought the president was lying about his role in the affair and a larger majority thought he was fulfilling his job as president. Tax revolts, the new politics of the 1980s, succeeded when they challenged not what governments should be doing but whether governments could be trusted with the money in the first place. In 1992 a jury refused to convict a former CIA administrator who lied to Congress because lying, the jury believed, was the way Washington officials did business.

Cynicism generated a compensatory romanticism. The most common variation looked to a leader—a Kennedy, Reagan, or Ross Perot—to transcend ordinary politics and take government in a new direction. Other alternatives envisaged equally dramatic changes coming in equally simple fashion. Instead of single leaders, some relied on elite groups. For example, the academically oriented Communitarians, who, they declared, were "not majoritarians," pictured a platonic community governance creating the good society, "whose moral standards reflect the basic human needs of all its members."[16] Several commentators demanded that leading politicians, apparently by fiat, eliminate from the national agenda the divisive cultural issues of the 1980s and 1990s and return—somewhat in the spirit of the old compromise—to what they called its real mission: economic management and social welfare. Others, on the contrary, never lost hope that the right president and the right Supreme Court could bring back the glory days of expanding universal rights: "the national uniformities some of us wished to impose on all of us," in the historian Barry Karl's phrasing.[17]

The basic limitations in majoritarian democracy, however, lay far beneath its level of leadership. The American electorate's class bias, already on a par with India's, grew even more pronounced in the polarizing years between the 1960s and the 1990s. In America's politics of distribution, most of those most in need did not participate at all. As a matter of policy, local middle-class majorities insisted on supervising them. As a matter of course, national-class publicists decided what rights were best for them.

Who were these Americans? Most of them belonged to America's multiethnic, multiracial, unskilled lower class, whose broad outlines appeared at the crossing of several statistical lines. Around 1990, perhaps 40 million Americans were eligible for food stamps. About 30 percent of the children in the United States lived in or on the edge of hunger. In the neighborhood of 70 million Americans had either patently inadequate health insurance or none at all. Recent studies suggested that about 35 million adults were illiterate and double that number could not understand simplified tax or consumer credit forms. Adding the chronically underemployed to the unemployed who were seeking jobs and those who had stopped looking totaled somewhere around 25 percent of the potential work force. A murder rate four times Europe's and an infant mortality rate twentieth among twenty-three industrialized nations did not mean that life was unusually risky for middle-class and national-class Americans, just shockingly so for lower-class Americans. In all of these categories, Native Americans, Latins, and African Americans constituted disproportionately high percentages. Blacks, for example, comprised more than half of those sunk in prolonged poverty.

Democracy's internal conflicts came into focus here. Although the struggle between universalizing individual rights and reclaiming community authority over them attracted almost all the attention, it obscured the fact that the national and local middle classes contesting these issues themselves colluded, as they had all century, in denying the lower class a voice in these or any other public debates. Together they short-circuited the democratic process. Yet contrary to their fears, reviving majoritarianism did not entail redistributing society's resources. The dream of the Left and the nightmare of the Right that the lower class, once activated, would force a radical remaking of the political agenda and a radical reapportionment of wealth remained just that: figments of ideology, with no discernible connection to the American experience. Nor did it mean managed competition, where other people arranged the terms of lower-class politics to produce outcomes that other people decided were just. Always the democratic issue was participation: no special rules, no hothouse environment, no mandated results. Just open wide the doors and let it happen.

||||||

CONCLUSION

|||||| **A**n agenda of concerns that came roaring out of the 1960s—America's divided society, its disappearing electorate, its atomized citizenry—continues to dominate contemporary discussions of democracy. These issues appeared more or less in that order: first polarization, then participation, then individualism. On each topic, the standard prescriptions have concentrated on changing what goes into democracy: the attitudes Americans bring to public affairs, the ways they mobilize to have an influence, even the frames of reference they take to their everyday lives. As both problems and solutions have accumulated over the years, however, their deeper message functions as a question: does American democracy have a future?

Initial responses to the polarized politics of the late 1960s, while certainly alarmed, proposed quite simple solutions. An abrupt, radical aberration required an equally quick return to the safe middle ground. In that spirit, such publicists as Samuel Lubell (1970) and David Broder (1972) called for a nationwide bootstraps operation, a collective effort of will, to draw the divided country together again.* What might seem evasive made sense on two conditions: first, that at heart the great majority of Americans remained moderates; and second, that they usually went where they were told to go. All else being equal, these commentators assumed, it should be easier for sound leaders, by tapping people's naturally decent impulses, to guide them home again than it

*Here as in the Introduction; citations to a core of works are by author and publication date. For full citations, see "Special Debts and Further Readings," section on Introduction and Conclusion, pp. 279–283.

had been for extremists to override those impulses and lead them astray in the first place.

This exceedingly attractive argument has lost none of its appeal in recent decades. No matter how grim the immediate circumstances or how extensive the necessary changes, some commentators still count on the right leadership mounting the right campaign to turn the country around. Hence James Davison Hunter (1991), who believes that propagandists have maneuvered Americans into artificially polarized positions on cultural values, looks for moderate messages from responsible leaders to pull the public back to the center; and E. J. Dionne, Jr. (1991), who believes the recent battling over cultural issues has hidden the serious social and economic problems that really matter, wants clear-eyed leaders to teach citizens how to distinguish a phony from a genuine politics.

An important subtext in these accounts has been the disputed place of America's liberals as national leaders. First radicals in the 1960s and 1970s repudiated liberals as just another kind of conservative trying to pacify the oppressed classes. Then conservatives in the 1980s and 1990s excoriated liberals as just another kind of radical catering to fringe groups at the expense of the majority. Those publicists who continue to believe in an inherently moderate American majority have had considerable difficulty defending the liberal faith. If liberals are the majority's natural leaders, they must have inflicted one political disaster after another on themselves through an almost perverse combination of public blindness and bad judgment. The champions of American moderation are beside themselves in frustration. Have liberals learned nothing at all from these mistakes? Are they even educable? In a particularly intense example of publicists as instructors, Thomas and Mary Edsall (1991) systematically walk liberals through every error they have made since 1964 in hopes that finally the lessons of experience will penetrate.

Right behind the initial reactions to political polarization came a second round of concerns, this one about popular participation, especially the missing voters. Some political scientists incorporated these latest cries of distress into a long-running campaign to make America's major parties responsible, along the lines of Britain's, and thereby compensate for the nation's high proportion of indifferent, ill-equipped citizens. Strong parties, such prominent figures as James MacGregor Burns (1990) and James Sundquist (Reichley 1987) still argue, are capable of turning public inertia into a mandate for effective government. Other critics, on the other hand, champion parties to overcome the weakness rather than the incompetence of ordinary citizens, to act not as their proxy but as their agency. In that vein, Walter Dean Burnham calls political parties "the only devices thus far invented by the wit of Western man which with some effectiveness can generate countervailing collective power on behalf of the many individually powerless against the [privileged] few."[1] Although policy-minded reformers now call for the revitalization of parties almost as a matter of course, their drastic remedies—eliminate primaries, stop ticket-splitting, monopolize campaign funds—suggest a doctor eyeing the artificial respirator.

Alternative strategies encourage the participation of the poor and discourage the participation of the rich. In an effort to redress the class bias in voting that Sidney Verba and Norman Nie (1972) identified and Burnham has emphasized, reformers attack rules that appear to be particularly inhibiting to lower-class participation. Advocating simplified, semiautomatic voter registration, a proposal recently identified with Frances Fox Piven and Richard Cloward (1989), has been the most popular of these campaigns, and the so-called Motor Voter Act of 1993, linking registration to the renewal of drivers' licenses, responds to it. At the other end of society, critics have targeted big money as popular participation's number one enemy. Here too proposals to diminish the influence of great wealth in popular communication, political campaigns, and government lobbying routinely appear in summaries of essential democratic reforms.

A quite different approach, equating genuine popular participation with a socialist overhaul of the system, has dwindled in recent years. World events have not been kind to traditional radicalism, and its heirs shy away from the prospect of massive upheavals. "The outcome of any thoroughgoing social revolution," warns the radical philosopher John Dryzek, "is almost always a strengthened state with a longer bureaucratic reach." At least temporarily, some socialist voices have fallen silent. After preparing five versions of his Leninist text on American democracy in rapid-fire sequence, for example, Michael Parenti has left it alone since the fall of the Soviet Empire. Another radical philosopher, John Dunn, has lapsed into a Barthian pessimism about political processes that he now considers "too complicated, too untransparent, and too unstable for the human mind to take in . . . In politics today, we do not really understand what we are doing and we do not grasp what is being done to, or for, or against us."[2] Even many of those who still advocate sweeping radical changes, such as Alan Gilbert (1990) and William Greider (1992), package them as reform. As if to avoid any taint of revolutionary intent, Gilbert wraps his Marxist program in sheaves of liberal proposals.

The third set of reactions required about fifteen years to materialize, a not uncommon gap between events and a considered scholarly response to them. Its focus, modern society's atomized individuals, has penetrated the farthest into American culture, and among the alternatives still lively in the 1990s its critique envisages the most profound changes. Although the ties between democracy and the individual have been matters of discussion throughout the 20th century, until well after midcentury almost no one challenged the individual's right to the central place. Even then, the lone individual as the core of democracy has never lacked eloquent champions. Robert Nozick (1974) has predicated a prize-winning study on the proposition that "no new rights 'emerge' at the group level, that individuals in combination cannot create new rights."[3] The Nobel Prize winner Kenneth Arrow's famous theorem about the logical unmanageability of individual choices presupposes an array of discreet actors, each making isolated selections from a complex menu of alternatives. Adam Seligman (1992) opens his important book on democratic life with a definition of society as a body of self-seeking atoms, and Robert Dahl (1989) ends his with a commitment to the primacy of the individual. Two late 20th century key words popularly linked with democracy—*meritocracy* and *the market*—celebrate the lone achiever and lone decision-maker respectively.

By the 1980s, however, an important group of commentators went on the attack against this position. Sometimes their attention fell on what American life was doing to the individual, as Christopher Lasch elaborated in *The Culture of Narcissism* (1978), sometimes on what the individual was doing to American life, as Robert Bellah and his associates discussed in *Habits of the Heart* (1985). Whichever way the influences moved, these critics found them corroding values and stunting lives. The very unattractiveness of the philosopher C. B. Macpherson's name for modern culture, "possessive individualism," helped to account for the phrase's popularity.

Taken one by one, most of the themes in these writings were familiar enough. Complaints about the self-indulgent individual with too much spending money and too few inner restraints, for example, hearkened back to the beginning of the century; so did laments about the loss of community. A rich literature on the individual's helplessness and anxiety flourished around the Second World War. A number of accounts late in the century of the individual without anchor or compass seemed merely to update old concepts of anomie and other-directedness.

In this case, however, the whole did exceed the sum of its parts. Taken together, these contemporary critiques of individualism oblige us to rethink the premises behind modern American culture and therefore of the democracy within it. Rather than designing theories of democracy in a universe of separate human beings—one person–one vote, one person's rights extending to the point where they infringe upon the next person's, and so forth—these commentators insist upon starting with something collective: a community, a tradition, a common need. What those who glorify the isolated individual ignore, John Dunn (1990) reminds us, is that the environment sustaining this individual requires the collective effort, "the skill and imagination of all its adult beneficiaries." In the same spirit, Benjamin Barber (1984) declares that, rightly understood, the individual's "freedom is a social construct based on a rare and fragile form of human mutualism that grants space to individuals who otherwise would have none at all." For "a *society of individuals*" to survive, Bruce Ackerman (1980) argues, it must "link individual rights to community processes."[4]

The controversy surrounding John Rawls' monumental *A Theory of Justice* (1971) illustrates the importance of that starting point. Although the main principles in Rawls' theory are clearly social—the three primary ones establish a bed of shared rights and a pair of checks against the unequal distribution of benefits and privileges—the origins of these principles as Rawls reasons about them lie in an imagined world of individuated, self-protective people who then create the just society. With a thunder that would certainly be excessive on any other grounds, his critics attack at the point of origin. A collection of "strangers" creates nothing of value, Michael Sandel (1982) has charged. Only through the politics of an already functioning community can we "know a good in common that we cannot know alone." The philosopher Richard Rorty (1979) makes a similar case: the process of knowing derives from the community, from "the confidence in our own assertions which the approval of our peers gives us." The Rawlsian imagery feeds into the "radical heterogeneous individualism" that Yaron Ezrahi (1990) condemns in late 20th century democracies. For Barber, it contains all the irremediable deficiencies of a "thin democracy" resting on "Man Alone."[5]

These philosophers reason in zero-sum terms: as the community gains authority, it retakes territory that has been lost to the individual. Charles Taylor (1992), on the other hand, holds out the prospect of a process enhancing to both. Individual fulfillment, the Western world's finest ideal, degenerates into mere self-indulgence for individuals in isolation, Taylor states. Fulfillment only has meaning by reference to a collective human record, in history and across cultures, enabling individuals to shape sets of values and through those values to understand their goals. In proper relationship, as the richness of modern society measures individual growth, the richness of individual growth ornaments modern society.

Beginning with a sense of culture's impoverishment, these critics end their argument with a call for society's revitalization. They imagine a

252

democratic life in common, a breaking down of old private barriers that hide gendered oppressions, property-based inequalities, silent controls over information, and the like, and an opening up of new public spaces where citizens meet, argue, decide, and meet again. It is a busy, assertive democracy of neighborhood gatherings, electronic votes, local initiatives, and national referenda. It places significantly less weight on an equality of conditions—lists of rights, leveled incomes, employment quotas—than on an equality in interaction, one that draws all of those who are living together, working together, or otherwise resolving problems together into pools of participants. The cardinal sin is exclusion. Once all the citizens have opportunities to gather, the process itself becomes sovereign: this democracy is what people make of it.

Benjamin Barber, John Dryzek, Philip Green (1985), Mickey Kaus (1992), Carole Pateman (1989), and Michael Walzer (1983) have been particularly impressive in this cause. Nevertheless, lacking a special vehicle to promote it, their vision has gained none of the prominence that the ACLU, for instance, gives to individual rights. It deserves better, for this composite account provides us with our finest description of what democracy entails and what efforts it requires.

What this impressive analysis lacks—what all three themes in the recent discussions of democracy lack, for that matter—is historical awareness, a sense of the particular experiences that particular people have had during a particular span of time. Although no one must ask history to forecast the future, we do need it to understand where we are and what alternatives actually exist for us. In orienting ourselves, history has three critical contributions to make. First, it frames the problems: it identifies their origins, it gives them an age, and in the process it goes a long way toward revealing how shallow or deep their place in a contemporary culture. Second, it reveals the conditions that each society has set for reconstructing itself. Under what circumstances, that is, has major social change occurred? Third, history inventories the possibilities for change. Which among the propositions now in the air have strong ties to a particular people's experiences and expectations, embedded values and common memories? Does such an inventory uncover some otherwise overlooked sources of change?

Notice how a simple chronology alters the perspective that a number of recent commentaries ask us to take. For example, the claim of E. J. Dionne, Jr., Thomas and Mary Edsall, William Greider, and John Davison Hunter, among others, that a unique crisis struck American democracy in the 1960s, or in a few cases the 1980s, obscures the depth and duration of the problems they want to resolve. Although politics did polarize between the 1960s and 1970s, the underlying divisions dated from America's restructuring early in the 20th century. Trying to manage those divisions, particularly through the compromise of the 1930s and its variations, determined the contours of public policy long before the 1960s, just as the collapse of the compromise set the limits afterward. By the same token, popular political participation, especially as measured by voting, did decline after 1960, but in the context of the 20th century this slippage was a relatively minor extension of the great slide that had more or less run its course four decades earlier. The class patterns in today's voting developed on the same timetable.

What follows is an attempt to combine this kind of historical understanding with the cultural analysis of democracy's latest cluster of critics. I refer to them collectively as *the democrat*. In the name of clarity, however, we must pause a minute first. Democracy is only one among many social objectives. There are ideals of personal freedom and human justice, programs for government efficiency and economic productivity, visions of international peacekeeping and global environmentalism, along with many others, whose pursuit may well run at odds with the quest for an invigorated democracy. But a history of American democracy does not speak to these alternatives; it has authority on just one subject. I apply that history to one cause not because this objective has claims precluding all others but because it has distinct claims requiring space of their own to be understood. By design, what follows is the democrat's brief. Balancing democracy's case against those of its competitors belongs in another book.

As my quick chronology indicates, we can establish at the outset that the basic problems confronting these critics trace well beyond Ronald Reagan, Richard Nixon, and John Kennedy to the days of Calvin Coolidge, Woodrow Wilson, and Theodore Roosevelt. They grew out of the social transformation occurring between the 1890s and the 1920s, which generated the two great constraints on modern democracy—centralization and hierarchy. Despite the capacity to accommodate a broad electoral base, centralization and hierarchy have consistently resisted the twin mandates for democratic participation—popular access to the governing process and a responsive governing system. The crucial first step on the democrat's agenda, therefore, is a relentless attack on those primary contraints. Wherever possible, the democrat exhorts, pull down on the hierarchies and pull away from the centers of power.

Of course there are those who say we must concentrate power to match concentrations of power elsewhere, and others who say we must amass power to meet massive human needs. "The ultimate test of a political system is performance," one leading advocate of concentrated national power has declared; performance on this grand scale, adds

254   CONCLUSION

another, depends inextricably on "hierarchy, inequality, arbitrary power, secrecy, [and] deception."⁶ The democrat responds: note carefully what you pay and what you get. Take, for example, these common justifications for the centralized state as a counterbalancing power. Only big government can regulate big business, one argument goes. In fact, the democrat responds, the record of public officials and private interests mingling and colluding has been repeated so often in the 20th century that the entire concept of regulation—a neutral state guiding private corporations in the public interest—lies bankrupt. Prohibitions, as on DDT, sometimes work; so do educational campaigns, as on the use of certain drugs; but regulation has not.

Or consider the argument that, with its separation of powers, big government polices itself. Have the War Powers Resolution of 1973 and the Intelligence Oversight Act of 1980 caused more than a ripple in the executive's ability to maneuver and make war as it chooses? Which ensconced bureaucracies have relinquished their power? Even centralized ventures with some initial promise have hung on to the point of disaster. If institutions, like individuals, cannot be properly assessed until they are dead, then TVA is a miserable failure.

Alternatively, large combinations of power are championed so that through government-business collaboration America can keep up in the race for global competitiveness. In fact, the democrat counters, competitiveness may well depend upon a radical decentralization of efforts. America's corporate hierarchies, once the world's pioneers in systematic organization, now stand as object lessons in self-protective, self-defeating business practices, snarled in the details of personal privileges, overwhelmed with top-down directives, and bunkered against reform. The tottering of corporate empires—General Motors, IBM, Sears, Roebuck—tells only the surface story. In diverse settings across the country, where human-scale work crews operate interactively rather than hierarchically, their productivity increases. Where skills are generalized and adapted instead of subdivided and repeated—that is, where greater responsibility falls to teams of workers in what Michael Piore and Charles Sabel call "flexible specialization"—industry commonly has prospered. The same prescription applies to government bureaucracies. For the democrat, the devolution of mainframe commuting centers into networks of small, adjustable work stations provides a metaphor as well as a model for success. Even detailed divisions of labor for highly complex tasks need not translate, as customary corporate wisdom would have it, into invidious hierarchies of atomized workers. In the face of any individual's absolute dependence on cooperation, humility is a more natural reaction.

Perhaps centralized power in the service of human rights is more appealing. Without firm national enforcement who would protect the Bill of Rights? We might as reasonably ask who would violate it, the democrat responds, for freewheeling agencies of the central government have been its most frightening abusers. Factoring human deaths into its balance sheet is one of the hallmarks of the modern state: take lives now, pay for them later, as in the case of numerous citizens caught in the lethal net of the government's nuclear power programs. What more extraordinary vision of lions and lambs than the judicial arm of the big state protecting the ordinary citizen's right to privacy. Efforts to determine fairness on a national scale are equally ominous, the democrat reminds us. In the most humanely motivated efforts, as Robert Nozick's principle of unintended consequences reminds us, new rules are forever sent after the old in a scramble to correct even more unfairness. Issuing from the top down, distributive justice means disruptive justice. In a centralized system, majorities find places for minorities; in a decentralized one, minorities have a chance of finding their own places.

Furthering human rights internationally raises other issues, the democrat tells us. We must not expect the national government to promote abroad what it has not accepted at home: a vigorous electoral democracy. Although the opposition of the United States to unusually repressive governments has a better chance of success, chasing the rainbow of security—ours or any other people's—has a dangerously inflating, coercing momentum to it, as we know from its pursuit during the last half century. In general, the democrat warns, sending more and more power in pursuit of bigger and bigger challenges—military, economic, demographic, ecological—dramatically increases the likelihood of disasters. While responsibility gets weakened, power still gets used. Whatever services supranational political structures may perform, they do not fundamentally alter that formula. Somebody's politics prevails—there are no platonic civil servants—and constituencies remain far away: their representatives' representatives' representatives are deciding for them. It is arguable, the democrat concludes, that a drastic reduction in the use of the world's resources, and an equivalent scaling back of the power to command them, would be America's greatest contribution to universal human rights.

The democrat pulls down the large structures so that ordinary citizens can move in and participate. The historical record and contemporary experience alike are eloquent in expressing how closely a rise in participatory energy correlates with a faith in local self-rule. Even in quite small nation-states, personal efficacy and popular activity rise at the local level. In these settings, the democrat places voting where it belongs—at the center of the political process. Nothing more effectively enforces popular judgments or heightens government responsiveness. Large turnouts at frequent elections simultaneously send a regular flow of messages to officials and keep them guessing. Between elections, moreover, officials stay alert to other kinds of popular politics. Starting here, citizens have a chance of achieving Benjamin Barber's definition of democracy: "a form of government in which all of the people govern themselves in at least some public matters at least some of the time."[7]

With voting once more central, the democrat turns to three important linkages that have become weak or ambiguous in modern times: between opinions and decisions, between decisions and actions, and between actions and determinations. The connection between forming an opinion and making a decision should be seamless, the democrat argues. Opinion polls, as pseudoparticipatory proxies that create an illusion of citizens actually having a say in their government, are particularly pernicious obstacles to that smooth joining. As if weak-willed citizens could only have genuine opinions apart from the give and take of everyday life, pollsters atomize and isolate them, turning opinions into artificially static thoughts offered in an artificially dead environment. Because expressing political opinions for opinions' sake simply ratifies public passivity, the democrat shuns them as personally degrading and publicly irresponsible. On political issues, citizens should presume that forming an opinion is always the prelude to making a decision. With a determinate outcome at hand—preferably with a ballot in hand—citizens would have reason to feel doubly responsible: responsible in their thinking, responsible for its consequences.

Again with voting in mind, the democrat seeks to sharpen the meaning of a second link: between deciding and acting. Needless obstacles between the two—marking a few special days to register voters, for instance—should be swept away. But in the name of shortening that connection, whatever merges the two is equally detrimental to the political process. Specifically, the several recent visions of electronic balloting, where future citizens would sit at home and give instant responses to unfolding events, take the muscle out of voting as a distinct, crucial act. Deciding is one thing in the democrat's scheme, acting another. In self-government, an act is not the same as a response; voting should not be confused with touching a key or punching the remote. Some effort is critical to its function.

Because voting is a collective effort that only acquires meaning through a quantity of ballots, the democrat needs to cement a third link, this one between acting and determining. By democratic standards, it is intolerable to accept whatever sprinkling of people may

appear for an election, then move on as if self-governing procedures
have been satisfied. Although coerced voting, thoroughly contaminated by authoritarian governments, is not an alternative, too few vol-
unteers also subvert the political process, just as surely as widespread
bribery and ballot-stuffing do. At some point on a curve of declining
turnouts, the system no longer functions. Nor does the democrat want
to sell the process short by setting this point too low. By tradition, a
majority has served as democracy's legitimizing principle. Therefore,
if a majority of the voters do not participate in an election, it should
be invalidated—that is, disqualified on democratic grounds—and re-
scheduled. As a last resort, an otherwise disqualified election might
stand with a formal disclaimer that it did not satisfy democratic procedures—a scarlet letter to disgrace the public, not the winners. Unless
elections are somehow bound into majorities, they only undermine
democratic responsibility: the responsibility of the community of voters who are electing and the responsibility of the government they
elect.

How much pulling down and pulling apart, how much popular participation is enough? At this stage, the democrat tells us not to worry:
with so far to go on all counts, the more the better. Advocating basic
changes, the democrat listens to the second important message from
history. Major changes in democracy rise only out of systemic break-
downs, not out of an accretion of many small adjustments. Broad processes of breakdown and rebuilding generated America's original democracy, destroyed slavery, and redefined democracy for the 20th
century. By contrast, a gradual decline in the authority of America's
governing institutions since the 1960s has done nothing to halt their
growing concentrations of power, despite quadrennial promises to reverse the trend. President Reagan, extraordinarily popular as the rhe-
torical champion of small government and private initiative, accelerated the growth of the federal budget and drowned the nation in
public debt. Competing over the levers of centralized power has never
humbled it. In the American experience, the essential corollary to the
often-cited iron law of oligarchy—the inevitable rise of a controlling
few in large organizations—is that only breakdown, never patchwork,
shakes the iron law's grip.

   From the voices of authority come incessant warnings about the dangers of this process. First, citing examples that range from South Asia
through the former Soviet Empire into Africa, they warn how easily
the passionate attachments of everyday life degenerate into anarchical
bloodletting unless a strong state restrains them. Nation-states with
delineated boundaries and fixed laws keep the peace; cultural group-

ings with fluid boundaries and negotiable rules subvert good order. The latest scare word is *Bosnia*. Second, bringing the case closer to home, they lament how severely the disruptive, centrifugal forces of liberty have hampered the United States government in trying to fulfill its normal functions. The political scientist Samuel Huntington has been particularly forceful: "the American people believe that government ought not to do things it must do in order to be a government and it ought to do things it cannot do without undermining itself as a government."[8]

The democrat rejects this entire argument. The terrible damage from a rampant tribalism has grown out of a mix of causes, not least of which is the the clash between artificial state systems and primary group identities. Whatever the sources, however, rendering illegitimate what is most important in people's lives is no solution. Nostalgia for big bosses like Tito simply obscures the fundamental problem of accommodating government to people's primary attachments. Moreover, holding citizens' rights in abeyance in order to free the hand of the central government is tantamount to losing them. Democratic rights do not survive in storage; kept in reserve, they deteriorate. People who want rights must act on them—take them into the world, apply them, then reacquire them over and over again through persistent use.

In that spirit, the democrat who insists upon major change exhorts citizens to activate their political rights wherever they go. In effect, they should politicize their lifeways—at work and at leisure, in clubs and in causes, by gender and by race, through ethnicity and through religion. The purpose is not to swamp America in politics but to diversify its politics; not to politicize all aspects of life but to use all aspects of life in politics—to spread it out as our lives spread out. James Mac-Gregor Burns throws up his hands in despair because "voters neither wish to, nor would be able to, cleanse themselves of family, neighborhood, ethnic, occupational, religious, and interest-group influences."[9] The democrat replies, of course. Politics should follow the voter, not the converse.

Multiple public identities mean multiple interests and loyalties; multiple attachments weave tapestries of political involvement that show different hues in the light of different issues. A politics reflecting what happens to people day by day, the democrat believes, will greatly expand the number of citizens who initiate and monitor, who raise the new issues and keep the old ones from getting lost. As it joins citizens in common causes, this kind of politics even makes human connections among people who have never seen or spoken with one another. Although the dynamics differ radically from face-to-face interaction, the bonds are by no means inconsequential.

Public spaces in this scheme are the spaces people make public. Wherever in the normal course of affairs numbers of them gather and mingle, the democrat argues, they create a public life. Shopping centers, for example, obviously qualify. From this perspective, the historian Daniel Boorstin's seemingly contrived notion of democratic "consumption communities" has a certain merit: common patterns of consumption do create opportunities for democratic action. So in their own way do electronic bulletin boards. And so do areas in most work places where the coffee and snack machines sit, where employees regularly chat as they cross paths, where notices are posted, and the like. Politics here would be no more restricted to work place issues than politics in a women's group would be to feminism. Whatever concerns people brought, from the hole in the ozone layer to the hole in the neighborhood street, would have their chance, the democrat emphasizes, and none could be dismissed as merely symbolic, as less real than the others.

An essential concomitant of guerrilla politics—which initially this would be—is a healthy disrespect. Those who deplore the declining public regard for government authorities, the democrat reminds us, miss two important points. First, officials have earned it. Against a backdrop of overweening rulers and their systematic lies, citizens use disrespect to make room for their own judgments. Second, American attitudes toward their national government are comparatively trusting. International polls indicate European skepticism running much deeper. Authority will require a good deal more deflation, the democrat argues, to prepare the way for major changes. Under current circumstances, as the philosopher Ian Shapiro describes it, democracy should be understood as "an ethic of opposition," a competitive, combative way of conducting public business that "best prevents the ossification of arbitrary entitlements and undermines entrenched power without collapsing into . . . chaos."[10] Democracy's target is always a superior power, never a vulnerable citizen. In no case does it have a stake in personal humiliation.

Subverting authority, the democrat's brief continues, must not spare the major political parties. Although they have the ability to gather otherwise ineffectual citizens into public alliances, in fact they too reflect the values of hierarchy and centralization. Both Republicans and Democrats feed at the grass tops; both exemplify the iron law of oligarchy. In modern America, both have organized around the principles in the compromise of the 1930s, principles that operate to exclude the lower class. That romantic moment when an underfunded candidate wins over the well-heeled incumbent no more alters these characteristics, the democrat stresses, than winning the lottery alters the distribution of national wealth. In 1990, when the shoestring candidacy of Paul Wellstone defeated the well-funded Rudy Boschwitz in Minnesota, Boschwitz was the sole incumbent to lose in that year's thirty-two senatorial races. As guerrilla politics succeeds, therefore, it almost always fills a vacuum at the grass roots. Its loyalties create their own kind of map: communities arising out of work, church, and recreation do not fit neatly into electoral districts.

The pulling-down process, the democrat adds, must cover what passes for private power as well. Large corporations sustain hierarchy and centralization, enter into myriad public activities, and affect the prospects for democracy at every turn. A guerrilla politics of everyday life would certainly insist upon corporate responsibility in at least two areas. First, corporate officers would become responsible to the citizens whom their actions affect. They would require endorsement from these constituents just as their political counterparts require validation from theirs. Second, corporations would be held responsible to the geographical communities with which they interact. For the valuable privilege of selling goods and services in the rich American market, the democrat might advocate a social tax for all companies, domestic or foreign, to be applied to the community's special stake in these transactions—educational, environmental, generational, recreational, and the like—with rebates for appropriate corporate initiatives. Finally, the democrat might turn the Jeffersonian principle of periodic renewal to corporate charters. Every fifteen years, say, a corporation would have to justify its existence, to demonstrate that it serves a desirable function in a socially responsible way. The more serious the public purpose behind this plan, the democrat predicts, the more routine its procedures would become.

As guerrilla politics subverts a centralized, hierarchical superstructure, the democrat anticipates it creating a human-scale world of its own: community breeds politics breeds community. Moreover, as Sidney Verba and Norman Nie reported more than two decades ago, politics breeds politics: the more active people are, the more active they become. Yet the standard wisdom still maintains that citizens, tiring quickly of politics, will simply tune it out. With no particular evidence, comedians, cartoonists, and commentators of all sorts agreed that the vigorous, three-way race for the presidency in 1992 utterly exhausted the electorate. For the poor Georgia citizenry, who still faced a late November runoff for a Senate seat, there was a national outpouring of sympathy. But in a politics that matters, why presume so little staying power? the democrat asks. Do basketball fans complain when their team makes the playoffs, forcing another round of games with a new opponent? Why should control over one's daily life somehow be less engaging?

Measuring the demands of the moment against a record of American experiences and traditions, history's third contribution is to find out what fits. Almost always, it turns out that a good deal does not. Take, for example, the oft-repeated insistence that democracy "critically depends on an informed electorate" who have heard "all worthwhile ideas and views."[11] Even if we accept the implausible proposition that a determinate body of knowledge lies out there to be learned, then agree on what in it passes the worthwhile test, why should citizens be obliged to sit there and learn it? At its most vigorous, American democracy has channeled existing sentiments. Rather than casting citizens as vacant-minded students in a civics class, democracy has mobilized what they bring to public life.

By and large, 20th century critics have defined an informed electorate by what the critics know. By their lights, they have recognized the complexities in modern policy; only others have oversimplified. Only others, never they, have succumbed to manipulative slogans and deceptive ads. In fact, the democrat points out, this informed opinion deserves exactly the same keen-eyed skepticism as any other opinion. It produced immigration quotas in the 1920s, defended the gold standard in the 1930s, and warned against precipitous desegregation in the 1940s. Who understood the war in Vietnam better, the democrat asks: the ordinary citizen who viewed it as a battle against Asian Communism, or the sophisticated advisers who thought they could create a nation of South Vietnam through a puppet Catholic in Saigon and forced relocation in the countryside? The modern application of Jefferson's famous conceit about the plowman grasping issues faster than the professor is that plowmen and professors understand differently, each with distinctive strengths and weaknesses for civic life and no fixed sum of knowledge out there to measure the difference between them.

History encourages a similar skepticism about the tone essential to democratic politics, especially the insistence upon a cool civility. As the recent enthusiasm for Jürgen Habermas's eerily detached rationality illustrates, contemporary commentators show an extraordinary aversion to emotion in politics. How we rule ourselves, the democrat responds, engages our deepest feelings. Draining emotions from politics drains it of life. Degendered, Ronald Dworkin's principle is unexceptionable: "A man cannot express himself freely when he cannot match his rhetoric to his outrage."[12] There are subtle issues at stake here, the democrat acknowledges, one of which is the possibility that Dworkin's

statement cannot be degendered. When speech batters a captive dependent who is allowed no voice and no recourse, it loses all claim to
be called free. And if emotions spill over into physical violence, another set of principles applies. Violence, the most pernicious legacy
from the 1960s, becomes democracy's mortal enemy at the point where,
directly or indirectly, it drives participants out of the political process.
Protecting access to that process overrides all other considerations, including, if it comes to that, the opposition to centralized controls. Nevertheless, from a long historical record of rude popular politics, the
democrat's rule of thumb holds: place just as few restraints as possible
on the expression of feelings.

The historical record also encourages critics not to grow apoplectic
over the issue of money in politics. Restrictions and more restrictions
do not keep them apart. Trying to get money out of politics is like
protecting sand castles from the tide: politics soaks it up. Seeking to
rechannel money in order to equalize its effects is just as delusive.
Inequalities of myriad sorts always exist, and using dollars to rebal-
ance the scales only complicates the problems. However, two guide-
lines suggest the possibility of diminishing its influence. First, big
money pursues centralized power. Scattering power through guerrilla
politics would sharply limit the attractions of the chase: too many elusive units, too little to gain from each. Second, because a privileged
access to mass media is money's most disputed influence, the democrat
has fewer reasons to fear the consequences than many of his contemporaries. The very term *mass media* implies an interpretation of its effects: simple messages implanted in the blank minds of countless ordinary citizens. The democrat has far more faith that receivers as much
as senders shape the messages.

For the democrat, the consequence most to fear is the power of
money to set an agenda for discussion. When popular media communicate on political issues, therefore, they must function as open public
spaces. The issue is not, as the Supreme Court presumed in *Buckley v.
Valeo* (1976) and ancillary rulings, that the public has a right to some
body of knowledge out there and that restrictions on the political uses
of money in the media might deny the public a part of this determinate
whole. Instead, the great danger is that unlimited spending may interfere with the public's right to speak and to hear—with the media's
openness, in Judith Lichtenberg's phrase, to a "multiplicity of voices."[13]
The democrat focuses on the narrow band of participants rather than
the narrow band of ideas: who gets a chance to talk instead of what
they say. Moreover, it makes less sense to crowd many additional
voices into a single national discussion, as Lichtenberg envisages, than
to welcome ways of scattering the venues. The democrat treasures the

American tradition of innumerable discussions, each with its own purpose, many tuned only to their own groups, and none blessed with a
distinctive national authority. The democratic objective, in other
words, is not to eliminate politics from popular media but to open the
media to political variety. Many voices generate many agendas.

These many voices come from many publics. Prominent figures such
as Ralph Nader and Ross Perot, who incessantly claim to be speaking
for a whole people, would turn them into a mere chorus. Popular government, the democrat reminds us, works up from those publics, not
down to them. To the national-class environmentalist slogan "Think
Globally, Act Locally," the democrat counters "Think Locally, Act Globally." Begin with people, not problems, with an understanding of
shared resources in small groups, then develop wider and wider networks through the connectedness that encourages. Those groups must
grow from people's lifeways. Simply declaring some geographical area
a neighborhood or community demeans its residents, especially since
such commandments often mask a desire to dissolve racial, ethnic, or
religious clusterings. Insisting that an electoral minority must be
"nothing more than a random collection of people who lost the last
vote," as Philip Green does in his account of local democracy, has unsettling implications.[14] Individuals who are separated from groups of
their choice become particularly dependent on others to act for them
and hence particularly vulnerable to coercion.

What the democrat seeks is a reaffirmation of the American heritage
that draws people with all kinds of identities and loyalties into a collective self-governing process. A national gathering of these participating
publics creates an exhilarating prospect: citizens divided by race and
nationality, sex and sexual preference, social class and physical condition, sundry gods and many lifestyles, contributing equally to decisions that some win, others lose, but all accept as a fact of life. It is a
civic affair. The self-governing process, as Rawls phrases it, "rejects
common views of voting as a private and even personal matter."[15] Universal love has nothing to do with it. It is a process compatible with
mutual exclusion, even mutual hostility. Although the ballot levels everybody for a moment, the election booth accommodates all the twist-
ing paths people take into it and out of it again. Elections leave diversity just as they found it. This politics of segmented unity—e pluribus
unum democratic-style—is the very antithesis of the bloody tribalism
running rampant elsewhere in the world: it is, on the contrary, a jewel
of democracy.

Which, finally, brings us full circle to the original definition. Invariably democracy entails some version of popular self-government that
assures citizens access to the political process, never bars losers from

that process, and keeps officials responsive to their constituents. It is this core that the democrat has been seeking to strengthen. But variably democracy is always something else, something specific to the culture in which it operates, and in America that additional component from the very beginning has been individualism, either as self-determination or as fulfillment. To this occasionally bending but un-broken tradition the democrat must pay particularly close attention. The substantial body of contemporary criticism that singles out indi-vidualism as the special curse of American democracy simply flies in the face of its history. Telling Americans to improve democracy by sinking comfortably into a community, by losing themselves in a col-lective life, is calling into the wind. There has never been an American democracy without its powerful strand of individualism, and nothing suggests there will ever be.

In America, democratic individualism has always meant abundant choices and has come to mean inviolable rights. A revitalized democ-racy must incorporate both. Demanding that other people make what we consider the right choices does not qualify. Many critics cite a pas-sionate attachment to consumerism as evidence of America's shallow, self-serving individualism; others cite a blind opposition to socialism as evidence of its narrow, self-defeating side. In each case, the roots lie deep in American culture; in neither case does a commandment from somebody's high ground change a thing. It matters, moreover, that some version of this cornucopia of choices has given hope to millions around the world. Under the best circumstances, as Charles Taylor has argued, personal choice from a range of alternatives defines human freedom, conferring dignity on choice and choser alike.

Inviolable rights, modern individualism's addition to the culture of choices, carry an equally firm but more complexly textured mandate for the democrat. The range and sacredness of rights that various Americans are claiming have increased dramatically during the past quarter century. If collective democracy is a common experience in shared space, a democracy of individual rights limits the experience and shrinks the space. When does the sum of rights removed from the realm of collective decisions bulk so large that it disables popular self-government? Nobody has a precise answer. Nevertheless, as the recent record of polarized politics illustrates, the perception that a majority has lost control over one important community issue after another does at some point sour the democratic process. In general, privatizing the exercise of democracy risks trivializing it: a thriving environment of consumerism and sexual preferences does not make Hong Kong a democracy.

But simply instructing Americans to set fewer rights aside would be as ridiculous as telling them to exercise fewer choices. As John Dunn and Herbert Gans have noted, individuals who ring themselves with protections and expect to rely on their own resources communicate a lack of alternatives, a sense of jeopardy in a manipulative environment. Lessening the conflict between a barricade of individual rights and a challenge from aggressive majorities depends upon those threatened individuals finding a setting where the group's agenda reinforces theirs, where either-or changes to both-and. In fact, the historical record provides a good deal of encouragement for that prospect.

Nothing in America's democratic tradition has greater persistence or force than a popular hostility toward distant, hidden centers of power, the natural enemy for both a democratic politics of everyday life and an individualism protective of its rights. Pulling away from those centers serves both causes. So does a second powerful democratic tradition, an opposition to exclusive status, to privileges inaccessible to a large majority of citizens. Here also a democratic group's stake in pulling down hierarchies and a democratic individual's stake in opening up opportunities mesh. That tradition certainly does not argue for equalizing wealth or returns. It claims a popular right to access, to a voice, to seizing the moment as an equal participant in a broad range of social enterprises. It harkens back to an axiom in America's original democracy: having rights means taking rights. The principle that democracy is something to do, not something to receive, that it is something citizens must enact for themselves, applies to individuals and groups alike. Finally, authority that takes itself for granted, that does not have to justify over and over again its right to respect, stirs another deep tradition of democratic distrust. Challenging that kind of authority nourishes both the democratic vitality of groups and the democratic self-respect of individuals.

Grounded in everyday life, then, guerrilla politics and individual rights are in a number of crucial ways natural allies. Would there be friction between them? Of course. Still, the fact that collective and individual democracy did interconnect in the 19th century and that in many localities they retained serviceable ties throughout the 20th reminds us that the American tradition contains alternatives, that nothing inherent to democracy sets majority rule and individual rights at odds. At the same time, nothing in this model of compatibility recommends either abandoning all individual protections or denying the establishment of new rights. To act without receiving harm in public and to act without doing harm in private are fundamental to democratic individualism. A woman's sovereignty over her own body may be sufficiently absolute to render anything that resembles mandatory childbearing "involuntary servitude." What the democrat asks is that just as few as possible of those rights be sealed apart from political life, just as many as possible embedded in a majoritian process. The rights themselves depend upon it. As recent events have demonstrated, those champions of individual rights who live by the judiciary die by the judiciary.

For contemporary critics who want to revitalize American democracy, in sum, history offers some advice and some encouragement. Neither an individualism that has always been intrinsic to American democracy nor a polarization that is only the recent manifestation of much deeper problems is their primary obstacle. On the contrary, it is the centralized, hierarchical structure of relations that first took shape between the 1890s and the 1920s, a structure that resists popular participation and at the least operates in tension with individualist democracy. No general renewal of democracy will occur, the record indicates, without a breakdown of the structure. Gradually accreting reforms could not meet the challenges of race and gender in the 19th century, nor have they reversed 20th century democracy's critical weakness, the long-term, class-biased decline in popular participation. At the same time, history provides a good measure of encouragement: specifically, a traditional distrust of distant, exclusive centers of power; a standing skepticism about self-proclaimed, self-perpetuating authority; an assumption that citizens have a right to act up and speak out; and an attachment to small, flexible groups as basic to democratic politics.

Nobody knows who might listen to these messages or what would happen if they were taken seriously. By nature, democracy is unpredictable. If a breakdown of centralized, hierarchial power is a precondition for democratic renewal, it is by no means a guarantee of one. The consequences might turn in altogether different directions. What democracy supplies is a way of conducting our common affairs. It is a gamble we take together. "In democratic politics," Michael Walzer reminds us, "all destinations are temporary."[16] Democracy always reveals who we are, never what we will become.

NOTES

INTRODUCTION

1. James MacGregor Burns with L. Marvin Overby, *Cobblestone Leadership* (Norman 1990), xiv; M. I. Finley, *Democracy Ancient and Modern*, rev. ed. (New Brunswick 1985), 100, 3; Sorauf (1992), 244; Christopher Lasch, *The True and Only Heaven* (New York 1991), 305; Bellah et al. (1991), 273.
2. Riker (1982), 241.
3. Morone (1990), 323; Cronin (1989), x.
4. Green (1985), vii; Fishkin (1991), 20.
5. Kristol (1972), 42.
6. Dworkin (1977), 205; Gutmann (1980), 198–99; Teixeira (1992), 3–4.
7. Seymour Martin Lipset, *Political Man* (Garden City 1960), 403; Dahrendorf presentation in Jerusalem, January 1987; Bellah et al. (1991), 176.
8. Barber (1984), xvi; Pateman (1989), 210.
9. Greider (1992), 14.
10. Verba and Nie (1972), 1; Walzer (1983), 310.

PART ONE

1. Bruce Ackerman, *The Future of Liberal Revolution* (New Haven 1992), 5–6.
2. Alexis de Tocqueville, *Democracy in America*, trans. Henry Reeve and Francis Bowen, ed. Phillips Bradley, 2 vols. (New York 1945), 1:208.

CHAPTER ONE

1. Calvin Colton, *History and Character of American Revivals of Religion* (London 1832), 218–19.
2. John Harley Warner, *The Therapeutic Perspective* (Cambridge 1986), 16.

268 NOTES TO PAGES 20–37

3. Henry D. Shapiro and Zane L. Miller, eds., *Physician to the West* (Lexington 1970), 199.

4. Francis Hilliard, *The Elements of Law* (Boston 1835), vi.

5. Allen Steinberg, *The Transformation of Criminal Justice* (Chapel Hill 1989), 3.

6. Alan M. Kraut, "Consensus and Pluralism: The Popular Will and the American People," in *The Will of the People*, ed. George R. Johnson, Jr. (Fairfax 1991), 55.

7. Yaron Ezrahi, *The Descent of Icarus* (Cambridge 1990), 69.

8. Alexis de Tocqueville, *Democracy in America*, trans. Henry Reeve and Francis Bowen, ed. Phillips Bradley, 2 vols. (New York 1945), 2:4.

9. Robert J. Steinfeld, *The Invention of Free Labor* (Chapel Hill 1991), 45.

10. William J. Cooper, Jr., *Liberty and Slavery* (New York 1983), 248.

11. Jan. 29, 1858, in *Letters and Recollections of John Murray Forbes*, ed. Sarah Forbes Hughes, 2 vols. (Boston 1900), 1:175.

12. U.S. House of Representatives, Executive Document No. 227 (25 Cong., 3rd Sess.), 607.

13. Irving Kristol, *On the Democratic Idea in America* (New York 1972), 57.

14. John Stuart Mill, *Principles of Political Economy*, in *Collected Works*, ed. F. E. L. Priestley et al., 33 vols. (Toronto 1963–91), 3:763.

15. James Fenimore Cooper, *Homeward Bound*, 2 vols. (New York 1854 [1838]), 2:125.

16. Adam Smith, *An Inquiry into the Nature and Causes of the Wealth of Nations*, ed. R. H. Campbell et al., 2 vols. (Oxford 1976), 2:784–85.

17. Frederick Grimke, *The Nature and Tendency of Free Institutions*, ed. John William Ward (Cambridge 1968 [1856]), 521.

18. [Horace Mann] *The Massachusetts System of Common Schools* (Boston 1849), 17.

19. Tocqueville, *Democracy*, 1:211.

20. John Adams quoted in Isaac Kramnick, *Republicanism and Bourgeois Radicalism* (Ithaca 1990), 138; Richard Henry Lee to Francis Lightfoot Lee, July 14, 1787, *The Letters of Richard Henry Lee*, ed. James Curtis Ballagh, 2 vols. (New York 1911–14), 2:424; John Marshall, *Life of Washington*, 2 vols. (Philadelphia 1848 [1804–7]), 2:447.

21. James Winthrop, "Letters of Agrippa," in *Essays on the Constitution of the United States*, ed. Paul Leicester Ford (Brooklyn 1892), 54, 86; Melancton Smith, in *The Complete Anti-Federalist*, ed. Herbert J. Storing, 7 vols. (Chicago 1981), 6:158; "Federal Farmer," ibid., 2:235; "Brutus," ibid., 2:381.

22. "Federal Farmer," 2:232–33, 282.

23. Thomas Jefferson to James Madison, March 15, 1789, *The Papers of Thomas Jefferson*, ed. Julian P. Boyd et al., 25 vols. to date (Princeton 1950–), 14:660.

24. Storing, *Anti-Federalist*, 5:257.

25. Quoted in John Phillip Reid, *The Concept of Representation* (Chicago 1989), 17.

26. "Federal Farmer," 2:304; [John Taylor] *An Enquiry into the Principles and Tendency of Certain Public Measures* (Philadelphia 1794), 55.

27. Smith, *Wealth of Nations*, 2:945.

NOTES TO PAGES 37–50   269

28. Thomas Jefferson to James Monroe, February 15, 1801, *The Writings of Thomas Jefferson*, ed. Paul Leicester Ford, 10 vols. (New York 1892–99), 7:491.

29. Quoted in Gordon S. Wood, *The Radicalism of the American Revolution* (New York 1992), 232.

30. *A Collection of the Political Writings of William Leggett*, ed. Theodore Sedgwick, Jr., 2 vols. (New York 1840), 1:262.

31. Grimke, *Nature*, 136; speech of October 23, 1850, in *Life and Speeches of Stephen A. Douglas*, ed. H. M. Flint (Philadelphia 1865), 27; Usher F. Linder, *Reminiscences of the Early Bench and Bar of Illinois*, 2nd ed. (Chicago 1879), 87; George Bancroft, *An Oration Delivered on the Fourth of July, 1826* (Northampton 1826), 19–20.

32. Leggett quoted in *Social Theories of Jacksonian Democracy*, ed. Joseph L. Blau (Indianapolis 1954), 83; Bancroft, *Principle*, 4; George Sidney Camp, *Democracy* (New York 1841), 183.

33. July 15, 1790, *Papers of Jefferson*, 17:195.

34. Stephen Douglas, "Speech . . . September 7, 1859," in *In the Name of the People*, ed. Henry V. Jaffa and Robert W. Johannsen (Columbus 1959), 139.

CHAPTER TWO

1. Cesare di Beccaria, *An Essay on Crimes and Punishments* (Edinburgh 1778), 16.

2. In this and succeeding chapters, reference notes to antebellum European travel writers are by author. For full citations, see "Special Debts and Further Readings," section on chapter 2, pp. 287–289. Stuart Wortley, 1:269–70; Grund, 202, 204; Chevalier, 205; Marryat, 43.

3. Grattan, 2:319, 98; Martineau, 2:183; Reid, 22; Trollope, 1:172; Chambers, 344, 222.

4. Trollope, 1:60–61; Mackay, 1:197; Buckingham, 2:3; Howitt, 217; Trollope, 2:110; Cather, 142; Adam Smith, *An Inquiry into the Nature and Causes of the Wealth of Nations*, ed. R. H. Campbell et al., 2 vols. (Oxford 1976), 2:943.

5. H. Murray, 1:198; Mackay, 1:40; Grund, 203; H. Murray, 1:17; Reid, 238.

6. Trollope, 1:173; Stuart, 1:468–69; B. Hall, 3:387–88; Howitt, 227–28.

7. Duncan, 209–10; C. Murray, 1:120, 2:88; Reid, 45.

8. Dickens, 1:147; Howitt, 223, 225; Reid, 49.

9. Cobden, 118; Pulzsky and Pulzsky, 1:285; R. Carlyle Buley, *The Old Northwest*, 2 vols. (Indianapolis 1950), 1:363; Dickens, 1:272.

10. Busch, 274; H. Murray, 2:371; C. Murray, 2:88; B. Hall, 3:151.

11. B. Hall, 3:166; H. Murray, 2:383; Dickens, 1:63; Grattan, 2:99; Tocqueville, 1:219.

12. Stuart Wortley, 1:301.

13. Tocqueville, 1:306.

14. Grattan, 1:134; F. Hall, 289; M. Hall, 24.

15. Buckingham, 3:38–39; H. Murray, 1:231; Arese, 9–10; Stuart Wortley, 1:13.

16. Rubio, 20–21; Hamilton, 48; C. Murray, 1:63n.

17. B. Hall, 2:406; Mackay, 1:151; Grattan, 1:66; Grund, 205.

18. Dickens, 1:205–7.

19. Trollope, 1:24; H. Murray, 1:195.

20. Howitt, 226–27.

21. Hamilton, 303; Stuart Wortley, 1:161.

22. C. Murray, 2:108; Buckingham, 2:80; C. Murray, 1:214; Tuckett, 13; Grattan, 2:86; H. Murray, 1:395; Reid, 68.

23. Cobden, 92; Howitt, 75; Cather, 100; Duncan, 242; H. Murray, 2:373.

24. Chambers, 285.

25. B. Hall, 3:41.

26. Hamilton, 212.

27. Edward Everett, *Oration Delivered on the Fourth Day of July, 1835* (Boston 1835), 13; Frederick Grimke, *The Nature and Tendency of Free Institutions*, ed. John William Ward (Cambridge 1968 [1856]), 655; Thomas Starr King, *The Organization of Liberty on the Western Continent* (Boston 1892 [1852]), 54.

28. Daniel Read, *Oration, Commemorative of the Life and Services of General Andrew Jackson* (Bloomington 1845), 14–15; Thomas Payne Govan, *Nicholas Biddle* (Chicago 1959), 20; *Oration of the Hon. Stephen A. Douglas . . . January 8, 1853* (n.p., n.d.), 3.

29. *The Diary of Philip Hone, 1828–1851*, ed. Allan Nevins (New York 1927), 93.

30. Trollope, 2:107; Bernhard, 2:238; Grattan, 2:106; Chambers, 344.

31. Stuart Wortley, 1:2; Dickens, 2:110; Cather, 80–81.

32. Chambers, 212; Cobden, 115; Buckingham, 1:46.

33. B. Hall, 2:94.

34. The Unitarian minister George Hosmer quoted in David A. Gerber, *The Making of an American Pluralism* (Urbana 1989), 25.

35. Duden, 43; C. Murray, 1:207.

36. Martineau, 2:170, 1:139–43.

37. Benton quoted in Daniel Feller, *The Public Lands in Jacksonian Politics* (Madison 1984), 163; *Boston Quarterly Review* (1840): 473.

38. James Bryce, *The American Commonwealth*, 2 vols. (London 1887), 2:851; Josiah Strong, *Our Country*, rev. ed. (New York 1891 [1885]), 203; John Swinton, *A Momentous Question* (Philadelphia 1894), 53, 55, 57.

CHAPTER THREE

1. F. Hall, 59; C. Murray, 2:297; Rubio, 43–44; Dixon, 170–71; A. Murray, 274.

2. Lyell, *Second*, 1:85; Reid, 55; Tuckett, 32; Hodgson, 221, 226; Grattan, 1:304–5.

3. Martineau, 2:200; Hodgson, 91; Rubio, 117, 4. The president to whom Rubio referred was probably James K. Polk.

4. Hamilton, xxiii–xxiv, 18.

5. Tuckett, 18; C. Murray, 1:143 (italics in original); Grattan, 1:168.

6. Klinkowström, 27; Andrew Jackson to George W. Martin, January 2, 1824, *Correspondence of Andrew Jackson*, ed. John Spencer Bassett, 7 vols. (Washington, D.C., 1926–35), 3:222; Hamilton, 229.

7. Tocqueville, 1:182, 210; H. Murray, 1:338.

8. Rynning, 86; Rubio, 39; Cather, 141; Stuart Wortley, 2:66–67; Martineau, 1:109; H. Murray, 2:163.

9. Trollope, 2:33; Dickens, 1:149; Cather, 141; Pulzsky and Pulzsky, 1:180.

10. F. Hall, 56; Reid, 53–54; Grund, 148 (italics in original).

11. Stephen A. Douglas, "Speech . . . September 16, 1859," in *In the Name of the People*, ed. Henry V. Jaffa and Robert W. Johannsen (Columbus 1959), 226.

12. B. Hall, 2:64

13. I am indebted to an unpublished paper by Gordon McKinney for this quotation.

14. Kenneth Cmiel, *Democratic Eloquence* (New York 1990), 12–13.

15. Tocqueville, 1:260; *A Collection of the Political Writings of William Leggett*, ed. Theodore Sedgwick, Jr., 2 vols. (New York 1840), 2:324.

16. F. Hall, 439.

17. Quoted in Carl Smith, *Urban Disorder and the Shape of Belief* (Chicago 1995), 80.

18. Klinkowström, 76 (italics in original).

19. Grund, 136; Ferguson, 48; Tocqueville, 2:202–3.

20. Fragment of a letter [1849]; Lincoln to William Herndon, January 5, 1849, *The Collected Works of Abraham Lincoln*, ed. Roy P. Basler et al., 9 vols. (New Brunswick 1953–55), 2:17, 19.

21. Usher F. Linder, *Reminiscences of the Early Bench and Bar of Illinois*, 2nd ed. (Chicago 1879), 82; George Booker to Robert Hunter, November 5, 1852, American Historical Association Annual Report (1916), vol. 2: *Correspondence of Robert M. T. Hunter, 1826–1876*, ed. Charles Henry Ambler (Washington, D.C., 1918), 150.

22. C. Murray, 2:86.

23. Quoted in Andrew Nelson Lytle, "The Hind Tit," in *I'll Take My Stand* by Twelve Southerners (New York 1962 [1930]), 213.

24. A. O. P. Nicholson to James K. Polk, December 20, 1835; Henry B. Kelsey to Polk, December 23, 1835, *Correspondence of James K. Polk*, ed. Herbert Weaver et al., 8 vols. to date (Nashville 1969–), 3:400, 409.

25. George Burnap, *Lectures to Young Men* (Baltimore 1848 [1840]), 109; Charles Crowe, *George Ripley* (Athens 1967), 132; Horace Bushnell, *The Northern Iron* (Hartford 1854), 26; James Bryce, *The American Commonwealth*, 2 vols. (London 1889), 2:67.

26. Margaret Bayard Smith, *The First Forty Years of Washington Society*, ed. Gaillard Hunt (New York 1906), 293.

27. *National Intelligencer*, quoted in Constance McLaughlin Green, *Washington: Village and Capital, 1800–1878* (Princeton 1962), 121.

28. Smith, *Forty Years*, 297.

29. Ibid., 294.

30. Dickens, 1:149; Kenneth J. Winkle, *The Politics of Community* (Cambridge, Eng., 1988), 177.

31. John Dunn, *Interpreting Political Responsibility* (Cambridge, Eng., 1990), 200.

32. Richard B. Stott, *Workers in the Metropolis* (Ithaca 1990), 237.

33. Lee Soltow and Edward Stevens, *The Rise of Literacy and the Common School in the United States* (Chicago 1981), 85.

34. Thomas Starr King, *The Organization of Liberty on the Western Continent* (Boston 1892 [1852]), 38; Mackay, 1:285–86.

35. Charles W. Eliot, *The Working of the American Democracy* (Cambridge 1888), 6–7; Howells quoted in Olivier Zunz, *Making America Corporate, 1870–1920* (Chicago 1990), 62; Grimke, *Nature*, 91; Henry Adams, *Democracy* (New York 1961 [1880]), 100.

CHAPTER FOUR

1. John Ware, *An Address* (Boston 1826), 15.

2. Nathaniel Southgate Shaler, *The Citizen* (New York 1905), 255.

3. Quoted in Chilton Williamson, *American Suffrage* (Princeton 1960), 219.

4. Chevalier, 361.

5. John S. Gilkeson, Jr., *Middle-Class Providence, 1820–1940* (Princeton 1986), 23; Iver Bernstein, *The New York City Draft Riots* (New York 1990), 242.

6. Grund, 236n; Eliza Potter, *A Hairdresser's Experience in High Life* (Cincinnati 1859), 34; newspaper quoted in Robin L. Einhorn, *Property Rules* (Chicago 1991), 162.

7. Harry Crews quoted in Jack Temple Kirby, *Rural Worlds Lost* (Baton Rouge 1987), 187–88.

8. Robert L. Rabin quoted in Lawrence M. Friedman, *Total Justice* (New York 1985), 57.

9. Quoted in Christopher L. Tomlins, *Law, Labor, and Ideology in the Early American Republic* (Cambridge, Eng., 1993), 151.

10. James Whiteside, *Regulating Danger* (Lincoln 1990), 56.

11. Drew Gilpin Faust, *A Sacred Circle* (Baltimore 1977), 112.

12. Herbert Aptheker, ed., *A Documentary History of the Negro People in the United States*, vol. 1: *From Colonial Times through the Civil War* (New York 1951), 413, 347–48, 274.

13. Calvin Colton quoted in Lori D. Ginsberg, *Women and the Work of Benevolence* (New Haven 1990), 95.

14. Aptheker, *Documentary History*, 453, 331, 137–38; editor quoted in Benjamin Quarles, *Black Abolitionists* (New York 1969), 122.

15. Quoted in Richard R. Beeman, *The Evolution of the Southern Backcountry* (Philadelphia 1984), 219.

16. Aptheker, *Documentary History*, 469.

17. Ibid., 523; Booker T. Washington, "The Educational Outlook in the South" [1884], in *Booker T. Washington and His Critics*, ed. Hugh Hawkins (Lexington 1974), 12.

18. Child to Francis Shaw, January 15, 1843, *Lydia Maria Child*, ed. Milton Meltzer et al. (Amherst 1982), 185.

19. Lyell, *Travels*, 1:57.

20. Ferguson, 48.

21. Susan B. Anthony, "Suffrage and the Working Women" [1871], in *Eliza-*

beth Cady Stanton Susan B. Anthony, ed. Ellen Carol DuBois (New York 1981), 142.

22. Quoted in Elizabeth Cady Stanton et al., eds., *History of Woman Suffrage,* 6 vols. (New York 1881–1922), 1:530.

23. Quoted in Norma Basch, "Equity vs. Equality: Emerging Concepts of Women's Political Status in the Age of Jackson," *Journal of the Early Republic,* 3 (Fall 1983): 309.

24. Elizabeth Cady Stanton, "Appeal for the Maine Law" [January 21 1853], in *Elizabeth Cady Stanton Susan B. Anthony,* 43.

25. Aptheker, *Documentary History,* 201, 324.

26. Elizabeth Cady Stanton quoted in Charles Royster, *The Destructive War* (New York 1991), 85.

PART TWO

1. Horace M. Kallen, *Culture and Democracy in the United States* (New York 1924), 42–43.

2. Karl Marx, "The 18th Brumaire of Louis Bonaparte," in *Selected Works,* 2 vols. (Moscow 1958), 1:340.

CHAPTER FIVE

1. Karl Marx, "The 18th Brumaire of Louis Bonaparte," in *Selected Works,* 2 vols. (Moscow 1958), 1:255.

2. George Sidney Camp, *Democracy* (New York 1841), 227.

3. "Laboring," *Boston Quarterly Review* (1840): 372.

4. Walter Licht, *Working for the Railroad* (Princeton 1983), 165.

5. Quoted in Stuart M. Blumin, *The Emergence of the Middle Class* (Cambridge 1989), 288.

6. George E. McNeill, "The Problems of Today," in *The Labor Movement,* ed. George E. McNeill (Boston 1887), 460; W. A. Peffer, *The Farmer's Side* (New York 1891), 196.

7. McNeill, "Problems," 465; Peffer, *Farmer's Side,* 9, 46, 123.

8. Powderly quoted in Susan Levine, "Labor's True Woman: Domesticity and Equal Rights in the Knights of Labor," *Journal of American History,* 70 (September 1983): 330.

9. Edward Bellamy, *Looking Backward, 2000–1887* (Boston 1926 [1886]), 231.

10. Quoted in Pete Daniel, *The Shadow of Slavery* (Urbana 1972), 94.

11. Walter Weyl, *The New Democracy* (New York 1912), 320.

12. Frederic C. Howe, *Revolution and Democracy* (New York 1921), 4–5.

13. John Swinton, *A Momentous Question* (Philadelphia 1895), chap. 3, "The People."

14. Richards O'Hare quoted in David Montgomery, *The Fall of the House of Labor* (Cambridge, Eng., 1987), 286; Upton Sinclair, *The Jungle,* ed. James R. Barrett (Urbana 1988 [1906]), 260; Charlotte Perkins Stetson [Gilman], *Women and Economics* (Boston 1910 [1898]), 201.

15. Quoted in Numan V. Bartley, *The Creation of Modern Georgia* (Athens 1983), 149.

CHAPTER SIX

1. Tocqueville, 2:200.
2. Grattan, 1:92, 117; Dickens, 2:253.
3. Andrew Carnegie, *Triumphant Democracy* (New York 1886), 117–18.
4. Cornelia Adair, *My Diary* (Austin 1965 [1874]), 16.
5. James Bryce, *The American Commonwealth*, 2 vols. (London, 1889), 2:666.
6. Horace M. Kallen, *Culture and Democracy* (New York 1924), 278; John B. Andrews quoted in Abraham Epstein, *Facing Old Age* (New York 1922), xiii.
7. Walter Lippmann, *The Phantom Public* (New York 1925), 100.
8. Mansel G. Blackford, *A Portrait Cast in Steel* (Westport 1982), 47.
9. Charles M. Sheldon, *In His Steps* (Pittsburgh 1979 [1897]), 82.
10. William R. Taylor, "The Launching of a Commercial Culture: New York City, 1860–1930," in *Power, Culture, and Place*, ed. John Hull Mollenkopf (New York 1988), 108–9.
11. Walter Lippmann, *A Preface to Morals* (New York 1929), 317, 257.
12. Carrie Chapman Catt and Nettie Rogers Shuler, *Woman Suffrage and Politics* (Seattle 1969 [1923]), 489.
13. Mary Gray Peck, *Carrie Chapman Catt* (New York 1944), 257.
14. Clyde Griffen and Sally Griffen, *Natives and Newcomers* (Cambridge 1978), 14.
15. William Howard Taft, *Four Aspects of Civil Duty* (New York 1906), 87.
16. Arthur Marwick, *Class* (New York 1980), 199.

CHAPTER SEVEN

1. Louis D. Brandeis, *Business—A Profession* (Boston 1914), xlv.
2. John Mitchell, "The Workingman's Conception of Industrial Liberty," *American Federationist*, 17 (May 1910): 405–6.
3. Jane Addams, *Twenty Years at Hull-House* (New York 1961 [1910]), 288.
4. I am indebted to John Thompson for this quotation.
5. Jacob A. Riis, *How the Other Half Lives* (New York 1957 [1891]), 159, 134.
6. Quoted in Elizabeth Cady Stanton et al., eds., *History of Woman Suffrage*, 6 vols. (New York 1881–1922), 5:292.
7. Rheta Childe Dorr, *What Eight Million Women Want* (Boston 1910), 49 (italics in original).
8. Carrie Chapman Catt and Nettie Rogers Shuler, *Woman Suffrage and Politics* (Seattle 1969 [1923]), 116.
9. Woodrow Wilson, "An Address to the Senate," in *The Papers of Woodrow Wilson*, ed. Arthur S. Link et al., 69 vols. (Princeton 1966–92), 51:158–59.
10. Wilson, "Remarks to a Group of Suffragists" and "An Address to the Senate," ibid., 51:190, 159.

11. Susan Anita Glenn, *Daughters of the Shtetl* (Ithaca 1990), 114.

12. Horace M. Kallen, *Culture and Democracy in the United States* (New York 1924), 10.

13. Edward Bellamy, *Looking Backward, 2000–1887* (Boston 1926 [1886]), 134.

14. Walter Weyl, *The New Democracy* (New York 1912), 137.

15. Harold Stearns, *Liberalism in America* (New York 1919), 80; Frederick Grimke, *The Nature and Tendency of Free Institutions,* ed. John William Ward (Cambridge 1968 [1856]), 387; George Creel, "The Ghastly Swindle," *Harper's Weekly,* 59 (Aug. 29, 1914): 196–97.

16. A. Lawrence Lowell, *Public Opinion and Popular Government* (New York 1913), 4, 109.

17. Frederic Howe, *Revolution and Democracy* (New York 1921), 70.

18. Walter Lippmann, *Drift and Mastery* (New York 1917 [1914]), xx, 274.

19. Walter Lippmann, *The Phantom Public* (New York 1925), 147, 146, 166; idem, *A Preface to Morals* (New York 1929), 278–79.

20. Lippmann, *Phantom,* 166, 30, 58; idem, *Public Opinion* (New York 1922), 270, 273, 232.

21. Lippmann, *Public Opinion,* 311–14.

22. A. Lawrence Lowell, *Public Opinion in War and Peace* (Cambridge 1923), 157, v.; L. H. Bailey, *What Is Democracy?* (New York 1923), 94, 25; V. O. Key, Jr., *Public Opinion and American Democracy* (New York 1961), 536.

23. John Dewey, *The Public and Its Problems* (New York 1927), 215.

24. Ibid., 109, 126, 82, 110, 166.

25. Ibid., 110; Allen quoted in David M. Kennedy, *Over Here* (New York 1980), 43; Lippman, *Phantom,* 52–53; Thomas Vernor Smith, *The Democratic Way of Life* (Chicago 1926), 8.

26. Julius Burrows quoted in J. Morgan Kousser, *The Shaping of Southern Politics* (New Haven 1974), 257.

27. Viola Paradise quoted in Elizabeth Ewen, *Immigrant Women in the Land of Dollars* (New York 1985), 27.

28. Ellwood P. Cubberly, *Changing Conceptions of Education* (Boston 1909), 15–16; Frances A. Kellor, "Americanization: A Conservation Policy for Industry," *Annals,* 65 (May 1916): 240.

29. Randolph Bourne, "Trans-National America," *Atlantic,* 108 (July 1916): 86–97; Kallen, *Culture,* 124, 198.

30. Walter Dean Burnham, *The Current Crisis in American Politics* (New York 1982), 121.

PART THREE

1. Quoted in Theodore Zeldin, *France, 1848–1945,* 2 vols. (Oxford 1973–77), 1:131.

2. Seppo Hentilä, "The Origins of the *Folkhem* Ideology in Swedish Social Democracy," *Scandanavian Journal of History,* 3 (1978): 329.

3. James Bryce, *The American Commonwealth,* 2 vols. (London 1889), 2:56.

CHAPTER EIGHT

1. Walter Lippmann, *A Preface to Morals* (New York 1929), 113.

2. Freda Kirchwey, ed., *Our Changing Morality* (New York 1924), vi.

3. *The Autobiography of Lincoln Steffens* (New York 1931), 328; Thomas Vernor Smith, *The Democratic Way of Life* (Chicago 1926), 135.

4. Gurowski, 1; Elizabeth Cady Stanton, "Speech . . . 1860," in *Elizabeth Cady Stanton Susan B. Anthony*, ed. Ellen Carol DuBois (New York 1981), 79; Charlotte Perkins Stetson [Gilman], *Women and Economics* (Boston 1910 [1898], 138–39, 147–48.

5. Quoted in Sheila M. Rothman, *Woman's Proper Place* (New York 1978), 137.

6. Quoted in Clarke A. Chambers, *Seedtime of Reform* (Minneapolis 1963), 68.

7. Walter Lippmann, *Public Opinion* (New York 1922), 253–54.

8. Richard Washburn Child, "The Great American Scandal: Youth and Felony," *Saturday Evening Post*, 198 (Aug. 29, 1925): 134. I am indebted to David Ruth for this citation.

9. Abbott quoted in Robyn Muncy, *Creating a Female Dominion in American Reform, 1890–1935* (New York 1991), 69; [Gilman] *Women and Economics*, 207.

10. Rheta Childe Dorr quoted in Nancy F. Cott, *The Grounding of Modern Feminism* (New Haven 1987), 46.

11. "Now We Can Begin" [December 1920], in *Crystal Eastman*, ed. Blanche Wiesen Cook (New York 1978), 54.

12. Smith, *Democratic Way*, 129.

13. Kenneth Fearing, "Dirge," in *Collected Poems* (New York 1940), 60–61.

14. Elizabeth Cady Stanton et al., eds., *History of Woman Suffrage*, 6 vols. (New York 1881–1922), 5:256.

15. Joseph Wood Krutch, *The Modern Temper* (New York 1929), 61.

16. Christopher N. May, *In the Name of War* (Cambridge 1989), 195.

CHAPTER NINE

1. W. A. Peffer, *The Farmer's Side* (New York 1891), 173–74.

2. Mackay, 1:198.

3. Arthur M. Schlesinger, Jr., *The Imperial Presidency* (Boston 1973), ix.

4. Michel Crozier, Samuel P. Huntington, and Joji Watanuki, *The Crisis of Democracy* (New York 1975), 93.

5. Helen Phelan quoted in Clarke A. Chambers, *Seedtime of Reform* (Minneapolis 1963), 148.

6. Henry A. Wallace, *New Frontiers* (New York 1934), 282.

7. Carl L. Becker, *Modern Democracy* (New Haven 1941), 14, 33.

8. Wallace, *New Frontiers*, 263, 20.

9. Abraham Epstein, *Facing Old Age* (New York 1922), 215; David E. Lilienthal, *TVA Democracy on the March* (New York 1944), 36.

10. Becker, *Modern Democracy*, 91; B. F. Skinner, *Walden Two* (New York 1976 [1948]), 251.

11. Joseph Tussman, *Obligation and the Body Politic* (New York 1960), 103.

12. Max Lerner, *America as a Civilization* (New York 1957), 355–56; Elmo Roper, *You and Your Leaders* (New York 1957).

13. Quoted in Roland Marchand, *Advertising the American Dream* (Berkeley 1985), 67.

14. Lilienthal, *TVA*, 36.

15. Austin Ranney and Willmoore Kendall, *Democracy and the American Party System* (New York 1956), 339.

16. Eleanor Roosevelt, *The Moral Basis of Democracy* (New York 1940), 59.

17. Arthur M. Schlesinger, Jr., *The Vital Center* (Boston 1949), 52.

18. Robin M. Williams, Jr., *American Society* (New York 1959 [1951]), 238.

19. William Jewell quoted in M. Christine Boyer, *Dreaming the Rational City* (Cambridge 1983), 272.

20. Morton Grodzins, *The Loyal and the Disloyal* (Chicago 1956), 246; Heinz Eulau, "The Politics of Happiness: A Prefatory Note to 'Political Perspective—1956,'" *Antioch Review*, 16 (Fall 1956): 259–64; Seymour Martin Lipset, *Political Man* (Garden City 1960), 181.

21. V. O. Key, Jr., *Public Opinion and American Democracy* (New York 1961), 547; Philip E. Converse, "The Nature of Belief Systems in Mass Publics," in *Ideology and Discontent*, ed. David E. Apter (New York 1964), 207 (italics in original).

22. Richard Hofstadter and Walter P. Metzger, *The Development of Academic Freedom in the United States* (New York 1955), 245; Hofstadter, *Anti-Intellectualism in American Life* (New York 1963), 407; idem, *The Age of Reform* (New York 1955), 23; idem, *America at 1750* (New York 1971), 106.

23. Richard Hofstadter, "The Paranoid Style in American Politics," in *The Paranoid Style in American Politics and Other Essays* (New York 1965), 31; Hofstadter and Metzger, *Development of Academic Freedom*, 11.

24. Lipset, *Political Man*, 115, 97.

CHAPTER TEN

1. Ruth Schwartz Cowan, *More Work for Mother* (New York 1983), 194.

2. Philip E. Converse, "The Nature of Belief Systems in Mass Publics," in *Ideology and Discontent*, ed. David E. Apter (New York 1964), 218.

3. William O. Douglas, *The Right of the People* (Garden City 1958), 161.

4. Mary Douglas and Aaron Wildavsky, *Risk and Culture* (Berkeley 1982), 75.

5. V. O. Key, Jr., *Public Opinion and American Democracy* (New York 1961), 178; Gabriel A. Almond and Sidney Verba, *The Civic Culture* (Princeton 1963), 500.

6. Converse, "Nature of Belief Systems," 233.

7. Donald G. Mathews and Jane Sherron DeHart, *Sex, Gender, and the Politics of ERA* (New York 1990), 210.

8. C. B. Macpherson, *Democratic Theory* (Oxford 1973), 51; Roberto Mangabeira Unger, *The Critical Legal Studies Movement* (Cambridge 1986), 26; Jones quoted in *New York Times*, July 18, 1993, sec. 4, p. 9.

9. *New York Times*, Aug. 9, 1992, sec. 1, p. 34.

10. Thomas R. Dye and L. Harmon Ziegler, *The Irony of Democracy*, 2nd ed. (Belmont 1972), 9, 20.

11. Ronald Dworkin, "The Reagan Revolution and the Supreme Court," *New York Review of Books* (July 18, 1991): 24, 23; Ira Grasser, in *Civil Liberties* (Fall 1991); Laughlin McDonald, ibid. (Summer-Fall 1992).

12. Nadine Strossen, ibid. (Winter 1991–92).

13. The Protestant fundamentalist Franky Schaeffer quoted in James Davison Hunter, *Culture Wars* (New York 1991), 103.

14. William Greider, *Who Will Tell the People* (New York 1992), 181.

15. Anna Quindlen, *New York Times*, June 21, 1992, sec. 4, p. 17.

16. Amitai Etzioni, *The Spirit of Community* (New York 1993), 255.

17. Barry D. Karl, *The Uneasy State* (Chicago 1983), 238.

CONCLUSION

1. Burnham (1982), 133.

2. Dryzek (1990), 80; Dunn (1990), 3, 8.

3. Nozick (1974), 90.

4. Dunn (1990), 208; Barber (1984), 100; Ackerman (1980), 100–101.

5. Sandel (1982), 183; Richard Rorty, *Philosophy and the Mirror of Nature* (Princeton 1979), 188; Ezrahi (1990), 282; Barber (1984), 100.

6. Burns (1984), 14; Huntington (1981), 39.

7. Barber (1984), xiv.

8. Huntington (1981), 41.

9. Burns (1984), 164.

10. Shapiro (1990), 266, 282.

11. Henry Geller in Lichtenberg (1990), 290.

12. Dworkin (1977), 201.

13. Lichtenberg (1990), 107.

14. Green (1985), 174.

15. Rawls (1993), 219.

16. Walzer (1983), 310.

SPECIAL DEBTS AND
FURTHER READINGS

In my situation it is not possible to credit people enough or credit enough people. I have drawn too much from too many over such a long period to hope that I can acknowledge all of it now. What follows is a compilation of works that have influenced me in ways I recognize and that provide readers with opportunities for additional inquiry.

INTRODUCTION AND CONCLUSION

The following core of works from the last quarter century has served both as a base for testing my own ideas about democracy and as a crucial resource for working them out. Like any such list, it expresses the particular paths I happen to have taken. The historian in me is embarrassed to acknowledge how the list leans toward more recent studies. Still, I have done my best to include any work about democracy over a twenty-five-year period that others on the list seriously debate. Philosophers are quite helpful in this regard. With a lone exception, I have limited each person to one publication. Although John Rawls deserves to be the exception simply for his unique influence in these discussions, in fact I include two of his titles because they need to be read as a pair. If publishing considerations did not interfere, they should be bound together as the revised edition of *A Theory of Justice*. Finally, with apologies to authors who feel jammed into a category, I have separated works into the three-part division I use in my introduction.

Publicists

Robert Bellah et al., *The Good Society* (New York 1991).
David Broder, *The Party's Over* (New York 1972).
E. J. Dionne, Jr., *Why Americans Hate Politics* (New York 1991).
Thomas Byrne Edsall and Mary D. Edsall, *Chain Reaction* (New York 1991).

279

Amitai Etzioni, *The Spirit of Community* (New York 1993).
Herbert J. Gans, *Middle American Individualism* (New York 1993).
William Greider, *Who Will Tell the People* (New York 1992).
Arthur T. Hadley, *The Empty Polling Booth* (Englewood Cliffs 1978).
James Davison Hunter, *Culture Wars* (New York 1991).
Mickey Kaus, *The End of Equality* (New York 1992).
Irving Kristol, *On the Democratic Idea in America* (New York 1972).
Judith Lichtenberg, ed., *Democracy and the Mass Media* (New York 1990).
Samuel Lubell, *The Hidden Crisis in American Politics* (New York 1970).
Ralph Nader, *The Concord Principles* (Washington, D.C., 1992).
Michael Parenti, *Democracy for the Few*, 4th ed. (New York 1983).
Kevin Phillips, *The Politics of Rich and Poor* (New York 1990).
Frances Fox Piven and Richard Cloward, *Why Americans Don't Vote* (New York 1988).

Philosophers

Bruce Ackerman, *Social Justice in the Liberal State* (New Haven 1980).
Benjamin Barber, *Strong Democracy* (Berkeley 1984).
John S. Dryzek, *Discursive Democracy* (Cambridge, Eng., 1990).
John Dunn, *Interpreting Political Responsibility* (Cambridge, Eng., 1990).
Ronald Dworkin, *Taking Rights Seriously* (Cambridge 1977).
Yaron Ezrahi, *The Descent of Icarus* (Cambridge 1990).
Alan Gilbert, *Democratic Individuality* (Cambridge, Eng., 1990).
Philip Green, *Retrieving Democracy* (Totowa 1985).
Amy Gutmann, *Liberal Equality* (Cambridge, Eng., 1980).
Jürgen Habermas, *The Structural Transformation of the Public Sphere*, trans. Thomas Burger and Frederick Laurence (Cambridge 1989).
C. B. Macpherson, *Democratic Theory* (Oxford 1973).
Robert Nozick, *Anarchy, State, and Utopia* (New York 1974).
Carole Pateman, *The Disorder of Women* (Stanford 1989).
John Rawls, *Political Liberalism* (New York 1993).
——, *A Theory of Justice* (Cambridge 1971).
William H. Riker, *Liberalism against Populism* (San Francisco 1982).
Michael J. Sandel, *Liberalism and the Limits of Justice* (Cambridge, Eng., 1982).
Adam B. Seligman, *The Idea of Civil Society* (New York 1992).
Ian Shapiro, *Political Criticism* (Berkeley 1990).
Judith N. Shklar, *American Citizenship* (Cambridge 1991).
Charles Taylor, *The Ethics of Authenticity* (Cambridge 1992).
Roberto Mangabeira Unger, *Politics: A Work in Constructive Social Theory*, part 1: *False Necessity* (Cambridge, Eng., 1987).
Michael Walzer, *Spheres of Justice* (New York 1983).
Robert Paul Wolff, *In Defense of Anarchism*, rev. ed. (New York 1976).

Social Scientists

Peter Bachrach and Aryeh Botwinick, *Power and Empowerment* (Philadelphia 1992).
Walter Dean Burnham, *The Current Crisis in American Politics* (New York 1982).
James MacGregor Burns, *The Power to Lead* (New York 1984).
Thomas E. Cronin, *Direct Democracy* (Cambridge 1989).
Robert A. Dahl, *Democracy and Its Critics* (New Haven 1989).
Thomas R. Dye and L. Harmon Ziegler, *The Irony of Democracy*, 2nd ed. (Belmont 1972).
Leon D. Epstein, *Political Parties in the American Mold* (Madison 1986).
James S. Fishkin, *Democracy and Deliberation* (New Haven 1991).
Benjamin Ginsberg and Martin Shefter, *Politics by Other Means* (New York 1990).
Russell L. Hanson, *The Democratic Imagination in America* (Princeton 1985).
Samuel P. Huntington, *American Politics* (Cambridge 1981).
Jane J. Mansbridge, *Beyond Adversary Democracy* (New York 1980).
James Miller, *"Democracy Is in the Streets"* (New York 1987).
James A. Morone, *The Democratic Wish* (New York 1990).
A. James Reichley, ed., *Elections American Style* (Washington, D.C., 1987).
Kay Lehman Schlozman and John T. Tierney, *Organized Interests and American Democracy* (New York 1986).
Frank J. Sorauf, *Inside Campaign Finance* (New Haven 1992).
Ruy A. Teixeira, *The Disappearing American Voter* (Washington, D.C., 1992).
Abigail M. Thernstrom, *Whose Votes Count?* (Cambridge 1987).
Sidney Verba and Norman Nie, *Participation in America* (New York 1972).
Joseph F. Zimmerman, *Participatory Democracy* (New York 1986).

Other works helped me to follow trends in the recent understanding of democracy but for one reason or another—less immediately relevant to this inquiry, otherwise represented on the list—were not included:

Herbert E. Alexander, *Financing Politics*, 2nd ed. (Washington, D.C., 1980).
Robert N. Bellah et al., *Habits of the Heart* (Berkeley 1985).
Samuel Bowles and Herbert Gintis, *Democracy and Capitalism* (New York 1986).
James MacGregor Burns with L. Marvin Overby, *Cobblestone Leadership* (Norman 1990).
Craig Calhoun, ed., *Habermas and the Public Sphere* (Cambridge 1992).
Michel Crozier et al., *The Crisis of Democracy* (New York 1975).
Robert A. Dahl and Edward R. Tufte, *Size and Democracy* (Stanford 1973).

M. I. Finley, *Democracy Ancient and Modern*, rev. ed. (New Brunswick 1985).

Benjamin Ginsberg, *The Captive Public* (New York 1986).

Mary Ann Glendon, *Rights Talk* (New York 1991).

Robert E. Goodin, *Protecting the Vulnerable* (Chicago 1985).

William Graebner, *The Engineering of Consent* (Madison 1987).

Mona Harrington, *The Dream of Deliverance in American Politics* (New York 1986).

Stephen Holmes, *The Anatomy of Antiliberalism* (Cambridge 1993).

Kenneth Janda et al., *The Challenge of Democracy* (Boston 1987).

Everett Carll Ladd, *Where Have All the Voters Gone?* 2nd ed. (New York 1982).

Christopher Lasch, *The Culture of Narcissism* (New York 1978).

Catharine A. MacKinnon, *Toward a Feminist Theory of the State* (Cambridge 1989).

Martha Minow, *Making All the Difference* (Ithaca 1990).

William N. Nelson, *On Justifying Democracy* (London 1980).

Benjamin I. Page, *Choices and Echoes in Presidential Elections* (Chicago 1978).

Robert D. Putnam, *Making Democracy Work* (Princeton 1993).

Richard Rorty, *Philosophy and the Mirror or Nature* (Princeton 1979).

———. "The Priority of Democracy to Philosophy," in *The Virginia Statute for Religious Freedom*, ed. Merrill Peterson and Robert Vaughan (Cambridge, Eng., 1988), 257–82.

Richard Sennett, *The Uses of Disorder* (New York 1970).

James L. Sundquist, *Dynamics of the Party System* (Washington, D.C., 1973).

Göran Therborn, "The Rule of Capital and the Rise of Democracy," *New Left Review*, 103 (May–June 1977): 3–41.

Michael Walzer, "Philosophy and Democracy," *Political Theory*, 9 (August 1981): 379–99.

Aaron Wildavsky, "Birthday Cake Federalism," in *American Federalism*, ed. Robert B. Hawkins, Jr. (San Francisco 1982), 181–91.

Daniel Yankelovich, *New Rules* (New York 1981)

My chronology meshed well with the concerns of the publicists and most exchanges among philosophers, but it interrupted a dialogue among social scientists, including some matters of political theory. Among the earlier publications critical to these conversations are:

Gabriel A. Almond and Sidney Verba, *The Civic Culture* (Princeton 1963).

Committee on Political Parties, "Toward a More Responsible Two-Party System," *American Political Science Review*, 44 (Supplement: September 1950): 1–96.

Bernard Crick, *In Defense of Politics* (London 1962).

Robert A. Dahl, *A Preface to Democratic Theory* (Chicago 1956).

Anthony Downs, *An Economic Theory of Democracy* (New York 1957).

Louis Hartz, *The Liberal Tradition in America* (New York 1955).
Seymour Martin Lipset, *Political Man* (Garden City 1960).
Theodore Lowi, *The End of American Liberalism* (New York 1969).
C. B. Macpherson, *The Political Theory of Possessive Individualism* (Oxford 1962).
Robert Michels, *Political Parties*, trans. Eden and Cedar Paul (New York 1962).
David Riesman et al., *The Lonely Crowd* (New Haven 1950).
E. E. Schattschneider, *The Semisovereign People* (New York 1960).
David Truman, *The Government Process* (New York 1951).
Sheldon Wolin, *Politics and Vision* (Boston 1960).

A few historians have taken long views of cultural or intellectual matters closely related to American democracy: John Patrick Diggins, *The Lost Soul of American Politics* (New York 1984); Christopher Lasch, *The True and Only Heaven* (New York 1991); David M. Potter, *People of Plenty* (Chicago 1954); Merrill D. Peterson, *The Jefferson Image in the American Mind* (New York 1960); and Daniel T. Rodgers, *Contested Truths* (New York 1987). The three volumes of Daniel J. Boorstin's *The Americans* (New York 1958–73) can be read as a full-scale history of the subject. Lawrence Goodwyn's study of the Populist movement, *Democratic Promise* (New York 1976), is one of the few histories to bring a theory of democracy to bear on its subject.

CHAPTER ONE

Robert H. Wiebe, *The Origins of American Society* (New York 1984), examines the transformation between the 18th and the 19th centuries as a national phenomenon. Gordon S. Wood, *The Radicalism of the American Revolution* (New York 1992), addresses many of the same themes in more detail. His reference notes are a valuable guide to further reading.

Two articles provide an excellent introduction to the meaning of democracy at the 18th century end of the transition: Richard Buel, Jr., "Democracy and the American Revolution: A Frame of Reference," *William and Mary Quarterly*, 21 (April 1964): 165–90, and Roy N. Lokken, "The Concept of Democracy in Colonial Political Thought," ibid., 16 (October 1959): 568–80. Willi Paul Adams finds positive associations with the concept in his careful *The First American Constitutions*, trans. Rita and Robert Kimber (Chapel Hill 1980). On the meaning of representation, see J. R. Pole, *Political Representation in England and the Origins of the American Republic* (London 1966); John Phillip Reid, *The Concept of Representation in the Age of the American Revolution* (Chicago 1989); and Charles S. Sydnor, *Gentlemen Freeholders* (Chapel Hill 1952). Although Edmund S. Morgan has burdened *Inventing the People* (New York 1988) with confusing ideas about what is fiction and what is reality, it remains an interesting study in Anglo-American political theory. Melvin Yazawa's introduction to *Representative Government and the Revolution* (Baltimore 1975) contains particularly useful comments on the sovereign people. Robert J. Dinkin, *Voting in Provincial America* (Westport 1977), supplies critical data on colonial elections. No account of the political process has greater value than Michael Zuckerman's explication of colonial town meetings in *Peaceable Kingdoms* (New York 1970).

The meaning of democracy has become entangled in the concept of republicanism. On republicanism, the essential books are Bernard Bailyn, *The Ideological Origins of the American Revolution* (Cambridge 1967), and J. G. A. Pocock, *The Machiavellian Moment* (Princeton 1975). Drew R. McCoy's understanding of political economy in *The Elusive Republic* (Chapel Hill 1980), and Michael Warner's explorations of the public sphere in *The Letters of the Republic* (Cambridge 1990), add texture to the concept. Soaring across time and space, some enthusiasts have assigned republicanism an almost magical explanatory power. James T. Kloppenberg, "The Virtues of Liberalism: Christianity, Republicanism, and Ethics in Early American Political Discourse," *Journal of American History*, 74 (June 1987): 9–33, and Daniel T. Rodgers, "Republicanism: The Career of a Concept," ibid., 79 (June 1992): 11–38, are indispensable in keeping the concept within bounds and, in the process, disentangling it from democracy. Both are excellent guides to further reading on the subject. Isaac Kramnick's *Republicanism and Bourgeois Radicalism* (Ithaca 1990) contains general criticisms of the concept.

The porous, malleable nature of America's 18th century hierarchies are revealed in a variety of ways in Fred Anderson, *A People's Army* (Chapel Hill 1984); Richard L. Bushman, *King and People in Provincial Massachusetts* (Chapel Hill 1985); Jon Butler, *Awash in a Sea of Faith* (Cambridge 1990); Robert A. Gross, *The Minutemen and Their World* (New York 1976); Jackson Turner Main, *Society and Economy in Colonial Connecticut* (Princeton 1985); and Gordon S. Wood, *The Creation of the American Republic, 1776–1787* (Chapel Hill 1969). Joseph H. Kettner's *The Development of American Citizenship, 1608–1870* (Chapel Hill 1978) has particular significance for a study of democracy.

Some assessments of the American Revolution's impact on these hierarchies have paid little attention to whether upheavals in the 1770s produced changes that endured. That problem limits the value of these interesting studies, for example: Edward Countryman, *A People in Revolution* (Baltimore 1981); Rhys Isaac, *The Transformation of Virginia, 1740–1790* (Chapel Hill 1982); and Richard Alan Ryerson, *The Revolution Is Now Begun* (Philadelphia 1978). Eric Foner's *Tom Paine and Revolutionary America* (New York 1976) is more attentive to long-range consequences. Other studies, such as Pauline Maier, *From Resistance to Revolution* (New York 1972), and Robert M. Weir, *"The Last of American Freemen"* (Macon 1986), describe an impressive hierarchical stability.

The standard line of argument explaining America's social changes between the 18th and 19th centuries attributes them to the transforming force of liberal capitalism and locates the pivotal years somewhere in the two decades following the War of 1812. For several ways of presenting this case, see Andrew R. L. Cayton, *The Frontier Republic* (Kent 1986); Christopher Clark, *The Roots of Rural Capitalism* (Ithaca 1990); Oscar Handlin and Mary Flug Handlin, *Commonwealth* (Cambridge 1947); Hendrik Hartog, *Public Property and Private Power* (Chapel Hill 1983); Morton J. Horwitz, *The Transformation of American Law, 1780–1860* (Cambridge 1977); J. Willard Hurst, *Law and the Conditions of Freedom in the Nineteenth-Century United States* (Madison 1956); and Steven Watts, *The Republic Reborn* (Baltimore 1987). Malcolm J. Rohrbough, *The Land Office Business* (New York 1968), pictures a weak, accommodating national government. See also Daniel Feller, *The Public Lands in Jacksonian Politics* (Madison 1984). For background to those new capitalist relations, see Allan Kulikoff, "The Transition to Capitalism in Rural America," *William and Mary Quarterly*, 46 (January 1989): 120–44; Kenneth Lockridge, "Land, Population, and the Evolution of New England Society," *Past and Present*, 39 (April 1968): 62–80; and Robert D. Mitchell, *Commercialism and Frontier* (Charlottesville 1977). Alan Taylor's *Liberty Men and Great Proprietors* (Chapel Hill 1990) demonstrates the stickiness of old hierarchical ways. In her important essay *Capitalism and a New Social Order* (New York 1984), Joyce Appleby finds the sources of transformation in the 1790s.

Accounts of the metamorphosis in politics usually follow a similar chronology. See in particular three basic studies: Lee Benson, *The Concept of Jacksonian Democracy* (Princeton 1961); Ronald P. Formisano, *The Transformation of Political Culture* (New York 1983); and Richard Hofstadter, *The Idea of a Party System* (Berkeley 1969). James S. Chase, *Emergence of the Presidential Nominating Convention, 1789–1832* (Urbana 1973), supplements those studies. James M. Banner, Jr., *To the Hartford Convention* (New York 1970); John L. Brooke, *The Heart of the Commonwealth* (Cambridge, Eng., 1989); and David Hackett Fischer, *The Revolution in American Conservatism* (New York 1965), give weight to changes very early in the 19th century, while Chilton Williamson's pioneering but sometimes imprecise *American Suffrage* (Princeton 1960) describes a gradual transition between the centuries.

On the transfer of authority from elites to ordinary white people, Samuel Haber's *The Quest for Authority and Honor in the American Professions, 1750–1900* (Chicago 1991) contains information about the losers. Nathan O. Hatch, *The Democratization of American Christianity* (New Haven 1989), is as superb account of how the process unfolded in one area. John B. Bowles, *The Great Revival, 1787–1805* (Lexington 1972), and Dickson D. Bruce, Jr., *And They All Sang Hallelujah* (Knoxville 1974), provide valuable information on the two sides of that transformation, and Harry S. Stout, *The New England Soul* (New York 1986), corroborates the timing of change. Sidney E. Mead, *The Lively Experiment* (New York 1963), remains the most feeling statement on the importance of religious pluralism to American democracy. The power of ordinary citizens early in the 19th century to make decisions about their lives that elites once monopolized is illuminated by two excellent books: Allen Steinberg, *The Transformation of Criminal Justice* (Chapel Hill 1989), and John Harley Warner, *The Therapeutic Perspective* (Cambridge 1986). W. J. Rorabaugh, *The Alcoholic Republic* (New York 1979), and Ian R. Tyrrell, *Sobering Up* (Westport 1979), help us see how empowering ordinary whites revolutionized American drinking habits. Audience authority in cultural matters is discussed in Mary Kupiec Cayton, "The Making of an American Prophet: Emerson, His Audiences, and the Rise of the Culture Industry in Nineteenth-Centry America," *American Historical Review*, 92 (June 1987): 597–620; Michael T. Gilmore, *American Romanticism and the Marketplace* (Chicago 1985); Lawrence W. Levine, *Highbrow/Lowbrow* (Cambridge 1988); and Donald M. Scott, "The Popular Lecture and the Creation of a Public in Mid-Nineteenth-Century America," *Journal of American History*, 66 (March 1980): 791–809.

Although Gordon Wood's *The Radicalism of the American Revolution* asserts the Revolution's centrality in undermining old authorities, its evidence actually reinforces the impression of a resilient hierarchy holding its own until the end of the 18th century, then major changes arriving with the 19th. If, as Wood claims (256), "the crucial moment in the history of American politics" occurred in 1786 with William Findley's argument that politics should express interests, Findley's cause—banks for western Pennsylvania—did not succeed until 1814. In Wood's account, the Revolution produced democracy in the same teleological way that it produced the Civil War: "The Revolution in effect set in motion ideological and social forces that . . . led inexorably to the Civil War" (186–87). James L. Huston makes a firmer case for the Revolution's influence on 19th century democracy in his discussion of ideas that underwrote a popularization of authority: "American Revolutionaries, the Political Economy of Aristocracy, and the American Concept of the Distribution of Wealth, 1765–1900," *American Historical Review*, 98 (October 1993): 1079–105.

On the crucial matter of spreading literacy and numeracy, with attention to the timing that reinforced the democratization of authority, see Patricia Cline Cohen, *A Calculating People* (Chicago 1982); Albert Fishlow, "The Common School Revival: Fact of Fancy?" in *Industrialization in Two Systems*, ed. Henry Rosovsky, (New York 1966), 40–67; Kenneth A. Lockridge, *Literacy in Colonial New England* (New York 1974); and Lee Soltow and Edward Stevens, *The Rise of Literacy and the Common School in the United States* (Chicago 1981).

For background on dependent labor on this side of the Atlantic, see Bernard Bailyn and Barbara DeWolfe, *Voyagers to the West* (New York 1986); Richard B. Morris, *Government and Labor in Early America* (New York 1946); and Abbot Emerson Smith, *Colonists in Bondage* (Chapel Hill 1947). For a sample of the restraints on the other side of the Atlantic, see Jerome Blum, *The End of the Old Order in Rural Europe* (Princeton 1978); Kerby A. Miller, *Emigrants and Exiles* (New York 1985); and Mack Walker, *German Home Towns* (Ithaca 1971). In establishing when white men everywhere in America took control of their working lives, two books are particularly important: W. J. Rorabough, *The Craft Apprentice* (New York 1986), and Robert J. Steinfeld, *The Invention of Free Labor* (Chapel Hill 1991). *Belated Feudalism* (Cambridge, Eng., 1991), Karen Orren's useful compilation of cases in labor law, pays too little attention to their 19th century chronology and historical context. The fluid world of wage earning in two settings is described in Thomas Dublin, *Women at Work* (New York 1979), and David E. Schob, *Hired Hands and Plowboys* (Urbana 1975). Jeremy Atack and Fred Bateman, *To Their Own Soil* (Ames 1987), and Clarence H. Danhof, *Changes in Agriculture* (Cambridge 1969), add specificity to the meaning of independent farming.

Four works further illuminate the New England difference: Robert A. McCaughey, *Josiah Quincy, 1772–1864* (Cambridge 1974); Gerard W. Gawalt, *The Promise of Power* (Westport 1979); Joseph Kett, *The Formation of the American Medical Profession* (New Haven 1968); and Randolph A. Roth, *The Democratic Dilemma* (Cambridge, Eng., 1987).

Joyce Appleby, "The Radical *Double-Entendre* in the Right to Self-Government," in *The Origins of Anglo-American Radicalism*, ed. Margaret Jacob and James Jacob (London 1984), 275–83, finds individual and collective rights interwoven in the late 18th century. The fact that the two sides in a sharp historians' debate over the original meaning of the constitutional right to bear arms are, in fact, both correct helps us see the ambiguous 18th century understanding of personal and group rights. Lawrence Delbert Cress, "The Armed Community: The Origins and Meaning of the Right to Bear Arms," *Journal of American History*, 71 (June 1984): 22–42, which argues that the Second Amendment denoted a collective militia right, expresses the antifederalists' understanding of the Bill of Rights as the community's protection against centralized tyranny. Robert E. Shalhope, "The Ideological Origins of the Second Amendment," ibid., 69 (December 1982): 599–614, which argues that the amendment secured an individual right, echoes those conservative federalists who wanted to bypass states and communities entirely and make the Bill of Rights exclusively a one-to-one connection between citizen and national government. T. Scott Miyakawa, *Protestants and Pioneers* (Chicago 1964), contains important insights into merging individual and community domains early in the 19th century. Yehoshua Arieli, *Individualism and Nationalism in American Ideology* (Cambridge 1964), is a thoughtful discussion.

CHAPTER TWO

The European commentary in this and the next chapters is drawn from the following sources. They are biased toward Britain, as they should be, for British judgments provided the primary external reference point for understanding the American experience. Dates in brackets following the title indicate the time of the visit; a date in brackets at the end of the citation indicates the original year of publication.

Count Francesco Arese, *A Trip to the Prairies and in the Interior of North America* [1837–38], trans. Andrew Evans (New York 1934).

Duke Bernhard of Saxe-Weimar Eisenach, *Travels through North America during the Years 1825 and 1826*, 2 vols. (Philadelphia 1828).

Fredrika Bremer, *America of the Fifties*, ed. Adolph B. Benson (New York 1924).

James Silk Buckingham, *The Eastern and Western States of America*, 3 vols. (London 1842).

Moritz Busch, *Travels between the Hudson & the Mississippi 1851–1852*, trans. and ed. Norman H. Binger (Lexington 1971).

Thomas Cather, *Voyage to America* [1836], ed. Thomas Yoseloff (New York 1961).

William Chambers, *Things as They Are in America* (New York 1968 [1854]).

Michel Chevalier, *Society, Manners and Politics in the United States*, trans. T. G. Bradford (Boston 1839).

William Cobbett, *A Year's Residence in America* (Boston [1819?]).

Richard Cobden, *The American Diaries* [1835, 1859], ed. Elizabeth Hoon Cawley (Princeton 1952).

Charles Dickens, *American Notes for General Circulation*, 2 vols. (London 1842).

James Dixon, *Personal Narrative of a Tour through a Part of the United States and Canada* (New York 1849).

Gottfried Duden, *Report of a Journey to the Western States of North America* [1824–27], trans. and ed. James W. Goodrich et al. (Columbia 1980).

Mary Lundie Duncan, *America as I Found It* (New York 1852).

William Ferguson, *America by River and Rail* (London 1856).

George Flower, *The Errors of Emigrants* (London 1841).

Thomas Colley Grattan, *Civilized America*, 2 vols. (London 1859).

Francis J. Grund, *The Americans, in Their Moral, Social, and Political Relations* (Boston 1837).

Adam G. de Gurowski, *America and Europe* (New York 1857).

Captain Basil Hall, *Travels in North America in the Years 1827 and 1828*, 3 vols. (Edinburgh 1829).

Francis Hall, *Travels in Canada and the United States in 1816 and 1817* (London 1818).

Margaret Hall, *The Aristocratic Journey* [1827–28], ed. Una Pope-Hennessy (New York 1931).

Thomas Hamilton, *Men and Manners in America* (New York 1968 [1833, 1843]).

Adam Hodgson, *Remarks during a Journey through North America in the Years 1819, 1820, and 1821* (Westport 1970 [1823]).

Emanuel Howitt, *Selections from Letters Written during a Tour through the United States in the Summer and Autumn of 1819* (Nottingham 1820).

Baron Axel Klinkowström, *America 1818–1820*, trans. and ed. Franklin D. Scott (Evanston 1952).

Charles Lyell, *A Second Visit to the United States of America*, 2 vols. (New York 1849).

———. *Travels in North America*, 2 vols. (New York 1845).

Alexander Mackay, *The Western World, or, Travels in the United States in 1846–47*, 2nd ed., 3 vols. (London 1850).

Frederick Marryat, *Diary in America*, ed. Jules Zenger (Bloomington 1960 [1839]).

Harriet Martineau, *Society in America*, 2 vols. (New York 1837).

Amelia M. Murray, *Letters from the United States, Cuba and Canada* (New York 1969 [1856]).

Charles Augustus Murray, *Travels in North America during the Years 1834, 1835, & 1836*, 2 vols. (London 1839).

Henry A. Murray, *Lands of the Slave and the Free: or, Cuba, the United States, and Canada*, 2 vols. (London 1855).

Francis Pulzsky and Theresa Pulzsky, *White, Red, and Black*, 2 vols. (New York 1853).

H. Reid, *Sketches in North America* (London 1861).

Ole Munch Roeder, *America in the Forties*, trans. Gunnar J. Malmin (Minneapolis 1929).

Rubio [Thomas Horton James], *Rambles in the United States and Canada during the Year 1845* (London 1847).

Ole Rynning, *Ole Rynning's True Account of America*, trans. and ed. Theodore C. Blegen (Minneapolis 1926 [1838]).

James Stuart, *Three Years in North America*, 2 vols. (Edinburgh 1833).

Lady Emmeline Stuart Wortley, *Travels in the United States, Etc. during 1849 and 1850*, 3 vols. (London 1851).

Alexis de Tocqueville, *Democracy in America*, trans. Henry Reeve and Francis Bowen, ed. Phillips Bradley, 2 vols. (New York 1945 [1835, 1840]).

Frances Milton Trollope, *Domestic Manners of the Americans*, 2 vols. (London 1832).

Francis Tuckett, *A Journey in the United States in the Years 1829 and 1830*, ed., Hubert C. Fox (Plymouth 1976).

Frances Wright, *Views of Society and Manners in America*, ed. Paul R. Baker (Cambridge 1963 [1821]).

Aspects of violence in American culture are discussed in Edward L. Ayers, *Vengeance and Justice* (New York 1984); Bernard Bailyn, *The Origins of American Politics* (New York 1968); Richard Maxwell Brown, *Strain of Violence* (New York 1975); Dickson D. Bruce, Jr., *Violence and Culture in the Antebellum South* (Austin 1979); John Hope Franklin, *The Militant South, 1800–1861* (Cambridge 1956); Thomas P. Slaughter, *The Whiskey Rebellion* (New York 1986); Richard Slotkin, *Regeneration through Violence* (Middletown 1973); and Russell F. Weigley, *The American Way of War* (New York 1973). Michael Kammen's *A Season of Youth* (New York 1978) has important comments on the conservative repackaging of America's revolutionary tradition.

CHAPTER THREE

Debates over the character and efficacy of 19th century democracy begin with elections. Was fraud common? Most students of the subject say no. See, for example, Howard W. Allen and Kay Warren Allen, "Vote Fraud and the Validity of Election Data," in *Analyzing Electoral History*, ed. Jerome Clubb et al. (Beverly Hills 1981); William E. Gienapp, " 'Politics Seem to Enter into Everything': Political Culture in the North, 1840–1860," in *Essays on American Antebellum Politics, 1840–1860*, ed. Stephen E. Maizlish and John J. Kushma (College Station 1982), 15–69; and Mark Kornbluh, *From Participation to Administration* (Baltimore 1995). From a present-minded, good-government perspective, Peter Argersinger counters with yes in "New Perspectives on Electoral Fraud in the Gilded Age," *Political Science Quarterly*, 100 (Winter 1985–86): 669–87; and, especially useful for the varied issues it raises, idem, "The Value of the Vote: Political Representation in the Gilded Age," *Journal of American History*, 76 (June 1989): 59–90. Are the commonly cited turnouts in the range of 70 percent to 80 percent inflated? Not significantly, concludes Walter Dean Burnham in his systematic analysis of the possible distorting factors, "Those High Nineteenth-Century American Voting Turnouts: Fact or Fiction?" *Journal of Interdisciplinary History*, 16 (Spring 1986): 613–44. Margaret Lavinia Anderson, "Voter, Junker, *Landrat*, Priest: The Old Authorities and the New Franchise in

290   SPECIAL DEBTS AND FURTHER READINGS

Imperial Germany," *American Historical Review*, 98 (December 1993): 1448–74, provides a fascinating international comparison on the meaning of the vote.

Four additional studies are particularly helpful in analyzing the origins of democratic parties: Michael F. Holt, "The Election of 1840, Voter Mobilization, and the Emergence of the Second American Party System: A Reappraisal of Jacksonian Voting Behavior," in *A Master's Due*, ed. William J. Cooper, Jr., et al. (Baton Rouge 1985), 16–58, on the economic roots of partisanship; Richard P. McCormick, *The Presidential Game* (New York 1982), on national mobilization; Michael Wallace, "Changing Concepts of Party in the United States: New York, 1815–1828," *American Historical Review*, 74 (December 1968): 453–91, on new democratic values; and Harry L. Watson, *Jacksonian Politics and Community Conflict* (Baton Rouge 1981), on the limits to democratization. Watson's *Liberty and Power* (New York 1990) and Holt's *The Political Crisis of the 1850s* (New York 1978) are superior accounts of antebellum party behavior. Two fine overviews, Richard L. McCormick's *The Party Period and Public Policy* (New York 1986), and Joel H. Silbey's *The American Political Nation, 1838–1893* (Stanford 1991), stress continuity across the heart of the 19th century. Sensitive studies of 19th century party behavior demonstrate how efficient they were in their own terms. See, for example, William N. Chambers and Philip C. Davis, "Party, Competition, and Mass Participation: The Case of the Democratizing Party System, 1824–1852," in *The History of American Electoral Behavior*, ed. Joel H. Silbey et al. (Princeton 1978), 174–97, on voter mobilization; and Robert Marcus, *Grand Old Party* (New York 1971), on information gathering. Although Margaret Susan Thompson's *The "Spider Web"* (Ithaca 1985) is also helpful, it exaggerates the significance of Gilded Age lobbying. The complex ways in which local, state, and sometimes regional impulses shaped national politics are illustrated by the role of nativism in William E. Gienapp's state-by-state study, *The Origins of the Republican Party, 1852–1856* (New York 1987); of ethnicity in Robert Kelley's *The Cultural Pattern in American Politics: The First Century* (New York 1979); and of economic interests in C. Vann Woodward's masterpiece, *Origins of the New South, 1877–1913* (Baton Rouge 1951).

Making the most of the differences between the Whig and Democratic parties is an old historical practice. See Wilfred E. Binkley, *American Political Parties*, 4th ed. (New York 1962), and Marvin Meyers, *The Jacksonian Persuasion* (Stanford 1957). Recent studies that rely on selected New England voices in describing a deeply conservative Whig party include John Ashworth, *'Agrarians & Aristocrats'* (London 1983); Daniel Walker Howe, *The Political Culture of the American Whigs* (Chicago 1979); and Lawrence Frederick Kohl, *The Politics of Individualism* (New York 1989). William H. Pease and Jane H. Pease, *The Web of Progress* (New York 1985), contrasts the styles of public life in Boston and Charleston, another center of opposition to democracy, by contrasting their styles of capitalism. For the South Carolina context, see Lacy K. Ford, "Republics and Democracy: The Parameters of Political Citizenship in Antebellum South Carolina," in *The Meaning of South Carolina History*, ed. David R. Chesnutt and Clyde N. Wilson (Columbia 1991), 121–45.

Evidences of a common 19th century democratic language abound. Kenneth Cmiel, *Democratic Eloquence* (New York 1990), finds it in popular speech; M. J.

Heale, *The Presidential Quest* (London 1982) in political campaigning; David Grimsted, "Melodrama as Echo of the Historically Voiceless," in *Anonymous Americans*, ed. Tamara K. Hareven (Englewood Cliffs 1971), in moral drama. The values that white men brought to war in Gerald F. Linderman's *Embattled Courage* (New York 1987) united northerners and southerners. So did the almost anarchic individualism that David Donald identifies in "An Excess of Democracy," in *Lincoln Reconsidered*, rev. ed. (New York 1961), 209–35.

Rowland Berthoff draws on the rhetoric of white fraternalism in "Conventional Mentality: Free Blacks, Women, and Business Corporations as Unequal Persons, 1820–1870," *Journal of American History*, 76 (December 1989): 753–84. Other aspects of white fraternalism are discussed from a social psychological vantage point in Mark C. Carnes, *Secret Ritual and Manhood in Victorian America* (New Haven 1989); and a Marxist perspective in Mary Ann Clawson, *Constructing Brotherhood* (Princeton 1989). Shifting sources of political identity in this fraternal world are nicely explicated in Ronald P. Formisano, "The Invention of the Ethnocultural Interpretation," *American Historical Review*, 99 (April 1994): 453–77, which is also a valuable guide to further reading.

A number of historians have tried to clarify the 19th century ambiguities between democratic assertiveness and violence. David Grimsted, "Rioting in Its Jacksonian Setting," *American Historical Review*, 77 (April 1972): 361–97, emphasizes its complex origins. Michael Feldberg, *The Turbulent Era* (New York 1980), is an overview; and Paul A. Gilje, *The Road to Mobocracy* (Chapel Hill 1987), a background for events in New York City. Two fine studies, Iver Bernstein's *The New York City Draft Riots* (New York 1990), and Michael Gordon's *The Orange Riots* (Ithaca 1993), stress the democratic impulses underlying those outbreaks. Paul Johnson, "'Art' and the Language of Progress in Early-Industrial Paterson: Sam Patch at Clinton Bridge," *American Quarterly*, 40 (December 1988): 433–49, explores the rough edge of working people's fraternal values. Workingmen struggle for their right to the streets in Susan G. Davis, *Parades and Power* (Philadelphia 1986). Rowland Berthoff, *An Unsettled People* (New York 1971), takes a broad view of social disorder in 19th century America.

CHAPTER FOUR

For useful material on new 19th century beliefs in the sanctity of the human body, see Myra C. Glenn's *Campaigns against Corporal Punishment* (Albany 1984); James Turner's examination of changing values related to pain, *Reckoning with the Beast* (Baltimore 1980); Ronald G. Walters' survey, *American Reformers 1815–1860* (New York 1978); and especially Thomas L. Haskell's stimulating essays, "Capitalism and the Origins of Humanitarian Sensibility," pts. 1 and 2, *American Historical Review*, 90 (April 1985): 339–61, (June 1985): 547–66.

On the ambiguous place of wage earning in the early 19th century, see Jonathan Prude, *The Coming of the Industrial Order* (New York 1983), and Howard B. Rock, *Artisans of the New Republic* (New York 1979). Paul E. Johnson, *A Shopkeeper's Millennium* (New York 1978), and Sean Wilentz, *Chants Democratic* (New York 1984), imaginatively recount the new demands for autonomy and self-respect among early 19th century wage earners. In *The "Lower Sort"* (Ithaca

1990), Billy G. Smith dispels the notion of an artisan's golden age in late 18th century Philadelphia.

White wage earners' drives for respectability included an assertive, free-labor, race-conscious politics, as discussed in Amy Bridges' *A City in the Republic* (Cambridge, Eng., 1984), Eric Foner's pathbreaking *Free Soil, Free Labor, Free Men* (New York 1970), and Alexander Saxton's *The Rise and Fall of the White Republic* (New York 1990); commitments to moral self-improvement, as the aspiring category of wage earners in Bruce Laurie's influential *Working People of Philadelphia, 1800–1850* (Philadelphia 1980) and the struggling ones in David Montgomery's superb "The Shuttle and the Cross: Weavers and Artisans in the Kensington Riots of 1844," *Journal of Social History,* 5 (Summer 1972): 411–46, demonstrate; a place in middle-class communities, as Michael Cassity's *Defending a Way of Life* (Albany 1989) and Brian Greenberg's *Worker and Community* (Albany 1985) illustrate; and a cap on the hours at work, a persistent theme in 19th century respectability, as David R. Roediger's and Philip S. Foner's *Our Own Time* (Westport 1989) reveals. Several books explore the centrality of autonomy and risk in the culture of skilled work: Keith Dix, *What's a Coal Miner to Do?* (Pittsburgh 1988); James H. Ducker, *Men of the Steel Rails* (Lincoln 1983); Walter Licht, *Working for the Railroad* (Princeton 1983); and James Whiteside, *Regulating Danger* (Lincoln 1990).

Grimmer pictures than mine of the lot of wage earners appear in Alan Dawley, *Class and Community* (Cambridge 1976); Susan E. Hirsch, *Roots of the American Working Class* (Philadelphia 1978); and Christopher L. Tomlins, *Law, Labor, and Ideology in the Early American Republic* (Cambridge, Eng., 1993), to which I am particularly indebted. From solid data, Robert A. Margo and Georgia C. Villaflor, "The Growth of Wages in Antebellum America: New Evidence," *Journal of Economic History,* 47 (December 1987): 873–95, argues that real wages rose very little. But because Margo and Villaflor concentrate on the least progressive trades, their conclusions do not supercede the most optimistic estimate of skilled workers' earnings in Peter H. Lindert and Jeffrey G. Williamson, "Three Centuries of American Inequality," in *Research in Economic History,* vol. 1, ed. Paul Uselding (Greenwich 1976), 69–123. In *Without Consent or Contract* (New York 1989), Robert William Fogel embellishes the Margo-Villaflor account with claims of a wage-earner depression in the mid-1850s, a hypothesis that does not square with simultaneous successes in the ten-hour movement and aggressiveness in urban workingmen's politics, both standard indices of good, not bad times. Much more persuasive is Richard B. Stott's excellent description of antebellum New York City's working world, *Workers in the Metropolis* (Ithaca 1990), which gives substance to the Lindert-Williamson sketch of skilled workers benefiting as the less skilled lagged.

The African American role in any aspect of 19th century history begins with the slave experience. Modern discussions of its meaning originate with Kenneth M. Stampp's *The Peculiar Institution* (New York 1956), which emphasizes the conflict between slaves and masters, and Stanley Elkins' *Slavery* (Chicago 1959), which analyzes the slaves' widespread acceptance of their lot. With greater appreciation for the ways slaves shaped their own lives, that debate continues in John Blassingame's account of slave resistance in *Slave Community*

(New York 1972), and Eugene D. Genovese's explanation of slavery as a reciprocal process between masters and slaves in *Roll, Jordan, Roll* (New York 1974).
One introduction to the complicated question of the slaves' physical conditions
combines Fogel's revised judgments in *Without Consent or Contract* and the
sharp criticisms spurring those revisions in Paul A. David et al., *Reckoning with
Slavery* (New York 1976). Bertram Wyatt-Brown, "The Mask of Obedience:
Male Slave Psychology in the Old South," *American Historical Review*, 93 (December 1988): 1228–52, explores the subtler battles inside slavery; and Deborah
Gray White, *Ar'n't I a Woman?* (New York 1985), concentrates on the often-
slighted lives of female slaves.

Carl N. Degler, *Neither Black nor White* (New York 1971), and Orlando Pat-
terson, *Slavery and Social Death* (Cambridge 1982), place the exceptionally harsh
lot of America's free blacks in perspective; Ira Berlin, *Slaves without Masters*
(New York 1974), and Benjamin Quarles, *Black Abolitionists* (New York 1969),
describe some of the consequences. What emancipation meant for African
Americans has been most closely examined in the immediate postwar south.
See, for example, Eric Foner, *Reconstruction* (New York 1988); Thomas Holt,
Black over White (Urbana 1977); and Leon F. Litwack, *Been in the Storm So Long*
(New York 1979). Although the longer-range passage from slavery to freedom
remains more obscure, some important books illuminate the process: Orville
Vernon Burton, *In My Father's House Are Many Mansions* (Chapel Hill 1985);
Barbara Jeanne Fields, *Slavery and Freedom on the Middle Ground* (New Haven
1985); Robert Higgs, *Competition and Coercion* (New York 1977); and James
Oakes, *Slavery and Freedom* (New York 1990).

The complex subject of how slavery affected whites seems to defy holistic
treatment. Among the aspects that have been illuminated are white workers
in Ira Berlin and Herbert G. Gutman, "Natives and Immigrants, Free Men
and Slaves: Urban Workingmen in the Antebellum American South," *American
Historical Review*, 88 (December 1983): 1175–1200, and, more subtly, David R.
Roediger, *The Wages of Whiteness* (London 1991); racial thought in George M.
Fredrickson, *The Black Image in the White Mind* (New York 1971); Winthrop D.
Jordan, *White over Black* (Chapel Hill 1968); and Bertram Wyatt-Brown, "Mod-
ernizing Southern Slavery: The Proslavery Argument Reinterpreted," in *Region,
Race, and Reconstruction* ed. J. Morgan Kousser and James M. McPherson (New
York 1982), 27–50; and the conscience of elites—women in Elizabeth Fox-
Genovese's *Within the Plantation Household* (Chapel Hill 1988), southern men in
Edmund S. Morgan's *American Slavery American Freedom* (New York 1975), and
northern men in Leonard L. Richards, *"Gentlemen of Property and Standing"*
(New York 1970).

Slavery as a deepening moral crisis is examined in David Brion Davis's *The
Problem of Slavery in the Age of Revolution, 1770–1823* (Ithaca 1975), and Ronald
G. Walters' *The Antislavery Appeal* (Baltimore 1976). William J. Cooper, Jr., *The
South and the Politics of Slavery, 1828–1856* (Baton Rouge 1978), William W.
Freehling, *Prelude to Civil War* (New York 1966), and Mark V. Tushnet, *The
American Law of Slavery 1810–1860* (Princeton 1981), analyze how slavery
shaped southern law and politics. Eugene H. Berwanger, *The Frontier against
Slavery* (Urbana 1967), and especially Leon F. Litwack, *North of Slavery* (Chi-

cago 1961), explain the consequences of slavery for free blacks in the north. J. Mills Thornton III, *Politics and Power in a Slave Society* (Baton Rouge 1978), is an outstanding study of slavery's relation to southern democratic politics. Peter J. Parish's *Slavery* (New York 1989) is a nicely presented overview.

Emancipation made a difference among white men too, Phyllis F. Field argues in *The Politics of Race in New York* (Ithaca 1982). How much of a difference is debated in constitutional terms by Harold M. Hyman and William M. Wiecek, *Equal Justice under Law* (New York 1982), on the side of cautious adjustments; and Garry Wills, *Lincoln at Gettysburg* (New York 1992), and Robert J. Kaczorowski, "To Begin the Nation Anew: Congress, Citizenship, and Civil Rights after the Civil War," *American Historical Review*, 92 (February 1987): 45–68, on the side of dramatic reconceptions. The turn toward violence among southern white men is described in George C. Rable, *But There Was No Peace* (Athens 1984), and Allen W. Trelease, *White Terror* (New York 1971).

Of particular interest on the marginalization of Native Americans, see Robert F. Berkhofer, Jr., *Salvation and the Savage* (Lexington 1965); Brian W. Dippie, *The Vanishing America* (Middletown 1982); Roy Harvey Pearce, *Savagism and Civilization* (Baltimore 1965); and Richard White, *The Roots of Dependency* (Lincoln 1983). See also Reginald Horsman, *Race and Manifest Destiny* (Cambridge 1981).

An understanding of white women in 19th century American life begins with an understanding of gendered spheres, which, in turn, begins with three formative studies: Nancy Cott, *The Bonds of Womanhood* (New Haven 1977); Carroll Smith-Rosenberg, "The Female World of Love and Ritual: Relations between Women in Nineteenth-Century America," *Signs*, 1 (1975): 1–29; and Barbara Welter, "The Cult of True Womanhood," *American Quarterly*, 18 (Summer 1966): 151–74. John Mack Faragher, *Women and Men on the Overland Trail* (New Haven 1979); Annette Kolodny, *The Land before Her* (Chapel Hill 1984); and Kathryn Kish Sklar, *Catharine Beecher* (New Haven 1973), add significantly to the subject. The current trend is to challenge or at least to complexify the concept of spheres: see, for example, Carl N. Degler, *At Odds* (New York 1980); Linda K. Kerber, "Separate Spheres, Female Worlds, Woman's Place: The Rhetoric of Women's History," *Journal of American History*, 75 (June 1988): 9–39; and Nancy Hewitt, "Beyond the Search for Sisterhood: American Women's History in the 1980s," *Social History*, 10 (October 1985): 299–321.

As background to the 19th century, Linda Kerber, *Women of the Republic* (Chapel Hill 1980), explains how little the Revolution's reform affected white women. See also Catherine L. Albanese, "Whither the Sons (and Daughters)? Republican Nature and the Quest for the Ideal," in *The American Revolution*, ed. Jack P. Greene (New York 1987), 362–87. By contrast, the dramatic extension of women's public activities in the 19th century is recounted in Barbara J. Berg's *The Remembered Gate* (New York 1978); Barbara Leslie Epstein's *The Politics of Domesticity* (Middletown 1981); Estelle B. Freedman's *Their Sisters' Keepers* (Ann Arbor 1981); Nancy Hewitt's outstanding *Women's Activism and Social Change* (Ithaca 1984); Mary P. Ryan's *Women in Public* (Baltimore 1990); and Carroll Smith-Rosenberg's *Religion and the Rise of the City* (Ithaca 1971). Ann Douglas, *The Feminization of American Culture* (New York 1977), addresses the expansion of middle-class white women's influence from another vantage point; and Mary H. Blewett, *Men, Women, and Work* (Urbana 1988), and Christine Stansell, *City of Women* (New York 1986), illustrate a new assertiveness among wage-earning women. The basic work on middle-class white women's turn into politics is Ellen Carol DuBois's *Feminism and Suffrage* (Ithaca 1978). See also Norma Basch, "Equity vs. Equality: Emerging Concepts of Women's Political Status in the Age of Jackson," *Journal of the Early Republic,* 3 (Fall 1983): 297–318; Beverly Beeton, *Women Vote in the West* (New York 1986); and Steven M. Buechler, *The Transformation of the Woman Suffrage Movement* (New Brunswick 1986).

Several books outline the limits men placed on these expansive activities late in the 19th century. Norma Basch, *In the Eyes of the Law* (Ithaca 1982); Amy Dru Stanley, "Conjugal Bonds and Wage Labor: Rights of Control in the Age of Emancipation," *Journal of American History,* 75 (September 1988): 471–500; and Michael Grossberg, *Governing the Hearth* (Chapel Hill 1985), emphasize the conservative force of the courts. Lori D. Ginsberg, *Women and the Work of Benevolence* (New Haven 1990), which also has an excellent discussion of women's petitioning, and James C. Mohr, *Abortion in America* (New York 1978), deal more generally with a repressive state. Ruth Bordin's *Woman and Temperance* (New Brunswick 1990 [1981]) demonstrates how the Woman's Christian Temperance Union rode with that conservative trend to create the most popular women's movement of the century. Ian Tyrrell's *Woman's World/Woman's Empire* (Chapel Hill 1991) follows the WCTU's influence abroad.

The best introduction to a comparison of the situations of African-Americans and white women is in William H. Chafe's *Women and Equality* (New York 1977). Stephanie McCurry, "The Two Faces of Republicanism: Gender and Proslavery Politics in Antebellum South Carolina," *Journal of American History,* 78 (March 1992): 1245–64, also helps.

CHAPTER FIVE

Michael Katz, "Social Class in North American History," *Journal of Interdisciplinary History,* 11 (Spring 1981): 579–605, is the best introduction to the 19th century two-class system. See also Katz et al., *The Social Organization of Early Industrial Capitalism* (Cambridge 1982), especially chaps. 1 and 9. Two works by Lee Soltow—"Economic Inequality in the United States in the Period from 1790 to 1860," *Journal of Economic History,* 21 (December 1971): 822–39, and *Men and Wealth in the United States, 1850–1870* (New Haven 1975)—lay out the economic ground for class. If property-holding did not determine class in the 19th century, class came close to determining property-holding. Hence disputes over what proportion of the white population owned significant property have a direct bearing on the proportions falling into each class. How does the fact that many propertyless young white men would eventually acquire it affect those estimates? Edward Pessen's *Jacksonian America,* rev. ed. (Homewood 1978), implying a majority in the lower class, and Robert E. Gallman's "Professor Pessen on the 'Egalitarian Myth,'" *Social Science History,* 2 (Winter 1978): 194–207, implying a majority in the middle class, disagree. On the congealing of classes around midcentury, see David A. Gerber, "Cutting Out Shylock: Elite Anti-Semitism and the Quest for Moral Order in the Mid-Nineteenth-Century

American Market Place," *Journal of American History*, 69 (December 1982): 615–37; Mary P. Ryan, *Cradle of the Middle Class* (Cambridge, Eng., 1981); and Sam Bass Warner, Jr., *The Private City* (Philadelphia 1968).

John Higham, *From Boundless to Consolidation* (Ann Arbor 1969), is indispensable for the cultural meaning of this midcentury change. Dolores Greenberg, "Reassessing the Power Patterns of the Industrial Revolution: An Anglo-American Comparison," *American Historical Review*, 87 (December 1982): 1237–61, examines its technological context; Karen Halttunen, *Confidence Men and Painted Women* (New Haven 1982), its cultural context; and Stephan Thernstrom, *Poverty and Progress* (Cambridge 1964), its social context. For more information on the 19th century work place, see Clyde Griffen and Sally Griffen, *Natives and Newcomers* (Cambridge 1978). On the culture of lower-class workers, see Perry R. Duis, *The Saloon* (Urbana 1983); Elliott J. Gorn, " 'Good-Bye Boys, I Die a True American': Homicide, Nativism, and Working-Class Culture in Antebellum New York City," *Journal of American History*, 74 (September 1987): 388–410; and Peter Way, "Evil Humors and Ardent Spirits: The Rough Culture of Canal Construction Laborers," ibid., 79 (March 1993): 1397–428. Milton Cantor, ed., *American Workingclass Culture* (Westport 1979), has more information on these matters.

A conception of social classes that draws the line between white- and blue-collar workers emerges in various ways from Stuart M. Blumin's important *The Emergence of the Middle Class* (Cambridge, Eng., 1989); Jonathan A. Glickstein, *Concepts of Free Labor in Antebellum America* (New Haven 1991); and Michael Katz, *The Irony of Early School Reform* (Cambridge 1968). David Brody, "The Old Labor History and the New: In Search of an American Working Class," *Labor History*, 20 (Winter 1979): 111–26, discusses a number of interpretive problems.

Studies of a late 19th century class crisis in rural America begin with C. Vann Woodward's extraordinary *Origins of the New South, 1877–1913* (Baton Rouge 1951). Lawrence Goodwyn's schematic *Democratic Promise* (New York 1976) offers a particularly bleak view of the collapse of agrarian protest. Other works on the sources and expressions of agrarian discontent are Peter H. Argersinger, *Populism and Politics* (Lexington 1974); Dwight B. Billings, Jr., *Planters and the Making of a "New South"* (Chapel Hill 1979); Lacy K. Ford, "Rednecks and Merchants: Economic Development and Social Tensions in the South Carolina Upcountry, 1865–1900," *Journal of American History*, 71 (September 1984): 294–318; Steven Hahn, *The Roots of Southern Populism* (New York 1983); Bruce Palmer, *"Men over Money"* (Chapel Hill 1980); and Norman Pollack, *The Just Polity* (Urbana 1987). For a more skeptical perspective on Populism, see Barton C. Shaw, *The Wool-Hat Boys* (Baton Rouge 1984).

Useful background to the class crisis of the 1880s among wage earners is provided by James Livingston's analysis of declining productivity in "The Social Analysis of Economic History and Theory: Conjectures on Late Nineteenth-Century American Development," *American Historical Review*, 92 (February 1987): 69–95, and David Montgomery's richly detailed account of changing technology and work in *The Fall of the House of Labor* (Cambridge, Eng., 1987). Bryan D. Palmer, *A Culture in Conflict* (Montreal 1979), offers a North American perspective on the struggle among skilled workers. For aspects of worker cohesion in the late 19th century, see David Bensman, *The Practice of Solidarity* (Urbana 1985); Leon Fink, *Workingmen's Democracy* (Urbana 1983); Richard Jules Oestreicher, *Solidarity and Fragmentation* (Urbana 1986); and Steven J. Ross, *Workers on the Edge* (New York 1985). These studies—in addition to John T. Cumbler's *Working-Class Community in Industrial America* (Westport 1979), Stanley Nadel's *Little Germany* (Urbana 1990), and Daniel J. Walkowitz's *Worker City, Company Town* (Urbana 1978)—also reveal the fluid ways in which work-place identities blended with ethnic, neighborhood, and partisan attachments. Susan Levine's "Labor's True Woman: Domesticity and Equal Rights in the Knights of Labor," *Journal of American History*, 70 (September 1983): 323–39, adds useful information on the urge to respectability.

The sinking of the lower class in the south has been particularly well documented. David L. Carlton, *Mill and Town in South Carolina, 1880–1920* (Baton Rouge 1982), describes the process among whites; Jacqueline Jones, *The Dispossessed* (New York 1992), and Gavin Wright, *Old South, New South* (New York 1986), explain how white and black fortunes were entwined. The collapse by the 1920s of an important biracial work arrangement—to the economic disadvantage of white wage earners—is analyzed in Eric Arnesen, *Waterfront Workers of New Orleans* (New York 1991), and Daniel Rosenberg, *New Orleans Dockworkers* (Albany 1988). William Cohen, "Negro Involuntary Servitude in the South, 1865–1940: A Preliminary Analysis," *Journal of Southern History*, 42 (February 1976): 31–60, and Pete Daniel, *The Shadow of Slavery* (Urbana 1972), detail the grim lot of the peons at the bottom of the pile. See also Amy Dru Stanley, "Beggars Can't Be Choosers: Compulsion and Contract in Postbellum America," *Journal of American History*, 78 (March 1992): 1265–93.

Three outstanding studies describe the success of white middle-class southerners in isolating African Americans: J. Morgan Kousser, *The Shaping of Southern Politics* (New Haven 1974); Joel Williamson, *The Crucible of Race* (New York 1984); and C. Vann Woodward, *The Strange Career of Jim Crow* (New York 1955). Charles L. Flynn, Jr., *White Land, Black Labor* (Baton Rouge 1983), deepens the story. White middle-class northerners were simultaneously distancing themselves from a much more diverse lower class, as Paul Boyer's valuable *Urban Masses and Moral Order in America, 1820–1920* (Cambridge 1978), John Higham's crucial *Strangers in the Land* (New Brunswick 1955), and Donald K. Pickens's *Eugenics and the Progressives* (Nashville 1968) explain. Kathleen M. Blee's *Women of the Klan* (Berkeley 1991), Robert Alan Goldberg's *Hooded Empire* (Urbana 1981), Kenneth T. Jackson's *The Ku Klux Klan in the City, 1915–1930* (New York 1967), and Nancy MacLean's powerful *Behind the Mask of Chivalry* (New York 1994) give different readings of the Ku Klux Klan's contributions. Alexander Keyssar, *Out of Work* (Cambridge, Eng., 1986), and Peter R. Shergold, *Working-Class Life* (Pittsburgh 1982), provide basic information on the consequences among wage earners. Melvyn Dubofsky's *We Shall Be All* (Chicago 1969), and Allan Kent Powell's *The Next Time We Strike* (Logan 1985), demonstrate the special vulnerability of isolated work forces, particularly in mining.

How the sinking process trapped blacks in northern cities is recounted in James R. Grossman, *Land of Hope* (Chicago 1989); Thomas Lee Philpott, *The Slum and the Ghetto* (New York 1978); and Joe William Trotter, Jr., *Black Milwau-*

kee (Urbana 1985). For background, see Roger Lane's speculative *Roots of Violence* (Cambridge 1986). As Cletus E. Daniel's *Bitter Harvest* (Ithaca 1981) demonstrates for Asian Americans and Frederick E. Hoxie's *A Final Promise* (Lincoln 1984) for Native Americans, minorities of color in the west fared little better.

On fragmentation and segmentation in lower-class life, see John J. Bukowczyk, *And My Children Did Not Know Me* (Bloomington 1987); Sarah Deutsch, *No Separate Refuge* (New York 1987); Herbert G. Gutman, *Power and Culture*, ed. Ira Berlin (New York 1987); and especially idem, *Work, Culture, and Society in Industrializing America* (New York 1975); David M. Katzman, *Seven Days a Week* (New York 1978); Ewa Morawska, *For Bread with Butter* (Cambridge, Eng., 1985); and Olivier Zunz, *The Changing Face of Inequality* (Chicago 1982).

Particularly useful accounts of a labor aristocracy are Andrew Dawson, "The Paradox of Dynamic Technological Change and the Labor Aristocracy in the United States, 1880–1914," *Labor History*, 20 (Summer 1979): 325–51; Helena Flam, "Democracy in Debt: Credit and Politics in Paterson, N.J., 1890–1930," *Journal of Social History*, 18 (Spring 1985): 439–55; Gwendolyn Mink, *Old Labor and New Immigrants in American Political Development* (Ithaca 1986); and Benson Soffer, "A Theory of Trade Union Development: The Role of the 'Autonomous' Workman," *Labor History*, 1 (Spring 1960): 141–63. Works that illuminate skilled labor's pulling-away process as they address other issues include Patricia Cooper's *Once a Cigar Maker* (Urbana 1987); Michael Kazin's *Barons of Labor* (Urbana 1987); David Montgomery's *Workers' Control in America* (Cambridge, Eng., 1979); and Mark J. Stern's *Society and Family Strategy* (Albany 1987). On company programs to entice skilled workers, see Stuart Brandes, *American Welfare Capitalism, 1880–1940* (Chicago 1976); David Brody, "The Rise and Decline of Welfare Capitalism," in Brody, *Workers in Industrial America* (New York 1981), 48–81; and Gerald Zahavi, *Workers, Managers, and Welfare Capitalism* (Urbana 1988). For a misleading account of skilled work in the early 20th century, see the influential book by David M. Gordon, Richard Edwards, and Michael Reich, *Segmented Work, Divided Workers* (Cambridge, Eng., 1982). Victoria C. Hattam, *Labor Visions and State Power* (Princeton 1993), emphasizes the unions' weakness in public affairs.

On the rise and fall of the Socialist party, see Eric Foner, "Why Is There No Socialism in the United States?" *History Workshop Journal*, 17 (Spring 1984): 57–80; Nick Salvatore, *Eugene V. Debs* (Urbana 1982); and James Weinstein, *The Decline of Socialism in America, 1912–1925* (New York 1967). Other aspects of Socialism and labor are discussed in John H. M. Laslett, *Labor and the Left* (New York 1970); Sally M. Miller, *Victor Berger and the Promise of Constructive Socialism, 1910–1920* (Westport 1973); and Michael Nash, *Conflict and Accommodation* (Westport 1982). See also Elliott Shore, *Talkin' Socialism* (Lawrence 1988).

The elusive subject of immigrant ambitions and community supports is analyzed in James R. Barrett's "Americanization from the Botton Up: Immigration and the Remaking of the Working Class in the United States, 1880–1930," *Journal of American History*, 79 (December 1992): 996–1020, and his valuable *Work and Community in the Jungle* (Urbana 1987); Harold Benanson's "The Community and Family Bases of U.S. Working Class Protest, 1880–1920: A Critique

SPECIAL DEBTS AND FURTHER READINGS

of the 'Skill Degradation' and 'Ecological' Perspectives," in *Research in Social Movements, Conflicts and Change*, vol. 8, ed. Louis Kriesberg (Greenwich 1985), 109–32; John Bodnar's *The Transplanted* (Bloomington 1985); John J. Bukowczyk's "The Transformation of Working-Class Ethnicity: Corporate Control, Americanization, and the Polish Immigrant Middle-Class in Bayonne, New Jersey, 1915–1925," *Labor History*, 25 (Winter 1984): 53–82; Susan Anita Glenn's *Daughters of the Shtetl* (Ithaca 1990); and Virginia Yans-McLaughlin's "A Flexible Tradition: South Italian Immigrants Confront a New York Experience," *Journal of Social History*, 7 (Summer 1974): 429–45.

For comparative perspectives on wage earners and class, see James E. Cronin and Carmen Sirianni, eds., *Work, Community, and Power* (Philadelphia 1983); John Foster, *Class Struggle and the Industrial Revolution* (London 1974); Dieter Groh, "Intensification of Work and Industrial Conflict in Germany, 1896–1914," *Politics and Society*, 8 (1978): 349–97; Seppo Hentilä, "The Origins of the *Folkhem* Ideology in Swedish Social Democracy," *Scandanavian Journal of History*, 3 (1978): 323–45; Gareth Stedman Jones, *Languages of Class* (Cambridge, Eng., 1983); idem, *Outcast London* (Oxford 1971); and Stephen Wood, ed., *The Degradation of Work?* (London 1982). Vernon L. Lidtke's *The Alternative Culture* (New York 1985), and Standish Meacham's *A Life Apart* (Cambridge 1977), deal with culture and class. Jean H. Quataert, "The Shaping of Women's Work in Manufacturing: Guilds, Households, and the State in Central Europe, 1648–1870," *American Historical Review*, 90 (December 1985): 1122–48, is best on the culture of discrimination against women in the 19th century.

There is a particularly rich, contentious literature on labor aristocracy in Britain before the First World War. For a sample, see Robert Q. Gray, *The Labour Aristocracy in Victorian Edinburgh* (Oxford 1976); Royden Harrison and Jonathan Zeitlin, eds., *Divisions of Labour* (Sussex 1985); E. J. Hobsbawm, *Labouring Men* (London 1964); idem, *Workers* (New York 1984); Henry Pelling, "The Concept of the Labour Aristocracy," in Pelling, *Popular Politics and Society in Late Victorian Britain*, 2nd ed. (London 1979), 37–61; Roger Penn, *Skilled Workers in the Class Structure* (Cambridge, Eng., 1985); and Alastair Reid, "Intelligent Artisan and Aristocrats of Labour: The Essays of Thomas Wright," in *The Working Class in Modern British History*, ed. Jay Winter (Cambridge, Eng., 1983), 171–86.

CHAPTER SIX

Anthony Giddens, *The Class Structure of the Advanced Societies* (London 1973), is a particularly relevant analysis. Arthur Marwick, *Class* (New York 1980), R. S. Neale, *Class and Ideology in the Nineteenth Century* (London 1972), and Raymond Williams, *Culture and Society 1780–1950* (New York 1958), are also valuable. For a sample of the confusion over a crucial term, see Lenore O'Boyle, "The Middle Class in Europe, 1815–1848," *American Historical Review*, 71 (April 1966): 826–45; Edward Shorter, "Middle-Class Anxiety in the German Revolution of 1848," *Journal of Social History*, 2 (Spring 1969): 189–215; and Peter N. Stearns, "The Middle Class: Toward a Precise Definition," *Comparative Studies in Society and History*, 21 (July 1979): 377–96.

Although information about an abortive plutocracy is scattered, Frederic Cople Jaher, "Styles and Status: High Society in Late Nineteenth-Century New

York," in *The Rich, the Well Born, and the Powerful*, ed. Jaher (Urbana 1973), 258–84, John F. Kasson, *Rudeness and Civility* (New York 1990), and Joseph F. Rishel, *Founding Families of Pittsburgh* (Pittsburgh 1990), are useful. In *Middle-Class Providence, 1820–1940* (Princeton 1986), John S. Gilkeson, Jr., takes a long look at America's respectable class. Mansel G. Blackford, *A Portrait Cast in Steel* (Westport 1982), Robert B. Davies, "'Peacefully Working to Conquer the World': The Singer Sewing Machine Company in Foreign Markets," *Business History Review*, 43 (Autumn 1969): 299–325, and Philip Scranton, *Proprietary Capitalism* (Cambridge, Eng., 1983), discuss traditional middle-class business practices. For community values in different venues, see Herbert J. Gans, *The Levittowners* (New York 1967); Ted Ownby, *Subduing Satan* (Chapel Hill 1990); and Robert A. Slayton, *Back of the Yards* (Chicago 1986). For local politicians in two settings, see Numan V. Bartley's *The Creation of Modern Georgia* (Athens 1983), and Philip R. VanderMeer's *The Hoosier Politician* (Urbana 1985). More on local middle-class politics can be found in John D. Buenker, *Urban Liberalism and Progressive Reform* (New York 1973); David Burner, *The Politics of Provincialism* (New York 1968); Henry C. Ferrell, Jr., *Claude A. Swanson of Virginia* (Lexington 1985); Dewey W. Grantham, *Southern Progressivism* (Knoxville 1983); William A. Link, *The Paradox of Southern Progressivism, 1880–1930* (Chapel Hill 1992); and David Thelen, *Paths of Resistance* (New York 1986). The place of white-collar women workers in the emerging class scheme has been examined with special care: Susan Porter Benson, *Counter Cultures* (Urbana 1986); Margery W. Davies, *Woman's Place Is at the Typewriter* (Philadelphia 1982); Ileen A. DeVault, *Sons and Daughters of Labor* (Ithaca 1990); and Lisa Fine, *The Souls of the Skyscraper* (Philadelphia 1990). Lynn Dumenil's *Freemasonry and American Culture 1880–1930* (Princeton 1984) describes a favorite local middle-class association.

Among the many points where national-class and local middle-class values clashed, Sydney E. Ahlstrom, *A Religious History of the American People*, vol. 2 (New Haven 1972), George M. Marsden, *Fundamentalism and American Culture* (New York 1980), and Ferenc M. Szasz, *The Divided Mind of Protestant America, 1880–1930* (University 1982), reveal conflicts in Protestantism. JoAnne Brown, *The Definition of a Profession* (Princeton 1992), Marjorie Murphy, *Blackboard Unions* (Ithaca 1990), and David Tyack and Elisabeth Hansot, *Managers of Virtue* (New York 1982), discuss the pulls of professionalism in education. The distance between urban professionals and the countryside is measured in William L. Bowers, *The Country Life Movement in America, 1900–1920* (Port Washington 1974); John Milton Cooper, Jr., *Walter Hines Page* (Chapel Hill 1977); and John Ettling, *The Germ of Laziness* (Cambridge 1981). How the new urbanites carried those old values with them to the suburbs is described in Peter J. Schmitt, *Back to Nature* (New York 1969). How new patterns in urban entertainment shifted power away from the local middle class is explained in Francis G. Couvares, *The Remaking of Pittsburgh* (Albany 1984); John F. Kasson, *Amusing the Million* (New York 1978); Kathy Peiss, *Cheap Amusements* (Philadelphia 1986); and Roy Rosenzweig, *Eight Hours for What We Will* (Cambridge, Eng., 1983).

James May, "Antitrust Practice and Procedure in the Formative Era: The Constitutional and Conceptual Reach of State Antitrust Law, 1880–1918," *University* of *Pennsylvania Law Review*, 135 (March 1987): 496–593, Walter F. Pratt, Jr., "American Contract Law at the Turn of the Century," *South Carolina Law Review*, 39 (Winter 1988): 415–64, and Melvin I. Urofsky, "State Courts and Protective Legislation during the Progressive Era: A Reevaluation," *Journal of American History*, 72 (June 1985): 63–91, describe class-conflicted adaptations and accommodations in the law. For background, see Thomas L. Haskell, *The Emergence of Professional Social Science* (Urbana 1977); Harry N. Scheiber, "Federalism and the American Economic Order, 1789–1910," *Law and Society Review*, 10 (Fall 1975): 57–118; Carole Shammas, "A New Look at Long-Term Trends in Wealth Inequality in the United States," *American Historical Review*, 98 (April 1993): 412–31; and Stephen Skowronek, *Building a New American State* (Cambridge, Eng., 1982). For alternative contexts, see Gabriel Kolko, *The Triumph of Conservatism* (Glencoe 1963), and Nell Irwin Painter, *Standing at Armageddon* (New York 1987).

There is a particularly rich literature on local middle-class preoccupation with city governance. For background, see Eric H. Monkkonen, *America Becomes Urban* (Berkeley 1988), and Jon C. Teaford, *The Unheralded Triumph* (Baltimore 1984). Samuel P. Hays, "The Changing Political Structure of the City in Industrial America," *Journal of Urban History*, 1 (November 1974): 6–38, and Martin J. Schiesl, *The Politics of Efficiency* (Berkeley 1977), explain the strains within progressive reform. For the triumph of the local middle class, see Blaine A. Brownell, *The Urban Ethos in the South, 1920–1930* (Baton Rouge 1975); Carl V. Harris, *Political Power in Birmingham, 1871–1921* (Knoxville 1977); Harold L. Platt, *City Building in the New South* (Philadelphia 1983); and Bradley R. Rice, *Progressive Cities* (Austin 1977).

For different points of view on Catt, Gompers, and Washington, see Robert Booth Fowler, *Carrie Catt* (Boston 1986); Louis R. Harlan, *Booker T. Washington: The Wizard of Tuskegee 1901–1915* (New York 1983); Stuart Kaufman, *Samuel Gompers and the Origins of the American Federation of Labor, 1848–1896* (Westport 1973); Bernard Mandell, *Samuel Gompers* (Yellow Springs 1963); Mary Gray Peck, *Carrie Chapman Catt* (New York 1944); and Bruno Ramirez, *When Workers Fight* (Westport 1978).

Alan Trachtenberg's *The Incorporation of America* (New York 1982) provides background for the emergence of hierarchies. Their prototypes in business are covered in Alfred D. Chandler, Jr., *The Visible Hand* (Cambridge 1977); Dan Clawson, *Bureaucracy and the Labor Process* (New York 1980); Daniel Nelson, *Managers and Workers* (Madison 1975); David F. Noble, *America by Design* (New York 1977); and JoAnne Yates, *Control through Communication* (Baltimore 1989). Daniel T. Rodgers, *The Work Ethic in Industrial America, 1850–1920* (Chicago 1978), discusses the implications in work values; and James Gilbert, *Designing the Industrial State* (Chicago 1972), the implications in collectivist theory. For the effects on women wage earners, see Alice Kessler-Harris, *Out to Work* (New York 1982); and Leslie Woodcock Tentler, *Wage-Earning Women* (New York 1979). For the assimilation of white-collar men, see Edwin Gabler, *The American Telegrapher* (New Brunswick 1988); Jürgen Kocka, *White Collar Workers in America, 1890–1940*, trans. Maura Kealey (London 1980); and Olivier Zunz, *Making America Corporate, 1870–1920* (Chicago 1990). Howard P. Chudacoff,

302 SPECIAL DEBTS AND FURTHER READINGS

How Old Are You? (Princeton 1990), Michael H. Hunt, *Ideology and U.S. Foreign Policy* (New Haven 1987), and James H. Madison, "Reformers and the Rural Church, 1900–1950," *Journal of American History*, 73 (December 1986): 645–68, suggest how generally hierarchical ideas spread early in the century.
The tenacity of hierarchical values and the rigidities they built into the corporate world are the subject of Sanford M. Jacoby's excellent "American Exceptionalism Revisited: The Importance of Management," in *Masters to Managers*, ed. Jacoby (New York 1991), 173–200. Steve Jefferys, *Management and Managed* (Cambridge, Eng., 1986), David F. Noble, *Forces of Production* (Chapel Hill 1984), Stephen P. Waring, *Taylorism Transformed* (Chapel Hill 1991), and William Bruce Wheeler and Michael J. McDonald, *TVA and the Tellico Dam, 1936–1979* (Knoxville 1986), are also useful. Michael J. Piore and Charles F. Sabel, *The Second Industrial Divide* (New York 1984), and Emma Rothschild, *Paradise Lost* (New York 1973), make important applications for contemporary America.

CHAPTER SEVEN
Some stimulating ways of looking at the 1890s as a fault line in American history are Walter Dean Burnham, *Critical Elections and the Mainsprings of American Politics* (New York 1970); John Higham, "The Reorientation of American Culture in the 1890s," in Higham, *Writing American History* (Bloomington 1970), 73–102; Richard Hofstadter, "Cuba, the Philippines, and Manifest Destiny," in *The Paranoid Style in American Politics and Other Essays* (New York 1964), 145–87; David P. Thelen, "Social Tensions and the Origins of Progressivism," *Journal of American History*, 56 (September 1969): 323–41; C. Vann Woodward, *Tom Watson* (New York 1938); and Larzer Ziff, *The American 1890s* (New York 1966).
The fullest account of a transformation in political practices is Michael E. McGerr's valuable *The Decline of Popular Politics* (New York 1986). John F. Reynolds, *Testing Democracy* (Chapel Hill 1988), is an excellent supplement. The introduction in Richard J. Jensen's *Grass Roots Politics* (Westport 1983) adds to our understanding. Aspects of the big change are discussed in John Buenker, "Sovereign Individuals and Organic Networks: Political Cultures in Conflict during the Progressive Era," *American Quarterly*, 40 (June 1988): 187–204; Michael H. Frisch, "Urban Theorists, Urban Reform, and American Political Culture in the Progressive Period," *Political Science Quarterly*, 97 (Summer 1982): 294–315; John F. Reynolds and Richard L. McCormick, "Outlawing 'Treachery': Split Tickets and Ballot Laws in New York and New Jersey," *Journal of American History*, 72 (March 1986): 835–58; and Lloyd Sponholtz, "The Initiative and Referendum: Direct Democracy in Perspective, 1898–1920," *American Studies*, 14 (Fall 1973): 43–64. Paul Kleppner, *Who Voted?* (New York 1982), provides important information.
James T. Kloppenberg's indispensable *Uncertain Victory* (New York 1986) places the transformation in social thought on a transatlantic canvas. Daniel Levine, *Poverty and Society* (New Brunswick 1988), does the same for specific welfare issues; and Mary O. Furner and Barry Supple, eds., *The State and Economic Knowledge* (Cambridge, Eng., 1990), for the workings of a new professionalism. Robert B. Westbrook, *John Dewey and American Democracy* (Ithaca 1991), is a basic source on American progressive values; and John Thompson,

Reformers and War (Cambridge, Eng., 1987), provides a sensitive account of changing progressive perceptions in the throes of war making and peace making. Wilbur Zelinsky's *Nation into State* (Chapel Hill 1989) offers a useful framework for understanding a new nationalism in the early 20th century. Related issues are covered in Thomas J. Archdeacon, *Becoming American* (New York 1983), and William Preston, Jr., *Aliens and Dissenters* (Cambridge 1963). On wartime itself David M. Kennedy's *Over Here* (New York 1980) is excellent.

Robyn Muncy's *Creating a Female Dominion in American Reform, 1890–1935* (New York 1991) is an outstanding account of the rise and fall of progressive women's public influence. Additional information on that progressive tradition is contained in Linda Gordon, "Social Insurance and Public Assistance: The Influence of Gender in Welfare Thought in the United States, 1890–1935," *American Historical Review*, 97 (February 1992): 19–54; Jacquelyn Dowd Hall, *Revolt against Chivalry* (New York 1979); Michael McGerr, "Political Style and Women's Power, 1830–1930," *Journal of American History*, 77 (December 1990): 864–85; and Sheila M. Rothman, *Woman's Proper Place* (New York 1978). While Theda Skocpol's *Protecting Soldiers and Mothers* (Cambridge 1992) demonstrates that early in the 20th century a substantial minority of northern white men over sixty-five received soldiers' pensions through an old-style, party-driven distribution system, it exaggerates the significance of new-style, bureaucratic benefits to mothers.

The place of a gendered progressive tradition as a backdrop for the suffrage amendment is illuminated in Paula Baker, "The Domestication of Politics: Women and American Political Society, 1780–1920," *American Historical Review*, 89 (June 1984): 620–47; Ellen Carol DuBois, "Harriot Stanton Blatch and the Transformation of Class Relations among Woman Suffragists," in *Gender, Class, Race, and Reform in the Progressive Era*, ed. Noralee Frankel and Nancy S. Dye (Lexington 1991), 162–79; and Richard J. Evans, *The Feminists* (New York 1977). The impact of the war on middle-class women's standing is suggested by William J. Breen, *Uncle Sam at Home* (Westport 1984); Ross Evans Paulson, *Women's Suffrage and Prohibition* (Glenview 1973); and Barbara J. Steinson, *American Women's Activism in World War I* (New York 1982).

For valuable international perspectives on these issues, see Peter Clarke, *Liberals and Social Democrats* (Cambridge, Eng., 1978); Steven C. Hause with Anne R. Kenney, *Women's Suffrage and Social Politics in the French Third Republic* (Princeton 1984); Sandra Stanley Holton, *Feminism and Democracy* (Cambridge, Eng., 1986); Susan Kingsley, *Sex and Suffrage in Britain, 1860–1914* (Princeton 1987); and Sonya Michel and Seth Koven, "Womanly Duties: Maternalist Politics and the Origins of Welfare States in France, Germany, Great Britain, and the United States, 1880–1920," *American Historical Review*, 95 (October 1990): 1076–108.

The difficulty of identifying the effects of women's ballots on American politics is revealed in Sara Alpern and Dale Baum, "Female Ballots: The Impact of the Nineteenth Amendment," *Journal of Interdisciplinary History*, 26 (Summar 1985): 43–67, and Paul Kleppner, "Were Women to Blame? Female Suffrage and Voter Turnout," ibid., 12 (Spring 1982): 621–43. Of the various ways in which women's influence was diminished after 1920, see Paula Baker, *The Moral*

Frameworks of Public Life (New York 1991); Felice D. Gordon, *After Winning* (New Brunswick 1985); William L. O'Neill, *Everyone Was Brave* (Chicago 1969); and Judith Sealander, *As Minority Becomes Majority* (Westport 1983). Sybil Lipschultz, "Social Feminism and Legal Discourse, 1908–1923," *Yale Journal of Law and Feminism*, 2 (Fall 1989): 131–60, and Joan G. Zimmerman, "The Jurisprudence of Equality: The Women's Minimum Wage, the First Equal Rights Amendment, and *Atkins v. Children's Hospital*, 1905–1923," *Journal of American History*, 78 (June 1991): 188–225, detail the frustrations of reform in the 1920s. For individuals in politics, see Dorothy M. Brown, *Mabel Walker Willebrandt* (Knoxville 1984), and Susan Ware, *Beyond Suffrage* (Cambridge 1981).

CHAPTER EIGHT

An understanding of the new sensibilities in modern American culture begins with Henry F. May's pathbreaking *The End of American Innocence* (New York 1959). In different settings these books add important information: Casey Blake, *Beloved Community* (Chapel Hill 1990); Lewis Erenberg, *Steppin' Out* (Westport 1981); Nathan I. Huggins, *Harlem Renaissance* (New York 1971); and Daniel Joseph Singal, *The War Within* (Chapel Hill 1982). Robert M. Crunden's *Ministers of Reform* (New York 1982) is helpful in emphasizing how different prewar and postwar sensibilities were.

The new values penetrated everywhere. James B. Gilbert, *Work without Salvation* (Baltimore 1977), discusses changing attitudes toward work. See also Harry Braverman, *Labor and Monopoly Capital* (New York 1974). Warren I. Susman, " 'Personality' and the Making of Twentieth-Century Culture," in *New Directions in American Intellectual History*, ed. John Higham and Paul K. Conkin (New Haven 1985), 212–26, traces the passing of 19th century character; and K. Austin Kerr, *Organized for Prohibition* (New Haven 1985), the last hurrah of a favorite 19th century reform. New meaning in marriage is suggested by Elaine Tyler May, *Great Expectations* (Chicago 1980), and William L. O'Neill, *Divorce in the Progressive Era* (New Haven 1967). For contrasting 19th century values, see Gillian Brown's *Domestic Individualism* (Berkeley 1990). Changing orientations toward youth and age are covered in Paula S. Fass, *The Damned and the Beautiful* (New York 1977); Carole Haber, *Beyond Sixty-Five* (Cambridge, Eng., 1983); and Gilman M. Ostrander, *American Civilization in the First Machine Age* (New York 1970).

The classic account of consumerism as the cultural cement for modern America is Daniel J. Boorstin, *The Americans: The Democratic Experience* (New York 1973). David E. Nye's *Electrifying America* (Cambridge 1991) is also a wide-ranging study of consumer culture. For the new consumer world as a self-conscious creation of the early 20th century, see Leigh Eric Schmidt, "The Commercialization of the Calendar: American Holidays and the Culture of Consumption, 1870–1930," *Journal of American History*, 78 (December 1991): 887–916; Susan Strasser, *Satisfaction Guaranteed* (New York 1989); and William R. Taylor, "The Launching of a Commercial Culture: New York City, 1860–1930," in *Power, Culture, and Place*, ed. John Hull Mollenkopf (New York 1988), 107–33. The role of advertising in this process, especially in the shift around the First World War to fulfillment appeals, is detailed in Roland Marchand,

Advertising the American Dream (Berkeley 1985), and James D. Norris, *Advertising and the Transformation of American Society, 1865–1920* (New York 1990). Ronald Edsforth, *Class Conflict and Cultural Consensus* (New Brunswick 1987), discusses the soporific effect of consumerism on labor activism; and Lary May, *Screening Out the Past* (New York 1980), explains the way in which Hollywood disguised modern values in conservative settings. Tania Modleski's *Loving with a Vengeance* (Hamden 1982), on the other hand, offers an interesting defense of psychic relevance in popular media.

Among the studies that give special attention to the place of women in modern culture, several highlight a generational divide that sorted out women around the First World War: Nancy F. Cott's *The Grounding of Modern Feminism* (New Haven 1987); David M. Kennedy's *Birth Control in America* (New Haven 1970); James R. McGovern's "The American Woman's Pre-World War I Freedom in Manners and Morals," *Journal of American History*, 55 (September 1969): 315–33; and Rosalind Rosenberg's *Beyond Separate Spheres* (New Haven 1982). Mary A. Hill's *Charlotte Perkins Gilman* (Philadelphia 1980) is the first volume of what promises to be an excellent biography of a major figure on the far side of that divide. How the politics of domestic space reflected changing values is the subject of Dolores Hayden, *Redesigning the American Dream* (New York 1984), and Margaret Marsh, "From Separation to Togetherness: The Social Construction of Domestic Space in American Suburbs, 1840–1915," *Journal of American History*, 76 (September 1989): 506–27. Jacquelyn Dowd Hall, "Disorderly Women: Gender and Labor Militancy in the Appalachian South," *Journal of American History*, 73 (September 1986): 354–82, Joanne J. Meyerowitz, *Women Adrift* (Chicago 1988), and Stephen H. Norwood, *Labor's Flaming Youth* (Urbana 1990), recount the contributions of workingwomen to the new spirit. Old values die hard in Ruth Rosen's study of prostitution, *The Lost Sisterhood* (Baltimore 1982).

The restraints—some old, some new—that went along with these changes qualify the picture of suddenly emancipated women: Regina Markell Morantz-Sanchez, *Sympathy and Science* (New York 1985); Mary P. Ryan, "The Projection of a New Womanhood: The Movie Moderns in the 1920s," in *Decades of Discontent*, ed. Louis Scharf and Joan M. Jensen (Westport 1983), 113–30; Carroll Smith-Rosenberg, "The New Woman as Androgyne: Social Disorder and Gender Crisis, 1870–1936," in Smith-Rosenberg, *Disorderly Conduct* (New York 1986), 245–96; Ellen Trimberger, "Feminism, Men, and Modern Love: Greenwich Village, 1900–1925," in *Powers of Desire*, ed. Ann Snitow et al. (New York 1983), 131–52; and Mary Roth Walsh, *"Doctors Wanted: No Women Need Apply"* (New Haven 1977). Lois W. Banner's *American Beauty* (New York 1983), and Joan Jacobs Brumberg's *Fasting Girls* (Cambridge 1988), focus on the costly culture of beauty. Campaigns that still had a long way to go are the subject of Susan D. Becker, *The Origins of the Equal Rights Amendment* (Westport 1981); James Reed's *From Private Vice to Public Virtue* (New York 1978) on birth control; and Margurete Sandelowski's *Pain, Pleasure, and American Childbirth* (Westport 1984) on natural childbirth. Linda Gordon, *Heroes of Their Own Lives* (New York 1988), explores domestic violence.

The effects of modern culture on the delivery of health care includes the transformation of the hospital, as Charles E. Rosenberg's *The Care of Strangers* (New York 1987), and David Rosner's *A Once Charitable Enterprise* (Cambridge, Eng., 1982), explain it. Elizabeth Fee, *Disease and Discovery* (Baltimore 1987), and David Rosner and Gerald Markowitz, *Deadly Dust* (Princeton 1991), describe the loss of vitality in public health, as, by implication, does Allan M. Brandt, *No Magic Bullet* (New York 1985). Edward H. Beardsley, *A History of Neglect* (Knoxville 1987), reveals the racial bias; and Richard A. Meckel, *Save the Babies* (Baltimore 1990), the class bias in health care delivery. On the state of reforms and social services generally, Clarke A. Chambers, *Seedtime of Reform* (Minneapolis 1963); and J. Stanley Lemons, *The Woman Citizen* (Urbana 1975), give more optimistic appraisals.

For new turns in the law, see Morton J. Horwitz, *The Transformation of American Law 1870–1960* (New York 1992), and Richard Polenberg, *Fighting Faiths* (New York 1987); and for the law generally, Lawrence M. Friedman, *A History of American Law* (New York 1973).

CHAPTER NINE

Almost everything written about public policy since the First World War speaks to the issue of distancing government from the public. Any sampling on the construction of the modern state in America is quite arbitrary. Some stimulating studies are Edward Berkowitz and Kim McQuaid, *Creating the Welfare State*, rev. ed. (Lawrence 1992); Alan Dawley, *Struggles for Justice* (Cambridge 1991); Michael J. Lacey and Mary O. Furner, eds., *The State and Social Investigation in Britain and the United States* (Cambridge, Eng., 1993); Ellis W. Hawley, *The New Deal and the Problem of Monopoly* (Princeton 1966); Richard Gid Powers, *Secrecy and Power* (New York 1987); Theda Skocpol, "Political Response to Capitalist Crisis: Neo-Marxist Theories of the State and the Case of the New Deal," *Politics and Society*, 10 (1980): 155–201; and William Appleman Williams, *The Contours of American History* (Cleveland 1962). Peri E. Arnold's *Making the Managerial Presidency* (Princeton 1986), and Thomas K. McCraw's *Prophets of Regulation* (Cambridge, 1984), deal with evolving bureaucracies. Ideas circulating around these processes are discussed in John P. Diggins, *Mussolini and Fascism* (Princeton 1972); Edward A. Purcell, Jr., *The Crisis of Democratic Theory* (Lexington 1973); and Sheldon Wolin, "The Idea of the State in America," in *The Problem of Authority in America*, ed. John Diggins and Mark E. Kann (Philadelphia 1981), 41–58. For the pulling away of government in other settings, see Robert A. Caro, *The Power Broker* (New York 1974), on metropolitan empire-building, and Sam Bass Warner, Jr., *The Urban Wilderness* (New York 1972), on distant city governments.

The leadership mentality in foreign affairs is described in John Lewis Gaddis, *Strategies of Containment* (New York 1982); Lloyd C. Gardner, *Architects of Illusion* (Chicago 1970); and Arthur M. Schlesinger, Jr., *The Imperial Presidency* (Boston 1973). Walter L. Hixson's *George F. Kennan* (New York 1989), and Ernest R. May's "Cold War and Defense," in *The Cold War and Defense*, ed. Keith Neilson and Ronald G. Haycock (New York 1990), 9–14, emphasize the antidemocratic streak in these policymakers. The process of isolating dissenters is revealed in Stanley I. Kutler, *The American Inquisition* (New York 1982); Mary

Sperling McAuliffe, *Crisis on the Left* (Amherst 1978); and Athan Theoharis, *Seeds of Repression* (Chicago 1971). How Americans projected visions of a domestic political economy on postwar Europe is nicely captured in Michael J. Hogan's "American Marshall Planners and the Search for a European Neocapitalism," *American Historical Review*, 90 (February 1985): 44–72, and Charles S. Maier's *In Search of Stability* (Cambridge, Eng., 1987), chap. 3. Christopher N. May's account of swelling state power, *In the Name of War* (Cambridge 1989), reminds us of the running start that the First World War provided.

By the same token, almost every study about American politics since the 1920s relates to allocations of authority between national and local middle-class leaders. For broad views, see Barry D. Karl, *The Uneasy State* (Chicago 1983), and two books by James T. Patterson: *America's Struggle against Poverty, 1900–1980* (Cambridge 1981), and *The New Deal and the States* (Princeton 1969). E. Digby Baltzell, *The Protestant Establishment* (New York 1964), and Peter H. Irons, *The New Deal Lawyers* (Princeton 1982), reveal changing ethnic sensitivities among national-class leaders.

Something of the malleability in state policy early in the New Deal is described in William W. Bremer, *Depression Winters* (Philadelphia 1984); Kenneth R. Philp, *John Collier's Crusade for Indian Reform, 1920–1954* (Tucson 1977); Janet Poppendieck, *Breadlines Knee-Deep in Wheat* (New Brunswick 1986); and Bonnie Fox Schwartz, *The Civil Works Administration, 1933–1934* (Princeton 1984). For the challengers, see David H. Bennett's *Demagogues in the Depression* (New Brunswick 1969), and Alan Brinkley's *Voices of Protest* (New York 1982). Although Arthur M. Schlesinger, Jr., had quite different purposes in mind, his *The Coming of the New Deal* (Boston 1959) and *The Politics of Upheaval* (Boston 1960) contain valuable information on the national end of the compromise. For aspects of its local applications, see Roger Biles, *Big City Boss in Depression and War* (DeKalb 1984); Nancy L. Grant, *TVA and Black America* (Philadelphia 1990); Phillip Selznick, *TVA and the Grass Roots* (Berkeley 1949); Douglas L. Smith, *The New Deal in the Urban South* (Baton Rouge 1988); and Bruce M. Stave, *The New Deal and the Last Hurrah* (Pittsburgh 1970).

Some conservative implications of the compromise are discussed in Mark H. Leff, "Taxing the 'Forgotten Man': The Politics of Social Security Finance in the New Deal," *Journal of American History*, 70 (September 1983): 359–81; John Salmond, *A Southern Rebel* (Chapel Hill 1983); and Bruce J. Schulman, *From Cotton Belt to Sunbelt* (New York 1991). For an example of how educational policies fit within the compromise, see Arthur J. Vidich and Joseph Bensman, *Small Town in Mass Society* (Princeton 1958). For an example of educational policies that did not, see Frank J. Munger and Richard F. Fenno, Jr., *National Politics and Federal Aid to Education* (Syracuse 1962). Paul E. Peterson's *City Limits* (Chicago 1981) explains the different socioeconomic logics at work in national-level and local-level budgeting.

Lizabeth Cohen's *Making a New Deal* (Cambridge, Eng., 1990), and Bruce Nelson's *Workers on the Waterfront* (Urbana 1988), emphasize the role of industrial unionism in wage earners' class consciousness. Limitations on organized labor are detailed in Nelson Lichtenstein, *Labor's War at Home* (New York 1982); Linda C. Majka and Theo J. Majka, *Farm Workers, Agribusiness, and the State*

(Philadelphia 1982); Daniel Nelson, "The CIO at Bay: Labor Militancy and Politics in Akron, 1936–1938," *Journal of American History*, 71 (December 1984): 565–86; and Richard Oestreicher, "Urban Working Class Political Behavior and Theories of American Electoral Behavior, 1870–1940," ibid., 74 (March 1988): 1257–86. Some articles in Steve Frazer and Gary Gerstle, eds., *The Rise and Fall of the New Deal Order, 1930–1980* (Princeton 1989), and Charles Stephenson and Robert Asher, eds., *Life and Labor* (Albany 1986), are also useful; as is Robert H. Zieger's reliable *American Workers, American Unions, 1920–1985* (Baltimore 1986). Joshua B. Freeman, "Catholics, Communists, and Republicans: Irish Workers and the Organization of the Transport Workers Union," in *Working-Class America*, ed. Michael H. Frisch and Daniel J. Walkowitz (Urbana 1983) , 256–83, demonstrates the imported nature of ideological radicalism; and Robert J. Norrell, "Caste in Steel: Jim Crow Careers in Birmingham, Alabama," *Journal of American History*, 73 (December 1986): 669–94, the record of racial protectiveness in particular unions. Howell John Harris, *The Right to Manage* (Madison 1982), and Sanford M. Jacoby, *Employing Bureaucracy* (New York 1985), combine into an excellent account of management's counterattack in the 1940s. How these patterns affected individual leaders and unions is illustrated in Melvyn Dubofsky and Warren Van Tine, *John L. Lewis* (New York 1977), and Ronald W. Schatz, *The Electrical Workers* (Urbana 1983).

For ways in which the compromise functioned in and around the Second World War, see John Morton Blum, *V Was for Victory* (New York 1976); Roger Daniels, *Concentration Camps USA* (New York 1972); Leonard Dinnerstein, *America and the Survivors of the Holocaust* (New York 1992); Peter Irons, *Justice at War* (New York 1983); Jacobus tenBroek et al., *Prejudice, War and the Constitution* (Berkeley 1954); and David S. Wyman, *The Abandonment of the Jews* (New York 1984). The importance of local middle-class elites to McCarthyism is explored in Don E. Carleton, *Red Scare!* (Austin 1985); Walter Gellhorn, ed., *The States and Subversion* (Ithaca 1952); and especially Michael Paul Rogin, *The Intellectuals and McCarthy* (Cambridge 1967). See also Alistair Cooke, *A Generation on Trial* (New York 1950), and David Oshinsky, *A Conspiracy So Immense* (New York 1983).

Peter Bachrach's *The Theory of Democratic Elitism* (Boston 1967) traces the development of midcentury democratic theory. Michael Kammen explains the place of the Constitution in his wide-ranging *A Machine That Would Go of Itself* (New York 1986).

CHAPTER TEN

Allen J. Matusow's *The Unraveling of America* (New York 1984) is a smooth, conservative account of failed compromise in the 1960s. Peter N. Carroll's *It Seemed Like Nothing Happened* (New York 1983) is an informed account of what followed in the 1970s. For a sample of contested issues, see Paul Boyer, "From Activism to Apathy: The American People and Nuclear Weapons, 1963–1980," *Journal of American History*, 70 (March 1984): 821–44, on peace politics; Brigitte Berger and Peter L. Berger, *The War over the Family* (New York 1983), Stephanie Coontz, *The Way We Never Were* (New York 1992), and Arlene Skolnick, *Embattled Paradise* (New York 1991), on family norms; Samuel P. Hays, *Beauty, Health, and Permanence* (Cambridge, Eng., 1987), on environmentalism; Kristin Luker, *Abortion and the Politics of Motherhood* (Berkeley 1984); and Frances Fox Piven and Richard A. Cloward, *Regulating the Poor* (New York 1971), on welfare.

Something of the energy on the Left in the 1960s is communicated in Wini Breines, *Community and Organization in the New Left: 1962–1968* (New York 1982); Vine Deloria, Jr., *Behind the Trail of Broken Treaties* (New York 1974); Kirkpatrick Sale, *SDS* (New York 1973); and two memoir histories, Sara Evans' *Personal Politics* (New York 1979), and Todd Gitlin's *The Sixties* (New York 1987). Anger on the Right is sampled in Sidney Blumenthal, *The Rise of the Counter-Establishment* (New York 1986); Michael Kazin, "The Grass-Roots Right: New Histories of U.S. Conservatism in the Twentieth Century," *American Historical Review,* 97 (February 1992): 136–55; Leo Ribuffo, *The Old Christian Right* (Philadelphia 1983); and Peter Steinfels, *The Neoconservatives* (New York 1979). Lloyd A. Free and Hadley Cantril, *The Political Beliefs of Americans* (New York 1968), and Michael Mann, "The Social Cohesion of Liberal Democracy," *American Sociological Review,* 35 (June 1970): 423–39, puzzle over the apparent confusion of economic liberalism and cultural conservatism in local middle-class circles.

The controversy over rights is explored further in Lawrence M. Friedman, *Total Justice* (New York 1985); Mary Ann Glendon, *Rights Talk* (New York 1985); and Bernard Schwartz, *Super Chief* (New York 1983). James C. Cobb, *Industrialization and Southern Society, 1877–1984* (Lexington 1984), and Gilbert C. Fite, *Cotton Fields No More* (Lexington 1984), explain forces integrating the south with the rest of the nation. For consequences in the major political parties, see David R. Mayhew, *Placing Parties in American Politics* (Princeton 1986); Kevin P. Phillips, *The Emerging Republican Majority* (New Rochelle 1969); and Martin P. Wattenberg, *The Decline of American Political Parties, 1952–1980* (Cambridge 1984).

A mustering of strength and a defining of issues among African Americans emerges from Kenneth W. Goings, "*The NAACP Comes of Age*" (Bloomington 1990); Charles V. Hamilton's thoughtful *Adam Clayton Powell* (New York 1991); Genna Rae McNeil, *Groundwork* (Philadelphia 1983); Robert J. Norrell's perceptive *Reaping the Whirlwind* (New York 1985); and Robert Weisbrot, *Father Divine and the Struggle for Racial Equality* (Urbana 1983). How the quality of life among Chicago's African Americans deteriorated for decades before the civil rights movement is detailed in Arnold R. Hirsch, *Making the Second Ghetto* (Cambridge, Eng., 1983); Michael W. Homel, *Down from Equality* (Urbana 1984); and Dianne M. Pinderhughes, *Race and Ethnicity in Chicago Politics* (Urbana 1987). Clayborne Carson, *In Struggle* (Cambridge 1981), and William H. Grier and Price M. Cobbs, *Black Rage* (New York 1986), explore aspects of the drive for black freedom. For a sample of unexpected outcomes, see James C. Cobb, " 'Somebody Done Nailed Us on the Cross': Federal Farm and Welfare Policy and the Civil Rights Movement in the Mississippi Delta," *Journal of American History,* 77 (December 1990): 912–36; and Jonathan Kaufman, *Broken Alliance* (New York 1988), on blacks and Jews.

On background to a resurgent women's movement in the 1970s, see William Henry Chafe, *The American Woman* (New York 1972); Ruth Schwartz Cowan, *More Work for Mother* (New York 1983); and Ruth Milkman, *Gender at Work*

(Urbana 1987), as well as a trio of extraordinary contemporary analyses: Betty Friedan, *The Feminine Mystique* (New York 1963); Kate Millett, *Sexual Politics* (Garden City 1970); and Robin Morgan, ed., *Sisterhood Is Powerful* (New York 1970). The fate of the ERA is anatomized in Mary Frances Berry, *Why ERA Failed* (Bloomington 1986); Joan Hoff-Wilson, ed., *Rights of Passage* (Bloomington 1986); Jane J. Mansbridge, *Why We Lost the ERA* (Chicago 1986); and Donald G. Mathews and Jane Sherron DeHart, *Sex, Gender, and the Politics of ERA* (New York 1990).

For some of the subtleties of class, see Gary Gerstle's *Working-Class Americanism* (Cambridge, Eng., 1989) on blue-collar patriotism; Phyllis Kaniss's *Making Local News* (Chicago 1991) on local-class sensibilities in the urban press; and John Tomlinson's *Cultural Imperialism* (Baltimore 1991) on the limitations of hegemony. Vicki L. Ruiz, *Cannery Women Cannery Lives* (Albuquerque 1987), and Rickie Solinger, *Wake up Little Susie* (New York 1992), examine intersections of class with race and gender. The burdens on the poor are analyzed brilliantly in Christopher Jencks et al., *Inequality* (New York 1972), and also in Richard Parker, *The Myth of the Middle Class* (New York 1972). For the erosion of self-respect in modern America, see Christopher Lasch's *The Minimal Self* (New York 1984). For the politics of nonvoting, see Robert S. Gilmour and Robert B. Lamb, *Political Alienation in Contemporary America* (New York 1975), and Norman H. Nie et al., *The Changing American Voter*, rev. ed. (Cambridge 1979).

More or less by definition, the core books for the Introduction and Conclusion, covering the last quarter century, also apply to this chapter.

||||||
INDEX

312

Bellamy, Edward, 124, 172, 178, 187
Berger, Victor, 132
Betterfield, Justin, 38
Bill of Rights, 35, 200, 226, 255
birth control, 192, 237
Blaine, James G., 81
Blatch, Harriet Stanton, 167
Boas, Franz, 190
Boorstin, Daniel, 217, 259
bourgeois democracy, 7
Bourne, Randolph, 178–79
Brandeis, Louis D., 146, 162, 197
bribery. *See* corruption
Broder, David, 247
Brownson, Orestes, 59, 119
Bryan, William Jennings, 123, 172, 208
Bryant, William Cullen, 38
Bryce, James, 75, 140, 183
Buckeye Steel, 144–45
Buckley v. Valeo, 244, 262
bureaucracy, 206
Burnham, Walter Dean, 8, 248–49
Burns, James MacGregor, 3, 248, 258
business
  corporate responsibility, 260
  local middle class and, 144–47
  20th century hierarchies, 155–61
  welfare programs, 160

Calhoun, John C., 64
Camp, George Sidney, 118
campaigning, 66–68, 205–6
  expenditures, 244
  See also elections; political parties;
    politics
capital investment, 159
Carnegie, Andrew, 139, 215
Catt, Carrie Chapman, 150–55, 167–69,
  170, 191
censorship, 191
central government, justifications for,
  254–55
character, 186
Chicanos, 127, 130, 133
Child, Lydia Maria, 105
Child, Richard Washburn, 191
child labor, 125
children's rights, 238
cities, 113, 146
  class identifications, 147–48

19th century European commentary,
  56–59
political machines, 163–64
citizenship
  bourgeoisie and, 14
  education and, 31, 178
  lower class and, 177–78
  participatory training, 82
  property and, 30–31
  See also voting
Civil Rights Act, 232, 234
civil rights movement, 232–38. *See also*
  progressive movements
Civil War, 54, 70, 81, 83–84
class, 114–15, 117–42
  African-American individualism,
    195–96
  character and, 143, 186
  civil rights movement and, 234
  creation of modern national class,
    141–49
  credit and, 118–21
  early 20th century citizenship and,
    135–37, 177–78, 180
  education and, 147
  European commentary, 138–40
  ideology of difference, 127–31
  labor movement and, 121–24
  local influences, 144–49
  lower-class changes, 119–21, 124–37
  majoritarian limitations, 245–46
  Marxist ideology of, 115, 117–18, 121
  minorities and, 125–27
  1960s politics and, 230–31
  progressive movement and, 164–65
  public space access, 136–37
  redressing voting biases, 249
  religious associations, 148, 149
  skilled workers, 131–32
  20th century hierarchies, 155–61
  upper-class realignment, 138–41
  urban culture and, 147–48
  U.S. economic policy and, 210–11
  wage earners, 88–96
  women's rights movement and,
    237–38
Clay, Henry, 22, 28, 64
Cleaver, Eldridge, 235
Cloward, Richard, 6, 7, 249
collective rights, 183–84, 188

private sector. *See* business
professionals, 20, 147, 157–58
progress, in 19th century America, 57–60
progressive movements, 150–55, 162–65
  Dewey and, 175–77
  hierarchies and, 167
  Lippmann and, 173–77
  lower-class disfranchisement, 164–65
  national leaders, 150–55
  war and, 168, 170, 172–73
  See also civil rights movement; labor
    movement
Prohibition, 149, 166, 189, 210
property qualifications for franchise,
  30–31
protest, 25, 213, 233
psychology, 188
public health, 189. *See also* health and
  medicine
publicists, 2–3
publicity, 163
public life, European visitor commentary
  on, 44–47
public opinion, 173, 217, 231
  post-Revolutionary discourse, 38
Public Opinion (Lippmann), 174
public order, 69–70
public spaces, 95, 136–37, 259
public sphere, 14–15
Pullman, George, 140

Quindlen, Anna, 244

race riots, 127
racial segregation, 125–26, 233
racism
  European democracy and, 182, 184
  immigrants and, 129–31, 179
  Socialists and, 133
  See also African Americans; slavery
radio, 228
railroads, 94–95, 122, 141, 146
Rand, Ayn, 240
rationalization, 156, 160
Rawls, John, 251, 263
Reagan, Ronald, 242, 245, 257
referendum, 163, 172, 174
religion
  African American organization and, 98
  class associations, 148, 149

intolerance, 81
  political inclusion and, 86–87
religious revivals, 17–19, 32
representation, 35–36
republicanism, 20, 34–35, 36–37
Republican party, 21, 29, 32, 66, 70, 231
revolution, Marxist ideology of, 115
rhetoric, 67–68, 261
Rice, Elmer, 194
rights, 5, 225–27
  abortion and, 238–39, 241–42
  collective vs. individual, 183–84, 188
  early 19th century wage earners, 89
  guerrilla politics and, 265
  health, 239
  individualism and, 184, 250–51, 264–66
  international human rights, 255
  judiciary and, 241
  justifications for centralized govern-
    ment, 254–55
  majority powers vs., 239–43
  privacy, 226–27
  self-ownership, 13, 91–92
  universalizing, 223–24, 234
  See also individualism
Riis, Jacob, 164
Riker, William, 4
Robins, Margaret Dreier, 169, 170
Robinson-Patman Act, 227
Roe v. Wade, 238
Roman Catholicism, 86–87
Roosevelt, Eleanor, 218
Roosevelt, Franklin, 206, 208, 212
Roosevelt, Theodore, 154
Rorty, Richard, 251
Rotary, 147
Royce, Josiah, 78
Russell, Charles Edward, 163

Sabel, Charles, 254
safety, 54, 91–95
Sandel, Michael, 251
Sanger, Margaret, 192
Saturday Evening Post, 228
Schattschneider, E. E., 221
Schlesinger, Arthur, Jr., 208
school desegregation, 233
Schumpeter, Joseph, 218
science and technology, 143, 148
scientific management, 158
segregation, 125–26, 233